24 ARCHITECTS IN JAPAN

interviews and photos by ROLAND HAGENBERG

なりたいのは建築家

柏書房

青木淳 アトリエにて、ライディング・プロジェクトの模型と |
Jun Aoki with model for Raiding Project at his studio, Tokyo (2010)

原広司 アトリエにて | Hiroshi Hara studio, Tokyo (2010)

隈研吾 ONE表参道にて | Kengo Kuma at Omotesando One, Tokyo (2005) with his design

妹島和世 アトリエにて | Kazuyo Sejima at her studio in Tokyo (2006)

藤森照信 茅野の茶室にて | Terunobu Fujimori with his teahouse in Chino (2010)

菊竹清訓 デスクにて | Kiyonori Kikutake at his desk, Tokyo (2008)

伊東豊雄 TOD'S表参道ビルにて | Toyo Ito at TOD'S building, Tokyo (2004)

なりたいのは
建築家

24 ARCHITECTS IN JAPAN
interviews and photos by
ROLAND HAGENBERG

contents

ローランド・ハーゲンバーグ
◎ 写真・インタビュー

はじめに Acknowledgments ……………12

001
安藤忠雄 Tadao Ando ……………16

002
青木淳 Jun Aoki ……………38

003
坂茂 Shigeru Ban ……………68

004
藤森照信 Terunobu Fujimori ……………82

005
藤本壮介 Sou Fujimoto ……………102

006
原広司 Hiroshi Hara ……………114

007
長谷川逸子 Itsuko Hasegawa ……………136

008
飯島直樹 Naoki Iijima ……………148

009
磯崎新 Arata Isozaki ……………160

010
伊東豊雄 Toyo Ito ……………172

011
菊竹清訓 Kiyonori Kikutake ……………192

012／013
アストリッド・クライン＋マーク・ダイサム／KDa
Astrid Klein+Mark Dytham ……………206

014
隈研吾 Kengo Kuma ……………218

015
黒川紀章 Kisho Kurokawa ……………244

016
槇文彦 Fumihiko Maki ……………256

017
内藤廣 Hiroshi Naito……………272

018
坂本一成 Kazunari Sakamoto ……………294

019／020
妹島和世＋西沢立衛／SANAA
Kazuyo Sejima+Ryue Nishizawa…………304

021／022
丹下健三＋丹下憲孝
Kenzo Tange+Noritaka Tange …………328

023
手塚貴晴 Takaharu Tezuka ……………350

024
山下保博 Yasuhiro Yamashita……………362

1960年以降の
建築家の系譜とムーブメント…………380

[ブックガイド]
建築家と建築学がわかる100冊 ………382

はじめに

2001年東京・BMWスクエアで、"sur|FACE"と題した展覧会が開かれました。そこでは日本の一流建築家を取り上げ、映像、写真とともに紹介。その後、カール・ノイバートと作ったドキュメンタリー映画は日本各地で上映され、バイリンガルのDVD（アップリンク）としてもリリースされました。2004年にはインタビュー集「職業は建築家 君たちが知っておくべきこと」（柏書房）を日英併記で刊行。2009年には台湾で「20 Japanese Architects」（田園城市）が、2010年にはその中国本土版（清華大学出版社）が出版されました。

本書は、これまでの写真やインタビューに加えて、ここ何年かの間に、"Architectural Digest"の取材や、展覧会のプロジェクトを進める中で撮りためた新しい写真やインタビュー、エッセイなどが入っています。展覧会の企画としては「素描：建築家のスケッチ」展（オーストリア・ウィーンのウィンター・ギャラリー）や、映像や模型を使って行われた「未来建築 日本からオーストリアへ」展（福岡・三菱地所アルティアム、2009年）、「日本—リスト—ライディング」展（ウィーン建築博物館、2010年）などがあります。なお、ミラノでの丹下健三氏とのインタビューは、1998年「BMV Magazine」に掲載されたものです。彼の最後のメッセージのひとつとして貴重なものだと思います。

本来であれば2011年3月に発行する予定で準備を進めていた本書でしたが、同月に東日本を襲った惨事により、2ヶ月遅れての完成となりました。もし、震災後に同じインタビューを行っていたなら、質問も答えも大いに違う部分があったことは疑いありません。にもかかわらず、日本の将来や安全であるということの意味、またシェルターという建築物本来の機能といった、どんな建築の議論にも欠かせない要素が、すでにここで十分に語られていました。そこにある建築家たちの言葉は、スタイルや流行についてどんなに多くの空論を並べるよりも、本質的な意味を持っていると思います。そんな彼らのスピリットに応えたいという想いから、本書の全収益を日本赤十字社に寄付します。

最後になりましたが、全ての建築家の方々に心からお礼を申し上げます。また、出版の機会を与えてくれた柏書房、Pei Liu氏、Sabrina Chen氏、赤星豊氏、佐々木南実さん、英文校閲をしてくれたKirsten Lawa氏、コーディネートを担当してくれた阪部恵子さんに御礼を申し上げます。

2011年5月
ローランド・ハーゲンバーグ

Acknowledgments

In 2001 the exhibition "sur|FACE" was held at BMW Square in Tokyo. It featured my video and photographs of Japan's leading architects. Since then the film documentary – co-directed by Karl Neubert – has been screened in theaters all over Japan and a bilingual version was released by Uplink in Tokyo on DVD. In 2004, Kashiwa Shobo published 14 Japanese Architects. The book featured my interviews in English and Japanese. In 2009 Garden City Publishers in Taiwan released 20 Japanese Architects and Tsinghua University Press in Beijing a mainland Chinese version in 2010.

24 Architects in Japan includes my photos and texts from the above projects but also complete new insights, images and interviews which I have compiled over the last couple of years when introducing the architects' works in Architectural Digest or when talking to the designers for exhibition projects. Events that I had organized included Sobyou with architectural drawings at Winter Gallery in Vienna; Architecture of the Future with models and videos at Artium Mitsubishi Jisho, Fukuoka, 2009; As well as "Japan-Liszt-Raiding" at the Museum of Architecture in Vienna, 2010. My interview with Kenzo Tange in Milan was originally published in BMW Magazine in 1998 – one of the last significant conversations with the master.

The catastrophe in Tohoku disrupted the original plan to publish this book in March 2011. And, if the interviews were conducted today, some of the questions and answers would undoubtedly be different. However, certain topics – the future of Japan, what it means to be safe, and the essential function of architecture as a shelter – remain relevant to any discussion of architecture nonetheless. These topics and the architects' ideas will outlive all speculations about style and fashion. In that spirit I donate all my earnings from this book to the Japanese Red Cross.

I would like to thank all architects and their staff for their generous support. My thanks go also to Kashiwa Shobo for making this project possible, to Pei Liu, Sabrina Chen and Yutaka Akahoshi, Nami sasaki as well as to Kirsten Law in Melbourne for checking on the English text, and to Keiko Sakabe for coordinating this project.

Tokyo, May 2011
Roland Hagenberg

24 ARCHITECTS
IN JAPAN
interviews and photos by
ROLAND HAGENBERG

なりたいのは建築家

安藤忠雄 | Tadao Ando

今、建築家になりましたが、やはり恐怖はあります。
"Today, as an architect, I still feel fear."

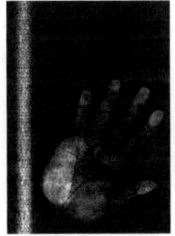

1941年大阪府生まれ。独学で建築を学び、1969年安藤忠雄建築研究所設立。イエール大学、コロンビア大学、ハーバード大学の教壇に立つほか、1997年から2003年には東京大学教授もつとめる。2003年から東京大学名誉教授。デンマーク・カールスバーグ建築賞、プリツカー賞、アメリカ建築家協会(AIA)ゴールドメダル、英国王立建築家協会(RIBA)ゴールドメダルなど、数々の賞を受賞。主な作品は、住吉の長屋(大阪)、淡路夢舞台(兵庫)、ベネッセハウス(香川県直島町)、フォートワース現代美術館(テキサス州)など。

Born 1941 in Osaka. Self-taught architect. Established his office in 1969. Taught at Yale, Columbia and Harvard University. Professor of Architecture at University of Tokyo, from 1997 to 2003. Professor Emeritus, University of Tokyo. Numerous awards such as Pritzker Prize, Gold Medal from American Institute of Architecture (AIA), Carlsberg Architectural Prize and Royal Gold Medal from Royal Institute of British Architects (RIBA). Major works include Row House in Sumiyoshi, Osaka; Awaji Yumebutai, Benesse House and Modern Art Museum of Fort Worth in Texas.

安藤忠雄 事務所にて | Tadao Ando at his office in Osaka, January 2011

安藤忠雄

安藤はのら犬の話が好きだ。それはある日、大阪にある彼の事務所に迷い込んできた。「妻の由美子と私は、その犬を飼うことにしたんです。でも、名前を思いつかない。その時、丹下健三さんのことを思い出した。でも、彼に因んだ名前をつけることなんてできないなと思いなおしました。そこで、その子犬をル・コルビュジエと呼ぶことにしたんです！」 その前に、安藤は大阪の古書店でコルビュジエと運命的な出会いをしていた。コルビュジエの貴重な画集がそこにあったのだ。それは安藤のバイブルになり、現代建築へと進むきっかけになった。1995年、安藤は世界で最も権威のあるプリッカー賞を受賞し、建築家人生のピークを迎える。（賞金の10万ドルは、すべて神戸の阪神大震災で被災した孤児たちに寄付された）。雑誌の記事では、安藤の10代の頃の経歴――トラックの運転手やボクサーなど、彼のバックグラウンドはタフで、建築は独学で学んだ大阪のストリートキッドだった――という紹介が必ずなされた。それは、東大を出たスノビッシュな建築業界のエリートたちとは一線を画すものだった。安藤は、この無法者のイメージを自ら受け入れ、生や死、怖れなどのたとえ話をするようになった。彼が事務所で人々を迎えるときは、彼のアシスタントたちがいつもスタンバイしている。彼らは黒いスーツに白いシャツを着て、安藤のすぐ横に並んで立ち、ノートを持って、先生の言うことは一言ももらさないようにとメモをとる準備をしている。会議室は有名な建築の模型でいっぱいだが、彼らはトレーニングの一環として、安藤のアドバイスを受けながら、それらを直す。たとえばルイス・カーンやレム・コールハース、ハンス・ホラインなどだ。昔から、安藤はハスキーでつやのあるトム・ウェイツのような声をして神秘的なのだが、いまやある意味、彼自身が現代の神秘になっている。人々を結びつけるような、同時的なイベントを重要視することについては、とくにそうだと言える。「モネとロダンは同じ年に生まれている。彼らは同時に新しい経験をし、新しい世界を作ったんです」。彼は言う。「ベルニーニの人生は、彼の敵であるボロミーニによって方向付けられていた。モンドリアンがいなかったら、リートフェルトは、シュレーダー邸を作らなかったかもしれない。カーンはバラガンに会い、一緒にどん底を経験した。だから私は、本を読んで、コルビュジエに会いにパリまでいったんです。でも、着いてみると、彼はちょうど亡くなってしまったところでした！」

[パート1]——2000-2004

ローランド・ハーゲンバーグ[以下 RH] 西洋文明では、美を計算しつくされた完璧なものと考えますが、建築家として美をどう捉えていますか?

安藤忠雄[以下 安藤] 日本人は移ろいやすく、はかないものを美しいと感じます。例えば、四季の移り変わりや、天候によって変わる陽の光、自然の色の変化などを、直感的に美しいと感じるのです。私自身は西洋と日本の中間ぐらいに美を位置づけています。

RH よく、建築家は環境にも責任を取るべきで、論理がすべてではないと発言していますね?

安藤 西洋の考え方では論理を重視します。論理とは、経済法則にもつながり、常に進歩しようとします。一方、東洋では自然から得る直感に頼っています。しかし、直感だけではだめで、世界で通用するには論理が土台にならなければなりません。
今、西洋の影響は世界中に及んでいて、特に第三世界には医薬品や科学技術の支援をして、良いことではありますが、それが人口の急増を招いているのも事実です。この危険な連鎖を断ち切るには、西洋の論理と東洋の直感を融合するしかありません。
個人レベルではありますが、私は常々、この2つの関係を考慮しながら、ものを創っています。

RH 論理とひらめきを組み合わせる、ということですか?

安藤 何かを創りたいと思っても、データと論理だけでは無理で、知恵が必要です。ただ知識さえ豊富なら何でも創れると思っている人が多すぎますが、知識だけでは不十分で、自分の仕事で人を感動させたいなら、まず自分が感動しなければいけません。

RH 以前に比べて、確信を得た様子ですね?

安藤 ここ、神戸には特別な愛着がありました。育った土地ですし、私が手がけた建物が30近くあります。その神戸が震災にあい、数千人が亡くなって、はっと気づいたのです。私たちの精神性に建築がどれほど深く関わっているのかということに。
震災は人々の記憶も奪ってしまいました。学校、図書館、アパート、街並み、あらゆ

る建物には記憶がつまっていて、失ってみて初めて、自分たちを取り巻いていた環境が何だったのかということに気がついたのです。風景というのは物理的に存在するだけではなく、心の中にもあったわけです。街は機能するだけではありません。人々の記憶を織りなす要素でもあります。

私が「ひょうごグリーンネットワーク」を始めたのも、そうした理由からです。

RH　目標は25万本の木を植えること、と聞いていますが……。

安藤　神戸の人々の記憶も復興させる必要があったのです。どうすれば、人々が心をひとつにして、互いの痛みを癒すことができるのか。街は自然と共存するべきだということを、どうすれば、皆にわかってもらえるのか、自問自答しました。答は実に単純で、木を植えることでした。毎年、たくさんの木が白い花を咲かせ、震災で亡くなられた方たちの冥福を祈ります。

その苗木は全国各地から取り寄せたもので、まず被災地の保育園に植えました。建設会社にお願いして、建物が完成するまでの数年間、水やりをして育ててもらっています。

RH　木の他には、何か集めていますか？

安藤　個人的には本や色鉛筆ですね。

RH　最近は鉛筆よりもコンピューターに頼る建築家が多いようですね？

安藤　美とはバランスです。設計する時、私はクリエイティブな想像の世界と物理的な現実の世界の間、言ってみれば、虚構と実像との間を行き来します。同時に、問題を解決するだけでなく、自分の理想に近いものを創りたいと思っています。というのも、これまでお話ししたように、建物は私たちが生きていく上での精神に深く関わっていて、記憶の根幹となるのですから。

RH　テキサス州のフォートワース現代美術館ではやはりコンクリートとガラスを使用していますね？

安藤　コンクリートとガラスは、20世紀を代表する建築素材です。フォートワース現代美術館では、外壁のコンクリートをガラスで被う予定です。そうすれば、巨大な建物のもつ威圧感は和らぐでしょう。

私は美術館とは貴重な美術品が保管されている場所というよりも、魂が触れ合う場所だと思っていますので、訪れた人が雑念にとらわれることなく、落ち着いて鑑

安藤忠雄 仕事机 | Tadao Ando's desk

賞できるような雰囲気を作り出すことが大切だと考えました。そういう空間なら、人は自分なりに美術と接することができるはずです。

建物とは子供の頃に植えた木のようなもので、人は一生、愛着を抱き続けられ、記憶もはぐくんでくれるのです。

RH 神戸の震災だけでなく、ニューヨークの大惨事の復興にも、建築家としてメッセージを発していますね？

安藤 ニューヨークのグラウンド・ゼロへの私の案は、日本の古墳のように、敷地の上に土をゆるやかに盛り、そこを芝が覆うというものでした。日本人は一目でお墓とわかるでしょうが、文化的な背景が違うアメリカ人には、何だか理解できないかも知れません。しかし、文化的な相違があっても、そこがメモリアルだと感覚的にわかる共通認識はあると思います。

私が想像するグラウンド・ゼロは、人々が芝生の上に座り、見知らぬ者同士が自分の体験を話したり、相手を慰めたりする場所です。そういう光景は、あの敷地に以前よりさらに高いビルを建ててしまっては望めません。高層ビルだけが、アメリカの強大な経済力を示しはしません。

9.11は、アメリカだけでなく世界の悲劇だと思います。だからこそ、政府がグラウンド・ゼロの敷地を買い取って、世界中から様々な人が集まり、瞑想にふけるような、平和で静かな場所にしてほしかったのです。

RH 危機に関してですが、もし自分のためにシェルターを作るとしたら、どのようなものになりますか？

安藤 地球上に生きている限り、私にはシェルターは必要ありません。松尾芭蕉は晩年に、「旅に病んで夢は枯れ野をかけめぐる」という句を読んでいますが。芭蕉は病に伏しても、生きることへの答を求めて旅したわけで、それは情熱以外のなにものでもありません。もし芭蕉のような情熱があれば、物やシェルターとは無縁に、生きることができるのではないでしょうか。

RH でも、どういうふうにして恐怖に立ち向かうのですか？

安藤 昔、私はボクシングをしていました。ボクシングというのは人を殺すこともできるわけで、当時、私は食べたり、眠ったりすることができず、嘔吐したこともありました。常に恐怖とともに生きていて、瞑想もしました。

今、建築家になりましたが、やはり恐怖はあります。すごいアイデアが浮かび、うまく設計ができて、理想的な建築物に仕上がったとしても、もし建物が倒れてしまったら、もう仕事はこないかも知れない。そうなったら私のスタッフは大丈夫だろうか、と不安になるのです。

しかし、私はボクシングを通して、自分の責任において、決定を下し、行動することを学んでいます。それは建築家にも通じることなのです。

RH　それに、グローバルなレベルでの脅威がありますよね。いわゆる戦争に加えて、経済戦争、テロもある。それに対して、どう対応していこうと思いますか？

安藤　繰り返しになりますが、やはり瞑想ですね。フェデリコ・マイヨール（ユネスコ元事務局長）も、瞑想を通して、異なった宗教の人々も平和に暮らすことができると信じていました。だから、私も1995年、ユネスコに瞑想のためのスペースを作ったのです。もちろん、そんな理想の、平和な世界を今すぐにつくることはできません。しかし、瞑想をすることは、その第一歩になると思います。私たちは、まずそれに気づかなければならないと思います。仏教の僧侶やイスラム教徒にとって、瞑想は常日頃やっていることです。建築家が家を建て、風景をデザインし、そのデザインの向こうにあるものについて考えています。それも、ある意味で瞑想だといえるのではないかと思います。

私たち日本人には、「浄土」という概念があります。仏教の言葉で、「清浄な場所」という意味です。浄土は西方にあるといわれています。私は、お寺の設計をいくつも依頼されたことがありますが、すべて西を向いていました。仏像も同じです。日が沈むときには、仏像に光が当たって輝くのです。この時間が瞑想に一番いい時間だと思います。

RH　アメリカの消費主義が世界中の問題の原因になっているとお考えですよね。それはテロの原因にもなっていると思いますか？

安藤　原因のひとつには、アメリカナイズされていくことへの反抗があるでしょうね。この50年間で、日本もアメリカ化された社会になりました。私たちは大量生産をし、社会も大量消費によって成り立っている。ハンバーガーショップ、ドーナツ店、ドライブスルーの店など……アメリカ社会への必要条件はすべて揃っています。そして、それが問題を起こしているのです。なぜなら、アメリカ化は、地域の多様性を

考えないからです。ただ、お互いの金のやりとりしか考えていません。

[パート2]──2011

RH　安藤さんにとって、戦後の日本の歴史で、2つのターニングポイントがあったと思います。ひとつは、1969年、学生たちが東京大学を占拠した、東大安田講堂事件。もうひとつは、その1年後、三島由紀夫のクーデターの失敗。そのとき安藤さんは、これがこの国で文化と経済が衝突した最後の事件だとおっしゃっていました。2つの葛藤が続かないということについて、残念がっていらっしゃいます。なぜですか？

安藤　1970年代から、日本は経済発展にばかり目を向け、文化については軽視してきました。そして私たちは、もうかつてのような経済大国ではないのに、いまだにこの状態を続けています。私は、日本が今の状況を直視し理解して、明治時代や第二次大戦が終わってすぐの20年間のように、もう一度、文化的な精神へ戻ることが可能になるのではないかと思います。

RH　150年も前の明治時代ですか？

安藤　その頃の日本は文化的な力もあったし、西洋からの劇的な影響を吸収するという意欲もありました。第二次大戦が終わった頃も、日本にはまだその力が残っていました。私たちの目的は、いつも安定した生活ができる、文化的な結びつきの深い安定した社会を作ることでした。この30年間、私たちはその哲学を捨てて、ただビジネスで成功すればいいとか、いい大学に入ればいいなどということばかりを考えてきました。詩人のポール・クローデルだったと思いますが「もし人類を代表する民族をひとつ選ぶとすれば、それは日本人だ」と言ったことがありました。今同じことを言ってくれるかと考えると、それは疑問です。

RH　ということは、日本には新しい明治維新が必要ということですか？　でも、そうだとすると、一体何が、あるいは誰がその原動力となるのでしょうか？　戦うべき相手は、もはや西洋諸国ひとつではありません。それは多種多様になっています。人々は、大量消費主義に足をとられていますし、隣国の中国は軍事力を誇示しているのに、日本はいまだに、4万人のアメリカ兵を抱える国です。この現状の中で変化はどのように起こるのでしょうか？

安藤　私は、変化は起きないと思います。日本人はもはや哲学の力を信じていないからです。日本特有の社会構造が極端な日本の国土開発を可能にしてきたことは間違いありません。もちろん、日本は世界第二の経済大国になり、経済力を誇るようになりました。しかし、文化価値の損失を恐れる民衆の声は、1970年代の田中角栄首相の日本列島改造論を自分なりに解釈するのに忙しい経済人たちの耳には届きませんでした。必要が疑問視される場所での開発が続きました。同時に日本の社会の知性は崩壊しました。もちろん日本は経済大国になりましたが、経済だけに頼っている国は長続きしません。日本の経済的発展は文化の衰退を同時に意味していたのです。残念ながら私たちが今、知っているような民主主義を通じては、変化は起こらないでしょう。

RH　人々が民主主義に積極的に関わらないのが原因だということですか？

安藤　アメリカが1945年に日本に落としたもうひとつの爆弾は、民主主義です。なぜなら、それは表面だけのものだったからです。18世紀のフランス革命を考えてみてください。あれが本来の姿です。外側からではなく、内側から起こった。民主主義は、自主的に動く個人によって、実際に機能します。日本では、そのような個人はいませんから、本当の民主主義もないのです。私は1968年パリに住んで、学生たちが古い体制に反対するのを見て、その事実に気づきました。そして私は思ったんです。日本は、ある意味で隠れた社会主義だなと……。

RH　それは、合理化されて、疑いを抱くことのない多くの中流層の人々のせいでしょうか？

安藤　たとえばアメリカでは、様々な階級があって、人々はそれぞれの階級に属することによって、個性を表現しています。しかし、日本では、多くの人々が同じ賃金で、同じ立場、そして持っている意見は皆同じです。この同質性があっては、明治維新や第二次大戦直後のように、国を立て直すために戦う、その最前線に立つなどということは、もはやできないでしょう。もう体力も知力も使い果たしてしまって、世の中を変えていかなくてはならない。今の30代や40代の人にそういう力があるようには見えません。一方で、60代を見てみると、たとえば日本で行われた国際デザイン会議では、菊竹清訓氏や黒川紀章氏、槇文彦氏のような、若い考えを持った人たちに多く出会います。でも、彼らは今どこにいますか？　彼らのような人たちなし

安藤忠雄 淡路夢舞台にて｜Tadao Ando at Awaji Island

では、日本は中国のスピードに追いつくことなどできないと思います。

RH 建築家の存在を変化のためのきっかけとご覧になりますか？

安藤 彼らは変化をもたらす可能性をもっていると思います。しかし、それも、ある程度までです。わたしは、自分の仕事はすべて、最前線に立つ試みだと思っています。たとえば、人はこう言います。「こんなコンクリートの箱に住めるわけがない。寒いし、殺風景で、灰色だ」などというように。そこから、ディスカッションが始まり、態度の変化が現れてくるのです。私にとって、家には2種類あります。ひとつは、体を休めるところ、もうひとつは、精神と魂が生きるところ。私はこの考えをずっと示し続けてきました。この意見を共有してくれる人もいれば、この考えを再評価し、もう一度考え直してくれる人もいます。私の思想に感動して、魅力を感じるといってくれる人もいます。私は子供の頃、親が家を修理していたときのことを憶えています。大工さんが細かいところまで丁寧に仕事をしているのを、ずっと見ていました。そのとき初めて、家には家の命や魂があるんだなと思いました。そしてその後、建築家になったときに、それが自分の仕事の指針になりました。私はいまだに、人々が家の中に入るとき、建築と一体になって感動してほしいと思っています。

RH 丹下健三氏が設計した広島の原爆慰霊碑を訪れたときに感じたように、感動するということは、恐れるということでもありますよね。

安藤 あのときは、まだ20代でした。慰霊碑には夜行ったんです。その頃、慰霊碑は今のようにライトアップされていませんでしたから、あたりは真っ暗で、ピロティからは、原爆ドームが見えました。人間の科学は、私たちの地球を滅ぼしてしまえるのだということに衝撃を受けました。20代のときに受けた恐怖の経験が、その後の私が世界をどう見るかということを決めたと思います。もちろん、何を恐いと思うかは人それぞれです。でも、今日の世界を作ったのは、ある時期に地獄を経験してきた人たちだと思います。だから、20代の学生は意識的に自分のその後を決めるような、決定的な瞬間を探し求めなければならないと思います。そして、そのような人がいつかこの世界を作り、変えていくのです。どんなガイドブックもそういうことは教えてくれません。私の場合、それはシベリア鉄道に乗って、ひとりきりで未知の世界を旅したことでした。ヨーロッパ、アフリカ、アジアをはじめてひとりで旅したことが、今日の私の世界観にも影響を与えています。

Tadao Ando

Tadao Ando likes to tell the story of a stray dog that walked into his office in Osaka one day. "My wife, Yumiko, and I decided to adopt him but couldn't think of a name. Kenzo Tange came to mind, but then I realized I couldn't order him around. And so I called the puppy Le Corbusier!" Previously and fatefully, the French architect had entered Ando's life in a second-hand bookshop in Osaka, where a rare catalogue of Le Corbusier's drawings fell into his hands. It became Ando's bible and set him on the path to modern architecture. In 1995 his career culminated with the world's most prestigious architectural decoration – the Pritzker Prize. (It came with a 100,000 dollar award, which Ando donated to orphans of the Great Hanshin earthquake in Kobe.) Magazines that write about Ando never fail to mention that in his teenage years he was a truck driver and a boxer, a background that sets him – a tough, self-taught street kid from Osaka – apart from the snobbish Tokyo university graduates that largely comprise the architectural elite. Ando has embraced this desperado image and feeds it into conversations through allegories of survival, killing and fear.

When he welcomes visitors to his office, a group of associates and assistants is always on stand-by. They line up next to him dressed in black suits and white shirts with notebooks, ever ready to collect any word or thought their teacher might offer. The meeting room is filled with models of famous houses they've had to rebuild as part of their training under Ando's guidance – works by Louis Kahn, for instance, or Rem Koolhaas and Hans Hollein. Over the years, Ando's voice has lost nothing of its mystic husky, Tom-Waits-like quality and, in a way, Ando has even become a modern-day mystic – especially when he speculates about synchronistic events that bring people together. "Monet and Rodin were born in the same year. They shared new experiences, created new worlds," he says. "Bernini's life is tied to his adversary Borromini. Without Mondrian, Rietveld would not have created the Schroder House. Kahn and Barragan experienced hell together. And me, I went to Paris to visit Le Corbusier because of a book and, when I arrived, he had just died!"

[**Conversation part one**]——2000-2004

Roland Hagenberg In Western civilizations the definition of beauty is close to the laws of geometry and synonymous with perfection. How would you define beauty in your work?

Tadao Ando Japan's interpretation of beauty is less static and it can be found in constant changes - in the coming and going of seasons for instance; in the fluctuations of light caused by the weather; in the colorful alterations of nature. We experience this through intuition. My own definition of beauty lies somewhere in-between the Western and the Japanese interpretation.

RH As an architect you have always emphasized your responsibility for the environment and warned us not to rely too much on "thinking by logic" alone.

TA Western thinking emphasizes logic and logic drives the economy. The keyword is improvement. In the East we rely more on intuition drawn from nature, but this alone does not allow us to act on a global scale. To do so, we must use the logic platform of the West. The Western influence has spread everywhere, especially into Third World countries, where medicine and technology support an out-of-control population growth.

This dangerous circle can only be broken if we blend Western logic with Eastern intuition. As a creative person I have to deal with this dilemma every day on a personal level.

RH To bring order into your creative chaos?

TA If you want to be creative, your work cannot be based on facts and logic alone. You need wisdom. Too many people believe they can be creative because they know a lot. But that's not enough. First you have to experience feelings yourself before you set out to move other people's hearts with your work.

RH Today you sound more radical. What happened?

TA I have a special attachment to the city of Kobe. I grew up there and conceived about 30 buildings in that area. After the devastating earthquake that killed thousands of people, I became suddenly aware how deeply architecture is rooted in our emotional lives. The disaster robbed people of their memories. Those memories were attached to schools, libraries, apartments, streets, and all kinds of structures. What I want to say is, that loss makes you become aware of your environment. You realize that it not only shapes your physical landscape but your mental world as well. The city is more than a pure functional arrangement; it is also a spiritual fabric for your memories. That's why I started the Hyogo Green Network...

RH ...with the goal to plant 250,000 trees.

TA Not only buildings and streets have to be restored but also our collective memory. I asked myself, what could bring people together and heal their pain, what could make them aware that the city should grow together with nature? The answer is as simple as planting a tree. Many of them bloom every year with white blossoms in memory of the people who perished in the quake. The trees come from all over Japan. We put some of them into a nursery school first. We asked the construction companies to take care of little seedlings – they water them and raise them until the construction work is finished.

RH Do you collect things other than trees?

TA Not in particular except books and color pencils.

RH Many architects today rely more on their computers than on their pencils.

TA Balance is beauty. In my work I am always traveling between the creative imagination and practical, physical reality – between fiction and substance. At the same time I hope that I not only can solve problems, but can stay true to my ideals. As I said before, architecture reaches out into our emotional lives, creates implants in our memories.

RH One of your current projects is the Modern Art Museum of Fort Worth, Texas. Again you prefer concrete and glass to other materials.

TA Concrete and glass are two of the representative materials of this century. In case of the Fort Worth Museum the concrete walls outside are covered with glass, which softens the appearance of the massive structure. Museums are first of all spiritual meeting places and not so much keepers of valued objects. It is therefore important to create a meditative atmosphere that allows the viewer to feel undisturbed, uninhibited and protected, so he can find his own unique relationship with art. To live with architecture is like living with a tree that we planted when we were kids. We will be attached to it for the rest of our life. Trees and architecture are the builders of our memories.

RH After Kobe, another disaster struck, this time in New York. Again you felt obliged to comment as an architect.

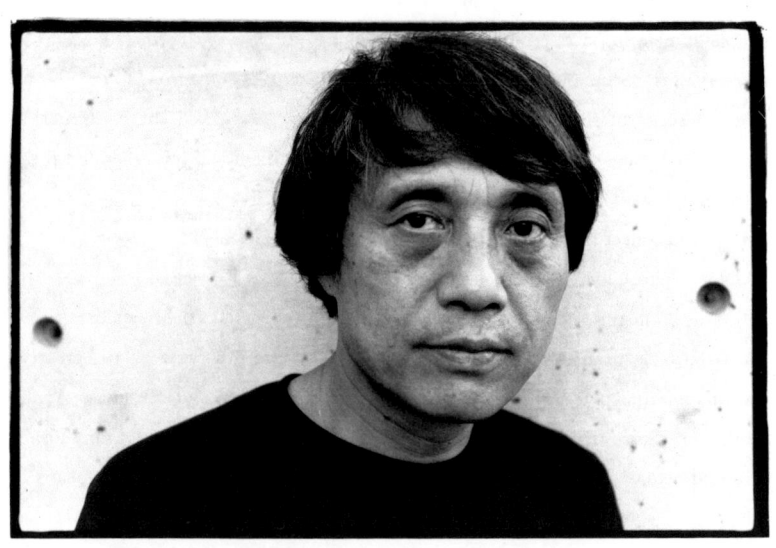

安藤忠雄 事務所にて ｜ Tadao Ando, Osaka, 2004
「日本は、明治時代のように、もう一度、文化的な精神に戻ることが必要だと思います」
"I wish the Japanese would turn back to the cultural spirit they enjoyed during the Meiji period."

TA My design for Ground Zero in New York is a simple, grass-covered mound of earth shaped like a traditional Japanese grave. Japanese people would recognize it as a burial site at once, but Americans might not. Perceptions change from culture to culture. But regardless of their cultural identity, people know instinctively when they enter a memorial. This is the result of a global sensitivity. At Ground Zero I imagined that people would sit on the grassy mound, and that these strangers would strike up conversations, talk about their experiences and take comfort in the company of others. This would never happen if they erect more skyscrapers — buildings that merely celebrate America's dominant economic power. 9/11 was not a purely American experience. It was a global tragedy. That's why I would have preferred that the government had bought Ground Zero. It could have turned it into a place of peace, tranquility and reflection to invite people from around the world to use it as a site for meditation.

RH If you had to build a shelter for yourself, how would it look like?

TA As long as I can stand on Earth, knowing consciously that I am alive, I don't need any shelter. In one of his last poems Matsuo Basho wrote: "Being ill while still on a journey/in my dream I'm still wandering around in the wilderness!" Basho was on a lifelong trip seeking for answers to life. That was his passion. If you are filled with passion like Basho you can live without objects, possessions and without a shelter.

RH So how do you address fear?

TA I once was a boxer. Boxing can kill. I could not eat. I could not sleep. I vomited. I lived in constant fear. So I meditated. Today as an architect, I still feel fear. I can come up with great ideas, draw up wonderful plans and use them to create impressive buildings. But all that is done alone in solitude. What if the building fails? Do I get another chance? If not, what happens to my employees? As a boxer I learned that I have to decide and act on my own and take on that responsibility. In that sense, the life of a boxer and the life of an architect are similar.

RH And fear on a global level – with conventional wars, economic wars, terrorism – how would you deal with that?

TA Again, with meditation. Federico Mayor (the former head of UNESCO) believed, too, that people of different religions could live peacefully next to each other through meditation. And that's why I built a meditation space for UNESCO in 1995. Of course, it is impossible to create such an ideal, peaceful world right away, but meditation could be the first step. We should be aware of that, always. Meditation is everyday work, as it is for Buddhist monks or Muslims. Architects build houses, design landscapes and think about what lies beyond their designs – that is a form of meditation, too. We Japanese have this concept of jodo (in Buddhist terms, 'the pure land'). Jodo is situated in the direction of the west. I designed several Buddhist temples and they all face west, as do Buddha statues, and when the sun sets it shines on them. This may be the best time for meditating.

RH You consider American consumerism the cause of worldwide problems. Is it also the cause of Terror?

TA Resistance to Americanization is one part of it. In the last fifty years, Japan, too, has changed into an Americanized society. We are mass-producing and society functions because of mass consumption. Hamburger shops, Mister Donut, drive-in stores; we have all the prerequisites of an American society. And that creates problems, because Americanization does not consider the diversity of local communities; it only considers the mutual denomination of money, the cultural imperialism of a certain currency.

[Conversation part two]——2010

Roland Hagenberg For you, there have been two important turning points in Japan's postwar history: the Yasuda Hall incident of 1969, where students occupied Tokyo University, and Yukio Mishima's failed coup d'état a year later. You say that was the last time that culture clashed with the economy in this country. You seem to regret that this struggle didn't continue. Why?

Tadao Ando From the 1970s, Japan focused on its economic development and neglected its culture. This is still going on, even though we are no longer the economic powerhouse we once were. I wish the Japanese would look at the reality of, and understand, the current situation. Then it might be possible to turn back to the cultural spirit we had during the Meiji period, or during the first two decades after World War II.

RH The Meiji period, 150 years ago?

TA At that time we had the cultural power and identity to absorb the impact of dramatic influences from the West. We still had the strength to do this after World

War II, when our goal was to create a balanced society and an affluent lifestyle with strong cultural bonds. But, over the last 30 years, we've thrown this philosophy overboard and instead have focused on becoming successful in business and attending the best universities. I think it was the poet Paul Claudel who said, "If we were to choose one people on earth to represent humankind, it should be the Japanese." I doubt he would say that today.

RH In other words, Japan needs a new Meiji revolution? But what, or who, would be the inspiring force? The challenge is no longer to compete with the West. It's now multifold: people are trapped in cycles of consumerism; China is showing off its military power next door, while Japan is still hosting 40,000 American troops. How can change occur in the present situation?

TA I don't think it can, because the people of Japan don't believe in the power of philosophy anymore. Japan's unique social structure made it possible to go to extremes with the National Land Development program. It was no surprise that the country showed a remarkable economic improvement and proudly became the second-most-powerful economy in the world. But the voice of the people, who were anxious about losing certain cultural values did not reach those who were too busy to realize late Prime Minister Kakuei Tanaka's plan of remodeling the Japanese Archipelago of the 1970s. We witnessed extensive construction at questionable locations and, meanwhile, watched the Japanese intellectual system collapse. We became an economic giant, but no national power can rely on business alone for longevity. The economic development of Japan happened at the cost of culture. Unfortunately, change won't come through the democratic system as we know it today.

RH You mean, because people are not actively involved in the democratic process?

TA The second-most-powerful bomb that America dropped on Japan in 1945 was democracy, because it set down only superficial roots. Look at the French revolution of the 18th century – that was a real revolution. It came from inside. Democracies work through individuals that act on their own. In Japan, we don't have those individuals and that's why real democracy doesn't exist. I woke up to this fact when I lived in Paris in 1968 and watched students rebel against the old order. I then thought, what we have in Japan is a kind of hidden socialism.

RH Because of the vast, streamlined, obedient middle class?

TA In America, for instance, you have people belonging to different classes who represent their class by expressing their individualities. In Japan, however, a wide range of people share the same income, the same position, and all express the same opinion. With this sameness, we cannot stand at the frontline anymore, as we did during the Meiji revolution or after World War II, when we were fighting to rebuild. We have run out of physical and intellectual power and it's not present in those who are now in their thirties and forties – the generation responsible for change. In the 1960s, when we had the international design debates here in Japan, we had young thinkers like Kikutake, Kurokawa, and Maki. But where are the Kikutakes, the Kurokawas, and Makis of today? Without people like them we cannot keep up with the speed of China.

RH Do you see architects as catalysts for change?

TA They have the ability to bring about change, but only to a certain extent. I consider all my work an attempt to stand at the very frontline. People have said, "I cannot live in this concrete box, it's too cold, there's no decoration, it's too gray," and so on. This discussion started and with it came a change of attitude. For me, there have always been two types of home – one where the body rests, and one where the mind and soul lives. I have been preaching this philosophy for a long time. Over the years, some people have come to share my opinion, others have reevaluated and reconsidered their own opinions or have been touched by and attracted to my ideas. I remember the time, in my childhood, when my parents renovated our house. I watched the carpenters; their devotion to details, to their work. I became aware for the first time that houses have a life of their own, a soul. Later, when I became an architect, this insight guided my work. I still think that, when an individual enters his house, he should be moved emotionally to become one with the architecture.

RH "Emotionally moved" can also mean being terrified, as you were when visiting Kenzo Tange's Hiroshima Peace Memorial Museum.

TA I was in my twenties when I visited it. It was nighttime, and the Hiroshima Peace Memorial Museum was not lit up as it is today. It was completely dark and through the pilotis I saw the burned-out dome. I was shocked by the thought that we now have the scientific knowledge to destroy our own planet. Terrifying moments in my twenties defined how I perceive the world. Of course, what is terrifying to us, depends on our individual personalities. I would say the world as it is today was defined by people who, at one point, experienced Hell. That's why students in their twenties should go out and consciously seek their own defining moment so that they too can shape and change the world one day. No guidebook can tell them how to do that. In my case, I took the Siberian railroad in my early twenties and headed for the unknown, all by myself. This experience – a challenging first trip through Europe, Africa and Asia – had a great impact on how I look at the world today.

安藤忠雄 デッサン中
「何かを創りたいと思っても、データと論理だけでは無理で、知恵が必要です」
Tadao Ando, Osaka, 2004
"If you want to be creative, your work cannot be based on facts and logic alone. You need wisdom."

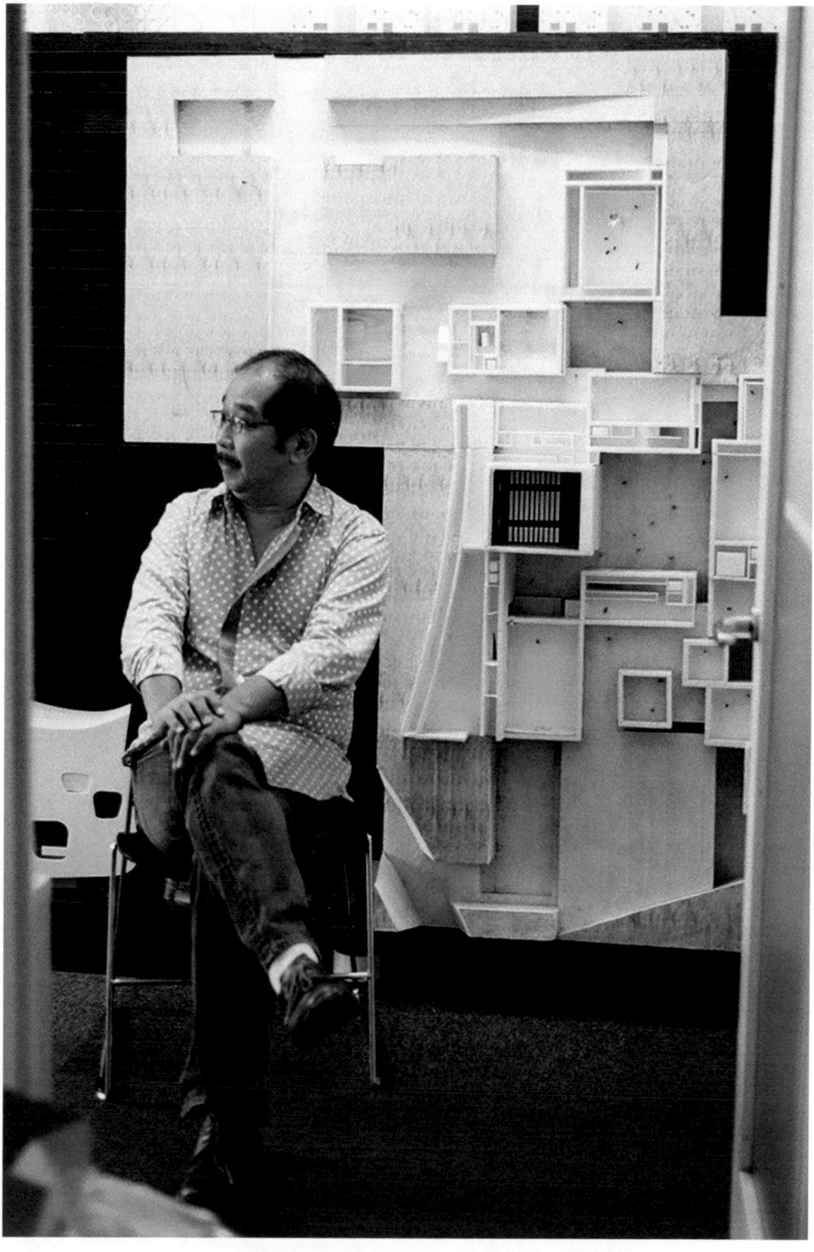

青木 淳 | Jun Aoki

セザンヌの風景画は
完璧な調和を表わしている。

"The sceneries in Cezanne's paintings represent perfect harmony."

1956年神奈川県生まれ。1982年東京大学大学院修了。1983年から1990年まで磯崎新アトリエ勤務。1991年青木淳建築計画事務所設立。東京大学、東京工業大学、東京理科大学の講師をつとめる。2004年度芸術選奨文部科学大臣新人賞を受賞。主な作品は、第8回くまもと景観賞の馬見原橋(熊本)、日本建築学会賞の潟博物館(新潟)、ニューヨーク、香港、東京のルイ・ヴィトン・フラッグシップショップ、青森県立美術館(青森)などがある。

Born in 1956 in Kanagawa Prefecture. Received master degree of Architecture at University of Tokyo in 1982. Worked at Arata Isozaki & Associates from 1983 to 1990. Established his own practice in 1991. Taught at University of Tokyo and Tokyo Institute of Technology and Tokyo University of Science. Received Minister of Education's Art Encouragement Prize. Major works includes Mamihara Bridge in Kumamoto, Fukushima Lagoon Museum in Niigata, Louis Vuitton Flagship Shops in New York, Hong Kong and Tokyo, and Aomori Museum of Art (Aomori).

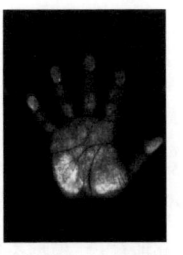

青木淳 事務所にて | Jun Aoki at his office in Tokyo's Jingumae district, 2011

青木 淳

彼は、クライアントの家の外壁を自分自身で塗る、おそらく唯一の有名建築家だろう。刷毛の風合いがきちんと出るかどうか確かめるためだという。青木淳は様々な点で型破りだ。毎朝、自分のオフィスまで一時間、リュックサックを背負って歩く。また、都市の環境にとってよくないと思ったとき、彼は同業者の建築を公然と批判することをためらわない。ひらめきを得るために、あるいはディスカッションをするときに、彼は時々クライアントと一緒に映画を見る。そうやって、多くの人たちと友だちになってしまう。青木の実験的な家「O」の施主である千賀香さんは、ある時青木と一緒に座って、ディズニーのアニメーションを見たことを覚えている。「彼は、私がどんな反応をするのか見たかったのでしょう。そして、私のこれまでの人生を感じとりたかったのだと思います。脚本家がある女優を念頭に置いて台本を書くように」。

青木の事務所で働くヨーロッパのインターンたちは、いつも、彼が使う模型の数に驚く。事務所には、模型を簡単に元に戻せるように青木が特別にしつらえた棚があり事務所内でスタッフが自由に持ち出せるようになっている。「私は『建設的ではない』形で解決方法を見つけます。クライアントが賛成しない部分をひとつずつ、家の模型からはがしていくんです」。そしてその過程で、青木は再び映画監督か、あたかも舞台演出家のように考える。「建築は光でできています。映画が建築と関係あるのは、その光という側面です。どちらも空間とその雰囲気を描写するという点で同じ性質をもっているんです」。

東京・銀座、もうひとつのルイ・ヴィトンのビルの照明をテストするために、青木は昔のパペット・シアターのようなキャンドルを使った。彼は、キャンドルを切り抜いた色紙の後ろに置いた。「私が一番好きな光の具合は、朝もやの東京です」。朝が早く、毎日4時か5時には起きている青木ならではだ。「ベランダに立って、朝の光の中で風呂に入るんです。どこに太陽が出ているかはわかりません。フランスのニームというところでは逆のことを経験しました。空気は乾燥していて、春の日はとても弱かったのですが、影はシャープで、強いんです」。

青木が映画監督のように物ごとを考えるとしたら、一番難しいジャンルはコメディ

「O」屋上につながる階段：
雨樋がデザインの一部となり、長さの違う棒はガードレールとして機能。壁面にあけられた、遊び心あふれる円形の穴は、クルト・シュヴィッターズのコラージュを思わせる。

Steps to "O" roof top:
Traces of rain water become part of the overall design. Uneven sticks serving as guard-rails and playfully placed circles in the wall evoke images of a Kurt Schwitters collage.

だ。ルイ・ヴィトンのビルを建てるとき、彼は『不思議の国のアリス』をテーマにした。そこでは、試着室の壁が、天井からロープで降りてくる。だから、VIPのクライアントは、スタッフが一緒についていれば、試着をするときに試着室を出たり入ったりしなくてもすむ。また青木は、ルイ・ヴィトンのインテリア・ディレクター、エリック・カールソンが認めるかどうかわからなかったデザインをこっそりしのびこませている。ルイス・キャロルの物語の中のウサギを思い起こさせる、ベージュ色の小さな人工の毛皮を使ったのだ(それが、最終的に天井に見つかったとき、店はすでにオープンしていた)。

結局、青木のユーモアのセンスが、クライアントに信頼を与えることになった。「いつだったか、彼が青いレインコートを着てそこに立っていたことがあります」。千賀香は覚えている。「でも、コートの内側はショッキングな赤だったんです。私は笑って、それから思いました。『絶対この人に家を建ててもらいたい!』って」。

[パート1] ── 2001-2007

ローランド・ハーゲンバーグ[以下RH] クライアントとは、どう仕事を進めるのですか?

青木 淳[以下 青木] まず、クライアントから希望をお聞きして、そこからたたき台としての案を考えて、それを模型にして見てもらいます。そうすると、最初に言葉で聞いた希望が実際にはちょっとズレていることがわかりますし、何がほんとうの希望なのかが、より正確に見えてきます。それで、また案をつくり直して、模型を見てもらいます。それを繰り返すプロセスを経て、案が固まってきます。模型が、コミュニケーション・ツールになっているのです。

RH 展覧会カタログの中に、建築家としての仕事は不可能の見極めとの記述がありますが、それは石材から不要なパーツを削り取っていく彫刻家のようなものでしょうか?

青木 ちょっと違います。あるプロジェクトで優先順位の高い要素を探る時に、同時に、優先順位の低い要素が何かも洗いだすのです。それは、最も重要度の高い要素の中に重要度の低い要素も含まれるということで、余分なものを削り取ることとは違います。クライアントには、僕の感じたこと、考えたことは、すべ

て伝えます。

RH すると、問題が発生しては解決する繰り返しに思えますが、どの程度クライアントの意向に従いますか？

青木 設計のどの段階でも、当然、クライアントの意向に従っています。ただ、自分が、いいと思えないものは設計したくありません。だから、言われた意向に字義通りに従うのではなく、まず、その意向のもとになっているものを探ろうとします。なぜ、そんな意向が出てきたのか、その根源がわかれば、別のかたちで意向に沿うこともできるはずで、自分にとっても納得がいく案ができる、と考えているからです。妥協するのも嫌ですし、自分の考えをゴリ押しするのも嫌です。クライアントとの間に共通の理解が生まれるまで、辛抱強く話し合い、変更を提案していくというアプローチをとります。

建築のプロジェクトは、長期間にわたり、予算規模も大きいので、お互いが納得できる土台を見つけることが重要です。例えば、住宅の依頼で、お金はないけれど頑丈な家を建てて欲しい、とクライアントが要望したとします。そういう場合は、内装にかける費用が足りないわけですから、内装のない殻のような住宅を提案し、それでほんとうに良いのか、それとも目標を変えるべきなのかよく判断してもらう必要があります。

RH 現代建築において、日本的なスタイルというものはあるのでしょうか？

青木 建築のスタイルが国ごとに違うという時代ではないと思います。しかし、不思議なもので、建築を雑誌で見て、その建築がどの国に建っているのか、だいたいわかるのです。ということは、建築のスタイルという次元ではありませんが、建築の風景という次元では、日本的なものがあるように思えるのです。

RH 日本とヨーロッパでは、建設のプロセスは違いますか？

青木 設計の期間を含めて、建設全体のプロセスが違うでしょうね。ヨーロッパの建築家の場合は、原理や原則を決めない限り、スタートしないようです。一方、日本人のやり方は、まず始めてみて、次々に変化する過程で、方針なり原則が生まれてくるのです。それは、東京という町の特徴でもあります。

あらかじめ決まった原則に従うのではなく、新たな事態が生じるたびに、秒単位で状況を把握して新しい作戦を考え、いつも最善の状態であろうとするのが、

日本での建築家の仕事なのです。サッカーと似ていますね。

RH　つまり、ヨーロッパ人の方が柔軟性に欠けるということですか？

青木　それは、柔軟性ということをどういうものとして考えるか、によりますね。ヨーロッパの建築家は、柔軟に課題に対応できるようながっちりとした原則を求める傾向があるし、ぼくは、仕事の過程でインスピレーションを得て、不断に変化し続け、結果として原則が見つかってくる、という仕事の進め方が気に入っています。

RH　そのやり方で、九州の馬見原橋も設計したと思いますが、ルイ・ヴィトンのフラッグシップショップとは対照的に、自然に満ちた山村の橋をデザインした真意は？

青木　人工が自然といちばん違うところは、それによってどういう感覚をもたらすかということなど、人の反応をあらかじめ想定しているところです。でも、僕は、人工のものでも、その想定がない人それぞれが違う受け取り方ができる、原っぱのような環境をつくりたいと思っています。その意味では、人工も自然も、そう変らないのです。

ぼくのそういう目標が、今まででもっとも素直に達成できているのが馬見原橋です。今の道はほとんど交通のためにつくられていますが、かつての道は、そこでいろいろなことが起きる場でした。橋は、そういう道が、川にぶつかって、それを跨ぐという特別な変形が成されたものです。それで、一本の道が、川のほとりで上下に分かれ、向こう岸でまた一本の道に戻る、というストーリーでこの橋をつくりました。結果として、道なのに宴会をしたり、お祭りの場所になったり、いろいろな使い方が生まれてきました。

RH　今、建築家は安全性や危機管理について再検証するべきだと思いますか？

青木　どうでしょう？僕が、ニューヨークのルイ・ヴィトンの店舗デザインをしていたのが、ちょうど9.11のテロの前後でした。案そのものは、その前後で変わっていません。僕は、人を煽り立てるような、これみよがしなデザインが得意ではありません。確かに、ニューヨークという町は強烈な欲望が生み出した都市でしょうが、そこには崇高さが強く醸し出されています。黒く重い石でできた崇高さですね。僕は、その崇高さを残したまま、それを白く透明な石に置き換え

られないか、と思って設計を進めていました。それは、ニューヨークの建物の根っこに戻るような方向でした。だから、テロの後、そのデザインが人々に安心感を与える方向に働いたのだと思います。安全性というのは、物理的なものだけでなく、拠り所となるような精神的なものも含んでいます。物理的な面での安全性や危機管理は、当然、考えていなくてはなりませんが、精神的な面もおろそかにできません。

RH 素材は設計に影響しますか？

青木 新しい素材からインスピレーションを受けて、そこから設計をすることがあるか、ということでしたら、そんなことはありません。最初にあるのは、もっ

SIA青山ビルディング スケッチ | Drawing for SIA Aoyama Building, Shibuya, Tokyo

と漠としたイメージのようなものです。その次に、そのイメージの達成のために、適当な素材を探します。

RH 素材は入念に調査するのですか？

青木 どんな表情をしているかということだけでなく、可能な大きさ、ジョイントの仕方、経年変化など、いろいろな側面が気になります。実は、一見地味な側面の方が、結果としての表情に大きな影響を与えるからです。特に、僕の場合は、日常とつながっているけれど、どこか日常とは違う、という感覚をつくってみたいと思っているので、そういう側面が重要になってきます。ひとつのピースの大きさだけで、スケール感はずいぶん変わってきます。夢としては、どこから始まって、どこで終わるか分からない均質でノン・スケールの素材があればなあ、と思うことが多いです。

RH もし自分のシェルターを作るとしたら、どのようなものになりますか？

青木 新しい形状の皮膚から成り、身体を覆うものはどうでしょう。自動的にサイズが変わり、時には、きつい手袋のように、肌にぴったりと張りつき、軟らかくなったり、硬かったり、見えなくなったり、ショッキングな表情になったり、まるでカメレオンのように周囲に合わせて色や模様を変えるような。伸縮自在で、泡や穴、大きな箱や暖かい部屋など、あらゆるものとなり、自分を包み込むことができて、また、負の感情やマイナスのエネルギーからも守る心理的なシェルターとしての機能があってもいいかもしれません。植物や動物は、数百万年かけて独自の複雑な自己防御機能を発展させてきましたが、そんな自然と同じように、シェルターという言葉には、無限の可能性があるように思います。

RH 2007年まで、10年間続けて、日本の現代建築は世界のデザインの舞台で、力を失っているという兆候が見られると思います。日本の官僚制度のもとにできた新しい制約が、建築の創造性をそいでいるのではないかと思うのですが？

青木 その通りです。悪い方向へむかっています。ネガティブ・チェックばかりで、前向きな夢がありません。おもしろいことを思いついてそれを実現させていく、という風土ではなくなってきています。ただ、これは官僚制度が問題というよりも、僕たち全体が問題なのです。まず、建築家はおもしろさばかりに目が行き、性能などを追求するという地道なことをおろそかにしてきました。それ

を両立させるには、時間とお金が必要です。つまり設計料がもっともらえなければ継続不可能です。だから、設計料を上げてもらうかわりに、もっと責任を持った仕事をするというように仕組みを変えていかなければならなかったのに、そういう努力を怠ってきました。そういうところに急に、もっと性能の検討・管理を、となると、機能不全になってしまう。法律の適用など、いろいろなところで、本音と建前は分けて考えていいんだ、としてきたのもまずかったことです。本音にあわせて建前も調整・改定していく努力と、建前にあわせた本音であろうとする努力を続けてくればよかったのですが、それをやってこなかった。今、建前としていることが本当に正しいのか検討していなかったところに急に、建前は絶対守らなくてはならない、となれば、間違った建前であっても、それを守らなくてはならなくなる。こういう環境では、安全な方へ安全な方へ流れていきます。建築家は実験をしなくなり、スムーズに認められる方法でのデザインをし、建築の過程で、遅れることがないように、ということに気を遣うようになります。

RH　それは、あなたが、自由な雰囲気で、普通とは違うコンセプトを実際の建築にすることができた、幸運な最後の世代ということですか？

青木　そうかもしれませんね。これからの時代、日本の大学を出たての若手建築家は、海外でキャリアをスタートすることも視野に入れ始めるのではないでしょうか。客観的に言って、ぼくはそれが正しい道だと思います。自分の創造性が発揮できるところでスタートした方がいいです。

RH　台湾の建物はどうですか？台湾でのプロジェクトもいくつか手がけていらっしゃいますよね。

青木　台湾の人たちは、自分たちがこうであってほしい、ということを素直に言います。彼らは、自分たちが美しいとか素晴らしいとか、モダンだと思っていること、資金的に実行可能かということをきちんと説明します。日本では、いいのか悪いのか曖昧なまま、進みます。日本では、クライアントが何を望んでいるのか、「感じ」「想像」しなければならない。

RH　台湾で実際に経験されたのは、どんなことですか？

青木　台湾の町では、モザイクタイルの古い建物がたくさんあります。とても素

敵に見えます。でも、僕は最初、そのモザイクがデザイン的に妥協の産物だということを知りませんでした。石はおろか、大きなタイルを使うお金がなかったので、仕方なくモザイクを使っていたことを知らなかったのです。だから、僕がプロジェクトの中で、モザイクを使うといったとき、皆がびっくりしました。「それだけは、やめてください！」って。そして、その理由を明確に言ってくれました。結局、議論を尽くして、今までネガティブに捉えられていたものをポジティブな捉え方に転換することこそ創造的ではないか、ということで、モザイクタイルが採用されました。

RH 中国ではどうですか？

青木 交渉にはとても時間がかかります。ルールも思いがけないところで変わったりします。たとえば上海では、光害がひどいために、ガラスの反射をおさえるという新しい法律ができました。それも突然です。だから、もう成り行きにまかせて、それに慣れるしかありません。そして同時に、粘り強く交渉を重ねなければいけないでしょうね。もしもともとのアイデアが強くなければ、建物が完成するまでにそのアイデアはどこかに飛んでいってしまうでしょう。

RH 日本では、創造性の表現がしにくくなっていると思います。それでは、建築の質はどうですか？まだ、世界でトップレベルにあるといえるでしょうか？

青木 それは言えると思います。アジアのほかの国々が追いつきつつありますけれどね。世界に誇る日本の建築技術と日本の秩序への誇りは、切っても切れない関係にあります。建設の現場はすばらしい。建設機械から、資材、道具、ネジからクギにいたるまで、全てのものが決められた場所に集められて、きれいに、規則正しく動いています。日本では、この仕事の哲学とでもいうべきものが、目に見えない美徳だと思われています。

RH 大手ゼネコンが寄り集まって、公共事業の入札価格を決める、いわゆる「談合」についてはどう思いますか？

青木 談合は、価格競争によって、自分の首を締めてしまわないものでもありました。大手ゼネコンは、ダンピングしないかわりに、その儲けの一部を技術力の向上に当てることができました。総合的な価格で言えば、談合はある意味、合理的な仕組みだったとも言えます。もちろん、談合には、対価以上の工事になって

しまうということなど、大きな負の面もありますから、それを禁止するのも当然です。でも、だとすれば、どうやってゼネコンの技術力を維持するのか、あるいは、設計者の技能向上など別の方法で技術力を維持するのか、そうした総合的なヴィジョンがないままだとまずいと思います。

RH そのほかに、日本の建築がこれまでの歴史で繰り返してきてしまった間違いの例をあげてもらえますか?

青木 たとえば、その時のニーズにぴったりあわせることがいい設計だとする姿勢は、そんな間違いのひとつだと思います。具体的には、学校や博物館、レストランなどです。もし、建物の使用目的が後になって変わったら、それがどんなによい建築であったとしても、壊されてしまうでしょう。でも、もっと一般的なことを大事にしてつくっていたら、もともと学校であったとしても、博物館にもレストランにも変わって、スクラップ・アンド・ビルドではない、豊かな町に育っていったのではないでしょうか。

[パート2]——2010

RH この10年間、近代的な建築が多く建てられ、ファッション業界の繁栄を表してきましたが、今後もこの大量消費が現代の建築のスタイルを支配するという状況が続くと思いますか?

青木 僕たちは、永遠に成長し続けるということが不可能であるということに、突如として直面しています。そして、それは日本の社会にとって大きな変化であると思います。僕たちは、かつてゼロから立ち上がり、急激な成長を経験してきました。僕たちは建てては壊し、建てては壊しということをいまだに続け、一度使ったものはほとんどを捨てています。この傾向を変えなければならないと思います。そして、短い期間使って終わりというものから、多機能で長く使えるものへと考えを変えていかなければならないと思います。長く使えるといっても、ただ単にその強度を上げればいいというわけではありません。それぞれのものが将来どういう使われ方ができるか、その可能性についてもう一度考え直すということです。現在、大量消費はもう行き詰まるだろうと言われていて、実

際のところ行き詰まっている状況だと思います。建築の世界では、僕たちはすでに新しい方向へと進んでいます。

RH それは、これまでの建築の方法から離れるということですか？

青木 スクラップ・アンド・ビルドをやっている限り、最大の価値は、新しさでしょう。他にはない、なにか新しいものを求める世界。つまり、流行の世界です。それでは、過去の建築を捨てることにもなりますし、周辺との差異を持つことに駆られた建築をつくることになります。これまでの建築の方法は、こうした新奇への希求と強く結びついています。今、僕が興味を持っているのは、その逆に、周辺と同化しながら、どこかわずかのところでズレていて、そのためにその周辺全体の見え方が変わってくるような、そんな建築のつくり方です。それは、個別の建築をつくりながらも、その個別が「作品」というのではなく、その個別を含む全体が「作品」になっている状態です。

RH これまで、ヨーロッパやアメリカで見られるような、大きな家や広いマンションをいいと言わない日本人に会ったことがありません。でも、そのような住居を基準にしようという全国レベルでの試みもまったく行われてきませんでした。これは、貧しい国についての話ではないんです。経済的に大きな国の話です。土地が足りないというのは、本当の理由ではないような気がします。東京への一極集中をなくし、様々な機能を地方へ分散させることはいつでもできることだと思うんです。

青木 僕にはそれがなぜだかわかりませんが、東京都の人口はこれからもっと増えるのではないでしょうか。それは、私たちのライフスタイルが大きく変わったことに原因があると思います。家族という単位がなくなって、多くの人が個人で暮らすようになっています。そういう人たちに広いスペースは必要ありませんから。一方で、狭い部屋に一人暮らしをするのは、あまり健康的ではありませんから、公共空間を共有するということがもっと増えてくると思います。

RH 青木さんの子どもの頃の経験で、今の建築家につながることはありますか？

青木 家族が引っ越し続きで、小学校を4つ替わりました。朝、目が覚めて、自分がいるところが一瞬わからず、どこにも帰属していない浮遊感をよく味わいま

した。その浮遊感は、その後、安部公房という作家の小説が好きになったことにもつながると思います。『燃えつきた地図』では、逃げた男が、いつの間にか、彼を追う探偵に入れ替わる。現実を前にしているのに、そこの非現実的な浮遊感が漂う、というのは、今、自分が建築家としてやろうとしていることのベースにあるような気がします。

RH 青木さんは、建築を説明するのに、よくヒッチコックの話を引き合いに出されますね？

青木 それは、もともと映画を見るのが好きだったことと、建築の仕事をしはじめた頃、たまたま、トリュフォーがヒッチコックにインタビューした『映画術』を読んで感銘を受けたからです。映画を観る人にある感情をあたえるために、どこでどういう方法をとったか、それがすごく具体的に書いてある。建築をつくるときも、このくらい明晰・意識的でありたいと思いました。もちろん、ヒッチコックの場合は、観客をひとつのサスペンスに巻き込むという目的であり、僕の場合は、ひとつの感情ではなく、人それぞれが別々の感情を持った方がいいと思うのですが、建築もまた、具体的な素材を使いながらある特定の質をつくりだす技術であることに気づかせてくれます。たとえば、ガラスはガラスとしてある、というのではなく、使い方次第で、建築にいろいろ質を与えることができる素材なのです。ちょうど、画家にとっての絵の具と同じで、赤という色自体が重要なのではなく、それをどう使うかに創造性があるということですね。

RH キャリアについて伺いますが、なぜ磯崎新氏のもとで働き始めたのですか？

青木 初めは、どこかで修業することなく、最初から自分で仕事を始められると思っていました。それで、東京大学で修士課程が終わって就職するのではなく、博士課程に進んで、1年ほど、大学と平行して設計事務所のまね事をしてみました。でも、ぼくの場合は、まるで展望が開けず、そもそも自分に建築の設計をするための基礎がまったくできていないのではないか、と180度逆の気持ちになり、ようやく修業先を考えるようになりました。磯崎さんは、ちょうどつくばセンタービルの現場の時期で、すでにエスタブリッシュした建築家でした。新進の建築家ではなく、磯崎さんのアトリエにと思ったのは、もちろん、氏を尊敬し

青木淳　馬見原橋にて｜
Jun Aoki at Mamihara bridge, Kyushu, 2000

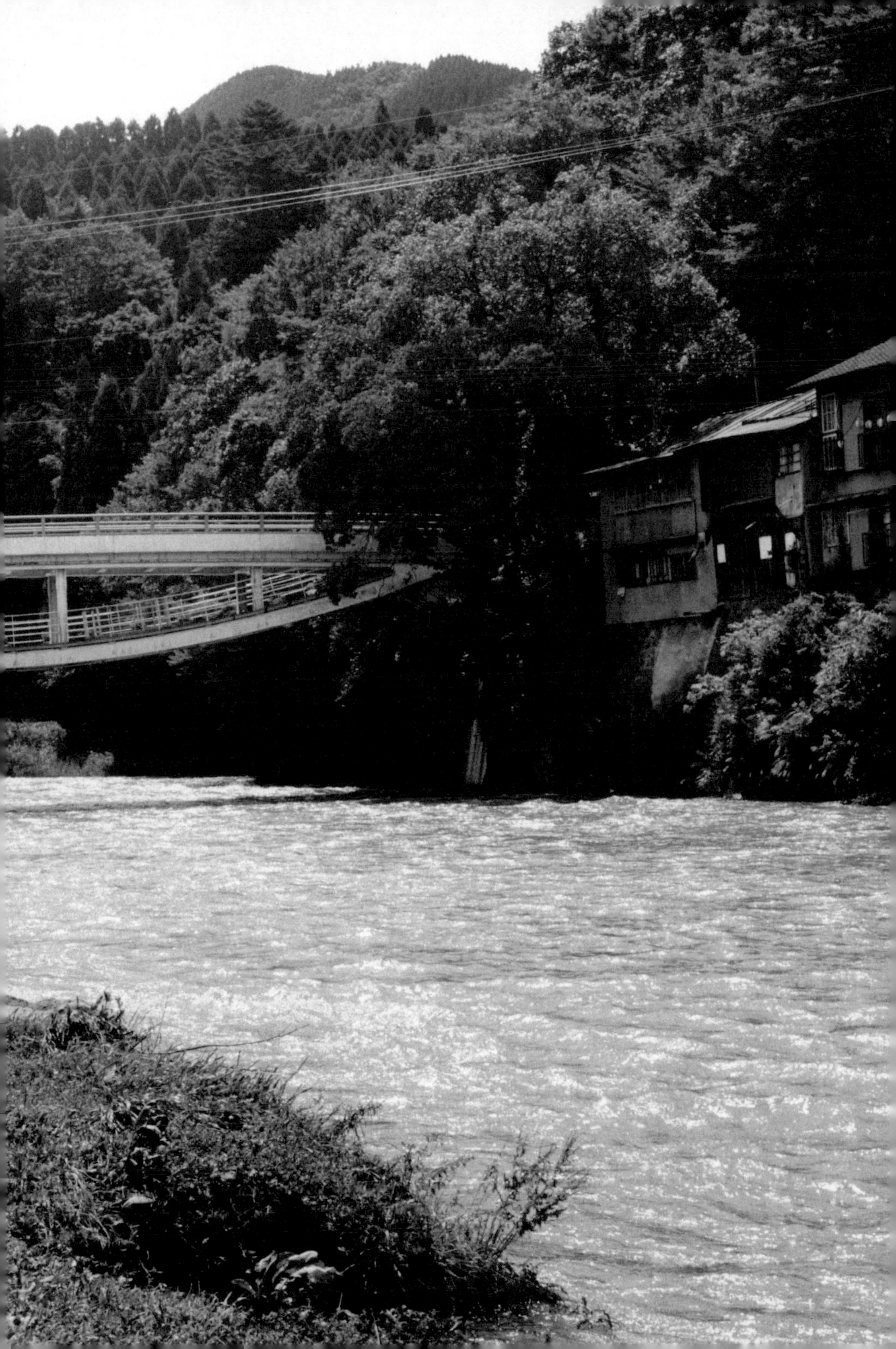

「不思議の国のアリス」をモチーフにした
ルイ・ヴィトン・フラッグシップショップにて（写真：高木淳）
At the Louis Vuitton flagship store in Tokyo
Jun Aoki's design refers to 'Alice in Wonderland'.
Photo : Jun Takagi

ていたからということもありますが、流行から離れて、まったくの白紙から建築について考え、設計できる場に入りたいと思ったからです。

RH　一方で、個人の家をたくさん手がけていらっしゃいますよね？　その仕事を完成させるのは毎回大変ですか？　施主とは絶えず連絡を取り合うのですか？

青木　どの仕事も大変ですけれど、個人の住宅は、住まう人にとって生活の基底部分にあたる空間になりますから、どうしても責任を感じてしまいます。その空間を気に入ってもらえなければならないだけでなく、その空間があるおかげで、もっと楽しく、拡がる感覚を感じられるようにしたい、と思います。深くつきあうことで、何を望まれているのかがわかってくるかもしれませんが、その反面、客観的になれなくなる気がします。ちょうどよい距離を保って、ある緊張感がある方がよい結果になるように思います。

RH　青木さんは、作曲家のリストと同じ誕生日（10月22日）ですよね？　リストの生まれた、オーストリアのライディングという町の郊外に、夢のような建物の模型を作りました。東京のような大都市からはずいぶん離れたこの町にどうして興味を持ったのですか？

青木　同じ誕生日であるとは知りませんでした。東京のような、よかれあしかれ、猥雑な町で生活し仕事をしていると、それと正反対の環境に憧れるものです。まわりにあまり建物がない田舎に、いつもの都会の空間を持ち込むのではなく、その環境に、ある意味で無防備なくらいに、ひたってみたい、と。ライディングという町は、さまざまな文明が交差する場にあったと聞きます。そのことと写真で観るのどかな景色とが、僕のなかではちょっとズレがあります。でも、きっとその風景を注意深く見つめていれば、またそこでの音や空気に敏感になれれば、過去から現代までのそういう時間を肌身で感じとれるのではないか、と思うのです。僕のバックグラウンドとはまったく別のところで、その土地にとっての「方丈記」の庵をつくる、というのは、実に挑戦的なことです。

Jun Aoki

He is probably the only renowned architect who has painted the outside wall of a client's house himself – just to make sure the brush-stroke texture came out right. Jun Aoki is unconventional in many ways. Every morning he walks an hour to his office with a rucksack on his back. He does not shy away from openly criticizing the works of his colleagues if he deems their buildings unhealthy to the urban environment. And to inspire, to start discussion, he sometimes watches movies with clients, many of whom become his friends along the way. Kaori Senga, the proprietor of Aoki's experimental O House, remembers sitting down one day with Aoki to go through the moods of a Disney animation clip. "He wanted to see my reactions, get a sense of my life's history, like a scriptwriter working on a film with a particular actress in mind."

European interns who work in Aoki's studio are always surprised at the number of models he uses. (For easy retrieval, Aoki developed a special shelf, where models stick into openings in a wall so they can float freely in his office.) "I find solutions in a deconstructive way. Step by step, I strip miniature houses of parts the client disapproves of." And in the process, Aoki thinks (again) like a movie or theater director: "Architecture consists of light, and films relate to architecture because of light. Both have the same quality of describing atmosphere and space."

To test illuminations for a Vuitton project in Tokyo's Ginza district, Aoki used candles like in old puppet theaters; he placed them behind cutouts and sheets of colored paper. "The light condition I like best is that of the Tokyo morning haze," says the early-riser, who has no problem getting up every day at four or five. "I stand on the balcony and take a bath in the particles of sunlight, not knowing where the sun is. I experienced the opposite in France, in the city of Nimes. The air was dry. The springtime light was weak but the shades sharp and strong."

If Aoki thinks as a cinematographer, than it is as one within the most difficult genre – comedy. He built the Vuitton flagship store around the theme of Alice in Wonderland. There, the dressing room walls descend from the ceilings on ropes, so that VIP clients, with store staff attending, do not have to go through the trouble of entering and leaving a booth when trying on clothes. Aoki also smuggled in a design that he was not sure Vuitton's interior style director, Eric Carlson, would approve of

「O」2000

– a piece of beige artificial fur that calls to mind the rabbit in Lewis Carroll's story. (When it was finally discovered on a ceiling, the store had already opened.)

In the end, Aoki's sense of humor can provide clients with the necessary confidence to build a house. "One day, he stood there in this blue raincoat," remembers Kaori Senga. "When he opened it, it was shocking red. I laughed and thought to myself, that's the person I want to build my home!"

[**Conversation part one**]——2001-2007

Roland Hagenberg How do you proceed when clients come to you?

Jun Aoki First I ask them to explain their ideas. Based on that information I produce a model. It serves as a springboard, so we can continue to communicate. Changes come up so I start modifying and the process repeats itself. Models can take on the roles of words.

RH When reading your essays I noticed, you often define your work by first explaining what is not possible. Are you a sculptor in front of a stone block chipping off what's unnecessary?

JA This is not quite correct. I put the priority on searching for the most important aspects. By doing so, I can identify all the lesser issues. These too should be included, but within the framework of the most important parts. So it's not just carving out. I tell the client everything I feel and think.

RH Architecture appears to be one continuous problem with constant solutions. How much do you let the client tell you what to do?

JA Of course, every step of the way the client comes first. I don't want to compromise or push my ideas either. I take a patient approach by negotiating and suggesting changes until we find a common ground. The most important thing is to have a bases for mutual understanding. The project usually takes a long time and involves a lot of money. For example, if a client says, I don't have a lot of money, but I want a solid, strong building, I give them a house that is an empty shell without any interiors. And then I ask them to decide if that is really what they want, or if they want to change the plan.

RH Is there something like a typical Japanese style in contemporary architecture?

青木事務所入口 | Entrance door to Aoki studio, 2011

JA The style of architecture is no longer different from one country to another. However, it is an interesting fact that, when I look at architecture in magazines, I can immediately understand which country it is from. This probably means that – not in an architectural style, but in the architectural atmosphere – something definitely exists that is unique to Japan.

RH Is the building process in Japan significantly different from that in Europe?

JA The working process of Japanese and European architects is very different. For Europeans principles come first and then the process happens. The Japanese way is to start creating and in the process principles will emerge within an environment which changes constantly. Just look at Tokyo. I often compare the situation with soccer. It works exactly like Japanese architecture. You cannot just follow a principle. Every split-second you must deal with a new situation, adjust and come up with a new strategy, which again might only be short-lived. That's how we work in Japan – like a soccer team.

RH You mean Europeans are less flexible?

JA That depends on how you define the idea of being flexible. European architects tend to look for a strong principle that can be applied to various themes in a flexible manner. For me there's only the working process from which I get inspired. Within that I make decisions and plans under the influence of an ever-changing situation.

RH This approach also applied to your Mamihara Bridge in Kyushu. Why would a contemporary architect who creates flagship stores for Louis Vuitton do a project in Japan's deepest, rural countryside?

JA The greatest difference between artificial and natural is that artificial products are calculated outcomes of projecting the future. My ambition is to create an artificial field of grass that people can react to in any way they want, because natural and artificial is not all that different anymore. Mamihara Bridge is one of the projects where this approach evolved naturally. Modern roads are mostly made for the purpose of commuting, but in the older days roads were stages for different dramas. When those roads reach the river, and are blocked by the river, and a bridge is built to connect the roads to the other side, the bridge changes according to that road. The story I had in mind when building Mamihara bridge was that the road would split into an upper and a lower part when it reaches the river and then would reunite on the other side. People now have parties on the bridge, and festivals, and they do so many other things there that they wouldn't otherwise do on a road.

RH   Nowadays, do contemporary architects have to re-think the meaning of "safety", "security" and "protection" in their work?

JA   There is no general answer to that. I was designing the Louis Vuitton store in NY just after 9/11. Before and after 9/11 the general plan remained the same. I am not so good at elaborate designs that challenge people. While it is true that New York is a city born of a strong will to always want more, it is also a very proud city and the pride is shown in the building's heavy stone black walls. I didn't want to lose that sense of pride, so my challenge was to change black stones into white transparent ones and retain the same feeling. The process led me back to the roots of New York's architecture, to a design that would give people a sense of comfort after the terrorist attack. This does not necessarily mean "safety", but more a "spiritual" comfort. Needless to say, the importance of safety in buildings must not be overlooked, but the spiritual part was very important to me.

RH   Do materials influence your style?

JA   If you are asking whether I ever get inspiration from materials and start my design from there, the answer is no. In the beginning, there is always just a vague image. After that, the task is to introduce the proper material to reality.

RH   Are there materials that you wish would be the subject of more research?

JA   I want to know not only about the texture of a material, but also how big a single piece of it could be, and how it can be connected to other things, and how it changes over the years, and so on. Those dry facts have a significant influence on how the materials look when the building is completed. In my case, this is especially important because I am always aiming for a design that is connected to everyday life and is, at the same time, different from everyday life. Even the size of one piece of material can have a big impact on the whole scale of the project. So, my dream material would be a material that is so consistent and out of scale that we actually don't know where it begins and where it ends.

RH   If you had to build a private shelter for yourself, what would it look like?

JA   My personal shelter is made of a new form of skin. It surrounds my body and adjusts itself automatically. Sometimes it's close to my own skin fitting like a tight glove: soft or hard, invisible or shocking and then again like a chameleon absorbing surrounding colors and patterns. Other times it expands and then I am inside a bubble, a cave, a bunker, a warm room - whatever. Maybe it can also turn into a psychic sphere that shields me from negative emotions and energies. The possibilities are endless like nature itself, where plants and animals have developed their own intricate protection systems over millions of years.

RH Now, in 2007, after ten successive years, there are growing signs that Japan's contemporary architecture is losing ground in the international design world. Japan's bureaucracy suffocates creativity because of new construction rules. Do you agree?

JA Absolutely. Japan is moving in a wrong direction. The bureaucrats only check on negative things and don't take into consideration dreams leading to the future. The whole society is becoming closed-minded and therefore cannot come up with an interesting new reality. We cannot entirely blame the bureaucrats – we must think of it as our own problem. Architects have focused too much on elaborate designs and not enough on the basics of design, such as usefulness and functionality. To balance interesting design and functionality we need time and money – in other words, we need bigger design budgets. The architects should change their attitude, they should take on more responsibilities and raise their budgets at the same time. When they fail to take on more responsibilities, they can't ask for more functionality. Another problem is that architects think they can bend the rules and not break them. We have not tried hard enough to unite regulations with the needs of the clients. And we have not put enough effort into examining and evaluating the rules and regulations. And now, suddenly, the government is enforcing their regulations more strictly and architects are having second thoughts about whether those rules are worth following. In such a situation, projects tend to drift to the "safe" side, because architects are not willing to experiment anymore. Their designs are made for the sake of passing regulations easily, so that the construction can be completed on time.

RH You mean you belong to that last, lucky generation of Japanese architects that started out in a free creative environment where unusual concepts on paper could be turned into real buildings?

JA You could say so. Today, young Japanese architects right out of university should seriously consider starting their careers abroad. I think that is the correct career path for them. They should start where their creativity has room to grow.

RH What about building in Taiwan? You have several projects there.

JA The main difference is that the Taiwanese tell you, directly, what they want.

They explain what they consider elegant, grand, modern or financially feasible. Not so in Japan. Here, many things remain unclear. You have to sense, guess and speculate about what your client wants.

RH   Can you give an example from first-hand experience?

JA   In Taiwanese cities, I see many old houses covered with mosaics. I find them very charming. But, in the beginning, I didn't know that those mosaics often represent a design compromise – when builders don't have enough money they use tiles. So, when I suggested using mosaics in one of my projects everybody was shocked, "No, no, not that, please!" We had big discussions and came to the conclusion that to have ideas that have been considered "negative" in the past changed and perceived as "positive" is the essence of being creative. And that's why we used the mosaic tiles.

RH   And in mainland China?

JA   Negotiations are very slow and rules can change unexpectedly. In Shanghai, for instance, with all the light pollution, new laws came up – to reduce the glare from

青木淳 東京のビルを背景に | Jun Aoki with Tokyo skyline, 2000

glass, for instance. It happened all of a sudden. So you go with the flow and adapt. At the same time, you continue to negotiate. If your original idea is not strong enough, it will not survive by the time the building is finished in China.

RH   The creative output might be suffering in Japan, but what about the construction quality? Is it still one of the best in the world?

JA   I would say so, although other Asian countries are catching up quickly. The famed Japanese construction quality and the Japanese pride in orderliness are inseparable; go to a construction site and it will never appear chaotic. From machines, materials and tools, down to screws and nails, everything has its designated spot, is clean and runs together like clockwork. In Japan, this work ethic is considered the invisible beauty of architecture. It is part of any finished building.

RH   What about the so-called 'dango system' in Japan, where big construction companies get together and secretly fix prices for public works projects?

JA   The bidding system was brought in so that the competition would not hurt the service providers. The construction giants would not be able to practice price-dumping and, instead, would put part of their profits into technology. The bidding system was logical, in a way. Of course, it had a big negative side to it in that the construction fee was very expensive, and that part needs to be taken care of. But then, how can the construction companies maintain their high-tech reputations? We need a general consensus on a way to maintain technological growth while improving the skills of the designers.

RH   Besides that, can you give an example of a mistake that has been repeated in the history of Japanese architecture?

JA   Such a mistake would be to accommodate in a building only one specific purpose. Let's say there is a school, or a museum, or restaurant. If the purpose of the building changes years later, even if it is a wonderful building, it will most likely be destroyed. If more thought was put into constructing buildings we could have schools that, if necessary, could easily be turned into museums or restaurants. Avoiding the "scrap-and-build" would lead to a richer urban environment.

[**Conversation part two**]——2010

Roland Hagenberg   During the last ten years, many modern buildings have been created to glorify the fashion industry. Will consumerism keep its grip on modern architecture?

Jun Aoki We suddenly see that eternal growth is impossible and this is a drastic change for Japanese society. We once started from zero and experienced rapid growth. We built and tore down, and we still build and scrap and do away with most of the used materials. This must change and we must switch from a flow of short-lived goods to creating things with multifunctional longevity. The modern concept of this longevity is not merely building strong objects but, rather, rethinking the potential future functions of each object. Right now, it is said that consumerism has reached a dead end, but this has been going on for a while now and, in the world of architecture, we are already shifting in new directions...

RH And leaving behind traditional building elements?

JA As long as we continue with a scrap-and-build process, the biggest value is always a completely new building – people long for something that did not exist before, and that is based on fashion. This leads to the discarding of historical architecture, just for the sake of being different to your neighbors. Recently, this process has gone to extremes. I don't say I want to be completely different, but just slightly different – still blending into the neighborhood. This approach should give the whole district a new look. At the moment we concentrate on individually constructed pieces. Instead, we should think of how they combine to create a unique atmosphere.

RH I've never met a Japanese person who doesn't admire the much larger apartments and houses available in Europe or America. And yet, there has never been an attempt to make that kind of living standard possible on a national scale. We are not talking about a Third World country here – Japan is the third largest economy in the world. Lack of space cannot be the real reason. Tokyo could be decentralized at any time.

JA I don't know. The population in metropolitan areas will further increase and, on top of that, our lifestyles will drastically change, because the family unit will disappear. More people will live alone and won't need larger spaces. On the other hand, to live alone in a tiny room is not healthy. So maybe the increased population will instead lead to more shared public spaces.

RH Was there a moment in your childhood that defined what you do as an architect today?

JA I attended four primary schools because my family moved constantly. Waking up in the morning, often I didn't know where I was for a second and then would experience a floating feeling of not belonging anywhere. That floating feeling led me to the works of writer Kobo Abe. In his story, "The Ruined Map", a fugitive trades places with the detective who's chasing him. What I am trying to do as an architect is based on this floating sensation of facing reality surrounded by surreal feelings.

RH You often refer to Alfred Hitchcock when explaining your architecture.

JA That is because I was always a movie fan and, when I was starting out as an architect, I read a book that featured interviews that François Truffaut did with Hitchcock and I was blown away. It was full of detailed ideas about how he constructed his movies to affect emotions. I wanted to become as clear and determined as him when designing buildings. Of course, in Hitchcock's case, the objective was to take the audience into a world of suspense. And, in my case, I don't aim for one general emotion, but rather an individual emotion unique to the building's user. I realized that architecture creates quality by using specific materials. Glass, for instance, should not exist merely as glass but be used in a multitude of ways to affect the texture of a building. It is like paint for a painter. What's important is not the color red itself, but how you use it in the creative process.

RH Why did you start working for Arata Isozaki?

JA At first I thought I could go to work without serving as an apprentice. So I started my own company while I was doing my Masters degree at the University of Tokyo. That didn't work out at all, and I ended up ignoring my personal voice as an architect. That's why I looked for a teacher. At that time, Isozaki was already an established architect working on the Tsukuba Center Building. I chose him, rather than a new star architect, not only because I respected him, but because he was beyond fashion and approached architecture from "point zero". That's why I wanted to be a member of his team.

RH You've built dozens of private houses. Is it always difficult to let them go? Do you stay in touch with the owners?

JA Every project is demanding. Private houses become the base of a person's life, so I feel very responsible for its design. It is essential that the client likes my ideas, but also that he understands that his house can lead to a better and happier life. When I get to know the client very well, I also get a very good idea of what he wants. But, at the same time, there's a danger of losing my objectivity. It is important to keep the right balance in my relationship with the client.

RH It is a wonderful coincidence that you share your October 22 birthday with composer Franz Liszt. For the village of Raiding in Austria, where Liszt was born, you recently created a model of a dreamy building in the countryside. What attracts you away from mega-cities like Tokyo?

JA I didn't know we shared the same birthday. Tokyo is a crowded city, for better or worse. As a person working in Tokyo, you sometimes long for the opposite atmosphere. I would like to let my guard down and jump right into the rural environment of the countryside, rather than try to bring city elements to the landscape. I hear that Raiding was a cross-point of different cultures. Looking at its peaceful surrounds, it is hard to imagine the exciting history of the place, but I am sure that if you look at it hard enough – and if you try to tune into the sounds and atmosphere – you would be able to feel it. It is a challenging project for me to build a hojoki hut (from Japan's ancient Kamakura period) in a land that is completely different to the land I come from.

青木淳 著者とともに「ライディング・プロジェクト」の模型と｜
Roland Hagenberg and Jun Aoki with model for "Raiding Project", 2010

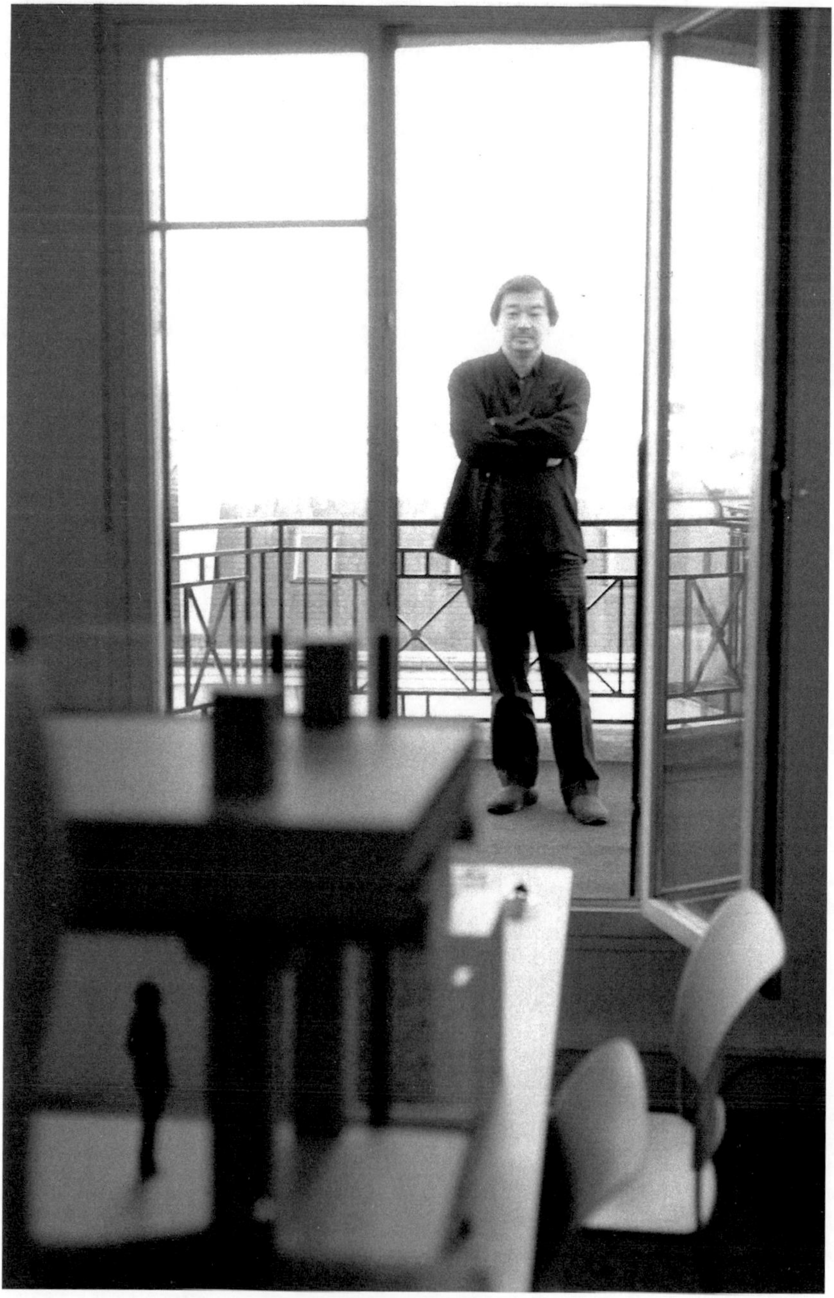

坂 茂 | Shigeru Ban

理想的には、私自身が継続して努力していかなければ乗り越えられないような、そんなプロジェクトがやりたいんです。
"Ideally, I would have insurmountable problems to solve so that I could train continuously."

1957年東京都生まれ。1982年から1983年まで磯崎新アトリエ勤務。1984年クーパー・ユニオン卒業。1985年坂茂建築設計設立。国連難民高等弁務官事務所コンサルタント、コロンビア大学を経て、慶應義塾大学環境情報学部教授(2008)。毎日デザイン賞大賞、日本建築家協会新人賞、世界建築賞2002など受賞多数。主な作品に、MDS│G(東京)、壁のない家(長野)、ハノーバー万博2000日本館(ドイツ)、ノマディック美術館(アメリカ)、ポンピドゥーセンター メス(フランス)などがある。

Born 1957 in Tokyo. Worked at Arata Isozaki & Associates from 1982 to 1983. Graduated from Cooper Union school of Architecture in 1984. Established his own practice in 1985. Consultant for UNHCR. Taught at Columbia University, New York. Professor of Keio University (2008). Among Numerous awards: Mainichi Design Prize, The Japan Intitute of Architects (JIA) Prize and World Architecture Awards 2002: Best House in the World. Major works include Paper Gallery (MDS│G) in Tokyo, Curtain Wall-less House in Nagano, Japan Pavilion at Hanover Expo 2000, Nomadic Museum, USA and the Centre Pompidou-Metz, France

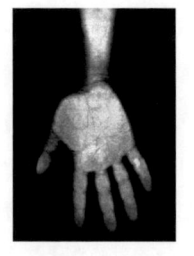

坂茂 パリの事務所にて | Shigeru Ban on the balcony at his office in Paris, November 2010.

坂 茂

「阪神淡路大震災の6カ月後、まだ多くの被災者たちが痛々しいテントで暮らしていました」と坂茂は当時を回顧する。「しかも、それが私の母国、日本での出来事だったのです！」1995年に起きたこの震災では、何千人もの人々が亡くなった。坂は大きな衝撃を受けた。彼はその影響を15年たった今もひきずっている。このスター建築家は、コンゴの殺戮の地、津波に洗われたスリランカの村、福島の瓦礫の山に向かう。建築家坂茂は、これらの土地で、家を失った人たちのために緊急避難住宅を建てている。

これらの避難住宅は次の3つの基準を満たす必要がある。単純な構造であること、再使用できる材料を使っていること、居住者によい影響をあたえること、である。現実には、金属製のコンテナやプラスチック製の陰気な色のバラックを使うことが多い。一方、坂茂の使う材料は面白く、ユーモアがあり、リサイクル可能で頑丈だ。たとえば明るい色で塗装した、砂を入れたビールケース。坂はこれを基礎として好んで使う。彼の原則はこうだ。「レンガに聞け！」、この言葉は伝説的な建築家ルイス・カーンによるもの。彼はよき建築材料を間違った場所に使うことを警告したのだ。フィンランドの建築家アルヴァ・アールトからは、環境が建物に対して優越的な時には、着実に施工しなければ成功しないということを学んだ。それらを活かして、坂は慎重に検討を重ね、アフリカの現地でダンボールの筒を使うというアイデアに行きついた。ルワンダの難民キャンプの状況を正確に把握した結果である。「目的を持って何らかの建物を建てるということは、とりあえず使うことができればいいということとはまったく違う」

国連難民高等弁務官が金属製のポールを難民のために配給した。思いがけないことには、援助物資がルワンダに到着すると、ポールは難民キャンプの資材としてではなく、通貨として使われた。現地では金属はとても高価なものだったのだ。それを知った坂は、紙管（ダンボールの筒）を送ることを提案した。最終的に、戦争難民たちは難民キャンプに戻ってきた。PTS（紙管構造）という材料を使用するアイデアが浮かんだのは、25年以上も前、坂茂がファックス用

紙を使いきった時のことである。紙管の芯を手にしたところ、とてつもなく頑丈そうに思えた。今度はもう少し太い筒を手に入れることにした。それは繊維メーカーのゴミ箱から持ってきた紙管だった。彼は荷重耐力を測定し、この環境にやさしい素材を使って6階建ての建造物が可能という結論に達した。5年後の1990年、坂茂のおかげで、日本の建築史上初めて紙管が建築材料として認可された。

現在までに、彼の作品の多くがすでに古典となっている。神戸の紙の教会、東京のファッションデザイナー・三宅一生の紙のギャラリー、2000年ハノーバー万博の日本館、フランス東部メス市のポンピドゥーセンター分館などである。坂茂のヒューマニズムに富んだ活動は、おしゃれな雑誌を読んでかけつけた学生やボランティアの支援を受けている。彼は2009年まで、国連のアドバイザーも務めている。

人々が彼を尊敬してやまない理由は、作品の魅力だけによるものではない。彼はあらゆる職務と格闘し、自ら現場に立ち、共感を示す。いやいやながらカリスマの役を引き受けさせられた坂茂は、「環境派建築家」のレッテルを貼られることに対してはしぶい顔をするばかりである。「私が環境にやさしい建物や

模型の人形 坂の事務所にて | Model detail with figurine at Ban's office in Paris, 2010

坂茂 パリにて | Shigeru Ban, Paris, November (2010)

人間の緊急時の建築に着手した時点では、これらに関心を持つ人は少なかった。当時はそれほど魅力的なテーマではなかったのです。しかし今では、多くの建築家たちが〈環境派〉を自称しています。彼らの多くは、トレンドから次のトレンドへとジャンプしている。ただそれだけのことなのです」

ニューヨークのクーパー・ユニオン建築学部を卒業した坂茂は、有名になることを嫌っているわけではない。むしろまったく反対だ。「有名になると仕事は円滑に進みます」と彼は語る。「信頼を得るために無駄な時間を費やす必要がなくなるんです。私の話をじっくり聞いてくれるし、技術的な問題をクリアするのもそう難しい話ではなくなるんです」

坂茂はふたつの世界に生きている。ひとつはスラムと難民キャンプの世界。ここに地球上の人間の7分の1が居住を強いられている。もうひとつは、現代的な美術館と魅力的なヴィラである。これらから抽出したアイデアを、彼は緊急避難の住宅に応用している。そして、応用を実践するにあたって、彼は常に「レンガに聞く」のだ。最近、スリランカであったこと。レンガは彼に次のように語りかけた。「今回は紙管を使わないでください。木材とレンガです。それを現地調達してください。レンガ用の土はたっぷりあります。そうすれば雇用が発生します。人々は新しい家について夢を見ることになり、それは彼らに希望を与えることになります」

2001-2003

ローランド・ハーゲンバーグ[以下RH] 1993年建築基準法第38条により、当時の建設省に恒久的な主体構造としての使用を認定させて以来、紙管を合法的な素材として使用していますが、そもそも、どうして紙の筒を使おうと思ったのですか？

坂 茂[以下坂] フィンランド人建築家、アルヴァ・アールトの展覧会のインスタレーションをした時ですが、高価な木材を使う予算がなかったのです。木材は、展覧会後にはゴミになってしまう点でも、気に入りませんでした。ちょうど、その前のプロジェクトで使った残り物の紙管が事務所にあり、捨ててしまうのはもったいないからアルヴァ・アールト展で使ってみようと思いついたのが、きっかけです。

正式に認定された建築素材として紙を用いた、恒久的な建築物の第1号は、東京にある三宅一生のMDS｜Gです。

RH 「地震は人を殺さない。殺すのは建物だ。我々建築家がもっと優れた建物を作れば人は死ななくて済む」というコメントを聞いたことがあります。

紙管の場合、神戸、ルワンダ、トルコ、インドなど、世界中の地震被災者や難民のために安価な住居を敏速に供給できたわけで、結果的に、日本から世界に向けて極めてユニークな建築スタイルを輸出することになったと思います。その延長線上に、ハノーバー万博の日本館があるようですが……。

坂 ドイツ同様、日本の都市はすべて戦争で破壊されました。その後、都市を再建する段階で、鉄やコンクリートを使った近代建築には、日本の伝統的建築様式の連続性を持たせることはできませんでした。日本の建築における近代化は、過去からの連続性のない唐突な西洋化と同義になったわけです。それに対し西洋諸国では、近代的な材料や構造を使っても、伝統的建築様式の延長線上の発展をとげられたわけです。日本の都市が無秩序なのはそのためで、それ自体は良い面と悪い面があると思います。良い面をあげると、建築家に自由があり、何でもできることです。

RH では、「何でもあり」が日本の現代建築の特徴ですか？

坂 その自由さゆえ、日本の現代建築には独特のアイデンティティーがあります。ここで言う自由とは悪い意味で、日本の建築家は甘やかされているのです。例えばの話ですが、有名な建築家に仕事を頼んだ場合、クライアントは設計に一切口

出ししません。クライアントは「なぜ、こんな形なのか?」とか「なぜ、こんな構造なのか?」といった質問はせず、建築家が提示する案を鵜呑みにしてしまうのです。ところが、外国で仕事をする場合は、筋の通った説明が必要です。どんなクライアントも「なぜ?」と尋ねてきますし、一般の人でさえ質問をしてきますので。要するに、日本の建築家は、説得力のある答えをしなくてもよい分、甘やかされているということです。その結果、日本では建物の形が極めて自由となり、それが日本の建築のアイデンティティーとなっているのです。

RH　つまり、日本で建築家をする方が簡単だということですか?

坂　私の場合、アメリカで建築を学んでいますから、日本でも外国でも特に違いはありません。ただ、若い建築家にとっては、日本の方がチャンスが多いと思います。世界各国を飛び回ってみてわかったのですが、この点は日本が特別で、例えば、アメリカでは若手はコンペにも参加できません。確かに、もっと建築家に質問を浴びせるべきですが、日本のクライアントは柔軟性があり、モダンで斬新なものを積極的に取り入れるので、若手建築家が実績をつくるには東京が一番だと思います。私は東京をベースに仕事を始めて、とてもよかったと思っています。

RH　今日のコンピューター・テクノロジーが建築を改善したと思いますか?

坂　コンピューターは道具としては使っていますが、設計そのものには使いません。コンピューターの恩恵が及ばない領域というのもがいくつかありますが、その1つが建築でしょう。構造計算は別として。コンピューターがなかった数百年前に、現在よりも優れた建築物が作られていたわけですから。より設計に時間をかければ、より優れた建物ができるということで、コンピューターの進化自体は建築の質の向上とは必ずしも関係ないのです。

RH　日本の将来を、どう見ていますか?

坂　正直言って、日本は危機的です。まず、教育制度がなっていない。おそらく、大学は世界最低レベルです。大学生は勉強する必要がなく、ひどい場合、学校にも来ないのですから。英語も話せないから、外国で仕事ができる人はほとんどいません。さらに、政治家が頼りないから政治家を志す者もいない。日本の将来は真っ暗です。

Shigeru Ban

"Six months after the earthquake in Kobe, many victims were still living in miserable tents," Shigeru Ban remembers. "And that was in my own country, Japan!" Thousands had lost their lives in the 1995 disaster. Ban was shocked. It was that shock that made him into what he still is today, 15 years on: an architectural star who is drawn to crisis zones like the killing fields of the Congo, the villages in Sri Lanka washed away by the tsunami, the piles of rubble in Fukushima. These are the places where Ban builds emergency housing for the homeless.

The buildings have to fulfill three criteria: the structure must be simple and the material reusable, and they must have a positive effect on the occupants - not depressing, as is often the case with metal containers and gloomy barracks made of plastic. Ban's materials are typically playful, humorous, recycled and stable - brightly colored beer crates filled with sand, for example, which the architect likes to use as foundations. Here his axiom is: "Listen to the brick!" It originated from the legendary architect Louis Kahn, who warned against using good building materials in the wrong place. From the Finnish housebuilder Alvar Aalto, Ban learned in turn that sound development can only succeed if the environment is brought into it. For this reason, Ban does not blindly send off cardboard tube designs to Africa, but first finds out for himself about the state of the refugee camps in Rwanda. "Building something with good intentions doesn't mean that it will work."

When the UN High Commission dispatched metal tent-poles for refugees, no one imagined that when the aid goods arrived in Rwanda they would be used as a barter currency and not as camping equipment. Metal is just too valuable there. So Ban suggested sending cardboard rolls. And after that, the war refugees did indeed go back to building shelters.

The idea of using the often undervalued building material known as PTS (paper tube structure) came to the Japanese architect more than 25 years ago, when he once ran out of fax paper. He held the empty roll in his hand. It was almost impossible to bend. Ban got hold of some larger examples; cardboard rolls from the refuse tips of textile companies. He tested their load-bear-ing capacity and came to the conclusion that this environmentally friendly substance could even be used to build six-storey houses. Five years later, in 1990, for the first time in Japanese history,

坂茂 MDS|Gにて | Shigeru Ban at Issey Miyake's MDS|G, Tokyo, 2000

paper tubes were permitted as a construction material - thanks to Ban.

By now, many of his buildings have become classics: the paper church in Kobe, the paper gallery for fashion designer Issey Miyake in Tokyo, the Japan Pavilion at the 2000 World Exhibition in Hanover, and of course the branch of the Centre Pompidou in the eastern French city of Metz. All these creations use paper as the supporting structure. Ban is assisted in his humanitarian initiatives - he was a UN adviser until 2009 - by students and volunteers, who came to hear of him from glossy magazines.

However, the reason why they admire him has nothing to do with glamour. "Ban never gives up," they say. "He tackles every job, gets his hands dirty, shows compassion." Forced reluctantly into the role of guru, Ban just grimaces when people try to label him as a "green architect". "When I started, only a few people were interested in ecological building and architecture for humanitarian emergencies. In those days, it wasn't sexy enough. Today many of my colleagues describe themselves as 'green', but only because they are constantly jumping from one trend to the next."

A former graduate of New York's Cooper Union School of Architecture, he has nothing against being famous - on the contrary: "It makes my work easier," he says. "I no longer waste so much time convincing people. They listen to me. Technical problems vanish over-night."

Ban lives in parallel worlds. One is the world of slums and refugee camps, in which every seventh human being on this planet is forced to live. The other is that of modern museums and cool villas. The ideas Ban picks up there, he uses for his emergency housing - and in doing so, of course, he always "listens to the brick". In Sri Lanka recently, the brick said to him something like: "This time, no cardboard tubes, please. Stick with the brick. Have them made locally. There is plenty of mud for that. It'll create jobs. The people will dream about their new houses and it will give them hope."

[**Conversation**]——2001-2003

Roland Hagenberg Under Article 38 of the Building Standards Law the Ministry of Construction in Japan approved your paper-tubes in 1993. Since then you have used paper legally as structural material in buildings. How did you come up with that idea?

Shigeru Ban I didn't have enough money to use expensive wood for the set-up of the exhibition for Finnish architect Alvar Aalto. The idea that wood is wasted after the show bothered me as well. At that time I still had some leftover paper-tubes from a previous project in my office. I thought what a pity to throw them away, better use them for Alvar Aalto. Issey Miyake's MDS Gallery in Tokyo became the first permanent paper-tube structure building, after I got the permission from the government.

RH "Earthquakes don't kill people. Buildings do! If we build them better, people

坂茂デザインの紙筒のいす |
Paper tube chair by Shigeru Ban

don't die!" is a famous quote of yours. Your paper-tubes provide quick and affordable housings to quake victims and refugees worldwide. Kobe, Rwanda, Turkey and now India. Seems like Japan is exporting a very unique architectural style after all, which culminated in your Japanese Pavilion at the Hanover World Expo (2000).

SB All cities in Japan were destroyed during the war – same as in Germany. When Japan rebuilt the cities, it used modern materials such as iron and concrete in its buildings, but it restricted Japan's historical continuation of its own architectural style. In other words, modernization of architecture was a synonym of westernization. On the other hand, European countries including your country – Germany could continue its architectural tradition, even though they used modern materials. For us Japanese, modernization was westernization, and that cut off our history. That's why our cities became chaotic. This has a positive and a negative side. On the positive side, it gives us the freedom to basically do anything we like in architecture.

RH "Anything goes" – is that what makes Japanese contemporary architecture different from other cultures?

SB Japanese contemporary architecture has a certain identity – because of freedom, and I want to use the word "freedom" in a negative way. In our country Japanese architects are spoiled. If somebody asks a famous architect to do a project, the client doesn't give him or her a hard time. Clients are not supposed to ask "why?" For instance, why this shape? Why this structure? The architect presents the client with a very serious building concept, and then the client is supposed to believe it without question. When I work abroad, I really have to come up with a convincing theory. Everybody will ask me 'why?' – even the general public. In that sense I think architects in Japan are spoiled – they don't have to convince people. That is the reason why there's such a freedom of shape. It provides Japanese contemporary architecture with a certain identity.

RH So it's easier for an architect in Japan?

SB For me there's no difference, since I studied architecture in the United States. There are so many opportunities in Japan especially for young architects. Since I have been traveling all over the world, I can say, we have a very unique situation here. In the United States there are practically no competitions for young talents and that's why I think Tokyo is one of the best places to start a practice. The Japanese client is flexible and really interested in something modern and innovative - although he doesn't quiz the architect enough. I was very lucky to start my own practice in Tokyo.

RH Did today's computer technology improve architecture?

SB I use computers as a tool but not for designing. Architecture is one of the very few fields where the advance of computers doesn't make things better - except structural design. Hundreds of years ago, without computers, we were building better architecture. The more time we spend in designing and building, the better architecture becomes. That's why the advance of computers doesn't necessarily mean it makes architecture better.

RH Is this openness towards modern styles that you mentioned, a reflection of Japan's modern lifestyle as a whole?

SB To be honest, we are having very critical problems. First of all, the education system is terrible. The universities are the worst in the world. Students don't have to study. They even don't come to school. They cannot speak English. We are generally not able to work in other countries. We have no strong leaders in politics. No one wants to be a politician. I don't see any future for Japan.

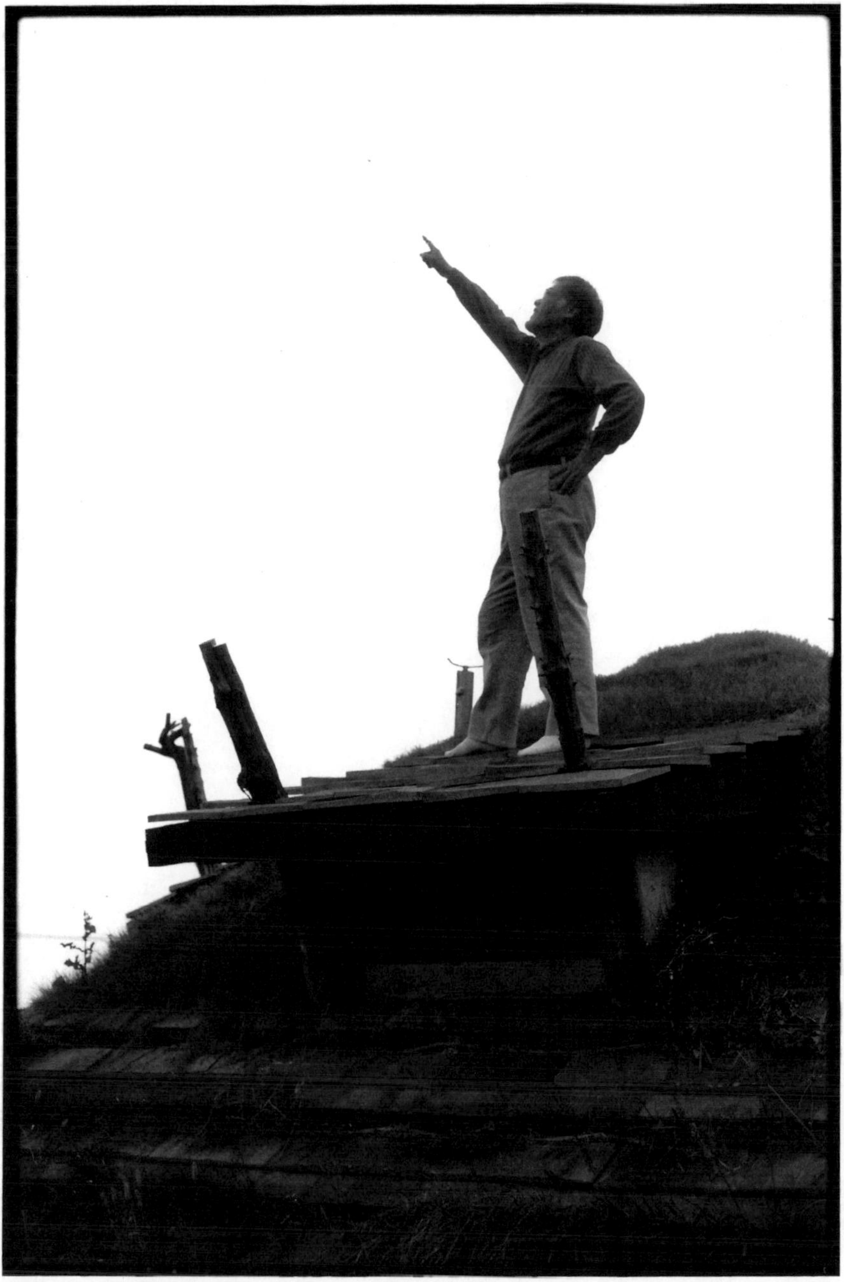

藤森照信 | Terunobu Fujimori

植物は手に負えず、頑固です。建築家は皆知っていることですが、そう、はっきり言うことを恐れたのです。

"Plants are uncontrollable and stubborn" all architects know that, but they are afraid to say it."

1946年長野県生まれ。東北大学工学部建築学科卒業。その後、東京大学大学院では近代日本建築史を専攻。1974年には「東京建築探偵団」を作り、日本各地の西洋近代建築を調査してまわる。現在、工学院大学教授。建築家としては、1991年に「神長官守矢史料館」でデビュー。日本芸術大賞、日本建築学会賞、毎日出版文化賞など数々の賞を受賞。おもな建築作品に、元首相である細川護熙のアトリエと茶室・不東庵工房と一夜亭、タンポポ・ハウス、高過庵などがある。2006年のベネチア・ビエンナーレ建築展では、日本館のコミッショナーを務めた。

Born 1946 in Nagano Prefecture. Graduated from Tohoku University Doctor of Engineering, specializing in the History of Japanese Architecture. Founder of the Tokyo Architectural Detective Agency (1974) that researches western style buildings in Japan. Professor of Kogakuin University. Started out as an architect in 1991 with Jinchokan Moriya Historical Museum. Numerous awards like the Japan Art Grand Prix, Architectural Institute of Japan Award (AIJ) and Mainichi Publishing Culture Award. Other works include the atelier and teahouse for former prime minister Morihiro Hosokawa: Futo-an Kobo and Ichiya-tei in Kanagawa, Tampopo House (Dandelion House) in Tokyo and Takasugi-an (Too-High Teahouse) in Nagano. In 2006 Fujimori represented Japan at the Venice Biennale.

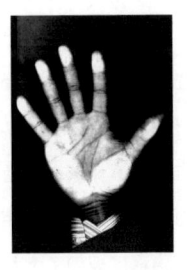

藤森照信 タンポポ・ハウスにて | Fujimori on the roof of Tampopo/Dandelion House (2003)

藤森照信

2005年、丹下健三の葬儀において、有名な建築家が大勢いる中、追悼文を読んだのは藤森照信だった。それは彼のことをよく物語っているだろう。コンクリート建築に支えられている日本の中で——歴史に残る丹下のデザインは、天からの恵みだったが——藤森には、敵も競争相手も、うらやましがる同僚もいなかったのだ。彼の建築はどうして木や土、植物や石で作られたのだろうか。そして、その多くが木の上にあったのか。彼は、デザイナーズブランドを着ることなく、高級レストランへも行かず、自分の手か、友人と一緒に建物を完成させた。東京大学の元教授でもある彼だが、実は自分自身を建築家であるとさえ考えたことはない。それよりも、自分は昔の住居を研究する、建築史家だと思っていた。つまり、藤森は日本で最も弱く、同時に最も影響力のある建築思想家だったのだ。彼のユーモアのセンスと、専門分野に対する謙虚なアプローチは有名で、作家や芸術家、僧侶や哲学者、そして細川護熙のような著名人をひきつけてきた。元首相で、現在は陶芸など自らの生活を楽しんでいる細川などは、藤森に彼のアトリエと隣接した木の上の茶室も依頼している。藤森のシナリオによると、このままいけば、東京の海面は上昇し、2101年までには洪水がおこるという。ただ、この想定は、彼が木のてっぺんに家を作ることとはほとんど関係ないようなのだが。

藤森照信 高過庵に上る｜Fujimori climbing up Takasugi-an (2007)

ローランド・ハーゲンバーグ[以下 RH]　なぜ、ツリーハウスにそれほどまでひかれるのですか？

藤森照信[以下 藤森]　子どもの頃、遊ぶために小屋を作ったことがあります。時には木の上に作ったこともある。板や棒で作って、カヤでカバーしました。最近私が作ったものに、長野県茅野市の「高過庵」があります。2本のクリの支柱の上に立っていて、厳密に言うと、ツリーハウスではないのですが、とにかく友人とこもって「遊ぶ」ことのできるスペースが欲しかったんです。どんなスペースでもよかったのですが、茶室がぴったりでした。

RH　あなたの作品でよく知られている茶室といえば、細川護熙元首相のものだと思いますが、あの茶室も木の上にありましたよね。建てられた時には、細川元首相自ら、作業員に混じって、ヘルメットをかぶり、かなづちと釘を持って加わったそうですね。建築家と依頼者、その友人たちが、実際に建設作業に参加するというのも、あなたの仕事の哲学のうちのひとつなのですか？

藤森　そうやって、子どもの頃わくわくしたことを今もやっています。それがコスト削減にもつながるんです。私は信州の田舎で育ちましたが、そこでは、村の人々は、ずっと荒々しい気候と自然に順応してこなければなりませんでした。ツリーハウスは、その苦労が反映されています。木の枝が二股になったところに板を置くと、土台ができて、そこから始めることになります。何を建てるかは、木が決めるんです。私が唯一できることは、屋根をどうするかということだけです。たとえば「高過庵」では、建物の屋根をヨーロッパのおとぎ話に出てくるような、とがった先端にしたいと思いました、見ての通り、建物は風ですごく揺れますが、地震がきても震度3くらいまでなら気づかないでしょう。

RH　屋根にある色づいた葉のあいだから、日の光が差してきて、茶室をやわらかい雰囲気で包みます。外国人が想像しているのとは逆で、ふつうの日本人は、自分の家に暖かく、やわらかい光を使うことはほとんどありません。寝室と居間は、冷たい蛍光灯の光で明るくしなければならない、という思い込みはどこからくるのでしょうか？

藤森　日本にガラスが入ってきたのは、江戸時代の終わり頃です。国内で生産が始

まったのは、1908年でした。その後、ガラスが障子に取ってかわりました。部屋はずいぶん明るくなったと思います。伝統的な日本の家には長いひさしがありました。日の光は、低い角度から家の中に入って、床を明るくしましたが、天井や部屋全体までは明るくなりませんでした。それは、障子がガラスドアに変わってからも同じでした。ランプの導入によっても——最初は30、40ワットに過ぎませんでした——部屋全体を明るくすることはできませんでした。しかし、蛍光灯ができて——私は小学生でした——驚きました。とても明るくて、天井のしみやクモの巣、ハエのフンや、ほこりまで見えました。それから、日本人は皆、明るい蛍光灯を使い始めたんです。まるでオフィスに住んでいるかのように。想像を越えたこの明るさを、人間はもう手放したくないと思っているのではないか、私はそう思っています。

RH　東京のような都会と、長野のような地方では、昼の明るさは違いますか？

藤森　日が沈む前の黄昏時が一番好きなんです。何だか時間が止まったように感じて、生と死の間に突然放り込まれたような気がするんです。村では、日が沈む時間には、道で人を見かけることはありません。東京では、モノと建物のコントラストがなく、全てが拡散していって、グレー一色になり、水平線はぼやけてしまいます。田舎に行けば、遠くのものがシャープに、クリアに見えます。山の稜線と空を見上げて、私は孫悟空が雲に乗って飛んでいくところを想像しました。東京では、日の光に気づくことはほとんどありません。天井の漆喰に反射した金色の光で、「高過庵」の中に自分だけの黄昏時を作りました。部屋の角を少し丸くしたので、ぼんやりした淡い光と白い壁で、角が見えなくなっているんです。これも、この部屋を実際より広く見せる工夫です。

RH　虫を珍味として食べるくらい、自然がお好きですよね。それはなぜですか？

藤森　昔、ひどい凶作のときなどは、信州の農家の人々は生きるためにやむなく昆虫を食べました。後になって、これが男性の習慣となりました。世代を越えて、父親が息子に虫がおいしいのだということを語り継いできたのです。

RH　どういうものがおいしいんですか？

藤森　ハチの子が一番だと思います。とてもおいしい。まずは巣を見つけなければなりませんけどね。たいがいが、木の枝や屋根の軒にあります。

RH　ツリーハウスのような……。

藤森照信 自宅の庭にて | Fujimori in his garden in Tokyo (2003)

藤森 そうですね！ ハチの巣を振って、地面に落とします。そうすると、ハチは逃げて、しばらくするともともと巣を作っていた場所にもどってきます。こちらはおいしい幼虫をいただく、というわけです。その一方で、トンボの筋肉はとても苦いんです。もし、蝶を食べてみたいと思ったら、手で羽をやさしくもみ、りんぷんを吹き飛ばしてから羽をむしり、残りを食べます。

RH とくに蝶は、あなたが屋根に花を植えるので、引き寄せられてくるのではないですか？ 建物のてっぺんに花を飾ったオーストリアのアーティスト、フンデルトヴァッサーを思い出します。

藤森 フンデルトヴァッサーというよりは、ル・コルビュジエのコンセプトだった、1926年の「近代建築の5原則」(ピロティ、屋上庭園、自由な平面、水平連続窓、自由な立面)に関係があります。コルビュジエは、すべての家は、屋上庭園をつくることによって完成する、と言いました。でも、コルビュジエは、いつも家の屋根に庭を作ったわけではありません。建築において、植物はいつも二の次にされがちですが、彼の初期の仕事においてはそうでないと思います。彼も屋上庭園を試みています。この「近代建築の5原則」という思考ゲームの後、彼は植物と実際の建築を調和することはできない、という結論にいたったのだと思います。植物は手に負えず、頑固であると。建築家は皆知っていることですが、そう、はっきり言うことを恐れたのです。フンデルトヴァッサーの場合も、植物と純粋な建築は、うまくおりあわなかったので、彼は装飾を基本にしてそれを結びつけるものを作った。私にとって、屋上庭園は機能上も環境調整上も必要なかったんです。それよりも、視覚的な意味について考えていました。たとえば、髪がのびるというような。私が家族と一緒に住んでいる家の屋根には、最初タンポポを植えたんですが、うまくいかなくて。だから今は年に2回花を変えて、あちこち、新しいものにチャレンジするようにしています。

RH 本によると、お家は「タンポポ・ハウス」と呼ばれているそうですが、有名になっていると……。

藤森 最初、子どもは嫌がったんです。同級生からバカにされるんじゃないかって。お前の父さんは、ちょっとおかしいとかなんとか。今はこの家も皆に受け入れられたのですが、逆にプライバシーがなく、子どもたちはあまり好きでないようです。知らない人が周りを歩いたり、窓からのぞく人がいたりするから。

RH　この家も、建設段階から、参加されていますよね。

藤森　私は、千年前の日本人がやったように、必要な木材すべてを、のこぎりで切らずに使ってみたいという考えをずっと持っていました。彼らは、木を割って使ったのです。つい第二次大戦の前までは、そういう技術をもっている大工さんたちがいました。そして、ようやく昔ながらの方法で材木を割って板にしてくれる親方を見つけたんです。処女作の神長官守矢史料館は手割りの板を使いました。タンポポ・ハウスの床はオーク材でできています。これは田舎でオークの丸太を探して入手し、ノコギリで製材してもらって使いました。天井のオークはちょうなで削り、壁はサンダー（紙ヤスリ）をかけています。オークは使う前に通常7年間は

藤森照信 タンポポ・ハウスにて｜Terunobu Fujimori at his family house Tampopo/Dandelion House (2003)

乾燥させます。私は1年しか乾燥させなかったので、ひびがはいって、割れてしまいました。そこで、割れ目に白い漆喰を流し込み、逆に面白い床の木目ができあがりました。これは、昔の遊郭の床に使われていた技法です。遊郭の非日常的な美しさを現すために、経営者は石臼の石や大きな石を床にはめ込んだのです。客がその上を歩くと、石臼の表面だけが見えます。大きさや重さは客の想像力を刺激しました。

RH　それから、ドアに桐材を選びましたよね。これも日本の歴史と関係があるのですか？

藤森　もちろんです。信州には、娘が生まれると父親が桐を植えるという伝統があります。21年後に父親はそれを切って、娘が嫁入りする時に着物を入れるための箪笥にして持たすんです。桐は湿気を吸収し、防虫効果があるんです。

RH　このように、歴史への言及がたくさんありますが、人が住む究極的な家とはどのようなものですか？

藤森　昔、建築家の吉阪隆正(元日本建築学会会長)のエッセイを読んだことがあります。彼は学生時代、土でできたモンゴル草原の小さな家を見たそうです。家といっても、簡単な盛り土のようなもの。簡単な木の枝と布の切れはしで作ったカバーを入口に立て、それが風にはためいていたそうです。吉阪さんの考えでは、これこそが人間の住居の、最もそぎ落とされた形だ、ということでした。私はいつもこの思想を自分の建築に移し変えようとしています。だから、私の建築はいつも昔の墳墓のようだといわれるのかもしれません。彫刻家のイサム・ノグチも、その形を好んだために、生きているうちに自分の墓としての土盛りを作ったのではないでしょうか。

RH　家をデザインするときに、身近な人の現実的な意見にはどう対処しているのですか。たとえば、奥さんのような方の意見には？

藤森　もちろん、間取りや部屋の話になると、たいてい女性の方がよく知っています。私の妻には、キッチンだけはまかせたのですが、それだけではゆるしてくれませんでした。私だけではないみたいです。自分たちの家族のために家を建てた建築家を訪ねると、きまって奥さんがデザインについて文句があると言っていますから。

RH 畳や障子、玄関など、伝統的な日本家屋の要素というのは、これからも残ると思いますか？

藤森 将来は、これまで日本で普通に行われてきたのとはまったく別のやり方で、客を自分の家に招くのではないかと思います。いまだに、マンションは客をもてなすように設計されていません。おそらく玄関は少し広くなり、そこでお茶を飲んだり、話をしたりして友人を出迎えるスペースになるでしょう。あるいは、茶室のようなもっと小さな空間が客をもてなすゲストルームになるか、玄関と組み合わせるようになるか。畳と障子は消えていくと思います。なぜなら、もう必要がないから。それに代わる何かがきっと出てくるでしょう。

RH それはいつ頃だと思いますか？

藤森 しばらくの間は、そのバラエティーを楽しんでいるものを、入れかえたり、作りかえたりするのではないかと思います。私は、少しずつ変化が起きて、その先にまったく新しいものが生まれてくるのを見るのが楽しみですが、10年か20年では、そ

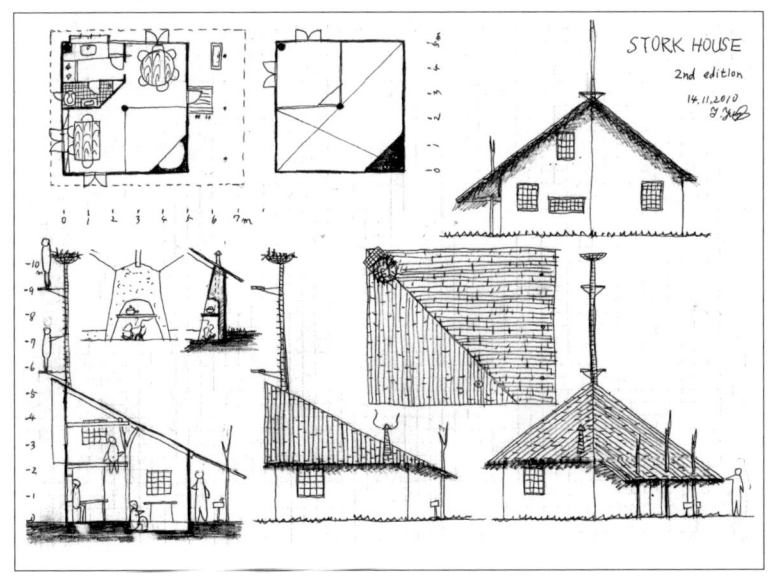

ライディングの「コウノトリ・ハウス」のスケッチ｜
Sketch for Stork House, Raiding (2011)

藤森照信 茅野にて | Fujimori in Chino, Japan (2010)

のような変化は起こらないでしょう。30年から40年はかかると思います。それまで、私たちは実験をすることをすすめていかなくてはなりません。

RH 藤森さんの場合、石や土、草や地元産の木材など、自然の素材との実験ですね。

藤森 建築では、いつも自然との関係を頭に入れておかなければならないと思います。建物の構造と使用方法は現代的でも、外にあるものを見て、触り、感じることは、周辺の環境とつながっていなければなりません。実はこれは簡単なことではないんです。たとえば、近くの自然から集めた素材を使って、屋根を作ったとしましょう。その屋根が雨漏りし始めたとき……何が一番効果的か、実験しているんです。

RH いつも、建設の過程に学生たちが関わることの重要性を強調していますね。教室だけでは不十分ですか？

藤森 建築を勉強するときに重要なことが2つあります。ひとつは自分の手で建てること、もうひとつは、自分のデザインについて論理的に考えることです。有名な建物をスケッチしている学生をよく見かけますが、これはよくありません。建築家は画家ではありません。どれだけうまく描けたとしても、それで満足するわけにはいかないのです。もしスケッチを描くのであれば、その建物を見て考えたこともスケッチに書き込まなくてはいけない。常に考えを言葉で言い表せるようにすること！ 日本の学生はもっと教室の外で学ばなくてはだめです。私はいつも学生を建設現場に連れて行きます。そしてその後すぐに、建築の知識と理論で、彼らの経験を補強してあげるのです。

RH オーストリアのライディングという村に、フランツ・リスト・フェスティバルを訪れる人たちのためのロッジをデザインされましたよね。これは1年の間に何度か行われるお祭りですが、今回はどんな実験を考えていますか？

藤森 建設は2011年の夏に始まります。このプロジェクトは、コウノトリ・ハウスと呼んでいます。オーストリアのこの地方では、コウノトリが家の煙突のてっぺんに巣をかけるんです。秋になって、彼らは南アフリカへ帰っていきます。今回は、このコウノトリが巣をかけるために、建物の屋根をどうやって選ぶのか知るための実験です。しかけとして、コウノトリには、基礎部分のみを与えて、巣を完成できるようにしてあります。これにはけっこう自信があります。なぜなら、コウノトリは私のように行動するからです。地元の素材しか使わないんです。

茅野にある茶室 | Fujimori teahouse in Chino, Japan (2010)

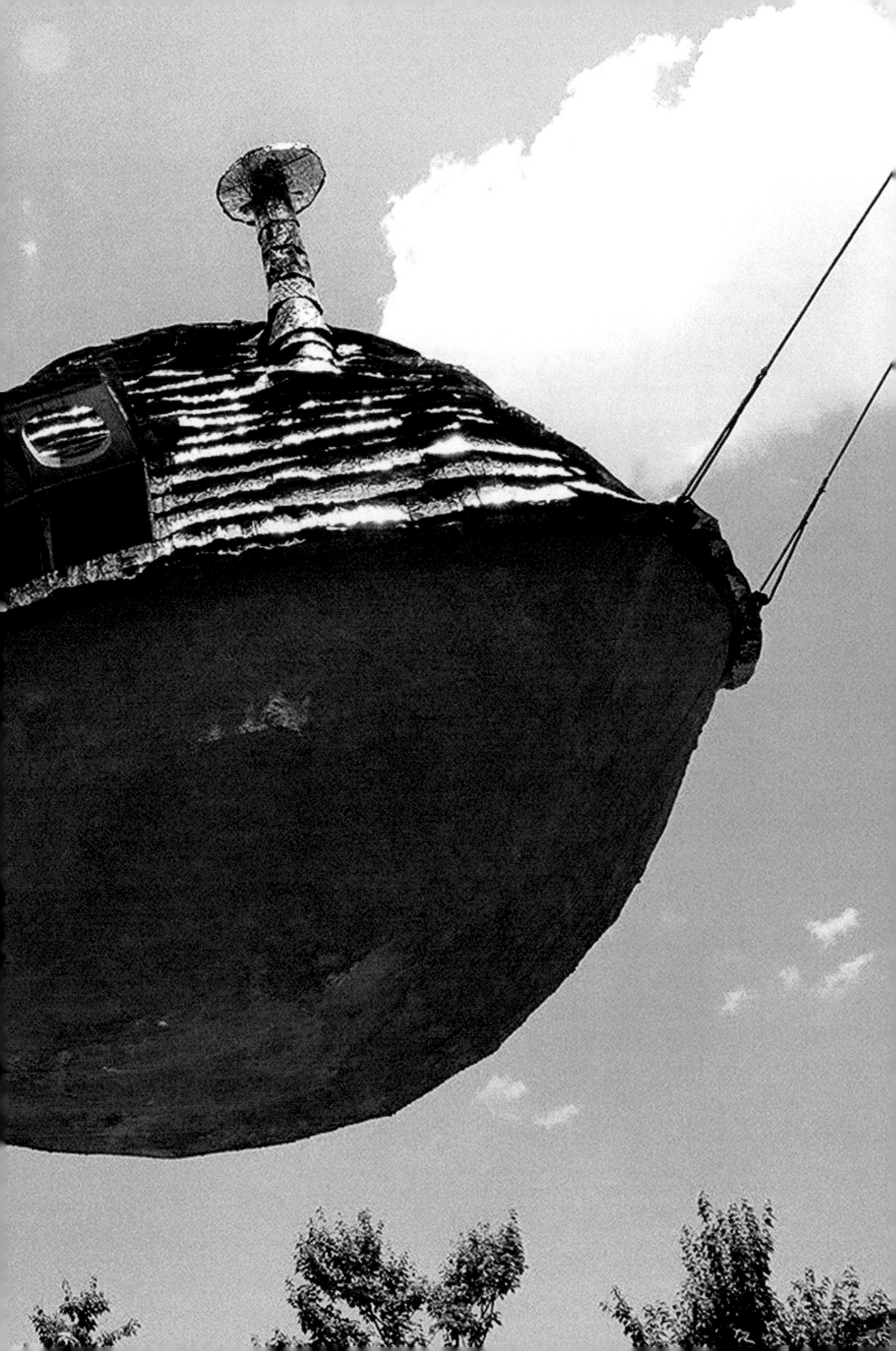

Terunobu Fujimori

How telling that Terunobu Fujimori, of all the renowned Japanese architects at Kenzo Tange's funeral in 2005, was the one to deliver the eulogy. In Japan's concrete-fueled construction world – for which Tange's monumental designs were heaven-sent – Fujimori has no enemies, no competitors, no envious colleagues. And why should he? His creations are made of wood, earth, plants and stones, and often sit on top of trees. He doesn't wear designer clothes or visit fancy restaurants and he builds his creations by himself, or "together with friends!" In fact, the former Tokyo University professor does not even consider himself an architect. Rather, he considers himself an architectural historian drawn to ancient housing solutions. In short, Fujimori is simultaneously one of the most powerless and one of the most influential architectural thinkers in Japan. His sense of humor and his humble approach to his profession are legendary and have drawn to him writers, artists, Buddhist priests, philosophers and luminaries like Morihiro Hosokawa. Hosokawa, the former Prime Minister of Japan who now devotes his life to pottery making, asked Fujimori to build his studio and an adjacent teahouse in a tree. According to Fujimori's scenario, rising sea levels will have flooded Tokyo by 2101. But this, as the visionary emphasizes, has little to do with his obsession to build houses in treetops.

藤森照信 ライディングにて | Terunobu Fujimori in Raiding (2011)

Roland Hagenberg Why are you so attracted to treehouses?

Terunobu Fujimori I built small huts to play in when I was a kid – sometimes in trees – using sticks and boards that I covered with hay. The one I constructed recently in Nagano prefecture is called Takasugi-an ('too-high teahouse'). It stands on two stilts, so, technically speaking, it's not a real treehouse. Anyway, I wanted a room where I could "play" with my friends. It could have been any space but a tearoom seemed just right.

RH Your best-known teahouse is probably that built for former Prime Minister Morihiro Hosokawa, which is also nestled into a tree. When it was built Hosokawa joined the construction crew with hammer, nails, and hardhat. Is hands-on collaboration between friends, client and architect part of your work philosophy?

TF That way I can keep the fun of childhood alive, and sometimes it helps to cut costs. I grew up in the countryside of Shinshu, where, for centuries, villagers had to adapt to rough weather conditions and nature. Building a treehouse reflects that struggle. When you put boards on a fork-end of a tree, you get a platform and you start from there. The tree pretty much decides what you can build – the only part where the plant lets me do what I want is the roof. For Takasugi-an, for instance, I wanted a pointed top like in old European fairytale illustrations. As you can see, the structure moves quite a lot in the wind. But an earthquake up to magnitude three you probably won't feel.

RH Sunlight enters through a gold-leaved shaft in the roof and covers the tearoom with a silky atmosphere. Contrary to what foreigners usually imagine, average Japanese people seldom use warm, soft lights in their houses. Where does this obsession come from, to brighten up sleeping and living rooms with cold neon tubes?

TF Glass was introduced to Japan at the end of the Edo period (1603–1867) and. domestic production started in 1908. After that, paper in traditional sliding doors (shoji screens) was replaced with glass. Rooms became much brighter. Traditional Japanese houses have deep eaves. They allow the sun to enter at low angles – enough to brighten floors, but not enough for ceilings or the whole room, even if they have glass sliding doors. With the introduction of lamps – in the beginning we had only thirty- or forty-watt bulbs – we still could not light up the whole room. But then fluorescent light arrived. I was in elementary school and we were shocked – it was so bright that for the first time we could see all the dirt under the ceiling, the spiders' nests, the flies' excrements and the dust. From then on, all Japanese have used bright fluorescent neon tubes at home, as if they were living in an office. My only explanation is that this brightness had so long been beyond our imagination that we decided to never let go of it again.

RH How would you compare daylight in Tokyo with that in the countryside, in places like Nagano?

TF I love the twilight hours, just before sunset. It makes me feel as if time has stopped, as if I suddenly exist somewhere between life and death. In villages, you can barely see anyone on the street at sunset. Time itself seems to stop. In Tokyo, objects

細川護熙元首相 藤森が設計した湯河原のアトリエにて |
Former Prime Minister Morihiro Hosokawa at his pottery studio in Yugawara, designed by Fujimori

and buildings have no contrast; everything is diffuse, a sea of gray. The horizon becomes blurry. Only in the countryside does the distant appear sharp and clear. And when I see the mountain rims and the sky, I imagine manga hero Son Goku riding and flying through the clouds. I am seldom aware of the sunlight in Tokyo. With the golden sunlight reflected on the whitewashed ceiling, I could create my own twilight zone inside Takasugi-an. Here, the corners of the space become invisible, because I curved them, and because of the dim light and the white walls. This also makes the room appear much bigger than it really is.

RH Your closeness to nature goes as far as eating insects like a delicacy. How come?

TF In the past, after a bad harvest, the farmers in Shinshu often had no other choice but to eat insects to survive. Later this habit changed into a 'male thing', where, over generations, fathers confided to their sons which insects tasted best.

RH And which do you prefer?

TF Probably wasp larvae; they are very sweet. However, you have to find their nest first, which is most likely attached to the roof or to tree branches.

RH ...same like a treehouse...

TF Exactly! So, you shake the nest, it falls to the floor, the wasps leave and later fly back to the spot where they originally built their home. In the meantime you can enjoy the sweet larvae. On the other hand, the muscles of a dragonfly are quite bitter. And if you want to try butterflies, first rub them softly between your hands, then blow away powder and wings and eat the rest.

RH Butterflies, especially, are attracted to your buildings when you plant flowers on roofs. This reminds me of Austrian artist Friedrich Hundertwasser, who promoted plants on top of houses.

TF It has less to do with Hundertwasser than with Le Corbusier's concept, 'Five Points of a New Architecture', from 1926, where he demanded that all houses should be topped off with a garden. But then again, Le Corbusier did not always build roof gardens. Plants have always played a secondary role in his architectural realm, except maybe in his earlier works, when he used rooftop gardens. After this five-point mind-game he probably came to the conclusion that plants and architecture can't be reconciled. Plants are uncontrollable and stubborn – all architects know that, but they are afraid to say it. In Hundertwasser's case, plants and pure architecture would not have worked either, and so he created ornament-based connectors and transitions.

I didn't need a roof garden for functional purposes or atmospheric effects. I was thinking more of a visual effect, like hair growing out of a body. On the roof of the house where I live with my family in Tokyo, I first tried dandelions but they did poorly – so now I change plants twice a year and try something new, here and there.

RH In architecture books, your family house is called Tampopo – 'dandelion'. It has become quite famous...

TF My kids hated it at first. They were afraid their classmates would make fun of them, "What a crazy dad you have," and such. Now, the house is accepted, but my kids don't like it because there is not much privacy left. Strangers walk around, some peek through the windows.

RH Here, too, you participated in the construction work.

TF I was obsessed with the idea of treating all the wood I needed like the Japanese did a thousand years ago: without sawing. They split the wood. Just before World War II there were still many carpenters around who used that technique. I finally found a master, who could split my logs the traditional way – into large planks. My first piece of work – Jinchokan – was made of hand-cut wood. The floor at Tampopo is made of oak. I found an oak log in the countryside and had it sawed by hand. The oak I used for the ceiling was carved out with traditional tools and the walls were sandpapered. One day, my historic carpenter had enough and I finished everything by myself. Oak wood should normally dry for seven years before it is used; I had only one year. And so it cracked. Which was fine with me – I filled the fissures with white plaster and this way achieved a wonderful floor pattern. It is a reference to floors in the ancient yuukaku [brothel]. To demonstrate its uncommon beauty, the brothel proprietors set into the floor heavy millstones or giant rocks. Spaces in-between were filled with earth or smaller stones. When guests walked on them, they could see only the surface of the millstones – size and weight were left to their imaginations.

RH And for the doors you selected Paulownia wood, which also refers to Japanese history?

TF Of course. According to Shinshu's tradition, when a daughter is born the father plants a Paulownia. 21 years later, when the daughter is leaving home to marry, he cuts down the tree and builds a cupboard with drawers for the kimono. Paulownia absorbs humidity and insects don't like it.

RH With so many historical references, what shape would symbolize the ultimate dwelling of humankind for you?

TF   I once read an essay by architect Takamasa Yoshizaka, the former president of the Architectural Institute of Japan. When he was a student he saw this small building made of earth in Mongolia, a simple mound. People had marked the entrance with a simple stick and a piece of cloth fluttered in the wind. In Yoshizaka's opinion, this was a human dwelling in its most reduced form. I carried on this thought in my own buildings, which often refer to ancient burial mounds. Sculptor Isamu Noguchi, by the way, admired their shapes, too, and probably worked on his own burial mound while he was still alive because of that.

RH   When it comes to designing a house, how do you deal with practical input from people close to you, let's say from your wife?

TF   Of course, women always know better when it comes to the distribution of floor-space and rooms. I let my wife do the kitchen, but she actually wanted to do more. I am not alone in this experience. Every time I visit an architect who had built a house for his own family, I hear that his wife had complaints about the design.

藤森照信 ライディングにて「コウノトリ・ハウス」の模型と |
Terunobu Fujimori with Stork House model, Raiding (2011)

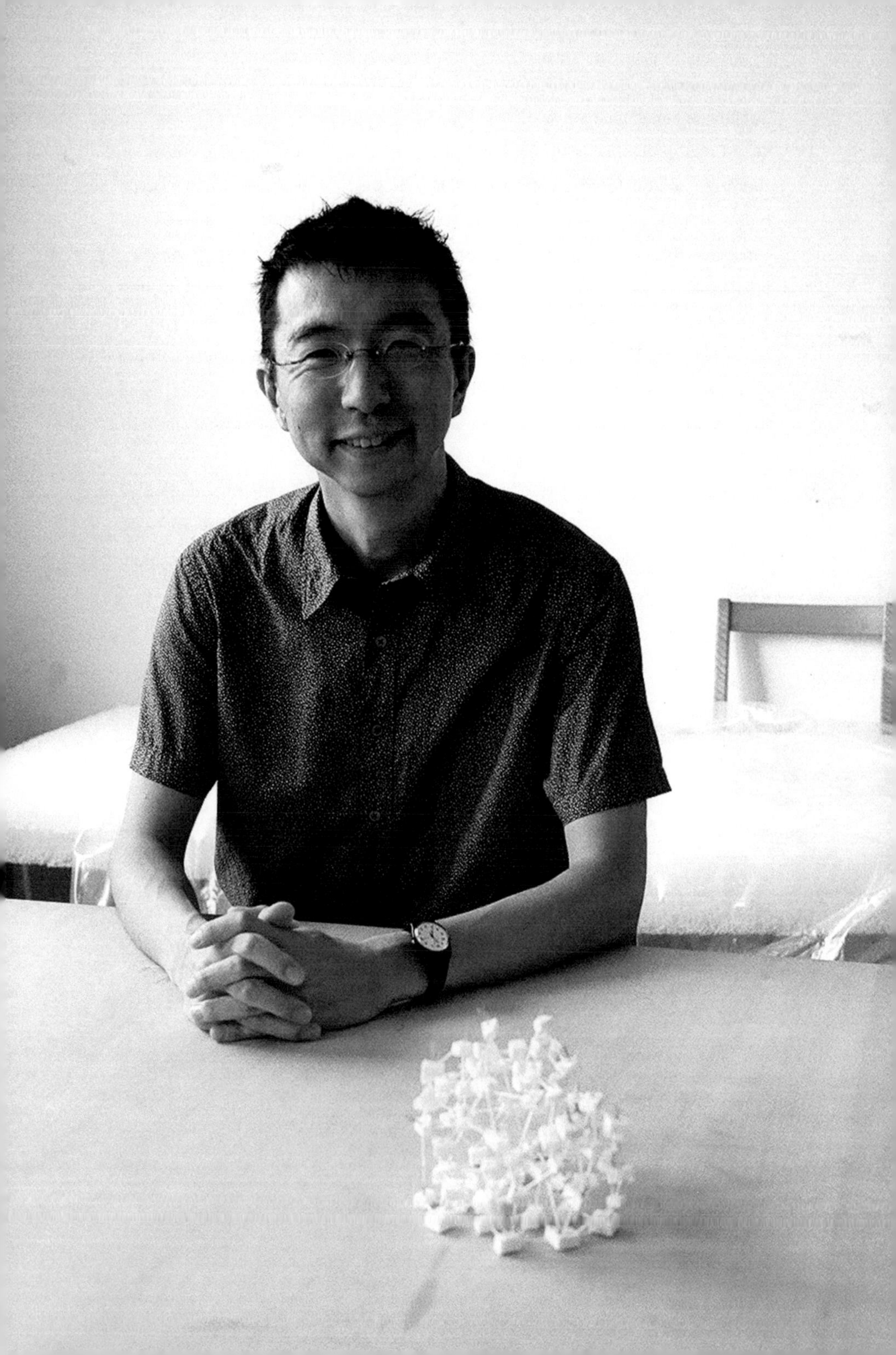

藤本壮介 | Sou Fujimoto

手つかずの洞窟だけが、
さらなる探検の余地を残しているのです。
"Only the raw cave leaves room for further exploration."

1971年北海道生まれ。東京大学卒業。2000年に藤本壮介建築設計事務所設立。2009年から東京大学特任准教授。主な作品に、次世代モクバン、house N、情緒障害児短期治療施設、武蔵野美術大学図書館などがある。

Born 1971 in Hokkaido. Graduated from department of architecture at University of Tokyo. Established his practice in Tokyo in 2000. Fujimoto has been a project associate professor at the University of Tokyo since 2009. Works by Fujimoto include Final Wooden House, House N, Children's Center for Psychiatric Rehabilitation and Library at Musashino Art University.

藤本壮介 アトリエにて | Sou Fujimoto at his studio, Tokyo (2010)

藤本壮介

スターはハリウッドやグラミー賞だけで生まれるものではない。建築の世界でも同じだ。ただ、それは一晩のうちにできるものではない。スピードが上がってはいるが、やはり時間がかかるものだ。ひとたびスターが出ると、どうしてそうなったのか、その仕組みや基準、そして新しい才能を見つけるにいたった現代の雰囲気とはどういうものかを想像するのは楽しい。藤本壮介（本書の中で最年少）が、最近、東京・ワタリウム美術館で行った展示では、6人の有名な建築家がやってきてレクチャーを行うなど、全力でイベントを支えた。その中には、妹島和世や伊東豊雄、磯崎新もいた。妹島や伊東、あるいは隈研吾や青木淳がこのようなサポートをするなどということは、15年や20年前には考えられなかったことだ。しかし時代は変わり、人々もなぜ妹島がプリッカー賞を受賞して、その師匠である伊東が受賞していないのか考えるようになってきたのだ。

「私は、ラフで生、荒々しい洞窟に影響を受けています」。藤本は言う。「そこには、人工的なものは何もない。それが私の空間探しの出発点になっているんです。少しずつ洞窟に感情移入していくと、そのシェルターとしてだけの機能から、実用的で快適な場所になり、最終的には巣になるんです」。彼の東京のアトリエは、日本のしゃれたデザイン事務所などではなく、むしろ建設現場のように見える。そこを訪れる人は、同じビルにある印刷会社のエレベーターを使わなくてはならない。コンクリートの壁はむき出しで、タイルもまばらな感じだ（意図的にそうしているのか、はぎとってしまうのが難しいからなのかは不明だ）。中に入ると、発泡スチロールでできた小さな模型が、そこらじゅうに積んである。「私はいつも模型の内装をのぞき見るんです。空間を感じとるために。そうして、その結果を想像するのです」。藤本は京都造形芸術大学でも教えている。しかし、少年のような外見のせいで、彼の方が学生のように見える。彼のデザインする家は「House "N"」やオーストリア・ライディングの模型のように、複雑で、カプセルの構造になっている。それは、障害を持った子どもたちのための「子どもセンター」のように、保護されているという印象を与えるのだ。

「彼らには、何か問題が起こった時に隠れることのできる曲がり角や、すき間、アルコーブなどが必要なんです。そこから同時に外の世界を見ることができるんです」。若い建築家はそう説明した。「それは、誰にでも言えることだと思います。でも、大人はなかなかそれを認めたがらないのですけれどね」。

藤本壮介とライディング・プロジェクトのための習作 |
Sou Fujimoto with study for "Raiding Project" (2010)

ライディング・プロジェクトのためのスケッチ | Fujimoto drawing for Raiding Project (2010)

ローランド・ハーゲンバーグ[以下 RH]　生まれ育ったのは北海道の郊外ですよね。東京からかなり離れています。だから、ご自身の建築について語るときは、いつも木について話をされるんですか？

藤本壮介[以下 藤本]　私はよく森の中で過ごしました。木々は、お互いにルールを作って生きています。自分だけが孤立することなく、それぞれの木が、お互いに心地よくいられる場所を尊重しています。木々の間には、枝や葉っぱによる相関性の影とグラデーションがあります。そして、木の上に登ると、その建築的な素材にもっと気づきます。抽象的な言葉で言うと、音楽の楽譜の五線をとったものと共通するところがあると思うのです。音符は空中に浮かび、それが、グラデーションのエッセンスになっている。まるで森の中の木の葉のように、時には深く暗く、そして、時にはゆったりと軽く。だから、私が家のデザインをするときには、たとえそれが街中でも郊外でも、プライバシーを守るだけでなく、自分のまわりへも手を伸ばす、その人が一番心地よいと思える場所を頭に置きながら考えます。私は「明確な区別」のかわりに、「緩やかに変化していくグラデーション」がさまざまな場所を生み出すような建築を確立しようと思います。

RH　それは近年、現代日本のほぼすべての建築家が言っているように、内側と外側の区別を壊して、伝統的な「縁側」のコンセプトを再び取り入れる、内と外の相関性ということですよね。そういう意味では、現代の日本人建築家は特段新しいわけではないと。

藤本　もちろん個人的には、全く新しいコンセプトによって日本が進化し、自分が少しでもそれに貢献できたらいいなと思います。しかし、私は同時に歴史的、伝統的な建築もとても好きなので、今の時代に関係が深く、未来に向けては動機づけとなるような要素を、歴史的なものの中から見つけたいと思っています。私たちは、これまでの経済体制や生態系が崩壊した時代に突入しています。私はこれこそが、新しい発見や変化の背後にある、一番の原動力ではないかと思っています。

RH　「原初的な未来」という言葉があります。それは将来を悲観的に見た言葉ですか？

藤本　むしろ反対に、とても楽観的な、新しい希望に満ちた未来を言い表してい

るつもりです。「原初的な未来」は、私たちが生まれてきたところ、洞窟で暮らしていた頃とつながっています。先のことを計画するときに、この、建築の初期の状況を頭に入れておくということは欠かせません。一方「巣」は洞窟よりもう少し洗練されたものです。「巣」は丁寧に作られて、機能的で手が込んでいます。だから、手つかずの洞窟だけが、さらなる探検の余地を残しているのです。そこには、新しい快適さと、新しいスペースの使い方があるのです。形のない形、洞窟の中の意図しなかったスペースが、将来の住居になるかもしれません。私は、経済が停滞し、消費の伸びが行きづまったときこそ、建築家が豊かな社会や生活の質を高めることに貢献できると信じています。

RH 現在、東京大学でも教えていらっしゃいます。学生たちに対して、どんなアプローチをしているのですか？

藤本 学生たちにはトピックを与え、それに対するプランを持ってきてもらうのですが、私はそれがいいか悪いか言いません。そのかわり、彼らのプランの中に、種が根を下ろすような点を探すようにしています。そして、それを育てていく方法も見つけるようにします。学生たちとは話をして、ディスカッションをする。これを繰り返します。実は私自身、あまり教えているという感覚はないんです。自分にとっても、これはトレーニングだなと。私もそれを楽しみ、大変なこともありますが、学生たちもそれを楽しんでできるようにします。最近、現代建築をもっと広い視野で見る必要がある、というふうに思っているのです。家のデザインだけにとらわれるのではなく、たとえば町全体、生態系全体など、もっと大きなイメージに気づくことに力を入れていかなければならないと思います。私は、日本の建築家——それは自分を含めてですが——は、スケールの大きな計画に関して、まだまだ未熟だと感じています。私は学生たちに、町全体のレベル、あるいは地球規模の総体として建築をとらえ、複雑な問題に取り組み、新しい豊かさを見出していってほしいと思っています。

ライディング・プロジェクトへの習作 |
Experimental study for Raiding Project (2010)

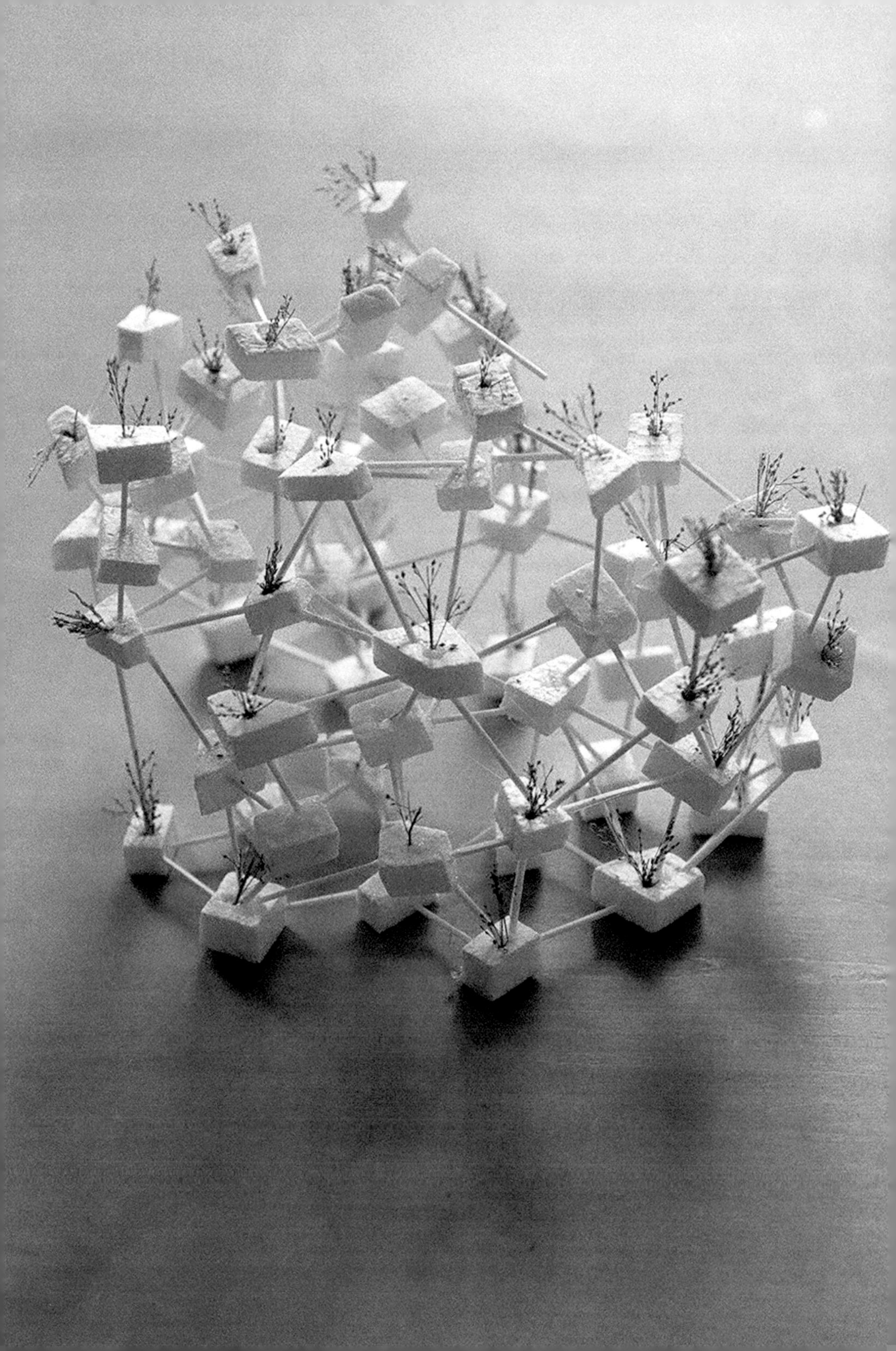

Sou Fujimoto

Stars are not only born in Hollywood, but also in the world of architecture. It used to be a slow process, but now some people are becoming star architects overnight. And whenever a star architect is born, it is exciting to speculate about what has gone on behind the scenes, in the discovery of the new talent.

When Sou Fujimoto (the youngest architect featured in this book) exhibited his work at the Watari-um Museum in Tokyo recently, six established architects came out in full force to support the event: Kazuyo Sejima, Toyo Ito and Arata Isozaki were among those who gave lectures. Though Sejima's generation wasn't as welcomed by their own predecessors, people nonetheless see some injustice in her being awarded the Pritzker Prize when her mentor, Ito, has never been recognized in this way.

"I am inspired by the roughness, rawness and robustness of caves," says Fujimoto. There's nothing artificial about a cave and so it has become the starting point for all my space-discovering journeys. When we attach emotions to a cave, the space outgrows its shelter function and becomes practical, comfortable and, finally, a nest." Fujimoto's admiration of caves is nowhere more obvious than in the layout of his Tokyo studio; it looks more like a construction site than a trendy Japanese design bureau. Visitors access it via a service elevator that belongs to a printing company in the same building. The concrete walls are bare and have tiles attached to them in sporadic fashion (whether on purpose, or because they were too difficult to remove is unknown). Miniature Styrofoam buildings are piled up everywhere. "I always need to have the ability to peek into the interiors of my models. Only then can I get the feeling of the space and imagine its implications."

Fujimoto also teaches at Kyoto Design University, but with his boyish looks he could almost pass for a student. Often his houses are complex, encapsulated structures – Tokyo Apartments, N-House, or the study-model for the village of Raiding in Austria – that appeal to our sense of needing protection. This is also the case with Fujimoto's Children's Center, an institution for young people with psychiatric disabilities. "They need corners, niches and alcoves where they can retreat to when they have problems, but from where they can watch the world outside at the same time," explains the young architect. "That need actually goes for any person, but grownups are mostly too embarrassed to admit it."

藤本壮介 アトリエにて | Fujimoto at his studio, Tokyo (2010)

Roland Hagenberg You grew up in the northern part of Japan, in the countryside of Hokkaido, a world apart from Tokyo. Is that why you always refer to trees when describing your architectural work?

Sou Fujimoto I spent lots of time in the forests there, where trees live together by established rules: they respect individual comfort zones without isolating themselves from each other. Between them are shades and gradations of interconnectedness, which are made possible by brushwork, branches and leaves. And when you climb trees you become even more aware of this architectural fabric. In abstract terms, I see similarities with a musical score that has had its five stave lines removed. The notes floating in the air are the essence of gradation; sometimes dense and dark, sometimes loose and light – like foliage in the forest. So, when I design houses for people I think about creating comfort zones that protect their privacy, but also reach out into the surrounding environment – be it a city block or the countryside. Instead of clear divisions, I try to create architecture in which gradation gives birth to various spaces.

RH This is what nearly all contemporary Japanese architects currently refer to: breaking down divisions and re-introducing the traditional concept of "engawa", the interconnectedness between outside and inside. In that sense, modern Japanese architecture does not represent something revolutionary or new.

SF Personally I hope, of course, that revolutionary new concepts will evolve in Japan and that I can contribute to some of them. But I am also a great fan of historical and traditional architecture. I want to distill certain historical elements that are relevant to our times and that inspire the future. We have entered a period where the old economic-ecological system is breaking down. This is the main driving force behind new discoveries and changes, I think.

RH You coined the term "primitive future." Is your outlook for the way we will live in the future pessimistic?

SF On the contrary, it means a very optimistic future full of new hope. The term "primitive future" relates to where we come from, to the human-cave situation. When planning for times ahead, it is fundamental to keep this embryonic state of architecture in mind. The nest, on the other hand, is a more refined cave. It is carefully assembled, functional, and well prepared. That's why only the raw cave leaves room for further exploration and development of new comforts and alternative uses of space. The formless form, the unintentional space of a cave, allows for the shaping of future habitats. I believe architecture can contribute to the richness of society and to quality of life, even when economic output declines and consumer growth comes to a standstill.

RH You also lecture at Tokyo University. What is your approach to teaching?

SF I give students a topic and they come back to me with a plan, but I don't judge whether it's a good or a bad plan. Instead, I try to identify the spots where my seeds have grown roots and together we figure out a way to nourish them. We talk, discuss, re-do. I actually don't feel that I am teaching – for me it is training too. I enjoy it and I make sure students feel the same, despite all the difficulties. Recently, I came to the conclusion that we should put more effort into seeing modern architecture under a broad perspective and not get caught up in house design alone: we should look at, for example, a whole city or a whole ecological system. We are then aware of the bigger picture. I think Japanese architects – and that includes myself – are still a little bit immature when it comes to big-scale planning. I want my students to catch up with their foreign counterparts, who are much better at solving complex problems on a city-sized scale. I hope the students will discover new richness through conquering complicated problems and by looking at architecture on a "cityscape" level, as well as on a "global" level.

藤本壮介と著者 | Roland Hagenberg and Sou Fujimoto (2009)

原広司 事務所にて、ライディング・キューブの模型と │
Hiroshi Hara working on model for Raiding Cube at his studio in Shibuya, Tokyo (2010)

原 広司 | Hiroshi Hara

私は、いまだに自分の中に
60年代の学生運動を抱えていきています。
"I still have the '60s revolution in me."

1936年神奈川県生まれ。1964年東京大学大学院修了。1970年よりアトリエ・ファイ建築研究所と共同で設計。1982年東京大学教授に就任、1997年より同名誉教授。日本建築学会賞、村野藤吾賞など受賞多数。主な作品は、新梅田シティ・梅田スカイビル（大阪）、京都駅ビル（京都）、札幌ドーム（北海道）、しもきた克雪ドーム（青森）など。

Born 1936 in Kanagawa Prefecture. Received Ph.D. from University of Tokyo (1964). Established "Atelier-phi" in 1970. Proffessor Emeritus, of University of Tokyo. Numerous awards such as Architectual Institute of Japan Award (AIJ) and Togo Murano Prize. Major Works include Umeda Sky Building in Osaka, Kyoto Station Building, Sapporo Dome, Shimokita-Kokusetsu Dome in Aomori.

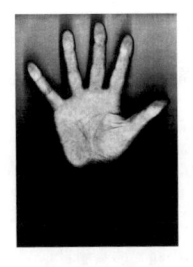

原 広司

東京・渋谷にある原広司のアトリエに入ると、一瞬、原自身が25年以上も研究していた、古代の村を訪れているような気持ちになる。

たとえば、入り口の道はとても狭く、肩幅の広い男性などは、脇にある道の方を歩くだろう（イエメン・ハジャラにあった石の要塞を思い出す）。その上、通れる隙間も一面生い茂った雑草でわからなくなっている（ペルー・トラニパタの葦の浮島のような感じだろうか）。そして、最後に階段を上がると、静かで落ち着いた場所にたどりつく。そこは、中国・福建の田螺坑土楼群にでも来たようだ。

原は大きなデスクに座っている。机の上には、紙や本、鉛筆などでいっぱいだ。彼が煙草に火をつけると、紫煙がその白い髪へと昇っていく。まるで、現代のシャーマンか、往年のハリウッド俳優のようだ。壁には「梱包するアート」で有名な彼の友人、クリストの作品がかかっている。本当はクリストはもっと大きなものを包みたかったのだという。原のデザインした大阪の梅田スカイビルだ（40階建ての高層ビルが2棟、空中にぶら下がるような形のエスカレーターでつながっている）。しかし、資金援助が実現せず、クリストはやむなく友人のオフィスの電話を包むことにしたのだった。

ライフワークについての話になると、原は自分でも驚き、おかしいのだと言う。自らを1960年代の学生運動の申し子と公言してはばからない原。そんな自分が京都駅や札幌ドームのような巨大な建築に行き着くとは。しかし、成功しても、彼はグローバルな放浪者、第三世界の漂流者という自らの人間性までは変えなかった。かえって、現代の都市の間違いは、古代の村の知恵を侵してしまったことにあるという思いを強くしたのだ。

最近オーストリア大使、ユッタ・シュテファン＝バストルとの夕食会のときに、原はこんな話を披露した。大使の夫、ピーターも建築家で、世界中を旅している。「アフリカでは外国人を最初にチェックするのは、いつも子供なんです。そして、相手が悪い人間ではないとわかると、親にそれを言いにいく。そうやって私は彼らの家の中に入っていったんです」。その後、ピーターが打ち明けた話を、原は忘れられない。「私たちはモーリタニアの砂漠の中を何日間も運

転していました。運転手が——イスラム教徒でしたが——私たちを、離れた村にいる自分の家族に紹介したいと言ったんです。おみやげに、袋に入った砂糖を車のトランクに入れて持っていったのですが、その隣には、自分たちの分として酒を何本かいれていました。ある日、そのビンが割れて、中の酒が砂糖にかかってしまったんです。運転手はパニックになって、大切なおみやげを投げ捨ててしまいました。私たちは結局手ぶらで村に着きました。彼の家族が持っているものといえば、生活のすべてを頼っている一匹の山羊だけ。しかし彼らは、その一匹の山羊をしめて、私たちをもてなしてくれたんです。本当に胸がつまりました」。原はその話を聞いて、うなずきながらも、ほかの人と同じようにずっと黙っていた。彼は、自己犠牲が古代の村の与えてくれた知恵であることを知っていた。同時に、現代世界がそれを受け入れるのにはまだまだ時間がかかりそうだということもわかっていたのだ。

[パート1]——2000-2007

ローランド・ハーゲンバーグ[以下 RH]　世界50カ国で現地調査をしているそうですが、その結果は建築にどう影響しているのですか？

原広司 札幌ドームの可動式サッカー場建設予定地にて｜
Hiroshi Hara overlooking future movable soccer field at construction site of Sapporo Dome (2000)

原 広司[以下原]　世界各地の集落に伝わるアイデアに関心があるので、旅行記やメモで記録は残しますが、デザインそのものを真似たりはしません。集落で発見した伝統的なアイデアを、現代のスタイルに転用したいのです。なぜ、ある時代に、あるアイデアが良いと思われ、建築に生かされたのかを分析し、そのエッセンスを、現代に適用しようと思っています。

RH　もし建築家として亡命するとしたら、どの集落を選びますか？

原　砂漠の集落でしょうね。日本人は、アラブの人を攻撃的だと思っているようですが、僕には非常に寛容でした。歴史的に、アラブの人は移動を繰り返してきたためか、心が広いのです。また、その移動の歴史は、建築にも反映されていて、テントのような可動式の住居が主流です。

RH　遊牧民に憧れているのですか？

原　僕自身が遊牧民ということですか？

そういえば、ちょっと前に、イエメンの遊牧民族を訪ねましたが、彼らの建物は地上10階建てなのです。砂の地平線の中に、突然、砂漠の摩天楼のような光景が現れ、

原広司 札幌ドームの建設予定地の中で ｜ Hiroshi Hara inside construction site of Sapporo Dome (2000)

驚きました。

その建物は、石の基盤の上に木と泥で上部が造られ、最上階が台所なのです。女性を守り、隠すために、お勝手を一番上にもってきたわけです。イエメンの女性は自由に外出できませんから、常に一番高い所にいて、世界を眺めるということになります。そんなイエメンの住居は、度重なる破壊と再建を経ながらも、2000年近く続いている建築様式で、その高さは京都駅ビルと同じぐらいです。

RH そのイエメンの住居に住んでみたいですか？

原 いえ、戦争のために、各家庭にマシンガンがあるような状態ですから……。調査の方も、なんとか6つの建物には入ることができたのですが、やはり内戦の最中ということで、それ以上は無理でした。ただ、集落の調査プロジェクトは、1970年代から続けているので、今後も継続する意向です。

RH そんな状況下のイエメンで、6つの建物の中に入ることができたのはなぜですか？ まさか、300ページもある自分のカタログを片手に「日本から来た建築家です」と、自己紹介して歩いたわけではないですよね？

原 調査の説明はしたのですが、なかなか理解してもらえませんでした。そもそも、あの辺の人々が知っている日本とは、トヨタだけなのですから。ただ、面白いことに、大人より子供の方がのみこみが早くて、僕が伝えたいことを砂に絵で描くと、それを理解して、親に伝えてくれたのです。

ところが、そのやり方は中米では使えませんでした。子供はまず、外国人から切り離されます。

RH 砂漠と類似した月面の研究もしていますね？ どのような経緯で宇宙での設計プロジェクトに携わったのか聞かせて下さい。

原 研究の題材として興味がありました。まず個人が、続いて集団が、地球外で生存できるかという問題ですが、宇宙空間でも砂漠でも同様の障害に突き当たります。考えていて面白いのは、文明から遠く離れた所で、いかに人間が生活するかという点ですが、人類が宇宙で生活するのは、かなり難しいと思います。というのも、砂漠ですら昼と夜の気温差が50℃もあるのに、宇宙では300℃にもなるわけですから。

RH 日本の建設会社が月に建物を造ろうとしている、というのは本当ですか？

原　　政府が調査を進めていたのは事実です。しかし現在では経済的に無理でしょうね。

RH　ということは、宇宙建築は個人的な趣味ですか？

原　　趣味として一人でやっているわけではなく、宇宙関係の専門家と共同で進めているプロジェクトです。しかし、まだ、研究は初期段階で、先程お話しした通り、興味深い理論上での実験ということです。

地球の人口は増加の一途をたどっているので、将来、ある時点で、宇宙進出が現実的なオプションとなる可能性はあります。しかしほとんど不可能だと考えられます。

RH　日本と外国では建築家としての仕事に違いはありますか？

原　　考え方に違いはありませんが、建設のシステムには大いに違いがあります。日本では建設会社が一から十までフォローしてくれますが、アメリカやヨーロッパではそんなことはありません。言い換えれば、日本の建築家は、建設のプロセスそのものには責任を持たなくても良いといった甘えた雰囲気があります。しかし最近では、かなり状況は違ってきました。甘えは通用しません。

RH　実際に設計するのは一日のうちどの時間帯ですか？

原　　真夜中に、やわらかい、4Bの鉛筆で描くのが好きです。

RH　近い未来に期待している素材はありますか？

原　　日本には、地震や台風など多くの天災がありますが、だからといって、ガラスの使用を控えるべきだとは思いません。必要なのは、ガラスが割れても、バラバラに飛び散らないようにする保護フィルムで、今後は、その種の安全フィルムでガラスを覆うべきなのです。

青森県にスポーツドームしもきた克雪ドームを建設しました。そのドームの屋根は、薄く、軽く、柔軟性のある四フッ化エチレン樹脂コーティングガラス繊維膜材で完全に覆われます。近い未来、フッ素樹脂ETFE(テトラフルオロエチレン・エチレン共重合体)のような素材は、建築の新たな可能性を開くでしょう。ただ、事前に、火や太陽光線に対して十分な耐性が得られるように、しっかりとしたリサーチをする必要はありますが。

RH　もし自分のシェルターを創るとしたら、どのようなものになりますか？

原　僕は自然に囲まれて生きてきました。長野県の田舎の山間で育ち、そのことは、自然環境への適応という意味で、自分の建築に大きく影響しています。
僕の理想は、山に囲まれて暮らすことですが、現代の都市において、それは難しいので、少なくとも自然を感じ、風に触れ、空を見て暮らしたいと思います。
シェルターについても同じで、ロビンソン・クルーソーのように、海辺に暮らし、気候が良ければ、外で釣りをします。暑くなったり、嵐がきたら、しばし身を守る建物を造るのです。そのように自然環境に適応し、快適な暮らしをするということです。

RH　2002年、ウルグアイのモンテビデオでのセミナーの後、ずっと海岸に住もうと思っていたとおっしゃっていました。大学をやめたときに、まだ研究費が残っていたので、それで海辺に小屋を建てたいと冗談でおっしゃっていましたよね？　海辺の小屋は実現しませんでしたが、そのかわりに、モンテビデオで、ホームレスの人々のための実験的な家を作られました。

原　友人の大江健三郎氏に聞いたんです。何にお金を使ったら、一番いいのか。そうしたら、彼が言ったんです。「世界中の村を調査したんだよね。そしてきみは建築家だ。新しい村をつくればいいじゃないか」。それを聞いて、私は、南米の都市

原広司 札幌ドームの建設予定地にて ｜ Hiroshi Hara at construction site of Sapporo Dome (2000)

では、5パーセントから30パーセントもの人々が占領地で非合法に住んでいる、ということを思い出したんです。そこで、私は彼らのために、3つの塔が橋でつながった、家族の住まいの試作品を作ったのです。1つ目の塔は夫、真ん中は妻、そして3番目は子どもたちのため。塔は、そこに住んでいる人たちが集まりやすいように設計しました。プレハブの材料はすべて、ひとりかふたりいれば運べるような軽いものにしました。

RH　どうして、塔はそれぞれ分かれているんですか？

原　実験的な建物は、"ディスクリート——離散"というコンセプトにもとづいたマニフェストとでもいうべきものです。一緒に住むということは、同じ場所をシェアしなければならないということではありません。別々のスペースは個々人の生活をサポートします。同時に、塔にかかる橋によって、同じグループの人々と密接につながりあうことができます。距離はもはや障害ではないのです。それは、地球規模でも同じことが言えます。現代のコミュニケーション技術を使えば、最も遠くにいる人でも、自分の一番近くにいると感じることが可能です。今私は東京にいますが、地球のちょうど反対側のモンテビデオの人々が私の「実験住宅」を組み立てている……そのことを考えると楽しくなります。モンテビデオの人々にとって、一番遠

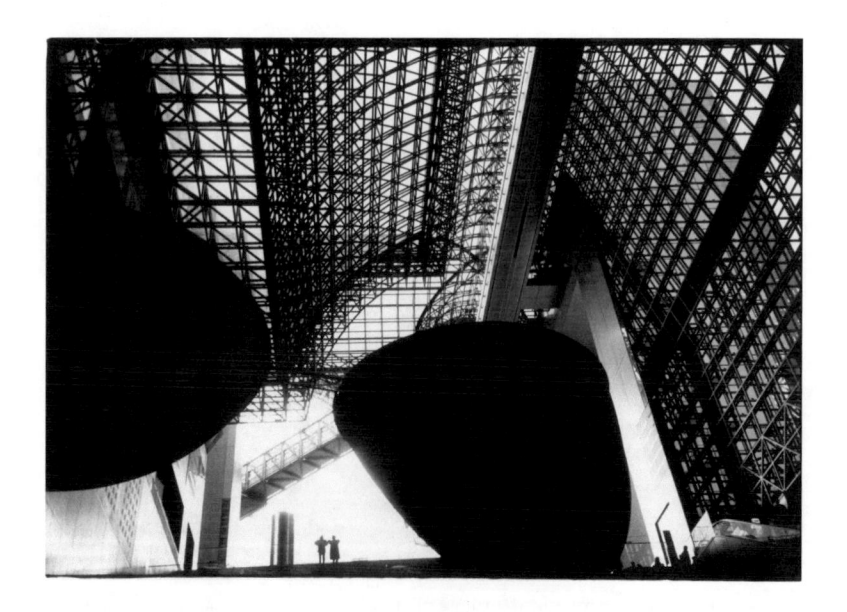

京都駅｜Kyoto Station Building

くにいる建築家が、自分たちの住居をデザインし、一番身近な人間になるのです。私はたとえ、彼らが関わることのない経済のために超高層ビルを建てたとしても、きっと彼らのことを忘れることはないでしょう。

RH あなたの社会的行動主義は、あなたが育った1960年代にその起源があるのですよね。

原 私は、いまだに自分の中に60年代の学生運動を抱えて生きています。あの運動のおかげで、私は世界に出て、各地の村を調査し、この地球の上で命がどのようにして成り立っているのか、見てみたいと思ったのですから。

RH では、今の若い建築家たちはどうですか？ ファッションや大量消費、スターに囲まれた状況が、彼らの創造の源泉なんでしょうか？

原 彼らにとっては、大変な時代だと思います。そのようなものの誘惑に負けずにいるということはとてもむずかしいと思います。ファッショナブルな建物を建ててもいいのです。でも、生活という、より大きな視野を忘れてはいけないと思います。大量消費社会の表層だけ見ていたら、きっと行きづまってしまうでしょう。資本主義の論理はすべてを説明してはくれません。それにとって変わる人間の行動が成功する「ニッチ」というものが必ずあるものです。私たちは、二層構造の世界に生きています。グローバリズムと資本主義という表面と、地域主義とヒューマニズムという底の面。建築はその中間に位置していて、両方を扱わなければいけないものだと思います。

RH これからの日本の都市計画はどうなっていくのでしょうか？

原 今までもそうでしたし、これからも、建築家はあまり口を出す余地はないのではないでしょうか。大きな建築会社がその役目を引き継いでいくのだと思います。彼らの力が強くなっていって、建築家の役割は少なくなり、私たちの仕事も減っていくのではないでしょうか。若い建築家たちはそのことに気づいています。「海外へ出ていき、仕事を見つけろ」なんて彼らに言う必要はないと思います。彼らはすでに知っていると思うので。

RH それでも、日本の建築家が中国で働くということは大変なことですよね。

原 日本は戦時中の残虐行為について、アジアの国々に謝罪していません。これは本当に残念なことです。申し訳ないことをしたと言うのには、さらに時間がかかるでしょう。日本の軍隊は中国でひどい行いをしました。だから、現地で日本の建築家

が歓迎されないということは、驚くことではありません。

RH　でも、あなたは例外ですよね。太原市では、3.3平方キロメートルにわたる大型開発計画を手がけていますし。建築のデザインは、規模によって変わるのでしょうか？　それとも、景観をそこなわずに、自由に縮めたり、拡大したりできるものなのでしょうか？

原　基本的に、規模が変わっても、デザインを変える必要はないと思います。村は小さな部分や要素がより集った複雑なシステムで成り立っています。私たちは長期にわたる調査でそれを明らかにし、観察しました。その結果、伝統的な村のバランスシステムは、何百万人もの住民がいる大都市にも移し変えることが可能だという結論に達したのです。私は、この村の知恵を京都駅のデザインにも応用しようと試みました。そして、京都駅から学んだことをまとめ、今行っている太原市のプロジェクトに生かしています。

RH　それはどんなふうにですか？

原　私は、京都の町を線路でふたつに分けてしまってはいけないと思ったのです。なので、太原では、線路上にデッキをつけ、町が一体になるようにしました。

RH　ご自分が設計している建物の夢を見ることはありますか？

原　プロジェクトのコンペで、相当ストレスがたまっている時以外には見ません。コンペが終わると、自然に頭の中、あるいは夢から消えていきます。

[パート2]——2010

RH　2050年までに、日本の人口は25パーセント減ると言われています。これは建築にはどういう影響が考えられますか？

原　人口の減少が、そのまま贅沢な生活や、スペースが増えるということにはつながらないと思います。近代化の経済のブームは去ったので、私たちの個人の生活空間というものが、より大切になってきています。今や、すでにある生活空間をさらによくするという話になると、ひとりの建築家の意見に重きを置くようになっています。私たちは、商業主義の時代の終わりにきています。しかし、世界の多くの人々がいまだに住む場所がないのです。そのような人々と一緒に働くことは（私はモンテ

ビデオとコルドバ、ラパスですでにやっていますが)将来の建築にとって、とても重要なことだと思います。そして、庭を取り戻すことも同じです。庭はかつての日本で、私たちの生活の中心にありました。数十年も経って、人々は以前より小さいマンションに移り、庭はだんだんとなくなっていったのです。

RH 何年もの間、この500メートルの立方体が何千人もの住居になるというアイデアにこだわってきました。今このアイデアは、規模を縮小して、南米だけでなく別の場所にも広がっています。オーストリアのライディングという村では、現在マイクロ・ハウスという、ミュージシャンのための5メートルの立方体の建物を作っていらっしゃいます。このプロジェクトは、建築家としての、今の興味をすべてまとめているような気がします。

原 若い頃、私たちは仕事がなくて、どうやって生きていったらいいのかと思っていました。そのときの経験が、私にいろいろなことを教えてくれました。大変なときでも建築家としての可能性を最大限に試してみるということ。困難な問題があったとしても、いつも大局から物を見るということ。日常生活での、不快で注意をそらすようなものにとらわれないこと。ライディングの立方体は、私が先ほどお話した、い

隈研吾、藤森照信、原広司と著者、リストフェスティバルのディレクターと
Kengo Kuma, Terunobu Fujimori, Hiroshi Hara, Roland Hagenberg and the directors of the Liszt Festival Eduard and Johannes Kutrowatz in Raiding (2010)

くつかの要素を組み合わせて作っています。たとえば、「モード・チェンジ」(札幌ドーム)「モデレーション」(イタリア・トリノ市庁舎)などです。「モード・チェンジ」は、変化する要求に、建物が常に適応していくということです。一方で「モデレーション」は、人工的なものを使わずに、建物の気候条件を変えることができるというものです。作曲家リストの生誕地であるライディングの立方体は、ピアノと、観客が座れる階段付きの小さなステージとして機能しています。その意味で、これは特定の場所のために作られたのですが、世界中のどこに建てられても大丈夫なのです。この立方体のサイズが小さいのも、簡単に組み立てられて、追加の目的に対応できるためです。そうです、ライディングの立方体は、今の時代にあっているのです。

RH これは、アルゼンチンの作家、ルイス・ボルヘスの短編小説に触発されたのですよね。

原 「エル・アレフ」という作品で、宇宙のすべてのものを、あらゆる角度から同時に見ることができる点について書いたものなんです。物語では、カイロのアムル・モスクの中にある石柱に隠された、アレフという、宇宙のすべてを包含するものについて書かれています。そこでは、宇宙を見ることはできませんが、その柱に耳をつければ、その音を聞くことができるのです。そこで私は、ライディングにくる人たちが、この立方体の外壁に耳をつけて、リストの音楽を聴いているところを想像するのです。

原広司と著者 ライディングにて | Hiroshi Hara and Roland Hagenberg at Raiding (2010)

Hiroshi Hara

To enter Hiroshi Hara's studio in Tokyo's Shibuya district feels – at least temporarily – like visiting one of the ancient villages that the architect studied for a quarter of a century. The entrance path, for instance, is so narrow, that a broad-shouldered man might prefer to walk sideways (stone fortresses in Hajjarah, Yemen, come to mind). Furthermore, the opening is camouflaged by rampantly growing plants (how about floating reed structures in Tranipata, Peru?). And, finally, after you pass the stairway, a bare space projects calmness and security, as if you had entered the sanctuary of an earth dwelling in Tian Luo Keng, China.

Hara sits at one of the broad desks covered with papers, books and pencils. He lights a cigarette and the smoke climbs up his long white hair, which adds to his appearance as a modern-day shaman or well aged Hollywood actor. On the wall are works by American wrap-artist Christo, who is friends with Hara. Originally, Christo wanted to package something much bigger: Hara's Umeda Sky Building in Osaka, with its two forty-floor landmark towers connected by escalators suspended in midair. But since the necessary funds never materialized, Christo resigned himself to wrap up one of his friend's office telephones instead.

Talking about his life's work, Hara expresses wonderment and finds it amusing that he, a proclaimed child of the '60s revolution, has turned out monuments of gigantean proportions, like Kyoto Station or Sapporo Dome. Success, however, never changed him as a person; the global nomad, the Third World country vagabond. On the contrary, it only fortified his belief that if an urban area fails today, it is because the wisdom of ancient village structures has been violated in one way or another. At a recent dinner Hara exchanged anecdotes with Austrian ambassador Jutta Stefan-Bastl and her husband Peter – himself an architect who has traveled the world. "In Africa, it was always the kids who checked out foreigners first," said Hara. "And if they felt they were pleasant, they told their parents. That's how I was allowed to enter their homes." Peter then shared an unforgettable story: "We were driving for days through the desert of Mauretania. Our driver, a Muslim, wanted to introduce us to his family in a distant village. We had sacks of sugar in the trunk to give them as a present and bottles of alcohol for ourselves, the Westerners. One day the bottles broke and their contents flooded the sugar. Our driver panicked and threw the precious gift away.

We arrived empty-handed at the village. The family had only one goat on which their lives depended, and they slaughtered it to welcome us. It broke my heart!" Hara listened, nodded, and kept silent like everybody else at the table. He knew that the concept of self-sacrifice is part of the wisdom that ancient village culture can offer the West. And he also knew that we in the modern world have a long way to go before we can accept it.

[**Conversation part one**]——2000-2007

Roland Hagenberg   You visited and studied villages in fifty countries all over the world. How did that influence your work?

Hiroshi Hara   I'm interested in collecting traditional ideas from villages. I keep a travel diary, make notes, but I don't copy. I translate historical notions into a modern style. I try to find out why certain things were the best solution at the time they originated. The essence of that I translate into modern thinking.

RH   Which village would you choose if you were forced to go into an architectural exile?

HH   Probably a desert village. In general Japanese people think Arabs are aggressive. I found them to be very kind. If you look back into their history, they were always traveling, so they have an open mind, which reflects in their architecture. They often live in tents, structures that shift constantly.

RH   Are you a nomad at heart?

HH   I guess, I am. Recently I went to Yemen to visit a nomad group. Their buildings were 10 floors high and looked like skyscrapers in the desert. It looked bizarre. There was nothing around except a horizon of sand. The base of the buildings was made of stone and the upper part of wood and mud. On the very top was the kitchen. To protect and hide their women, they put them on the highest point of the structure. Women cannot go outside freely, so they constantly perceive the world from above. The Kyoto Station structure is about as tall as those desert dwellings, which were often destroyed and then rebuilt. Their style is about 2000 years old.

RH   And that's where you could live yourself?

HH   Well, today there are machine guns in every house because of the war. I managed to enter about six buildings, but not more. Tribes are constantly fighting.

My village study-project started in the 1970s and it still continues.

RH   How did you manage to enter those six desert buildings? Did you bring one of your 300-page-catalogues with you and said "Hello, I am an architect from Japan?"

HH   I tried to explain what I do, which was of course difficult.

In these parts of the world, if you mention Japan, they only know the word "Toyota". It was interesting to find out, that children always have a better sense of understanding than adults. Sometimes I just drew what I wanted to say in the sand and they understood. They were the translators between their parents and myself. In Central America I often had trouble communicating because children there are kept away from foreigners.

RH   From the desert it's not so far to the lunar landscape, which is also the topic of an ongoing project of yours. How did you get involved in outer space design?

HH   I love to explore how people can live, first by themselves, later in a group in outer space. It features similar obstacles like the desert. How to carry on our lifestyle far away from civilization is an interesting exercise in theoretic thinking. It's almost impossible for humans to survive in space. In the desert there are 50-degree differences between day and night, but on the moon we are talking 300.

RH   Are Japanese construction companies really planning buildings up there?

HH   The government did research, but now today's the economic situationy would not permit it.

RH   So it's more a private hobby?

HH   This is not a project I work on by myself, but together with others specializing in space. It's all in the first stage, and as I said, an interesting thought experiment. The world population is still increasing – so this could be one of our options sometime in the future. But at this point it seems nearly impossible.

RH   Is there a difference when you work as an architect in Japan or abroad?

HH   Not so much in the philosophy but within in the construction system. Here, there are big construction companies who follow up on everything that you're are designing, which is not the case in America or Europe. Architects in Japan are kind of spoiled and they think that they don't have to take full responsibility for the construction process. But in these days situations are changing. We are not being spoiled anymore.

RH   When is the best time for you to work?

HH   After midnight, with a very soft pencil, 4B, I love to draw.

RH   Are there construction materials that you hope will be developed in the near future?

HH   Earthquakes, typhoons – there are lots of dangers in Japan. However, I don't think we have to stop using glass because of that. All we need is a protective film which keeps glass together when it breaks. From now on we should cover all glass constructions with this kind of safety film. I built a sports dome in Aomori prefecture: Shimokita-Kokusetsu Dome. Its roof is entirely made of a thin, light and flexible foil, a coated glass fiber film. In the future materials like ETFE will open new doors and possibilities for architects, but a lot of research has to be done first to make them more resistant to fire and sunlight.

RH   If you would have to build a protective structure for yourself, a shelter, what would it look like, where would you build it?

HH   I have always been close to nature. I grew up surrounded by valleys in the country side of Nagano prefecture and my design makes references to these valleys. My work is about moderating nature. The ideal way would be to live completely immerged in it – a difficult thing to do in our modern cities. So I want at least to be able to feel the environment, touch the wind, and see the sky. The same goes for any shelter. I imagine living like Robinson Crusoe on the seaside, in the open, fishing in a warm climate. And when it gets too hot or stormy, I just build something that moderates nature for a few hours so I can live comfortably.

RH Living on the beach was also on your mind after a seminar in Montevideo, Uruguay, in 2002. You mentioned, jokingly, that you would like to build a bungalow on the seaside because you had university funds left when you retired as a professor. The beach bungalow never happened; instead, you created the Experimental House Montevideo for homeless people.

HH I asked my friend, Kenzaburo Oe – the Nobel laureate for literature – how to best spend the money and he said, "You researched villages around the world. You are an architect. Shouldn't you make a new village?" That made me think about the five-to-thirty percent of people in South American cities living illegally on occupied land. So I created for them a prototype of a family dwelling, three towers connected by bridges: one for the husband, the middle one for the wife, the third for the children. The towers can be easily assembled by the people who will live there – I made sure that all prefabricated parts are light enough for one or two persons to carry.

RH Why are the family towers separated?

HH The Experimental House was based on the conceptual manifesto "Descrete". To live together does not mean you must share the same room. Separate spaces support individual lives – at the same time you stay closely connected to your group, with bridges. Distance is no barrier anymore, even on a global scale. With our communication technologies, the farthest person away can feel like the closest person to you. It is amusing to think that where I stand right now in Tokyo, exactly under me – on the other side of the planet – is Montevideo, for which I created this do-it-yourself house. For people there, the farthest architect away from them designed a dwelling and became the closest to them. I wanted to say I have not forgotten them, even though I build mega-skyscrapers for an economy that they can never be part of.

RH Your social activism goes back to your upbringing in the '60s.

HH I still have the '60s revolution in me; it drove me out into the world, made me research villages, made me see what life is made of on this planet.

RH What about young architects today, surrounded by fashion, consumerism and stardom – is that their only inspiration?

HH It's tough for them. To resist those temptations is difficult. To build a fashionable house is fine with me, but never forget the broader perspectives of life. If you look only at the surface of commercialism, you are already stuck. The logic of capitalism does not explain everything and there will always be niches where alternative human activities thrive. We are living in a world of double layers, with globalism and capitalism on top and regionalism and humanism below. Architecture, in the middle, has to deal with both of them.

RH What about the future of Japanese city planning?

HH In the future, as it has always been the case, architects will not have a lot of opportunities to voice their opinions. Big corporations will have taken over; their pressure mounting, the role of architects diminishes – our work becomes less. Young architects are well aware of that. I don't even have to tell them, "Go and find a job abroad!" They know it already.

RH To work as a Japanese architect in mainland China is not easy either.

HH Japan has not apologized to Asian countries for its war atrocities – that's a pity. To say that we are sorry will probably take more time. The Japanese army behaved badly in China, so it comes as no surprise that Japanese architects are still not always welcome there.

RH But you are an exception, working on a giant development proposal for the city of Taiyuan encompassing 3.3 square kilometers. Does design depend on size? Or, can design be shrunk or enlarged at will without losing its esthetic properties?

HH Basically, you don't have to change the design when changing its size. A village is an intricate system of smaller parts and elements. We identified and observed them through our long research period. And we came to the conclusion that the balance system of a traditional village is transferable to a metropolis with millions of inhabitants. I also tried to apply the village wisdom to the Kyoto Station Building. And what I learned from the Kyoto Station Building I integrate now into the Taigen project.

RH And what is that?

HH Kyoto should not have been devided by train tracks and so in Taigen, I covered the train tracks to keep the city united.

RH Do you ever dream about your buildings?

HH Never – except during project competitions, when I am under a lot of stress.

But, once a competition is over, my buildings are out of my system and out of my dreams.

[**Conversation part two**]——2010

RH It is expected that by 2050 the population of Japan will have decreased by 25 percent. How does that affect your profession?

HH I don't think that a population decrease will automatically lead to a richer lifestyle and more available space in Japan. A new economic boom of modernization is out of sight and, therefore, our personal living space will become more important to us. The opinion of an architect will carry more weight when it comes to creating a better version of an already existing living space. We have come to the end of an era of commercialism. Many people in the world don't have a place to live at all. To work with those people – as I have already done in Montevideo, Cordoba and La Paz – is an important aspect of future architecture. And so is bringing back our gardens. They

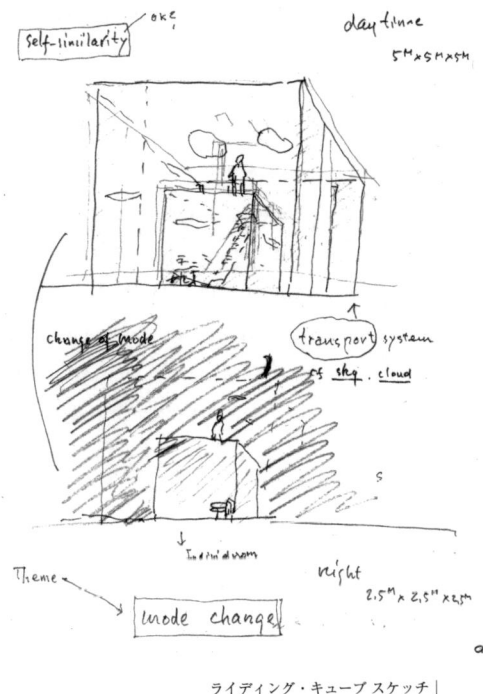

ライディング・キューブ スケッチ |
Hiroshi Hara sketch for Raiding Cube (2010)

were the center of our lifestyle in Japan. Over the decades, people moved into smaller apartments and gardens gradually disappeared.

RH For many years you were obsessed with the idea of this 500-meter square cube that could house thousands of people. Now you are scaling back – and not only in South America. For the village of Raiding in Austria you are currently creating a micro-house equivalent to a five-meters-squared cube, a shelter for musicians. This project seems to summarize all the current concerns that you have as an architect.

HH When I was young, many of us were out of jobs and wondered how to survive. This taught me to push forward in exploring the full potential of architecture, in spite of difficulties, and to always look at the big picture, not get caught up in the unpleasant distractions of daily life. The Raiding Cube combines several elements that I have previously addressed. For instance, "mode-change" (Sapporo Dome) and "moderation" (Palazzo Regionale in Torino, Italy). Mode-change allows the building to be constantly adapted to shifting requirements. With "moderation", on the other hand, you can affect the climatic conditions of a building without using artificial energy. In Raiding – the birthplace of composer Franz Liszt – the Cube functions as a micro-stage with a piano and a staircase for an audience to sit on. In that sense it is site-specific, but it could be built anywhere in the world. The cube's small size also means it can be easily assembled or adapted for additional purposes. Yes, you could say the Raiding Cube fits our time.

RH And it was inspired by a short story by Argentinean writer Jorge Luis Borges.

HH It is called "The Aleph," which Borges describes as a point in space where you can see everything in the universe from every angle simultaneously. The story also tells of an aleph hidden behind a pile of stones inside the Mosque of Amr in Cairo that contains the whole universe. Although you cannot see the universe there, if you put your ear to the pile you can hear it. So I imagined visitors to Raiding listening to Liszt's music by pressing their ears to the outside wall of the cube.

ライディングの風景におかれた「ライディング・キューブ」模型 | Hiroshi Hara model for Raiding Cube placed in the landscape at Raiding, the birthplace of composer Franz Liszt (Photo: Gianmaria Gava, 2010)

長谷川逸子 新潟市民芸術文化会館にて
Itsuko Hasegawa with her chair design at Niigata City Performing Arts Center. (2000)

長谷川逸子 | Itsuko Hasegawa

建築とは、
使いながら完成させていくものだと思っています。
"A building is only finished through the process of living in it."

1941年静岡県生まれ。1964年関東学院大学卒業後、東京工業大学を経て菊竹清訓建築設計事務所勤務。1979年長谷川逸子・建築計画工房設立。1992年から1993年までハーバード大学客員教授をつとめ、2001年より関東学院大学客員教授。日本建築学会賞、日本文化デザイン賞、日本芸術院賞などを受賞。主な作品に、藤沢市湘南台文化センター(神奈川)、すみだ生涯学習センター(東京)、新潟市民芸術文化会館(新潟)、静岡大成中学・高等学校などがある。

Born 1941 in Shizuoka Prefecture. Graduated from Kanto Gakuin University in 1964. Became a research student in Department of Architecture at Tokyo Institute of Technology. Worked at Kiyonori Kikutake & Associates. Established her own practice in 1979. Taught at Harvard University from 1992 to 1993. Professor of Architecture at Kanto Gakuin University since 2001. Many awards from Architectual Institute of Japan Award (AIJ), Japan Culture Design Award and the Japan Art Academy Award. Major works include Shonandai Culture Center in Kanagawa, Yutoriya in Tokyo, Niigata City Performing Arts Center and Shizuoka Taisei Junior & Senior high school.

長谷川逸子

本や雑誌でよく言われているように、長谷川逸子はフェミニスト建築家だとここでも言いたい誘惑にかられる。彼女は、この男性中心のデザインの世界において成功している数少ない女性だからだ。しかし、彼女の作品は男女間の戦いとはほとんど無縁である。たとえ、要求を選んだり、専門分野を女性に開放することが、ジェンダーについての認識を高めることにつながっているとしてもだ。1941年に生まれた長谷川は、東京から西に車で1時間ほどの距離にある静岡県で育った。そこで彼女と姉妹は、母の母校でもあり、もともとエリートの子女が通った女子校、静岡大成中学・高校に進む。彼女の兄弟は、父の石油関係の仕事を継ぐはずだったが、突然亡くなってしまう。家長を失い、会社は解体。長谷川は別の道を歩むことになる。そこで出会ったのが、ふたりの個性的な建築家、メタボリズムを提唱した菊竹清訓と(彼自身がエリートだった)、混沌とした都市の性質を見つめたことで有名な篠原一男だった(長谷川は彼が亡くなる2006年まで、毎年4月に一緒に誕生日を祝っていたという)。1979年に独立した長谷川は、国際的な建築の世界で急速に注目を集めていく。山梨フルーツミュージアムや新潟市民芸術文化会館、藤沢市湘南台文化センターといった建築で、受賞が続いた。

今日、長谷川の母校は変わり、何年も前に一般の学生の入学も認められるようになった。日本の人口が大きく減少したこともあり、男子にも門戸を開くようになった。長谷川はその変化をずっと見つめてきた。そして、2004年に新しい校舎をデザインする。広く開放的な空間に、バウハウスを思わせるカラフルで面白いアレンジメントやアシンメトリの窓。教室の壁は、廊下に面したガラスになっている。透明な壁は、男女共学や近年日本の学校に多く起きている校内暴力に対する管理のやり方なのかもしれない。しかしどんな場合であれ目立たないように監視をしても、私たちが見学に訪れたときのように、生徒が授業中に居眠りをすることを完全に防止することはできない。長谷川は、自分の身の回りにかつてあった風景をもう少し気楽に考えている。あたかも一生かけて世界中をまわる長い旅から帰ってきたかのように、彼女はノスタルジアと自由の混じった感情を放っている。もはや誰に何も証明してみせる必要がないのだ。彼女が語るかわりに彼女の建築が語り、もし彼女

が語るときでも、彼女は建築の邪魔をしないよう小声でささやく。写真をとろうとすると、彼女に断られた。「何年か前にとってもらったポートレートでいいです！」彼女は、生徒たちがサッカーをしている校庭を見やり、言った。「もし、プロジェクトが面白くなくなってしまったら、私はやめようと思います。ただ、立ち去ろうと」。私は聞いた。「たとえそれが建設の真っ最中だとしても？」「ええ、たとえそれが建設の真っ最中だとしても」、彼女はそう答えた。

新潟、2000

ローランド・ハーゲンバーグ[以下 RH] 日本で女性建築家として仕事をするというのは、どのような感じなのでしょう？

長谷川逸子[以下 長谷川] よく、そういう質問を受けますが、もう日本ではこういう質問はないですよ。私の年代の女性はどこの国でも建築家へのスタートは大変だったと思います。男性の進む工学部などは反対され、良妻賢母であることが求められました。戦後、日本は急速に工業化したわけですが、その流れを支配したのは男性中心の社会でした。例えば、キッチンセットも洗濯機のような家電製品も一斉に登場しましたが、女性消費者のことを考えては作られなかったのです。布を大切に扱ってきた感覚が取り込まれるようになったのは、この頃のことで、工業化社会は弱者の思想も排して進められました。

RH でも、洗濯機のおかげで女性は楽になったのでは？

長谷川 それはそうですが、メーカーが女性消費者に意見を求めるようになったのは、1990年代前半にバブルがはじけてからなのです。だから、現在の洗濯機は、手洗いに近いこともできます。このような密なコミュニケーションは、建築においても必要です。私の建築家としての出発点は使用側の視点を加えることでした。

RH 結局、大学に進学したのですよね？

長谷川 はい、希望する国立には担任に反対され、姉に無理に入れられましたが、しょっちゅうさぼっていました。当時、祖父が船の部品を作る工場を経営していたこともあって、私は船の設計図に惹かれていました。船の設計をしたいとも思っていましたので、大学のヨット部の集まる横浜の本牧でヨットに乗りながら、ヨットの

デザインに夢中になっていました。

大学3年と4年の春休みに菊竹清訓建築設計事務所でアルバイトをしました。京都国際会議場のコンペのパースと浅川アパートの設計に参加し、初めて建築を設計している現場に参加して興奮しました。そのお礼にと、奥様が有名なスカイハウスを見せてくださったのですが、スカイハウスは生活装置としての建築だと知りました。その帰り道、建築家になろうと決意したのです。建築の勉強も急に始め、そして建築は社会も伝統も自然もあらゆるものと関係して成立する総合芸術にしたいと考えるにいたりました。そして、藤沢市湘南台文化センターの公開コンペに参加し、一等になったのをきっかけに、公共プロジェクトを手がけるようになったのです。最近では30代、40代の女性が大活躍しています。私の事務所には多くの女性がいます。女子学生も私のところにたくさん応募してきます。

私の若い頃と違って、大学の理工系には女子学生が増えました。女性はすごく元気ですね。とにかく彼女たちのパワーには感心させられます。彼女たちの能力は社会にもっと生かされるべきだと思います。パートナーシップで仕事をする人が増えていますが、今のところ最善策のようです。

RH　どんな時にアイデアが浮かびますか？

長谷川　アイデアが浮かぶと、すぐにノートに書き留めるようにしています。まあ、24時間フル操業という感じですね。ベッドのそばにもノートを置いています。

RH　新潟市民芸術文化会館は、今までの建築の中で最も大がかりなプロジェクトだと思いますが、ここでも、建物と使う人との関係づくりを重視しているように感じます。

長谷川　コンペ案を公開してシンポジウムを行い、利用者とのコミュニケーションを通して、設計をまとめていきました。その後も、工事中の期間を使って、パフォーミングアーツ・センターの運営方法について語り合ったり、新しい場をイメージしてのワークショップを、市の職員にも、市民にも参加してもらい、やってきました。このように、利用者、クライアントに加えて、プロフェッショナルな人、様々な人たちとの関係の中でコラボレーションを行いながら、建築を実現してきました。ここでの建築のテーマも、プロとアマチュア、伝統と建築、音楽と演劇など、異分野のクロスオーバーによって、新しい創作を立ち上げることでした。実際、そうした自主創作が約半

分にもおよびます。こうしたことができるのも、建築のランニングコストの低減が関わっています。そのために考えた新しいテクノロジーが、外壁やエンジニアリングの中に組み込まれています。埋立地でアスファルトだった、このエリア全体を100％緑化し、ヒートアイランドを解消して、敷地の性能を上げ、さらに既存の建物をつなげる空中歩道の導入でネットワーク化を図り、これまで途切れていた街とウォーターフロントをつなげるなど、都市環境のデザインによって、市民に快適な公共空間を提供できたと思っています。

建築とは常に未完である、というのが私の考え方です。大いに使いながら完成させ、時代に合わせて創り続けていくプロセスの中で、生かし続けたいと思っています。

長谷川のデザイン | Itsuko Hasegawa design

長谷川逸子は、かつて女子校だった静岡大成中学・高校の校舎を2004年に改築。今では、現代的な建物が男子たちを迎える。

Not only girls: Itsuko Hasegawa rebuilt the former all-female Taisei Junior & Senior High School in Shizuoka in 2004. Now, the modern structure welcomes boys too.

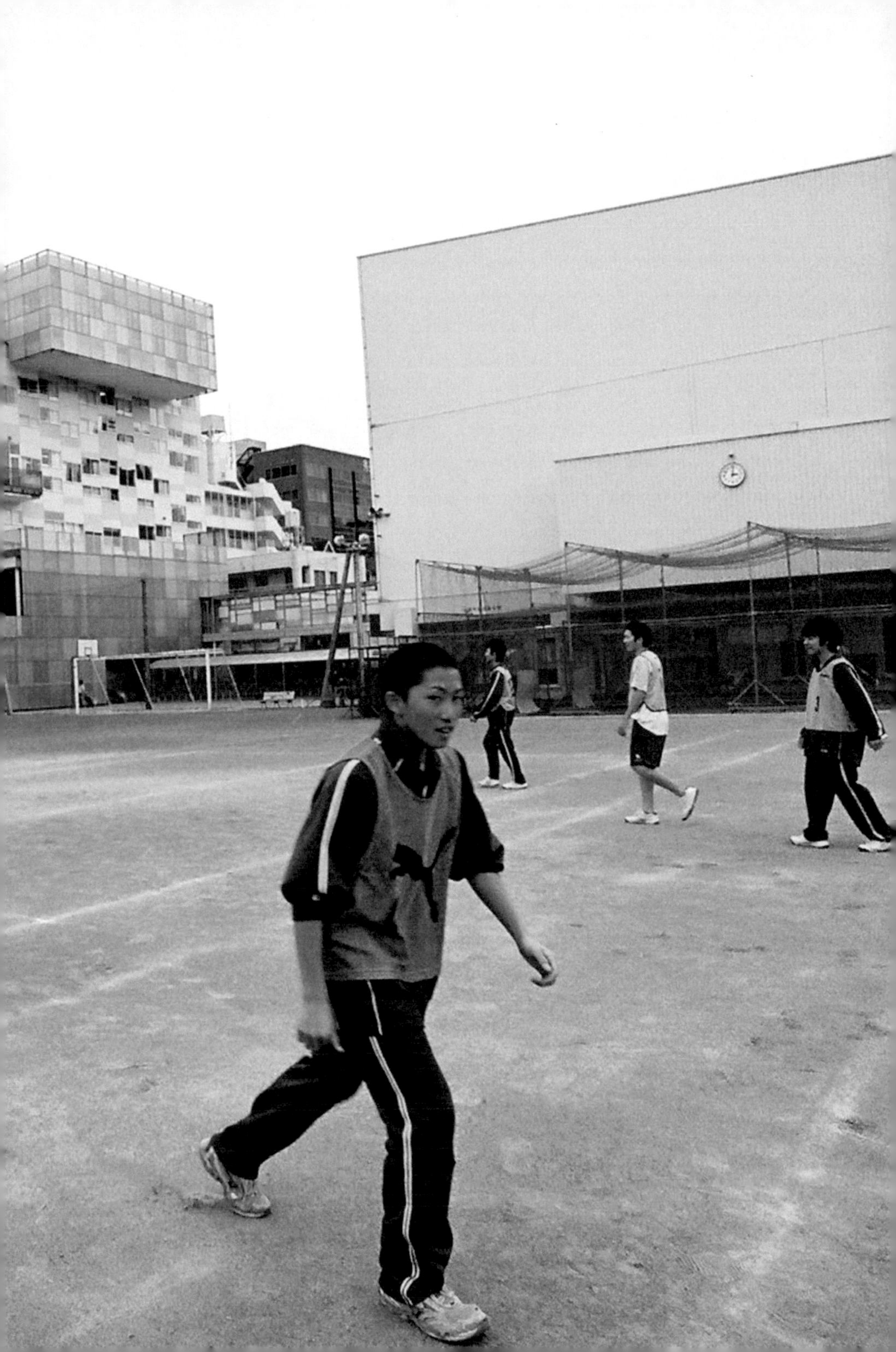

Itsuko Hasegawa

To call Itsuko Hasegawa a feminist architect, as books and magazines have done, is tempting because she is one of the few women who has succeeded in the male dominated world of house designers. But Hasegawa's oeuvre has little to do with gender politics – although her decision to choose a commanding, liberating profession might have resulted from a heightened awareness of her gender. Born in 1941, Hasegawa grew up in Shizuoka prefecture, an hour's drive west of Tokyo, where she and her sisters followed in their mother's footsteps through Taisei Junior & High School – an all-girl institution originally reserved for aristocratic families. Her brother was to take over the family-owned oil business from his father, but died unexpectedly. Deprived of leadership, the family enterprise dissolved and Hasegawa found a new source of guidance in two unique architects: Metabolist Kiyonori Kikutake (himself an aristocrat) and Kazuo Shinohara, the famed observer of chaotic urban qualities. (Until his death in 2006, Shinohara and Hasegawa celebrated their birthday together every year in April.) When she opened her practice in 1979, Hasegawa quickly caught the attention of the international world of architecture. Awards followed for Yamanashi Fruit Museum, Niigata City Performing Arts Centre and Shonandai Culture Center.

Today, Hasegawa's old school in Shizuoka has changed. Commoners were admitted quite some time ago and since the population in Japan is shrinking drastically, the institution has had to open its doors to boys. Hasegawa witnessed the transformation and, in 2004, designed the new school building with wide-open spaces, playful color arrangements reminiscent of Bauhaus patterns and asymmetrical windows. The classrooms now have glass walls that face onto corridors; boys and girls peered out at us as we passed, though they didn't recognize their architect. The transparent walls might be the management's way of dealing with co-education, or with the recent rise of violence in Japanese schools. Whatever the case, discreet surveillance has not deterred students from sleeping during class, as we witnessed during our visit. Hasegawa seemed at ease in her former surrounds and, as if she were returning from a lifelong trip around the globe, radiated a mix of nostalgia and freedom – she no longer needed to prove anything to anyone. Now, Hasegawa's work speaks for her instead and if she does speak, she whispers, so as not to disturb her work. Asked to be photographed on this occasion she declined, saying, "I think the portrait you took a couple of years ago is just fine!" She looked over to a courtyard where students were playing soccer. "You know, if a project is not interesting for me anymore, I just stop. I just walk away!"

"Even in the middle of construction?"

"Even in the middle of construction!"

Niigata, 2000

Roland Hagenberg How does it feel to work as a female architect in Japan?

Itsuko Hasegawa I always come across this kind of question. I believe any female architect of my generation had a difficult start in this world. People were against the idea that girls attend male dominated schools like those of technology. During the postwar period Japan's goal was to industrialize quickly and this resulted in a male-dominant society. For example, all these products like kitchen sets and washing machines were put on the market to be sold to households, but the manufacturers did not pay much attention to the female consumers. It took them a long time to find out, for instance, that households are cautious when washing fabrics. Our industrialized society excluded the point of view from minorities.

RH The washing machines didn't help women?

IH They did, but the manufacturers did not seriously ask consumers for ideas and comments. After the collapse of the bubble economy in the 1990s they realized that they should ask users too. Washing machines are now as sensitive as human hands. In architecture too, there should also be this intimate relationship. My starting point as an architect was to collect users' opinions on design.

RH What obstacles did you face when entering university?

IH My high-school teacher opposed the idea to enter a national university – but my sister made me go anyway. As a result, I was not very motivated and didn't attend regularly. My grandfather had a factory, which produced parts for ships. I was very attracted by ship drawings. In wanted to design them too so I often went yachting at Honmoku harbor in Yokohama as a member of the university yacht club. I was totally into yacht design then. I worked at Kiyonori Kikutake's studio as a part-time worker during spring vacation after I completed my the third year of university. I made perspective drawings for a competition for the international convention center project in Kyoto and for the Asakawa apartment building project. I was very excited to see how architectural design is produced. Kikutake's wife was very grateful and showed me their famous "Sky House". I was touched by the way it is designed to serve human life. On my way back I thought, I really want to become an architect. Immediately after that experience, I started to study architecture. I concluded that architecture is a very inclusive art – serving society, tradition and nature. It was a big turning point for me when I started to design a series of public buildings. I participated in an open architectural competition of Shonandai Culture Centre in Fujisawa and won the first prize. Women in their 30s or 40s are very active nowadays. I have many female architects at my studio, receive many resumes of women students. More and more female students study at science and technology colleges. Women are very energetic. Their energy and power is admirable. I think they should be evaluated more in society. It seems that women currently benefit most when working in a partnership (with a man).

RH When do you have your best ideas?

IH There's no specific time. Whenever I come across an idea I write it down in a notebook immediately. I guess I work 24 hours nonstop! I also have a notebook at my bedside.

RH The Niigata City Performing Arts Center has been one of your most ambitious projects. Here too, it was important to build up relationships with people who then use your architecture.

IH First of all we made our competition project transparent, open to everybody, and we had symposiums. We developed the design through communication with performers. During the construction period we discussed freely how to best manage new activities and organized hundreds of workshops with city officials and citizens. Thus we made architecture happen through collaboration with users, clients and professionals. The concept of this project is creation through crossover, when different fields join, like amateurs and professionals, tradition and (modern) architecture, music and theater. In fact, 50 percent of the programs are produced by the Performing Arts Center. This is possible, because it is financially in good shape. For energy efficiency we applied a new technology on the façade. The reclaimed land was originally covered with asphalt, which we replaced with greeneries to work against the heat-island-phenomenon. A network of pedestrian bridges connect buildings and support the relationship between city and waterfront. I believe that this urban strategy provided public amenities effectively to the citizens. In my opinion, architecture is always incomplete – people who live with it carry it on. It is only completed through the process of living in it and through appropriate renovation.

長谷川逸子の影 | Itusko Hasegawa's reflection, Niigata, 2000

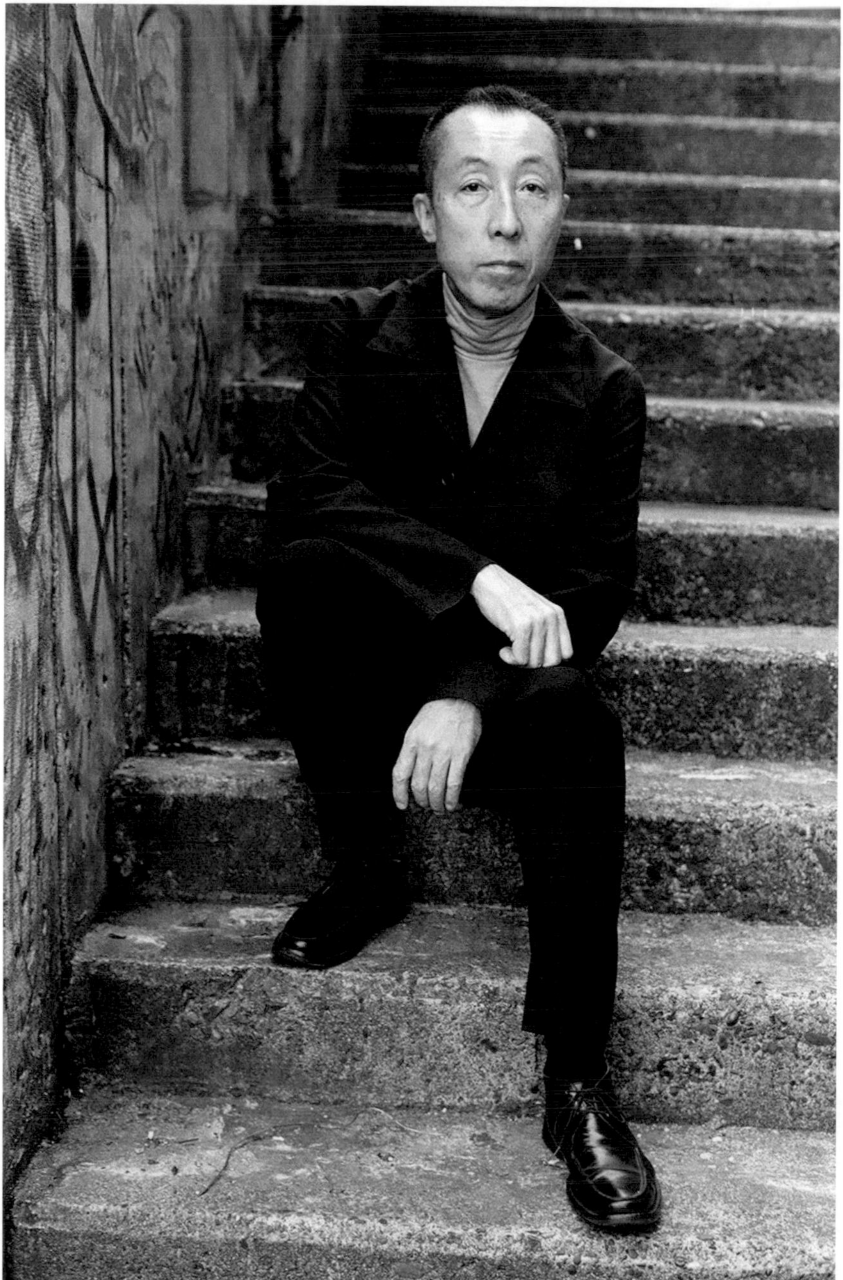

飯島直樹 | Naoki Iijima

色から考え始めるということはありません。
色は力がありすぎるんです。
だから、最初は白と黒だけで考えています。

"I never start out with colors. They are too powerful.
So, in the beginning, I only think in shades of black and white."

1949年埼玉生まれ。武蔵野美術大学卒業。1985年に飯島直樹デザイン室を設立。JCDデザイン賞、「Best Store of the Year」など数々の賞を受賞。伊丹十三邸のほか、大野邸、ソニアリキエル京都ブティック、資生堂ビューティーギャラリーなどがある。

Born 1949 in Saitama. Graduated at Musashino Art University in Interior Architecture. Established Iijima Design in 1985. Numerous awards, among them JCD Design Award and Best Store of the Year. Works include Juzo Itami House, Ohno House, Sonia Rykiel Kyoto and Shiseido Beauty Gallery.

飯島直樹 東京にて | Naoki Iijima, Tokyo (2009)

飯島直樹

飯島直樹が今の仕事を始めてから25年。そのお祝いの会が友人たちによって、八芳園で開かれた。江戸時代、八芳園は将軍の家臣の住まいだった場所だ。レセプションが進むと、はっぴを着て、提灯を持った人々が何百人もの客の間を縫ってステージに上がった。その中には飯島もいて、まるで天皇のように威厳のある笑みを浮かべながら、観衆に手を振っている。この突然のユーモラスな演出で、まじめなその場の雰囲気がいっぺんになごやかになった。人々はくつろいで、笑い、拍手をした。これはまた「もちろんあなたは成功した建築家だけれど、そのことを深く考えすぎないで」というメッセージでもあった。そのほかにも、飯島には一風変わったところがたくさんある。たとえば、彼は事務所に一日中座っていることにたえられない。そのかわり、彼は無数にある東京の日常生活の中から、仕事へのインスピレーションを受ける。だから、新宿や六本木、池袋などを何時間も歩くのだ。ウインドサーフィンにも熱心で、波や風と闘ったときの傷を誇らしげに見せてくれた。一番影響を受けた建築家は誰かと聞かれて、彼は答えた。「実は建築家ではないんですが……画家のマーク・ロスコです。彼の作品を見たときに、自分の選択が間違っていなかったと思ったんです。建築は、私たちがそこに入るたびに気持ちが変わるような、そんな環境をデザインするものですから」。

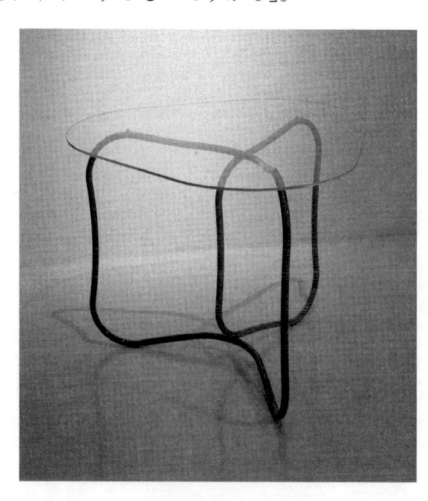

飯島直樹デザインのテーブル |
Naoki Iijima, Chinese Table (2007)

ローランド・ハーゲンバーグ[以下 RH]　デザイナーと映画監督には共通することが多いと感じていらっしゃるんですよね？　彼らのどんなところが重なるのですか？

飯島直樹[以下 飯島]　子供の頃、よくチャンバラ映画を見ました。平日には特別な切符を売っていました。朝の8時に映画館に行くと、3本のチャンバラ映画をまとめて見ることができたのです。今でも映画を見るときは、筋立てよりも画面のなかのセットそのものをじっくり眺めるのが大好きです。いつも思うのですが、カメラのフレームに限定せざるを得ない、映画監督のシーンやアングルの選び方は、私の仕事、インテリアデザインにある意味で似ていると思います。なぜなら、私も内部空間という限定された不自由なフレームの中で場面をカットし、シークエンスとなるように編集しているからです。内部に限定されるインテリアデザイン＝不自由なカメラワークというわけです。たとえば「グラン・トリノ」という映画があります。クリント・イーストウッドが車を運転していて、車の中から外を見ているシーンがあります。それはほんの数分の場面なのですが、クリント・イーストウッド——この映画の監督でもあります——は、何台ものカメラを使って撮影しています。こんな短いシーンにもかかわらず、なぜこんなに複雑な撮影をするのだろう？　少ないカメラではヴィジュアルインパクトが弱まってしまうから？　実はイーストウッドはこのどうでもいいような短いシーンで映画的としか言いようのない「空間」をねつ造するのですね。「グラン・トリノ」の何台ものカメラは、場面を複雑に切り刻むことで、驚くほど豊かな空間を生み出しています。建築家やインテリアデザイナーのレス・モアの問題にも関係しますね。イーストウッドはときに複雑さのデザイナーであり、私にとっては、店やアパートの空間への視線と映画のセット（画面空間）への視線との架け橋になります。

RH　でも、映画監督は観客を誘導しているので、観客は監督が思ってほしいと思うように感じているだけではないのでしょうか？　その一方でデザイナーは、それを見る人を理解しようとして、その人の心の中に入り込んでいきますよね。そういう観点からすると、デザイナーはクライアントを喜ばせるための選択肢をいくつも考えていると思います。

飯島　できあがった店の前に立つとき、時々私は、自分勝手な映画監督のような気持ちになることがあります。でも、それは一瞬のことで、何かもっと大きなものに現実が方向付けられているなと感じます。スクリーン上の映画は、映画そのものが生きています。監督を越えてパワフルです。それは、パブリックデザインにも言えることです。その作品を評価するのは、それを見る人、観客です。映画監督も、デザイナーもとても無力な存在なのです。

RH　初めてクライアントに会ったとき、第一印象で彼らの求めているものがわかるものですか？

飯島　ラッキーなときには、クライアント自身がクリエイティブな人であるということがあります。でも、ほとんどの場合、デザインの過程や、私のこれま

飯島直樹 建設現場にて｜Naoki Iijima at a construction site, Tokyo (2009)

での仕事のクリエイティブな側面についてよく知らない方との仕事になります。たとえばそれは、役所の人であったり、不動産投資家、デパートやレストラン、アパートをデザインしてくれと依頼してくる企業の人たちです。彼らには「空間」というのは抽象です。言葉で説明したり、概念化してもあまり意味がない。具象的な事実が一番です。素材のことや予算のことに話を変えます。そして、彼らに模型を見せます。いつも驚かされるのですが、目の前に、触ることができて分解でき、中をのぞくことができる「物体」模型がくると、彼らはすぐに体を投げ入れ理解してくれるのです。

RH 一方で、クライアントの中には、伊丹十三監督のようなデザインの専門家のような人もいます。そういう人にはどうやって接するんですか？

飯島 私たちの世代にとって伊丹十三という人は、とても大きな影響を与えた人です。1964年に、おそらく日本ではじめて「スタイル」を標榜した本『ヨーロッパ退屈日記』を出版したときには、半分神格化されていました。完璧主義で読者をとまどわせ、ある車の名前をどうやって正確に発音するかというような細部にまでこだわりました。日本語では皆、「ジャガー」といいますが、伊丹さんは「ジャ・ギュ・アー」だと主張しました。監督になる前は一時期精神分析学にのめり込み、日本人の男性はすべて子供なんだと通告する雑誌まで作っています。一流中華料理店で注文した北京ダックの焼き具合を見て眉間にしわを寄せ、それをつき返したりしていました。このようなクライアントは大変ですよね。でも、伊丹さんだけでなく、彼ら大変なクライアントからはとても刺激を受けます。いまだに覚えていますが、伊丹監督のアパートのデザインをしているときです。障子に特異な形を提案したんです。監督は一言だけ「だめ、だめ」と。その仕事は一切の注文がない奇妙なものでした。伊丹さんは映画に気持ちが行ってしまっている様でした。このときの「だめ」はその仕事の唯一の応答だったかもしれませんが、それはその通りでした。

RH 伊丹監督に合ったのはいつですか？

飯島 お互い共通の知り合いを通してです。彼は伊丹監督の映画のポスターを作っていました。監督の第一作が大成功をおさめた後、私は伊丹さんの事務所をデザインしたんです。それは監督に気に入ってもらえました。その後、書斎

とご自宅のアパートをデザインさせてもらいました。私はいつも彼のまわりに「空」とでもいうような感じを受けました。仕事の場面でも、どこか違うところを見つめているようでした。監督から直接答えをもらうことは難しかったんですが、模型や図面の前でもそうでした。彼は信じられないほどの才能の持ち主ですが、いつもほんやりとした壁の向こう側に居る、そのような感じでした。

RH　飯島さんの場合、創造性は、日常の仕事や仕事の流儀と密接に結びついていますか？

飯島　私は度を超さないタイプなので、創造的になるということは、自分自身のバランスをプッシュする作業になります。そうしたことは人それぞれのタイプにもよりますよね。私の場合、一日中机の前に座っているというのはうんざりです。なので、私はなるべく事務所から抜け出して、外に出ています。散歩するだけでも東京の街は面白いものです。時々プッシュのために、深夜に新宿歌舞伎町のコンビニエンスストアに行ってみたりする。実に様々な人たちと、様々な色、ミックスカルチャーがあふれていますよ。

RH　飯島さんのデザインのプロセスは、いつも「色」が一番最後の出番ですね。

飯島　色から考え始めるということはありません。私にとって色は力がありすぎるんです。色は、デザインのほかの要素をすべて支配してしまう。だから、最初は黒と白、グレーだけで考えます。色より線の合理性、ラショナルな側面のほうが身近ですね。でも、つまるところ空間の生成に色は欠かせません。たとえば線と色彩を融合させ、特別な感情に達した画家にサイ・トゥオンブリーがいますね。以前、マーク・ロスコの大きな展覧会に行きましたが、色彩の感情が原初的な空間を形成する神秘的な体験でした。共に感覚が空間の原初的な起点であることをあらためて指し示してくれました。

RH　原初的な空間体験について触れましたが、人間はDNAの中にそのような感覚を記憶させているのかな？

飯島　人には細胞のレベルまでたどれる先天的な感覚の資質があるんじゃないかな。私たちは分子生物学の素人だから論理的、数量的に説明ができません。でも、どうやら細胞の末端は、何が調和がとれていて、何が調和がとれていな

いか、「動的平衡」の内に知っているようです。

RH この原初的な空間の感覚は、洞窟住居（ラスコーの洞窟）のなかでの生存や快楽に繋がっているのかもしれませんね。

飯島 おそらく、生存のためというより、快楽の側面が大きいのではないでしょうか。面白いと思うのは、年を経るにしたがって、空間の見えない側面、アウラや物質の不可思議さに敏感に反応するようになったこと。マーク・ロスコ

東京糸井重里事務所 | Naoki Iijima design for Tokyo Itoi Shigesato office (2005)

の展覧会の他にも、近年何度か、物質的なリアリティーの向こう側に現前する「格別な空間」に驚きました、今更なんですが。たとえば奈良の法隆寺、そしてスイスの建築家、ピーター・ズントーのブラウダー・クラウス野外礼拝堂です。ロスコの世界はユダヤの継承から、法隆寺は仏教、そして、ズントーの礼拝堂はキリスト教から発展してきたものです。私が原初的な体験をしたこれらの建築に出会ったきっかけは、もともと宗教とは何の関係もありませんでした。そこに確かにあった見えない空間は、本当に不思議な偶然の一致だと思います。

Naoki Iijima

When friends of Naoki Iijima celebrated his 25 years of architectural work last year at Happo-en, the former residence of a Tokugawa shogunate minister in Tokyo, the reception began with a procession. A group of solemn associates dressed in traditional happi workman's coats led the way, with paper lanterns, through the crowd of hundreds of guests, up to the stage. In their midst was Iijima, wearing a dignified smile and waving to the crowd like an emperor. The humorous gesture changed the atmosphere of the black-tie event – people relaxed, laughed, and applauded. It also sent a message: don't take yourself too seriously, even if you're a successful architect.

Iijima is unusual in other ways too. For one, he cannot stand sitting in his office all day and instead finds inspiration for his work in the myriad shapes of daily life in Tokyo; he will stroll for hours through districts like Shinjuku, Roppongi or Ikebukuro. He is also a passionate windsurfer and wears the scars of his on-sea battles proudly. Asked which architect has had the biggest influence on his work, Iijima says: "Actually, it's not an architect, but a painter – Mark Rothko. When I see his work, I feel confident that I chose the right profession, which is to design an environment that transforms how we feel every time we enter it!"

飯島直樹 渋谷にて |
Naoki Iijima, Shibuya, Tokyo (2009)

Roland Hagenberg You believe that designers and filmmakers have a lot in common. Where do their interests overlap?

Naoki Iijima As a child I saw many samurai movies. On weekdays, theaters offered special tickets. I used to go at eight in the morning so I could watch three films for the price of one. I still love going to the movies and observe the sets very carefully. I wonder, for instance, why the director has chosen certain scenes and angles. In a way, my work is similar, because I also cut and edit within single frames. The freedom of interior design, limited to the inside of rooms, is equal to a camera's limited freedom. There is this scene in Gran Torino, for instance, where Clint Eastwood is driving and observing from inside the car. It lasts only a few minutes, but Eastwood – who is also the director – used numerous cameras just for this short chapter, and I still wonder why. Would the visual impact really be lessened by fewer cameras? The fact is, Eastwood created an imaginary space with this short scene that can only be described as a "typical movie world". Gran Torino created amazingly rich spaces by using many cameras and applying complicated cuts. This relates to the problem of an interior designer dealing with considerations of using less or more. Eastwood can complicate things, but he also provides visual bridges that connect the real world with the movie set. Actually, entering a store or an apartment can be like entering a movie set.

RH But aren't movie directors manipulating viewers so that they think and feel as the directors want them to think and feel? A designer, on the other hand, enters the mind of a viewer to understand the viewer. From that understanding, he develops choices to please the client.

NI When I stand in front of my finished shop design I sometimes feel like a selfish movie director, but that lasts only for moments because reality is defined by something bigger. The movie on a screen always takes on a life of its own, is much more powerful than its director. And the same goes for public designs. It is the viewer, the audience, that appropriates the work to their liking. So, in a way, movie directors and designers are both quite powerless.

RH Do you know what a client wants based on your first impression of them?

NI If I am lucky, the client is a creative person himself. But most of the time I deal with people who are not familiar with the design process or the creative aspects of my work. They are bureaucrats, real estate investors or business people who want me to design a department store, a restaurant or an apartment. In that case, it does not make sense to theorize and explain options in abstract terms. So I quickly switch to subjects they can easily relate to: the merits of a specific design, for instance; the materials; the budget. As soon as possible, I show them a model. It always surprises me how quickly they understand once they have something in front of them that they can touch, take apart or look inside.

RH On the other hand, you've had clients like film director Juzo Itami who are experts in design themselves. How do you deal with them?

NI Itami had a big impact on my generation. When he published his Diary of Boring Days in Europe in 1965, it was the first Japanese book to focus on style. And with this book he became a demigod, preaching perfectionism down to details like how to correctly pronounce the name of a car. In Japan we all say "Jaggar", but Itami insisted on "Ja-gu-ar". He studied psychology, thought that all Japanese men were stuck in their childhoods, and, if the Peking duck in a restaurant was not correctly prepared, he sent it back. So, yes, such clients are always a challenge, and that is inspiring. I remember when I designed one of Itami's apartments, I proposed certain patterns for the paper screen. "No, no," he said. "That wouldn't work." It was a strange project without any specific requests from the client. Itami seemed to be too focused on his movie project to get involved. And that "no" he gave me was his only comment throughout the whole project. Anyway, in that instance, he was right.

RH How did you meet him?

NI Through a mutual friend, who created Itami's movie posters. After his first film had become a big success I designed his office, which he liked very much. I always sensed this big emptiness around him. Even when he was working he had this distant look. It was difficult to get a response from him, even in front of models or drawings. He was a man with incredible insights, but was always surrounded by walls.

RH In your case, is creativity tied to strict routines, discipline and working rituals?

NI I am a pretty steady person, so to be creative means to push myself constantly out of balance. It depends on one's character. In my case, it would be deadly to sit at the desk all day long. The feeling of being at work is counterproductive. And so I try to escape from the office environment as much as possible. Just walking through Tokyo's streets can throw you off, not to mention visiting a convenience store in Shinjuku at night with its strange mix of people, culture and colors.

RH Actually, in your design process colors are always the last thing you want to deal with.

NI I never start out with colors. For me they are too powerful – they can dominate all other design aspects – and so, in the beginning, I think only in shades of black, white and gray. I am more at ease dealing with lines. Lines are rational. But once a space is defined, I let the colors gradually in. For example, Cy Twombly is an artist who combines lines and colors to reach unique heights. I admire how he combines the linearity of handwritten words with colorful intonations of oil paint to create spatial sensations. Not long ago, I went to an exhibition of works by Mark Rothko. It was a mystical experience, where colors and emotions created an archaic field in space.

RH When you talk about this archaic experience of space, do you mean that humans have a sense for an ideal proportion built into their DNA?

NI I think there is an instinct that goes down to the cell level. We know what's proportionally right and wrong, although a non-professional might not be able to rationalize it and bring it down to mathematics. But it seems there is a sense of balance built into our cells, they know the state of dynamic equilibrium.

RH I would relate this archaic instinct either to survival or to pleasure, or maybe both – like when the cave turned into a nest.

NI Probably more pleasure than survival. I find it interesting that over the years I became more sensitive and attracted to the invisible aspects of space – to its aura, to the magic in-between solid objects. Besides the Mark Rothko exhibition, I was overwhelmed by space beyond its physical reality on two other occasions. Once in Nara at the Horyuji Temple, and then at the Field Chapel by Swiss architect Peter Zumthor. It is a strange coincidence: Rothko's world evolved from a Jewish heritage, Horyuji is for Buddhists, and Zumthor's chapel is Christian. But my encounter with those spaces had nothing to do with religion, although it came close to a religious experience.

磯崎新 水戸芸術館にて ｜ Arata Isozaki at Art Tower Mito (2001)

磯崎 新 | Arata Isozaki

東京のように知性のかけらもない建築が無節操に並んでいると、誰も何も気にしなくなってしまいます。
"If architecture is so dumb and irrelevant like in Tokyo, nobody cares."

1931年大分県生まれ。1961年東京大学大学院修了。1963年磯崎新アトリエを設立。東京大学、UCLA、ハーバード大学などの客員教授や国内外のコンペの審査員、展覧会のコミッショナー等をつとめる。日本建築学会賞、英国王立建築家協会ゴールドメダル、米国・アーノルド・ブルンナー記念賞など数々の賞を受賞。主な作品は、ロサンゼルス現代美術館、水戸芸術館(茨城)、チーム・ディズニービル(フロリダ)、バルセロナ市オリンピック屋内競技場、証大ヒマラヤ芸術センター(上海)など。

Born 1931 in Oita Prefecture. Received Ph.D. from University of Tokyo (1961). Established his practice in 1963. Taught at University of Tokyo, UCLA and Harvard University and others. Numerous awards including Architectural Institute of Japan Award (AIJ), Gold Medal from Royal Institute of British Architects (RIBA) and Brunner Memorial Prize. Important works: the Museum of Contemporary Art, Los Angeles (MOCA), Art Tower Mito in Ibaraki, Team Disney Building in Florida, Olympic Sports Hall (Palau Sant Jordi) in Barcelona and Zendai Himalayas Art Center in Shanghai.

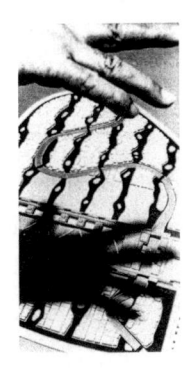

磯崎 新

1980年代前半、ニューヨークのパラディウムで人々がお祭り騒ぎをして踊り、熱狂のさなかにいたとき、この伝説的なディスコのデザイナー、磯崎新の名前を聞いたことのある人はほとんどいなかった。もし、彼の名前を知っていたならば、彼らはその後のアート・スター、ジュリアン・シュナーベルやフランシスコ・クレメンテ、ロバート・メイプルソープたちのような、VIP席の常連になっていたかもしれない。「その当時、アメリカで日本人の建築家がダンスステージを設計することは、フィリップ・ジョンソンが日本に行って、芸者の家を建てるようなものでした。超高層ビルではなく」。ニューヨーク・タイムズの批評家ポール・ゴールドバーガーはそう言う。「パラディウム」はアメリカで磯崎の最初の仕事だった。その後、ロサンゼルスの近代美術館や、フロリダのチーム・ディズニービル（エンターテインメント大手ディズニーの本社）などをたて続けにデザイン。80年代に磯崎が海外で評価されていく時期は、日本が経済的大国へと変化していく時期と重なっている。彼の建築は、先端がとがっていて直線的。最後に角錐がついて、甘い色がそれをやわらげている。それは彼の名前のように、つまり爆発しそうな子音「K」と「Z」（カミカゼの「K」「Z」）のような鋭い刃であり、同時に彼の穏やかなしゃべり方のように知的な雰囲気（シロップのような甘い部分）もあわせ持つ。

それから四半世紀が経って経済の中心が移り、それに呼応するかのように、磯崎も活動の拠点を移す。現在、彼の主なプロジェクトは中国だ。最近、展覧会のオープニングで会ったとき、まわりがすべて黒いスーツを来た要人たちの中で、彼はひとり目立っていた。グレーの髪を後ろでしばり、「長衫」と呼ばれる茶色の伝統的な中国服をまとっている。まるで、日本人の国籍を捨ててしまったかのように。その近くには、理想郷の迷宮、ヒマラヤ芸術センターの模型があった。夢のように変形する洞窟や柱が中央にあり、両端にある二つのブロックの壁は漢字でできた集積回路を思わせる模様で覆われている。私は、証大グループのCEO・載志康に話をしたことがある。日本人の建築家は、戦争という過去があるので、中国ではなかなか活躍できないでいると。若い起業家はそんな私に笑い

建設中の上海・証大ヒマラヤ芸術センター│
Isozaki's Zendai Himalayas Center in Shanghai (under construction, 2010)

ながらこう言った。「磯崎さんとは何の問題もありませんよ。彼はすでに私より中国人ですから！」

水戸、2000

ローランド・ハーゲンバーグ［以下 RH］　ニューヨークの写真家、アーヴィング・ペンのスタジオで話して以来ですが、その後、建築写真についての考え方は変わりましたか？

磯崎 新［以下 磯崎］　いいえ、変わりません。写真家は建物を美しく撮りますが、私の建築についていえば、一流の写真家が撮影したとしても、満足できません。そもそも、建築写真とは、写真家の解釈で編集された建物の姿であり、私自身が建築に託した思想や意図は、とうてい写真には映らないのです。

私が創りたいのは、目で見るだけでなく、五感を使って体験する空間なのであって、建物の中に入って感じて欲しいのです。そうすることで、人は過去に経験した何かを思い出すかも知れません。そうした、あらゆることが建築を体験するということなのです。しかし、写真というものは、表面だけしか捉えていません。

RH　コルビュジエは、コンピューター・ソフトがなかった当時、手で自分の建築の写真を修正してから出版した、と伝えられていますね？

磯崎　コルビュジエは、メディア世代の最初の建築家ですからね。ビアトリス・コロミーナは、建築とマスメディアについての著書で、メディアの中では、対象そのものよりも、対象の映像の方が、よりリアルになるメカニズムが働いている、というようなことを指摘していますが、的確だと思います。それは、かつて、ゲーテが『イタリア紀行』中で、パラディオの本にある古代建築のドローイングは間違いだらけと気付き、いかにコミュニケーションが当てにならないかを嘆いていたのと同じ問題です。

RH　展覧会「間(MA)」で空間の概念を扱っていますが、出品作品の中に、有名な京都の龍安寺の石庭で、カメラが石から石へと動いていくビデオ作品がありましたね？

磯崎　間は点と点の間、あるいは、物と物の間に存在します。からっぽで静寂な無です。見ることも、聞くこともできませんが、感じることはできるのです。だからこそ、空間を体験することの本質となるのです。物というのは、取り替えることもできる

ので、たいして重要ではありません。禅僧の教えのように、何も持たないということは、世界のすべてを持つということです。

RH　京都には感動的な古い建物があると思うのですが、あれは建築ではない、と指摘していますね？

磯崎　もともと、日本には建築という概念はありませんでした。もちろん、建物や居住空間はありましたが、建築という概念では捉えていなかったのです。したがって、いわゆる建築を歴史的な文脈に、どう位置づけるかという、根本的な疑問が出てきました。桂離宮や御所などは、それぞれ価値のある美しい建物ですが、建築というものではないのです。

著者 水戸芸術館にて
Roland Hagenberg at Art Tower Mito (2010)

RH　東京の景観については、どう思いますか？

磯崎　建築が過度に威圧的だったり、美しすぎたりすると、くつろげません。かといって、東京のように知性のかけらもない建築が無節操に並んでいると、誰も何も気にしなくなってしまいます。

東京の人は、どんな建物もすぐになくなると思っていて、実際、新しく何かが建っては、翌日、消えていくわけです。そんな環境で暮らしているためか、若者には驚かされます。私自身は、とてもついていけませんが、若者のライフスタイルは興味深いですね。東京の未来図なのでしょう。

RH　東京での典型的な一日の過ごし方を教えてください。

磯崎　コルビュジエには数々の逸話があります。午前中はもっぱら、時には午後まで、自分のアトリエで絵を描いていて、夕方になる頃、事務所で少し話をして、終わるとすぐに帰った、というものです。そんな生活には、私も学ぶところがあり、コルビュジエのようなスタイルで仕事をしたいと思っています。なぜなら、私にとって、設計は仕事の一部でしかなく、文章を書いたり、絵を描いたりすることも建築なのですから。

私の一日は3つに分かれます。午前中は自宅の書斎で本を読んだり、原稿を書いたり、スケッチをしたりして過ごします。一人で過ごす貴重な時間ですから、なるべく確保するようにしています。午後はずっと事務所でスタッフやクライアントと打ち合わせです。夕方からはオープニング・パーティなど、社交をこなさなくてはなりません。

RH　現代建築に関して、国家はプロセスの中から学んでいくもの、と発言していますね？

磯崎　フランスのミッテラン元大統領が良い例です。就任直後はほとんど外国人建築家を起用していましたが、それは、明らかにフランス人建築家を信頼していなかったことの現れでしょう。しかし、途中で方針を変更して、フランス人建築家を起用するようになったのです。

似たようなことが、現在、中国でおこっています。もちろん、中国の政治情勢はもっと複雑で、外国人建築家を起用する際には、中国を侵略したり、植民地化した歴史のある国の出身者は避けるという配慮をしていますが。

磯崎新 水戸芸術館にて
Isozaki at Art Tower Mito (2001)

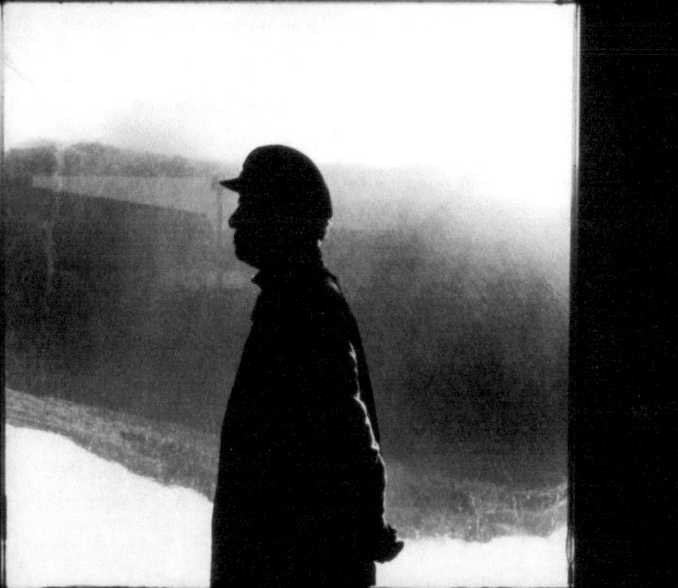

Arata Isozaki

In the early '80s, when revelers danced themselves into a frenzy at New York's Palladium, few had heard of Arata Isozaki – the designer of the legendary discotheque. If they did know him, they were most likely upcoming art stars like Julian Schnabel, Francesco Clemente or Robert Mapplethorpe – the VIP-booth regulars. "At that time, to have a Japanese architect build a dance stage in America was as if Philip Johnson were to go to Japan to design not a skyscraper, but a geisha house," observed Paul Goldberger, critic for The New York Times.
Palladium was Isozaki's first endeavor in the US, which he followed with the Museum of Contemporary Art in Los Angeles and the Team Disney building (the entertainment giant's headquarters) in Florida. Isozaki's rise to international fame in the '80s overlapped with Japan's metamorphosis into a global economic powerhouse. His buildings were sharp-cornered and linear, with pyramids to top them off and syrupy colors to soften them up – kind of like his name, with the sharp-edged, explosive consonants 'k' and 'z', as in kamikaze (the syrupy part being the aura of a soft-spoken intellectual).
A quarter of a century later, economic power centers have shifted again and so has Isozaki. His main projects are now in China. When I met Isozaki recently in Japan, at the opening of an exhibition of his works, he stood out from all the dark-suited dignitaries. With his gray hair tied back in a small ponytail, Isozaki wore the traditional Chinese brown cheongsam – as if he was about to renounce his Japanese citizenship. Nearby was a model of the Himalayas Center, a utopian labyrinth with dreamily deformed caves and columns, sided by two blocks and covered with a pattern that might remind one of Chinese characters serving as computer circuits. I mentioned to Dai Zhi Kang, CEO of the Zendai Group, that many Japanese architects still have difficulties working in China, because of Japan's wartime past. The young entrepreneur smiled and said, "We have no problem with Mr. Isozaki. He is already more Chinese than I am!"

Mito, 2000

Roland Hagenberg In the beginning of the 90s we met at Irving Penn's photo studio in New York. Has your opinion about architectural photography changed since then?

Arata Isozaki Actually no. Photographers take beautiful pictures of my buildings but I am never satisfied, even with the best in their field. Photographers have their own style so my buildings are interpreted and edited with their eyes. I have my own intentions, my own ideas, which photography cannot express. My intention is to create space that can be experienced, not only with your eyes but also with all of your senses, with all of your body. You have to come inside this space and you have to feel it and when you do that, you might even include images that you remember from the past. All that together is the experience of architecture. Photography can only capture the surface.

RH Le Corbusier went so far as to modify the photographs of his buildings that he wanted to be published – at that time by hand, without "Photoshop".

AI He was the first modern architect to emerge through the media. In his book about modern architecture and the mass media Beatriz Colomina rightly points out that within the media there is a mechanism at work that transforms an image into something more real than its actual subject. Goethe complained in his "Italian Journey" about how unreliable communication is, because he found drawings in Palladio's book on ancient architectural buildings that featured obvious mistakes.

RH In your exhibition "Ma" you explain your concept of space. Among other exhibition items was a video of Kyoto's famous stone garden, the Ryoanji, with the camera gliding smoothly from stone to stone.

AI "Ma" exists between points or objects. It is nothingness - blank, silence, you cannot hear or see it but you can still feel its existence. This is for me the essence of experiencing space. Objects are not so important – they are replaceable. Just as a Zen priest would say: "Having nothing, means having everything in the world."

RH We admire the beauty of Kyoto's old buildings, these are not architecture.

AI In the history of Japan there was no concept of architecture. Of course there are buildings, there are living spaces, houses, but the concept of architecture did not exist. So from the beginning this was a major contradiction for us, how we should understand so-called architecture within our traditional context. Each building has its own quality like the Katsura Detached Palace - beautiful buildings but they cannot be called architecture.

RH What about the urban landscape in Tokyo?

AI If architecture is too dominant and beautiful, people cannot expand their own life. On the other hand, if it is so dumb and irrelevant like in Tokyo, people don't care at all. They know that buildings won't last anyway. All the time something new comes up and disappears the next day. Life is there and goes on and when I look at the young people in the streets, it just amazes me. I must say, I can't follow them, but looking at them is fascinating. I guess that's what the future has in store for Tokyo.

RH How does a typical day in your Tokyo life unfold?

AI There are all these stories about Corbusier. In the morning or afternoon he was in his studio, mostly painting. And in the late afternoon he would come to his architecture office, talking to his people and then he left. That's what I have learned from his studio life. Maybe in a similar way I would like to follow his work style. The reason is because architecture for me includes more then just designing a building. Designing is only one part, but so is writing and painting. My daily life is divided into three parts. In the morning I stay at home in my study. I read books and write articles and sometimes I make sketches. This private time I try to protect. All afternoon I have to work in the office, talk with my associates and clients. In the evening I have my social obligations, go to opening parties and so on.

RH You mentioned that when it comes to contemporary architecture nations have to go through a learning process.

AI A good example was Mitterrand. At the beginning of his term as French president important contemporary buildings were mostly created by foreigners. He obviously didn't feel confident enough to commission their own nationals. At the end of his career Mitterrand changed and preferred French architects. You can see similar things happening now in China. But there the politics are more complex. If they choose foreign architects, they are careful not to select anyone from countries that were former aggressors or colonial powers.

水戸芸術館 | Art Tower Mito, suspended stone

「間は点と点の間、あるいは、物と物の間に存在します。からっぽで静寂な無です。
見ることも、聞くこともできませんが、感じることはできるのです。
だからこそ、空間を体験することの本質となるのです。」

"Ma" exists between points and objects.
It is nothingness – blank, silence. You cannot hear or see it but you can still feel its existence. For me this is the essence of experiencing space!"

伊東豊雄 東京にて ｜ Toyo Ito, Tokyo (2011)

伊東豊雄 | Toyo Ito

頭だけで考えたアイデアは数日で変わっていってしまいます。でも、心から出てきたアイデアは、一生残るんです。

"Ideas straight from the brain can change in a couple of days. Ideas from the heart will last a lifetime."

1941年京城（現ソウル）生まれ。1965年東京大学卒業。1965年より1969年まで菊竹清訓建築設計事務所勤務。1971年アーバンロボット（URBOT）を設立し、1979年に伊東豊雄建築設計事務所と改称。東京工業大学、早稲田大学、東京電機大学などで非常勤講師をつとめる。日本建築家協会新人賞、米国・アーノルド・ブルンナー記念賞、日本建築学会賞など数々の賞を受賞。主な作品は、風の塔（神奈川）、せんだいメディアテーク（宮城）、TOD'S表参道（東京）など。

Born 1941 in Soul, Korea. Graduated from University of Tokyo 1965. Worked in Kiyonori Kikutake Associates until 1969. Opened his practice in 1971. Taught at Tokyo Institute of Technology, Waseda University and Tokyo Denki University. Awards from such as The Japan Institute of Architects (JIA): Best Young Architect of the year, Brunner Memorial Prize and Architectual Institute of Japan Award (AIJ). Major works include Tower of Winds in Kanagawa, Sendai Mediatheque in Miyagi and TOD's Flagship Shops in Omotesando in Tokyo.

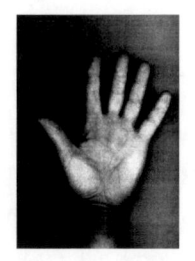

伊東豊雄

彼は、数学の公式におさまらないような、予想もしなかった動きというのも大好きだ。奔流、風にそよぐ葉、情報の流れと、広がっていく自然。建築家は、こういうものにどうしてもひかれてしまう。

伊東豊雄の言葉は、液体が急に冷えて固まった時にできる表面とたわむれるかのようだ（それは、分子が完全に結晶をつくってしまう直前の時間だ）。その結果、せんだいメディアテークの柱のように、「非晶質的」な構造がねじまがった建築や、台湾・台中市のメトロポリタン・オペラハウス（2013年に完成）のように、湾曲している建築ができあがる。簡単な言葉で言えば、伊東の建築の中を歩くと、60年代に流行った、不規則に並んだでこぼこがあるラーヴァ・ランプの中にいるような気がしてくるのだ。非晶質の溶岩の形は、伊東の展覧会にも出てくる。そこで、見る人は、波の形をしたフロアの中の小さな洞窟から、彼の模型を見ることになる。「建築は、社会の多様性に従っていかなければならない」と彼は言う。「しかし、立方体も正方形も、それを表わすことはできないのだ！」（ひとつだけ例外があるとすれば、オーストリア・ライディングのために彼がデザインした立方体がある〔表紙の写真〕。中が空洞になっているので、外部からの多様性は吸収されて、解消していく）。彼は、流体のやわらかなカオスと、その「Generative Order（生成する秩序）」に頼るのだ。（「Generative Order」は、2008年、台北市立美術館で行われた伊東の展覧会のタイトルでもある）。これは、もともと量子物理学者のデビド・ボームが作った言葉だ。彼はこう言っている。「自然と宇宙の中での自由運動は究極的にGenerative Orderになる」。木の影が動いて、TOD'Sビル正面のような最終形態になるとき、これも伊東の言う「Generative Order」の一表現なのだ。これは、なぜ伊東が、小さくてカラフルなジェフ・クーンズの彫刻をオフィスの棚に目立つようにずっと飾ってあるのか、ということの説明にもなる。それは風船であり、ひとつのかたまりであり、一定の形を持たないものだからである。

[パート1] —— 2000

ローランド・ハーゲンバーグ[以下 RH]　今日、人は2種類の身体を持っている、と発言していますが、どのような意味なのでしょうか？

伊東豊雄[以下 伊東]　ひとつめの身体は、古来から我々が持ち続けてきたプリミティブなもので、水がなくては生きていけない身体です。昔から、人は水辺で生活してきましたが、水を飲み、水を排泄するというように、川の支流のような身体を維持してきました。近代になるにつれて、人々は、身体が環境から自立しても存在できると考えましたが、不思議なことに、コンピューター・ネットワークの発達は、再び、身体は自然の一部であるという近代以前の思想を思い起こしつつあるように思われます。

RH　では、もうひとつの身体とは？

伊東　バーチャルな身体と呼んでいるもので、情報のような、いわば目に見えない流れが、我々の身体を通過しています。その流れを、もうひとつの水と呼ぶことができると思います。

その考えは、友人のデザイナーの言葉でひらめきました。彼は、一日中、コンピュータに向かって仕事をしてるのですが、スクリーンに映し出されている映像が、自分の脳から出てきたものか、外の世界からやって来たものなのか定かでなくなり、そのときまるで、自分の足が水に浸っているみたいだ、と言っています。彼は、体外のもうひとつの水、つまり情報と結ばれる印象を語ったわけです。

RH　その理論は、せんだいメディアテークにも活かされていますか？

伊東　せんだいメディアテークでは、建築が身体のようにあるべきだと考え、プリミティブな自然の流れと、バーチャルな情報の流れを協調させようとしました。ここでは、13本のチューブが、樹木のように7層の床を支えています。建築というより、人工の森にラップトップコンピューターを持った人々が集まり、コミュニケーションが発生するような場所にしたかったのです。

RH　それは、生物と電子が結びつく建築ということですか？

伊東　バーチャルな身体、つまり、情報によってつくられる身体は、日々拡張し続けていますが、我々はあいも変わらず、プリミティブな身体がなくては生き

ていけません。たとえ、携帯電話やインターネットで世界と24時間つながるようになっても、生の身体はほぼ太古のままで、重力に逆らうこともできないし、睡眠なしでは生きていけません。そんな、2つの身体をつなぐ建築です。

RH 人に理解されないことをどんどんやる、がモットーでしたね？

伊東 その通りです。理解されやすいものをつくってもクリエイティブとは言えないと思います。

RH だから、予測不可能なものに惹かれるのですか？ 先程、言及があった水の流れにも、横浜に造った風の塔における音や光の動きにも通じるようですが……。

伊東 ええ、確かに流動的な要素には関心があり、正方形や円のような完璧な形より、非対称的な方が好きです。せんだいメディアテークで使ったチューブ状の円柱13本にしても、まっすぐなわけではなく、曲がったり、歪んだりしていて、その配置もランダムです。

RH コルビュジエやミース・ファン・デル・ローエを巨匠と仰いだ世代だと思いますが、

伊東豊雄 せんだいメディアテークにて | Toyo Ito at Sendai Mediatheque, Japan (2000)

今でも彼らの影響を受けていますか？

伊東 今ではもう、彼らの影響はないと思います。むしろ、仏教など東洋的なものを、無意識に受け入れている気がします。かつて教科書で学んだ建築から離れ、もっと日常生活に直結した事柄に向き合っているように思います。

RH 菊竹清訓氏の影響は大きいのですか？

伊東 大学卒業後、菊竹清訓建築設計事務所で働きましたが、そこで学んだ最大のことは、デザインはある瞬間に進化するということです。決して、毎日スタディするから少しずつ進歩するのではなく、一夜にして、アイデアが生まれ、その瞬間にデザインが変わるということです。ほとんど設計が終了しかかっていても、新しいアイデアのためには、設計を白紙に戻して、まったく新しく始めることもしばしばでした。それは、今でも、私が設計をするうえで、とても大事なことだと思っています。

RH 雑誌に写真が掲載され、そのスタイルがはやることがありますが、写真は建築に影響を与えると思いますか？

伊東 若い頃は、ずいぶん建築写真に神経を使っていて、どの位置から、どのアングルで、どのように撮るべきか、ハッキリした希望がありました。しかし、最近では、あまり写真のことは気になりません。おそらく、私自身の関心が、空間を完璧に見せたいということから、ただ1枚の写真では表現できないコンセプチュアルな次元に移ったからだと思います。

RH 朝型の生活をする建築家が多いようですが、やはり朝は早いのですか？

伊東 だいたい朝は5〜6時に起きて、考え事や読み物、スタディをします。その後、オフィスに行き、昼はミーティングが続きます。遅くまで仕事をすることもありますが、毎日というわけではありません。

RH 9.11から立ち直りの兆候が見える今となっても、グラウンド・ゼロの再建案を出さない数少ない建築家となりましたね？

伊東 9.11のテロ後に感じたのは、災難に立ち向かうために、人は何かリアルなものを求めるということです。私自身も軽く透明な建物でなく、がっしりと強いものを考えるようになりました。

グラウンド・ゼロですが、あのような悲劇の場に、建築家として何かアイデアを出すの

は困難で、むしろ、私は平和と平穏のために静かに瞑想しようと思ったのです。

生と死については、パリのコニャック・ジェイ病院の設計をする際にも考えましたが、それぞれが別のものではなく、一つの流れでつながったものだと思います。コニャック・ジェイ病院は、不治の病に侵されている患者もいるので、自然で穏やかに魂が移りゆく環境を創ろうとしました。人生の最期を過ごす場所として、一般的な病院の雰囲気が薄く、パリの街と自然、そして、綺麗な中庭のある自宅が混在し、夢のような雰囲気を感じる空間にしたかったのです。

RH もうひとつのセキュリティーの問題は、建物そのものの安全性の問題だと思います。日本の役所は建物の安全性について、より厳しい基準を設けています。それによる設計への影響というものはあるんですか？

伊東 もちろん、私がやるものは全て安全にしたいと思っています。でも、厳しい規制が創造性をそいでいる面もあります。ただ、新しい規制のせいで、私の建築の創造性が落ちているということはありません。私のコンセプトはいつも、既成の概念から自由になることです。私はいつも人々を解放し、リラックスさせたいと考えています。でも、今はユーザー側からの視点よりも、管理者側の視点からものを作ることが当たり前になっている時代です。たとえば、図書館を建てるとしましょう。親たちは本を読み、くつろげる。子どもたちは走り回って、楽しい環境で遊べる。お年寄りは、居心地のいいコーナーなどに座り、学生たちは、床にでもグループでも座りたいところにすぐ座りたい。そのような環境では、ユーザーの自由度はとても高いと思います。しかし、管理者（この場合は図書館のスタッフ）の視点からすれば、そんなスペースは悪夢のような場所です。管理するのが大変だし、多大な労力を必要とします。だから、自治体の人々は当然そうした管理者の要求を受け入れることを欲します。こういう場合、どのくらい設計案に対して妥協できるのか？ もし、外の国がもっと自由に建築家に任せるのだとしたら、もちろん日本人の建築家たちは、日本ではなく海外での仕事を選ぶようになると思います。

RH 台湾で新しい「自由」を見つけたようですね？

伊東 台湾の人たちにはとても感謝しています。今年、高雄市の5万人収容のスタジアムが完成しましたし、台中市のオペラハウスや台北市にある国立台湾大学社

会科学院のデザインも進行中です。

RH 建物によっては、家具のデザインもご自分でやっていますよね。そのほかにも、表参道のTOD'Sビルの場合、ザハ・ハディドの不定形のソファなんかがおいてありますが、ほかの建築家のものも加えたりしています。誰が何をやるかは、どうやって決めているのですか？

伊東 実は、TOD'Sビルのソファはクライアントのアイデアです。誰が家具について決めるかは、そのプロジェクトによります。私にとって、いすやテーブルなどをデザインすることは、建物を造るより難しい。建物を造るほうがより複雑ではあるのですけれどね。建物の構造やクライアント、デザインや安全性について考えるとき、いつもひとりでは考えません。ほかの人と話し合っている時にアイデアは生まれてくるんです。でも、家具は私ひとりで考えるのです。ほらちょうど今あなたが座っているこのベンチのような。水面に広がる波紋のようなパターンが見えますよね。私の空間についての考え方とその空間がどう建築と結びついていくかということは、水滴が、静かに水面に落ちていく様子に似ています。水滴は、水面に落ちて消えます。でもそれによって、水面の波紋があらわになるのです。これは矛盾なのですが、私は空間に何かの形を作りたいのではない。その結果として形が現れてくるようなものを作りたいのです。

RH 建築家としての出発点は、どのようなものだったんですか？ 新しいスタッフを募集するときに、どうしていますか？

伊東 1960年代後半、東京では学生運動が盛んに行われていました。私は大学に戻って、勉強したかったのですが、大学は閉鎖されてしまいました。だから、思ったんです。それじゃあ、自分で始めるしかない。私は実家の片隅に製図板を置きました。それが全ての始まりでした。今、新しいスタッフを雇うのは、1年に1回、3月です。応募者に課題を与えます。フリーハンドの製図、作文、そして面接。前もって、志願者がコンピューターで作成したポートフォリオを見てはいるのですが、それはその人が本当にどのようなことを考えていて、何ができるのか、それほど参考にはなりません。コンピューターで作ったもののさらに向こうにあるものを知りたいんです。だから、選抜方法を変えたんです。

[パート2]──2010

RH 2010年から建設が始まった、台湾・台中市のメトロポリタン・オペラハウスはこれまでで最も大きなプロジェクトのひとつだと思います。2000席と800席、さらに200席という3つの劇場を包含し、床面積は43,000平方メートル。これは未来に向けて、ひとつの指針になる建物ではないかと考えていらっしゃるそうですが、やはりそのエコロジーの考え方からですか？

伊東 洞窟の連続体のような空間は元々人間の身体にたくさんあるチューブのような存在です。つまり内部と外部を結ぶものなのです。このように建築と自然をどう関係づけていくかを考えることこそ、私にとってはエコロジーを考えることだと思います。でも、このような考えは世界中の建築家が今考えて、実行しなければならないことです。台中メトロポリタン・オペラハウスのビジュアルメッセージと、その斬新な方向性は、外側の世界と内側の世界を結びつける新しい定式になると思います。そして、もちろんそれは自然と調和したものでなければなりません。

RH 伊東さんは、同じことを、オーストリアの郊外にある小さな村、ライディングのプロジェクトでもおっしゃっていましたよね。スイスチーズのように切り出されて、自然にはめ込まれた、白い「Cube」は、その力強いメタファーだと感じました。

伊東 一緒につけたコメントでは、「立方体がただの立方体である限り、それは自然から孤立してしまう。しかし、立方体に、それをつらぬく穴があけられて、ひとつながりの管のネットワークができると、立方体は自然と結合を始め、その一部になっていく」。伝統的な日本の木造建築では、建築と自然の間に引かれた線は曖昧です。将来の建築を考えるとき、私たちはこれを無視できないと思います。これまで現代建築は、建物の内側と外側に明確な線引きをしてきました。これからは、その逆を行かなければならないと思います。私たちはもう一度、曖昧にならなければいけないのです。ふすまや障子、そして縁側は建物の内と外との境界を曖昧にします。すべての人が環境保全への取り組みについて話をするこの時代に、私たちはこのような日本の伝統的なものの役割についてもう一度考える必要があると思います。それは、必ずしも伝統的なやり方でやらなければならないということではなく、新しい技術を使って、もう一度その使い道を作り出せばいいということです。

RH 日本の若い建築科の学生たちは、そういうアイデアに対してオープンですか？

伊東 私はそう思います。日本の学生たちはよく知っていて、よく調べていますので。しかし、彼らは自分自身の哲学や思想の手がかりになるものをもっていません。もし彼らが、グローバルなレベルで仕事をしたいと思ったら、誰のために、そしてなぜ、そのデザインをするのか、より明確なビジョンが必要だと思います。身体全体で考えなくてはだめです。頭だけで考えたアイデアは数日で変わっていってしまいます。でも、心から出てきたアイデアは、一生残るんです。

RH 快楽を求めて次々に新しいものを求める、この大量消費社会の世界で、何が難しいのでしょうか？

伊東 建築の世界では、大量消費からはほとんど得るものがありません。大量消費に頼ってしまった建築は、表層的なものになってしまいました。とにかく形が斬新で格好がいいというだけで建ててしまった。日本はすでに大量消費におぼれてしまっているので、私は大量消費社会を越えたところに新しい場所を探したいと思っています。ヨーロッパでも同じです。大量消費に侵食されていない場所を見つけるのはもう難しくなっています。今後、私はそのような時代の波からは遠ざかっていたいと思います。私は意味のある役割をもって社会に貢献できる、公共の空間をつくりたいと思っています。日本では、個人の生活は小さなままでしょう。一方で町は刺激的な方法で成長し続けると思います。なぜなら、人々は自分の小さな家の外にある公共空間を、共有しなければならないからです。

伊東豊雄 せんだいメディアテークの建設現場にて

Toyo Ito at construction site of Sendai Mediatheque, Japan (2001)

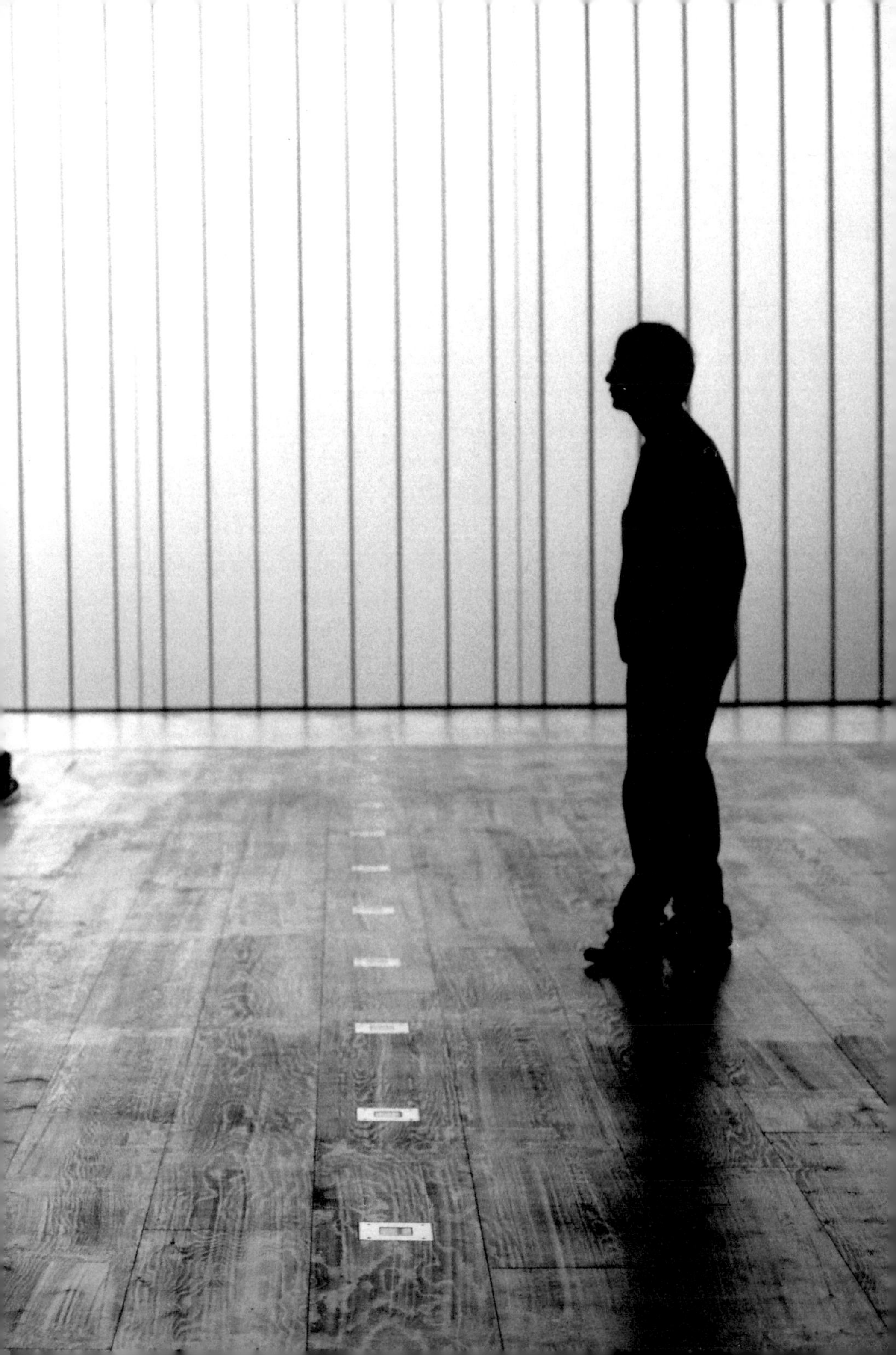

Toyo Ito

He is in love with unpredictable movements that are difficult to pack into mathematical formulas: rushing water, leaves in the wind, the flow of information and nature expanding. If you are an architect – such tough love is hard to hide. Toyo Ito's language plays with surfaces that form when fluids are shock frozen (when molecules run out of time to organize into crystals before coming to a standstill). The resulting amorphic structures can be twisted like Ito's columns inside Mediatheque in Japan; Or curved like the Taichung Metropolitan Opera House in Taiwan (when completed in 2013). In simplistic terms, walking through Ito's creations can feel like being inside one of the lava-lamps that were popular in the 1960s (with randomly-shaped blobs rising and falling). Amorphous lava formations show up also in some of Ito's exhibitions, where visitors observe his models from tiny caves inside a wave-shaped floor. "Architecture has to follow the diversity of society," he says. "Cubes and squares, however, cannot express that!" (An exception is the cube Ito designed for the village of Raiding in Austria, depicted on the cover of this book. It is so hollowed-out that it seems as if it has absorbed diversity from outside, and that this had started to dissolve it.)

Ito relies on the mellow chaos of fluidity and its "generative order" (which was the title of his exhibition at the Taipei Fine Art Museum in 2008). Quantum physicist David Bohm originally coined this term, when he stated that "free play in nature and cosmos ultimately results in a generative order (of things)." When tree shadows move and then morph into a final shape like the façade of TOD'S building in Tokyo, then this too is an expression of Ito's generative order. Which might explain why he has kept this little colorful Jeff Koons sculpture for so many years prominently on a shelf in his office in Tokyo's Shibuya district: it's a balloon, it's a blob, it's amorphous.

[**Conversation part one**]——2000

Roland Hagenberg You say that there are two kinds of human bodies. I don't understand.

Toyo Ito One is the primitive body, part of nature and the same as it has always been over the ages. Its most important substance is water. Humans have always gathered around water. We drink it. We excrete it. Our body is maintained as if it were a part of a river. When the modern age approached, people thought that their bodies could be independent from nature and that they would not need nature anymore. Amazingly enough, nowadays, because of highly developed computer networks, people are realizing again that the human body is part of nature. That way of thinking was forgotten in modern days.

RH And the other body?

TI I started to have this idea of an electronic body when I heard the comment from a designer describing his work. He said, "I sit in front of my computer all day and when I look at the screen I sometimes get confused and don't know anymore if what's on the screen comes from my mind or from outside. When that happens I feel like my feet are dipped in water."

When I heard this, I thought that the electronic flow is just like water - a different kind of water, fluid but invisible, mediating between humans and the world.

RH Did you integrate this theory in your building Sendai Mediatheque?

TI I thought that architecture should be like the human body. It should be in relationship with the natural flow and the electronic flow. 13 tubes are used to hold 7 stories of the building just like a tree. In my mind I actually envisioned this building not so much as architecture, but more like an artificial wood, in which people can stroll around with laptops in their hands and, here and there, they gather with other people, and then communication happens.

RH Architecture as an interface between biology and electronics?

TI The virtual body that is made up of information keeps expanding every day, but we reside inside a primitive body, which cannot change much – even if we are connected to people all over the world for 24 hours through mobile phones or the Internet. Our living body is almost as same as it was thousands of years ago. We can't overcome gravity and we cannot escape sleep. Architecture can be the interface

伊東豊雄 事務所にて | Toyo Ito at his studio with miniature glass models, Tokyo (2002)

between these two bodies.

RH For you the motto was always to go forward and pursue things that can't be understood.

TI That's the point. I think, something that is easy to understood is not worthy to be called creative.

RH Does this explain your love affair with randomness? The unpredictable flow of water that you mentioned is a good example – or the uncontrolled sound and light movements in the Tower of Winds that you built in Yokohama.

TI I do have some orientation towards fluid states of being. I also have some orientation towards asymmetrical space rather then perfect squares and circles. The Mediatheque features 13 tubes that are not straight, some are crooked and warped and pretty much laid out at random.

RH: For your generation Corbusier and Mies van der Rohe were giants. Are you still under their influence?

TI Today I feel free from their influence, because now I unconsciously follow discourses that are more oriental, such as in Buddhist thinking. I better deal with issues that relate to everyday life, than to textbook architects.

RH Another important architect in your life was Kikutake. What did you learn from him?

TI After graduating from the university I worked at Kikutake's office. The most important thing I learned there was that when the design process takes a leap forward it can happen in a split second. That's the crucial point. It is not that you study design every day and it gets better step by step. Important steps often happen overnight and designs are immediately and completely changed. It was very common for us to erase an almost-finished design and start again from zero. This is an important element in my work process, even today.

RH Do you think photography can influence architecture?

TI When I was younger, I was quite nervous about architectural photography. I always had these specific ideas about how my buildings should be photographed, from which angle, which room etc. But nowadays I don't really mind how photos are taken. Maybe my interest has shifted from the need to impress people by showing a perfect space – towards being more concerned about conceptual issues, which cannot be expressed by just a photograph.

RH   Are you a morning person, like most of your colleagues?

TI   Yes, I am. I get up between five and six. I think, I study, I read. After that I go to the office and through the day it is all meetings. Some days I work until late at night, but not every day.

RH   A regular office day started when people's lives were shattered by the 9/11 attack. You were one of the architects who didn't submit a design for rebuilding the WTC.

TI   People desire something real when they have to confront a disaster – that's what I felt after 9/11. I started to think more about strength and intensity in my work instead of transparency and lightness. Regarding Ground Zero itself – as an architect – it's impossible for me to think what to build on such a tragic site. I wanted to meditate for peace and serenity. I also think it would be wonderful if life and death were not two separate entities but forever connected in a continuous way. I thought about it when I redesigned the Cognacq-Jay Hospital in Paris. Some of its patients are terminally ill so I created an environment where life transcends naturally, calmly. It's a place where patients have to spend the rest of their lives. They should not feel the atmosphere of a hospital; instead they should experience a dreamlike reality, a mix of Paris, nature and a private home with a beautiful courtyard.

RH   Another aspect of security is the safety of a building itself. Now, in 2008, Japan's bureaucracy is applying stricter building-safety rules. Does that affect your design?

TI   I want all my buildings to be safe, no question, but in the end stricter rules impede creativity. It does not mean that I become less creative because of the new rules. My concept has always been to be free from existing norms and expectations; I have always wanted to liberate and relax people. But we are now entering a phase where it is becoming more common to create from the controller's point of view than from that of the user. Let me give you an example. Say I build a library; parents can read and relax, their kids run around and have fun in the playful environment. Old people can retreat to comfortable corners and students can sit down spontaneously, if they want to, on the floor and in groups. In such an environment, the degree of freedom for the user is very high. But from the controller's point of view (in this case the library staff), such a space is a nightmare – so the people responsible for the building would naturally want to follow the rules laid out by the controllers. In such situations, how much are architects willing to compromise their original ideas? If other countries offer more freedom, then of course Japanese architects will prefer to work abroad than in Japan.

RH It seems like you found a new freedom in Taiwan.

TI I am very grateful to the Taiwanese. We recently finish a fifty-thousand-capacity stadium in Kaohsiung City and are building now the new opera house in Taichung as well as the Social Science department at the Taiwan National University.

RH For some of your buildings you designed the furniture yourself. In others – like at TOD'S in Tokyo, where Zaha Hadit's amorphous sofas welcome visitors – you let other architects participate. How do you decide who does what?

TI The sofas at TOD'S were actually my client's idea. Who takes care of furniture depends on the situation of each project. For me, designing chairs and tables, for instance, is more difficult than creating buildings, despite the fact that it is a less complex task than architecture. But when you deal with structures, clients, design and safety, you are never alone and solutions come during discussions with people. Furniture, on the other hand, is something I think about all by myself – like this bench you are sitting on right now, where you can see patterns in the wood structure like ripples in a pool of water. My understanding of space and how space relates to architecture is best expressed by the image of a drop falling onto a smooth water-surface that is nearly invisible. The drop represents architecture; the water-surface is space. The drop dissolves on the surface and by doing so makes the surface visible. This is my contradiction: I never want to create shapes in space and, as a result of that, shapes happen.

RH How did you start out as an architect? How do you hire new staff?

TI At the end of the 60s there were big student demonstrations in Tokyo. I wanted to go back to university and study, but all the universities were closed. So, I thought, the only way is to start my own business. I put a designers desk in my parents' house and that's how it all began. Today, when we hire new staff, we do so once a year – in March. I give the applicants a subject to work on. Freehand drawings, a written essay, followed by an interview. I used to have the applicants turn in a computer generated portfolio beforehand, but that did not give us much of an idea what they were really thinking and what they were capable of. I wanted to know what was behind this computer façade, and so I changed the screening system.

[Conversation part two] —— 2010

Roland Hagenberg   From 2010 construction began on the opera house in Taichung, Taiwan – one of your biggest theater projects. It features 800 seats, a floor space of 43,000 square meters, and it is a building that you consider exemplary for the future. Is this because of its ecological considerations?

Toyo Ito   We collect rainwater from roofs for landscape irrigation, for instance, and use greywater for flushing toilets. And, should the building be torn down again, all its materials can be reused. But those are considerations that any builder in the world should have adopted by now. The visual message – and the progressive direction – of the Taichung Opera House is a new formula that interconnects outside and inside. And, of course, you can only do that when synchronizing with nature.

RH   You addressed the same topic in a project for Raiding, a small village in the countryside of Austria. Your white "cube", carved out like Swiss-cheese is a powerful metaphor.

TI   The accompanying statement reads, "As long as a cube is just a cube, it isolates itself from nature. However, the moment holes are drilled through the cube to form a continuous network of tubes, the cube begins to merge with – and becomes part of – the natural systems." Traditional Japanese wood houses have always created a blurry line between architecture and nature. We cannot ignore this when thinking of architecture for the future. Until now, modern architecture has drawn a clear line between the inside and the outside of a building. In the future, we have to go in reverse. We have to become blurry again. Fusuma (paper doors), shoji (paper screens) and engawa (open space connecting house and garden) helped to create vagueness between the building and the outside. In times when everybody talks about efforts to conserve the environment, we should rethink the roles of these traditional Japanese elements. It does not necessarily mean we have to use them in their original format, but we can recreate their purpose with the help of new technologies.

RH   Are young architecture students in Japan open to such ideas?

TI   I think Japanese students are well informed, and they are good researchers. However, they don't have a clue about their own philosophy and what they stand for. If they want to perform on a global level, they must have a clearer picture of why they are designing and for whom. They should work with their whole body. Ideas straight from the brain can change in a couple of days. But ideas from the heart will last a lifetime.

RH Not an easy feat in a world where consumerism constantly demands the euphoria of the new.

TI For the world of architecture, there is little positive input from consumerism. Reliance on consumerism has resulted in architecture becoming superficial; built only for the sake of cool new shapes. I try to select places beyond the ocean of consumerism because Japan has already drowned in it. In Europe too it is hard to find places untouched by consumption. From now on, I want to isolate myself more from these waves; I want to build public spaces with meaningful functions. In Japan, the personal way of life will continue to be compact, and the city will continue to grow in stimulating ways, because people must share spaces outside their small homes.

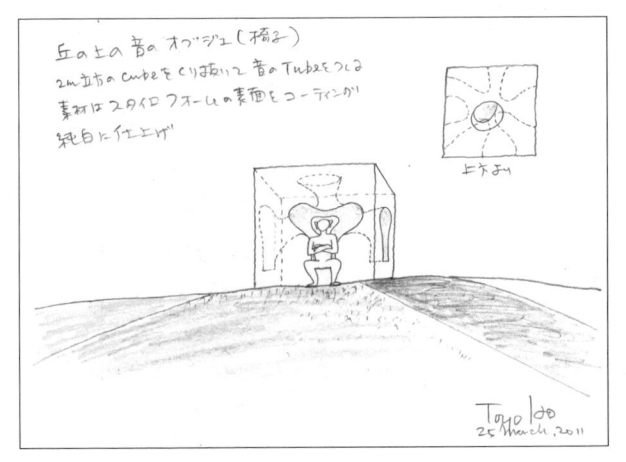

ライディングプロジェクトのための模型図 サウンドキューブ |
Toyo Ito drawing for Raiding Project : "Sound Cube on the Hill" (2011)

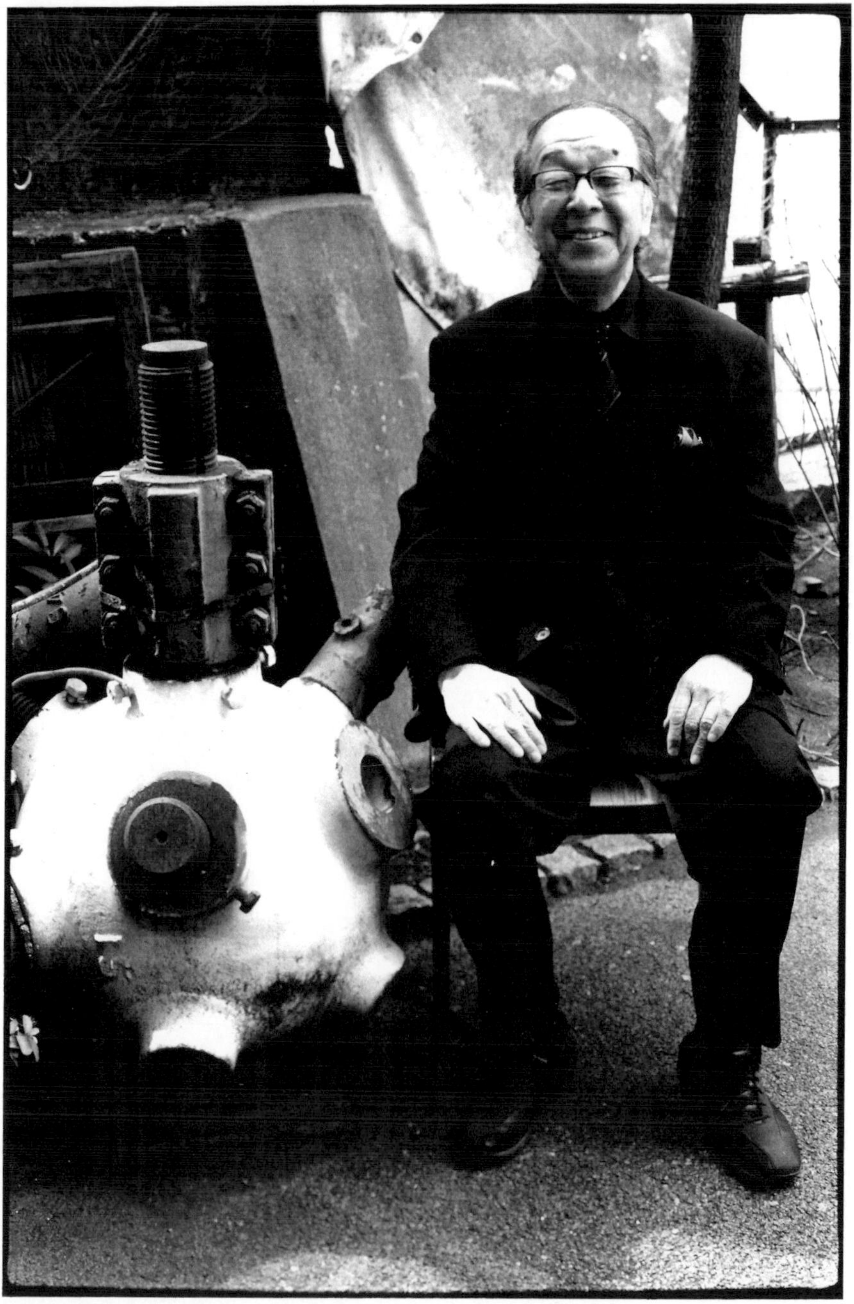

菊竹清訓 | Kiyonori Kikutake

**私は建築家になるつもりはありませんでした。
でも、ほかに何ができるでしょう？
土地を取り上げられて、私は、高い建物を作れば、
スペースができると思ったんです。**

"I never planned to become an architect, but what else could I do? The Americans took our land. I thought that I could create space by erecting towers."

1928年、福岡県久留米生まれ。早稲田大学卒業。1953年に独立、日本での「メタボリズム」ムーブメントの生みの親のひとりでもある。1958年からの「海上都市」プロジェクトは彼の考える都市のユートピアの出発点であり、「海洋都市」のように、人や物が都市に一極集中する問題を解決するために考えられた。彼は、日本で最初に超高層建築を推進したうちのひとりであり、超高層建築の研究委員会の代表もつとめている。今日影響力のある多くの建築家たちが菊竹建築事務所から輩出している。かかわったプロジェクトは「スカイハウス」(東京)、「海上都市」計画(ハワイ)、2005年の「愛・地球博」(愛知)など自宅から新しい都市開発まで数百におよぶ。

Born 1928 in Kurume (Fukuoka Prefecture). Studied at Waseda University. Started his office in 1953. Co-founder of the Metabolism movement in Japan. His "Marine City Project" from 1958 became a starting point for his urban utopias like "Ocean City" to solve problems associated with high-density urban centers. He was one of the first architects to promote skyscrapers in Japan and heads the Hyper Building Research Committee. Many of today's influential Japanese architects started out at Kikutake's office. His career encompasses hundreds of projects – from private homes to new town developments – like Sky House in Tokyo, Floating City Prototype in Hawaii and the 2005 World Exposition, Aichi, Japan.

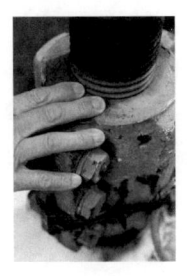

菊竹清訓 アトリエ前にて、廃棄された大阪万博の建物の一部とともに
Kiyonori Kikutake in 2008 in front of his studio next to a decommissioned building-part from the 1970 Osaka World Expo where he participated

菊竹清訓

ベビーブルーのクレヨンがぴかぴかの机の上にきちんと置かれ、黒いスーツの胸ポケットからは赤いハンカチーフがのぞいている。笑顔は若々しく、とても83歳には見えない。学生のときの写真を見ると、スタイルと決断力を放つ、目鼻立ちのはっきりした顔は、まるで若い頃のイヴ・サン・ローランのようだ。

「はら、今準備をしているところ」と、図表とイラストを指しながら菊竹が言う。日本では、西洋と違ってインタビューの質問をあらかじめ相手に渡しておく。その方が安全だと思われているし、日本のジャーナリストたちは、質問のリストから決して脱線しない。でも、今回は別だ。話題はつい1950年代末、菊竹たちが起こした有名なメタボリズム運動へと移っていく。そして未知の領域、政治的にも正しくない領域へ……。右翼だと言われずに、アメリカから独立した強い軍隊をつくるためにはどうしたらいいか、などと誰が話題にするだろう? それ以上に、慰安婦の問題など、日本の戦争犯罪について近隣の国とまだ決着していない時期に、ふつう誰もそんなことを話題にしたりはしないだろう。建築家、菊竹清訓はそれをやる人だ。しかし、それは民主主義をもっと進めたいからにほかならない。「政治に関して、日本の若者はまったく読み書きができていないと言っていい」。彼は言う。「彼らは世界の情勢についてまったく知らない。だから民主主義の一番の脅威は日本なんです!」

菊竹の将来の展望は常に気高く、清浄で、エコだ。50年代のSF映画の世界──重力に逆らって雲を突き抜ける超高層ビル、人口増加の対策としての水中都市、公害のない、空中の交通機関──に今もこだわり続けている。メタボリズムは、再利用可能で、柔軟性のある部分が都市を進歩させ、都市に恩恵を与える無限のシステムだ。土地が足りないということに突き動かされて、メタボリズムは常に空や海へその出口を求めている。(菊竹は建築家になった理由を、アメリカ軍に家族の土地を奪われたからだと言っている)。

学生の頃から住み、今も仕事を続けている東京・文京区の菊竹の家の外には、かわいらしい鉄製の像が建っている。錆びてペイントがはがれているが、レジェ、ブラック、ピカソあたりの彫像、あるいはジュール・ヴェルヌの『海底二万里』に出てくる潜水艦の一部のようにも見える。実はこれは、使われなくなった菊竹のデザインの

一部だ。屋根と鋼索がついているコネクターは、70年の大阪万博で使われたもの。「このがらくた、きれいでしょ?」と彼は言う。そして、昼寝をしている猫をなでるかのように、鉄の表面をこつこつとたたく。「誰もいいと思わないみたいなんだけど……いいと言ってくれたのはあなたが最初ですよ!」そして、その喜びを表現したかったのだろうか、彼はベビーブルーのクレヨンをおみやげにくれた。

大阪万博の建物の一部 | Old building-part from the 1970 Osaka World Expo

ローランド・ハーゲンバーグ[以下 RH] 菊竹さんの人生は、ハリウッド映画の脚本を読むようですね。14代も続いた地主が、アメリカによって土地を奪われ、その息子は新しい土地に移り住むほかなく、高層建築と町を作った……。そしてそれが、日本の新しい顔になった。

菊竹清訓[以下 菊竹] 日本が戦争に負けたとき、アメリカは地主から土地を取り上げました。何世紀にもわたって、私の祖先は土地と、そこに住む人々を守ってきました。病院を作り、社会保障もきちんとしたのです。しかし、徐々に私の家族はそれができなくなっていきました。最初は家や倉庫を貸し出したのですが、最後には新しい税金も全く払えませんでした。番頭さんと、一緒に住み、働いてもらっていた人たちには、出ていってもらわなくてはならなくなりました。日本では「同じ釜の飯を食う」（まわりにいる人々と、全てを分け合う）とよく言いますが、そのような精神は死んでしまったのです。

RH 「地主」はもう過去の遺物ですか？

菊竹 私が話したのは、外国の力によって、日本の農業の基盤が組織的に破壊された、ということです。日本はその文化の一部をあきらめざるを得ませんでした。その文化とは、米と水田が中心にある文化です。マッカーサーがアメリカに帰ったときに、彼は、議員の前で嘘の証言をしたのです。彼は日本の農業を救ったと。

RH 米は、まだ日本でも作っていますが……。

菊竹 私が言っているのは、米の文化についてです。米は私たちのコミュニティーを結びつけていました。灌漑をするため、畑仕事をするため、収穫をするため、皆いっしょに集まりました。私たちは、米の助けによってコミュニケーションをとっていたのです。農業は、自分たちの土地で育った人々によって続いてきました。アメリカのように、奴隷や移民を酷使して続いてきたわけではありません。アメリカは、日本の米のDNAまで奪ってしまいました。彼らは、米をカリフォルニアまで持っていきました。広い土地があって、工業生産の設備があり、低コストで農業ができる場所です。ついには、日本も自国の主要産品である米を輸入しなければならなくなりました。輸入税を作ったのも、残された米の文化的な遺産を守るためです。

RH もし1950年代のアメリカが、外国の農業の基盤を組織的に壊したがってい

もし、軍がなければ、自分から、国際的に声をあげることはできないと思います。そして、庇護者か、占領者のものの見方を身に着けなければなりません。

If you have no army you cannot speak up for yourself. Internationally you have to adopt the view of your protector or occupier!

たのだとしたら、今のアメリカも同じだと思いますか？

菊竹　もちろんです。ドイツは様々な国に占領されたので、ある意味、幸運でした。それに加えて、親や祖父母がドイツからきているアメリカ兵も多くいたので、彼らはドイツを日本の広島や長崎のようには扱いませんでした。

RH　菊竹さんの家族は全てを失いました。だから、建築家になったのですか？

菊竹　私は建築家になるつもりはありませんでした。でも、ほかに何ができるでしょう？　土地を取り上げられて、私は、高い建物を作れば、スペースができると思ったんです。それは小さな土地が重なり合った壁のようなものに過ぎませんでしたけれど。私は空中へ土地を求めていったようなものです。この考えは、1950年代に私が東京で学生だった頃、さらに具体的になっていきました。池袋周辺に、高層ビルをまとめて建てるという計画を立てたんです。当時の規制では、私たちが想像していた十分の一の高さしか立てることができませんでした。でも、ある雑誌とテレビが私の考えを面白いと思ってくれて、後押ししてくれました。私は形と構造を想像するだけではなく、慎重に計算しました。

RH　こうして、大衆社会と都市の住宅問題に新しい解決方法を提案する、メタボリズムが生まれたのですね。メタボリズムは、有機的な成長をサポートする、大規模で多機能型の構造に焦点を当てていましたが、当時日本はそれを受け入れる態勢になっていましたか？

菊竹　いいえ、まだでした。私はたたかれたんです。規制に阻まれました。その一方で、当時日本建築学会の会長だった高山英華先生には、励まされました。「心配するな」って。「いずれ法律は変わる。今から、どうやって高層建築を弱い地盤の上に建てるか、どうやったら地震に強い高層建築ができるかを考えておきなさい」と言われました。現在は、高くしようと思えば、いくらでも高くできます。しかし、必要なのはその周りの緑です。これはヨーロッパでは簡単なんです。貴族たちは、狩場を持っていて、それが公園に変わりましたから。日本ではそういう習慣がないので、都市緑化がなかなか進まないのです。

RH　それから、海上都市も考えていらっしゃいましたよね？

菊竹　土地が足りないのならば、海へ移動して、町や工場を海の上に建てたらどうかと思ったんです。浜辺は製造業のために開放されるでしょう。さもなければ、風

景を壊してしまうことになるでしょうから。それに加えて、物を海外に運ぶことも簡単になるでしょう。日本の主要な産業——自然の原料がない——は原料を輸入し、加工し、製品を輸出するということで成り立っています。

RH 40年前にあなたが予想した未来は、今と違っていましたね。今では、日本の海岸線の50パーセントが、コンクリートで固められています——熱帯の島である沖縄でさえそうです。農業を中心としたコミュニティーは、コンクリートに依存した社会になっています。コンクリートが米に取って代わられてしまったんです。これは日本に進駐した4万人かそこらのアメリカ軍から守られたものなんでしょうか？

菊竹 私は、アメリカからきたすべてのことが悪いとはいいたくありません。いいことだってあったでしょう。でも、戦後アメリカは、日本の軍隊を解体しました。私はいまだに「日本は軍隊を持とう」などとは言えません。もし、軍がなければ、自分から、国際的に声をあげることはできないと思います。そして、庇護者か、占領者のものの見方を身に着けなければなりません。最も恐ろしいことは、今の日本人の若者が、自分の身の回りにはいつでも助けてくれる人がいる、と思い込んで育っているということです——自分の身は自分で守るということがわからない。だから、彼らは政治にもあまり関心がありません。私などは、ベトナム戦争の最中、アンカレッジに立ち寄ったときに見たアメリカ軍を今でも憶えています。空港で彼らは、ユニフォームをカジュアルに着こなし、銃を平然と担いでいました。そこで私は思いました。「なぜ彼らはこんなにひ弱に見えるんだろう？」彼らは戦争に行くようには全く見えなかったのです。自分の国のために戦う者だけが、戦争に勝つのだと思います。

RH 安藤忠雄さんが、日々の仕事を戦争のようなもの、自分自身との戦いだと言っていました。建築に対して同様のアプローチをしていると思いますか？

菊竹 私は朝早いほうが、仕事がはかどるんです。とてもリラックスできます。ある科学者が発見したのだそうですが、人間の脳の働きがその日、ピークに達しているのは、たった5分間だけなのだそうです。また、「馬の背」理論というものもあるそうです。馬に乗っているときは、普段より高い視点から、物を見ることになります。あなたの周りにあるものが動き、あなたの脳も活性化されます。今日それに当たるものといえば、車でしょう。だから私は車を運転するときは、いつもテープレコーダーを持っています。

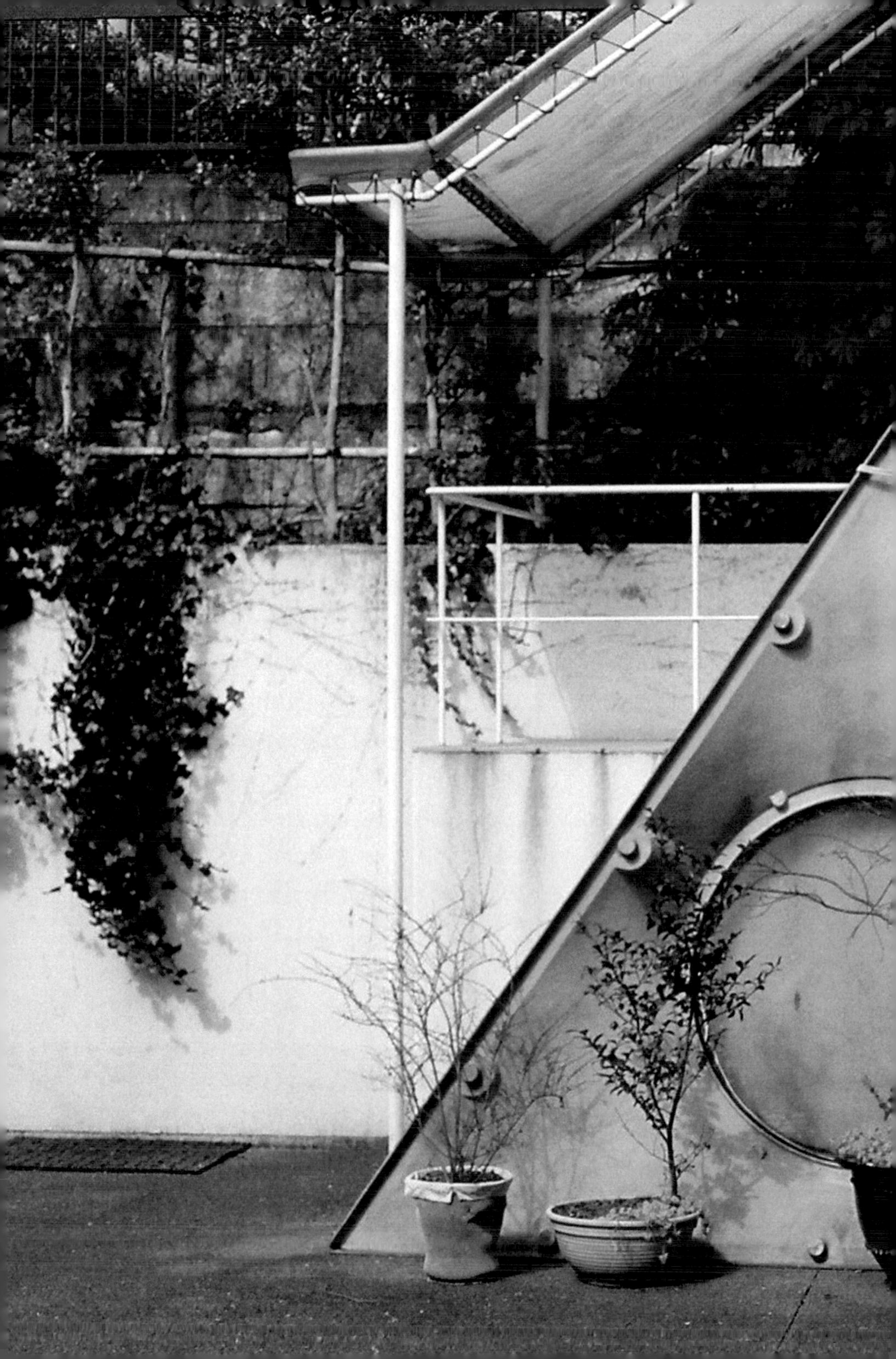

菊竹清訓のアトリエ入口 | Kiyonori Kikutake studio entrance, Tokyo, 2008

Kiyonori Kikutake

Baby-blue wax pens are neatly arranged on his shiny desk, a red handkerchief sticks out from the breast pocket of his black suit and a youthful smile disguises his real age (83). In photographs from his time as a student, Kiyonori Kikutake looks like the Japanese version of a young Yves Saint Laurent, with a sharp-featured face radiating style and determination.

"You see, I'm prepared," he says, pointing to charts and illustrations. Unlike in the West, questions for interviews in Japan are submitted beforehand with topics that are considered safe, and Japanese journalists never deviate from the list during interviews. Not so this time! Quickly, the conversation drifts off Kikutake's famed Metabolist movement (which he co-founded at the end of the 1950s) and into uncharted – even politically incorrect – territories. Who would argue for a strong Japanese army (independent from the US) without running the risk of being labeled a right-wing nationalist? Moreover, who would argue this at a time when issues surrounding the forced prostitution and other war crimes committed by the Imperial army have not yet been resolved with Japan's neighbors? Kikutake, the architect, does just this, but reasons as someone who wants to strengthen democracy. "Politically speaking, the young in Japan can neither read nor write," he explains. "They are uneducated in world affairs and therefore the biggest threat to the democratic future of Japan!"

Kikutake's vision of the future has always been noble, clean and green – stuck in a science fiction movie from the '50s, where skyscrapers built above clouds defy gravity; where cities under water are the answer to overpopulation; where transportation in midair is pollution free. Metabolism is an infinite system of reusable and adaptable parts that advance and benefit a healthy metropolis. Driven by a lack of land, it details constant escapes to the skies and the oceans. (As Kikutake explains, he became an architect because the Americans took land from his family.)

Outside Kikutake's house in Tokyo's Bunkyo ward, where he has lived and worked since his student days, stands a charming piece of cast iron. Rusty with peeling paint, it could be a sculpture by Leger, Braque or Picasso – or a submarine machine part from Jules Verne's Twenty Thousand Leagues Under the Sea. It is actually a decommissioned part from one of Kikutake's designs; a connector that held roofs and steel ropes together at the Osaka World Expo in 1970. "Isn't this junk beautiful?" he says, and strokes the iron surface like the fur of a sleeping cat. "Nobody seems to appreciate it. You are the first!" And then – as a sign of his appreciation – Kikutake hands me one of the baby-blue wax pens as a parting gift.

Tokyo, 2008

Roland Hagenberg   Your life reads like a Hollywood movie script: a 14-generation-strong aristocratic family loses its land to the Americans. Son sets out for a new place and has no other choice but to build skyscrapers and cities that eventually change the face of Japan!

Kiyonori Kikutake   When Japan lost the war the Americans expropriated the landowners. For centuries, my family had taken care of the land and the people who lived there. They established hospitals and took on social welfare responsibilities. Gradually, my family could not afford that anymore. In the beginning we rented out houses and storages, but in the end we could not pay all the new taxes. We had to let go of our banto-san, the people who lived with us and worked our land and farms. In Japanese we say, "Onaji kama no meshi okuu" [to eat the same food], meaning, "to share everything with the people around you". This philosophy died.

RH   Isn't 'aristocracy' a past relic?

KK   I am talking about the systematic destruction of Japan's agricultural base by a foreign power. Japan was forced to give up part of its culture, which has always been centered on rice and rice fields. When General MacArthur went back to America, he testified falsely in front of congress that he had saved Japanese agriculture.

RH   Rice is still growing in Japan...

KK   I am talking about the culture of rice. Rice anchored our communities; people came together to organize water irrigations, to tend the fields, to harvest. We communicated with the help of rice. Agriculture was sustained by people who grew up on their own land and not, as it was in America, by slaves and immigrants. America even stole the DNA of Japanese rice – they took it to California, where they have lots of land, industrialized production and low costs. In the end Japan was forced to import its national food staple. To protect what was left of our cultural rice heritage we established import taxes.

RH If the America of the '50s was out to systematically destroy the agricultural base of a foreign country, would it do the same again today?

KK Absolutely. In a way Germany was lucky, because it was occupied by several countries. In addition, many of the American soldiers had parents and grandparents that came from Germany, so they would not have treated Germany as they treated Japan – Nagasaki and Hiroshima could never have happened there.

RH Your family lost everything; that's why you became an architect?

KK I never planned to become an architect, but what else could I do? Deprived of land, I thought that I could create space by erecting towers, which are nothing more than walls with small pieces of land stacked over each other. I reclaimed my land in the air, so to speak. This idea took further shape when I was a student in Tokyo in the '50s. I drew up a plan for bundled skyscrapers in the district of Ikebukuro. At that time, the height regulation permitted buildings only a tenth of the size I had envisioned. But magazines loved my ideas and so did television and that encouraged me. I not only imagined shapes and forms, I also calculated very carefully.

RH It was the birth of the Metabolist Movement, which suggested new habitat solutions for a mass society and their cities. It focused on large scale, multi-functional structures that supported an organic growth process. Was Japan ready for that?

KK Not yet. I was attacked. Regulations were against me. On the other hand, people like Takeyama-sensei, the head of the National Institute of Architecture encouraged me. "Don't worry," he said. "The laws will change. For now, find out how you can build skyscrapers on soft soil and find out how to make them earthquake proof!" Well, today we can go as high as we want, but we need more green around. This has been easier in Europe, where the aristocracy had hunting grounds that were turned into public parks. The Japanese did not have that and a green urban strategy never developed.

RH You also envisioned populating the oceans.

KK With lack of land, I thought, why not move out to the sea and build cities and factories there? Beaches would be freed of manufacturing sites that otherwise disturb the landscape. It would also make it easier to transport goods offshore; Japan's core business – in the absence of its own natural resources – consists of importing, refining, and then exporting again.

RH Your imagination of the future 40 years ago did turn out differently. Today, concrete covers fifty percent of Japan's coastal lines – even on tropical islands like Okinawa. Your agriculture-based community changed into a concrete-addicted society. Concrete replaced rice. Is that what is protected by the forty thousand or so American troops in Japan today?

KK   I am not saying that everything coming from America is bad. There are good things, too. But after the war America demobilized the Japanese army. We still cannot say, "Let's have an official army!" If you have no army you cannot speak up for yourself, internationally, you have to adopt the view of your protector or occupier. The most frightening part in this scenario is that today's young Japanese have grown up thinking there is always going to be someone around to protect them – that protecting themselves is not their job – and so they have become politically oblivious. I still remember watching American troops when I was on a stopover in Anchorage during the Vietnam War. At the airport they wore uniforms casually and carried guns nonchalantly and I immediately asked myself, "Why do they look so weak?" They didn't seem to be going to war – only those who fight for their own land can win a war.

RH   Architect Tadao Ando describes his day-to-day work as a kind of war, a fight with himself. Do you take the same approach to architecture?

KK   I work best in the early morning, very relaxed. Some scientists found out that the human brain can only function five minutes a day in peak-performance mode. There is also this so-called 'horseback' theory. If you ride a horse, you see the world from a higher perspective; things around you move and so your brain gets stimulated. Today's equivalent would be driving a car. That's why I always have a tape-recorder at hand when I drive.

アストリッド・クラインとマーク・ダイサム | Astrid Klein and Mark Dytham, Tokyo (2010)

アストリッド・クライン | Astrid Klein
マーク・ダイサム | Mark Dytham / KDa

イギリスでは、デザインは細部から発展していくと教えられます。
"British education teaches you that design evolves from details."

アストリッド・クライン

1962年イタリア生まれ。ロイヤル・カレッジ・オブ・アート修了。1988年から、マーク・ダイサムとともに日本に渡る。伊東豊雄の事務所を経て、1991年にダイサムと、クライン・ダイサム・アーキテクツ（KDa）を設立。日本国内の大学のほか、イギリス、アメリカ、オーストラリアやヨーロッパの国々で講義を行う。

Astrid Klein

Born 1962 in Italy. Masters in architecture from Royal College of Art in London. With her partner Mark Dytham since 1988 in Japan. Worked at Toyo Ito and established KDa with Dytham in 1991. Lectures and teaching positions at universities in Japan, the UK, the USA, Australia and throughout Europe.

マーク・ダイサム

1964年イギリス生まれ。ロイヤル・カレッジ・オブ・アート修了。2000年には大英帝国勲章を受ける。伊東豊雄の事務所に勤務した後、1991年にアストリッド・クラインとKDaを設立。KDaの作品に、「Undercover Lab」「ブリラーレ」「セルフリッジ」の内装「トマムタワー」などがある。またアストリッドとともに「PechaKucha Night」を考案。

Mark Dytham

Born 1964 in England. Masters in architecture from Royal College of Art in London. Awarded by the Queen with Member of the British Empire medal in 2000. Worked at Toyo Ito before establishing KDa in 1991 with Astrid Klein. Works by KDa include Undercover Lab, Brillare, Selfridges and The Tomamu Towers. Astrid and Mark are the inventors of PechaKucha Nights.

アストリッド・クライン、マーク・ダイサム

素晴らしいアイデアというのがいつもそうであるように、「Pecha Kucha」は、とてもシンプルなので、なぜこれまで誰も思いつかなかったのか、不思議に感じてしまうようなアイデアだ。デザイナーやアーティスト、建築家が限られた時間の中で、プレゼンテーションを行う。いつまでもだらだらと話をし続けるということがないから、聴衆を飽きさせるということがない。「Pecha Kucha」は、東京を拠点に活動している、アストリッド・クラインと、マーク・ダイサムの発案によるもの。「Pecha Kucha Night」(PKN) の中で、話し手はプレゼンテーションをするのだが、全部で20個のイメージしか使ってはいけない。加えて、ひとつのイメージを説明するのに、与えられた時間は20秒。制限時間を過ぎてしまうとマイクが離れていく。そして、次の話し手がステージにあがる。誰もがこんなみじめな屈辱を味わいたくないと、頑張るのだ。「近頃は、ノートパソコンに何でも保存できる。集めた写真や情報など、データ量にもはや限界はない」。イギリス出身のダイサムが言う。「私たちは、ハムスターのように物を集めるだけで、編集するとか、どうやって不必要なものを消すか、すっかり忘れてしまっている」。「Pecha Kucha」の成功は、オンラインマガジンの『Architecture』で、アップルの製品やモレスキンのノートと並べられたほど。国際的なデザインの世界で、ひとつの独立した動きを生んだもの、と証明されたのだ。(PKNは、今や世界210の都市に広がっている)。20という数字は、アストリッドとマークのマジックナンバーだ。今からちょうど20年前、彼らはふたりで日本に移り住んだ。東京という都市そのものも、20年を一区切りとして生まれ変わり、ファッションなどの流行も20年サイクルでやってくる。ロンドン・ロイヤルカレッジ・オブ・アートを卒業したふたりは、日本のことは雑誌で知るだけだった。そんな彼らの目に、日本は無限の可能性が広がっている土地に映った。しかし、それは、ゆとりを優先させることに敬意を払う国でもあった。マークは次のように言う。「建築家の長谷川逸子が日本建築学会賞をとったとき、彼女の有名な同僚たちは皆、彼女にお祝いを言いにいきました。イギリスでは考えられないこと。リチャード・ロジャーズが、ノーマン・

フォスターを口に出してほめるなんていうことはありえない。ふたりとも、世界的に有名な建築家だとしても」。彼とアストリッドは、伊東豊雄の元で2年間働いた。彼らが最終的に独立するとき、伊東は彼らの最初の仕事を見つけるために骨を折ったという。それは、銀座のショッピングエリアにある優雅な美容院だった。

ローランド・ハーゲンバーグ［以下 RH］　クライン・ダイサム・アーキテクツを1991年に設立する前は、おふたりとも伊東豊雄さんのところにいましたが、そこでの2年間の経験は今の仕事に生かされていますか?

マーク・ダイサム［以下 MD］　私自身は、リチャード・ロジャーズの思想を受け継いでいるので、プロジェクトの詳細がわかっていないときでも、まず直感で探ります。そして、そこから方向性を決め、こだわっていきます。伊東さんの事務所では、途中で方向性がまったく逆転したり、プロジェクトも何度か方向性を変えながら進行していくことが常でした。西洋では、ひとつのコンセプトをじっくりと検討しますが伊東さんの事務所では、常に様々な角度から検討を重ねます。そうやって、私たちが処理しなければならないこの巨大で複雑なアイデアの雲を作っていきます。そこからエッセンスとなるアイデアが出てくるのです。どちらのやり方がいいというわけではありませんが、とにかくふたつのやり方は全く異なっていました。伊東さんからは、そのときにやっている現実のプロジェクトに直接関係ないとしても、探求し続けることを学びました。

アストリッド・クライン［以下 AK］　自分の心の中の『データバンク』に持っている情報を探求し続け、疑問を持ち続け、見続け、蓄積し続けることが大切だと思います。その後で締切のことを考え、それをはき出せば、すべてがうまくいくと思います。

MD　イギリスの学校では、デザインは細部から発展していくと教えられています。どの部分とどの部分が関わりあっているかを見つけること、これが建築を決めるのです。伊東さんの事務所でも、細部について考えましたが、それは機能としての部分であって、物ごとを推進する要素としての細部ではありませんでした。もちろん、物ごとの出発点でもありませんでした。

RH　今「現代建築」ときいて、すぐにイメージがわく国というのはそう多くありません。その中でも日本の現代建築は、細かい説明をする必要がなく、人々が思い浮かべる

ことのできるものに、急速になってきていると思います。これはどこからきていると考えますか？

MD ひとつには、今の時代と経済状況があると思います。そのために、ある一定の素材を使って、ある一定の建物を作る。そして、建築工法も似たようなものになる。見た目と雰囲気はその決まりによって規定されてくると思います。

RH それは、アメリカについても同じように言えることですよね。でも、「アメリカ現代建築」というと、何かあいまいな感じがします。

AK 1960年代から70年代の日本の建築は、2010年の建築とまったく違っています。

マーク・ダイサムとアストリッド・クライン | Mark Dytham and Astrid Klein, Tokyo (2010)

その時代の経済がトレンドや建築に影響を与えることは確かです。しかしそれに加えて、日本の建築には、日本の文化に根付いた何かがあると思います。そして、それは現代の建築様式が世界的に常に混ぜ合わされ、すりつぶされているときにもかかわらず、その個性を残していると思います。簡素な茶室などはそのいい例です。茶室は、たとえば不思議な形をした小さなものがひとつその空間にいれられただけで、突如として驚きと緊張感に満ちた空間になります。それに、漆器などもそうです。もちろんこれはただのお椀に過ぎないのですが、うるしが30回も重ね塗りをされているということを知ったときに、それを身近に感じ、その目に見えない領域に引き込まれてしまうのです。

RH 目に見えない、と言えば、北海道のホテルアルファトマム ザ・タワーホテルは、目に見えないというのがポイントではないでしょうか。

AK トマムの2つの塔、ザ・タワーは、80年代終わりのバブル期に建てられ、私たちはその改装をしました。建てられてから20年が経ち、建物は老朽化して、持ち主は外壁の断熱工事をしようとしていたところでした。クライアントから、配色の構想を聞かれたので、私たちは周囲の風景にとけ込むようなカモフラージュパターンを考えました。こういう仕事は、日本でますます増えています。時代遅れの大きな建物は、すべて簡単に取り壊してしまうわけにはいきません。そこで、それをどうやってアップデートし、もう一度、今の時代に合うようにするか。これは、将来に向けての大きなチャレンジです。

RH クライン・ダイサム・アーキテクツで、おふたりは仕事を分けているのですか？男・女で役割を分担している部分はあるのでしょうか？

MD 色については、アストリッド(クライン)が見ています。多少の例外はありますが、基本的に私は関知しません。

AK 形や構造、テクスチャーについては、私たちはもちろんそれぞれの感性からアプローチします。もしそう呼びたいのであれば「女性の視点」というものはありますが、私たちはチームとして、ひとつの仕事をやっていますし、リスクを負っています。アイデアに収拾がつかなくなるときには、どちらかがいつも言うんです。「ちょっと待って！」とね。私たちは、常にアイデアのキャッチボールをしていると、真実が見えてくるので、いやな方法で自分たちをさらけ出さずにすむんです。そうやってうまくやっています。

RH　なぜ日本のクライアントは、日本に住む外国人の建築家を使いたがるのでしょうか？

AK　私たちと仕事をすると、物の見方が広がるからではないでしょうか。ヨーロッパのバックグラウンドに日本人の解釈が合わさっているので。私たちは「日本人的」なものを別の角度から見て、また違った方法で強調します。私たちがヨーロッパに戻ったときなど、逆の場合も同じです。私たちは日本に20年以上いて、再びロンドンに住んだとき、より広い視野と、一歩ひいた視点から、そうしました。化粧品会社が最近男性の客に声をかけているように、あるクライアントも、私たちが男女のチームであることを評価してくれました。私たちのこの関係が工夫されたものなので、多くの人に訴える力を持っているのではないかと思います。

RH　おふたりは、今や世界中で使われている「PechaKucha（ペチャクチャ）」という、プレゼンテーションのフォーマットを発明しました。これは、おふたりの専門から出てきたアイデアなんですか？

MD　そうですね、ひとつには、私たちがだらだらと長く続き、早く要点にたどりつかないプレゼンテーションを聞くのに疲れてしまったということがあります。

AK　「PechaKucha」はワクワク感と情熱を伝えるためのもので、情熱を持った人がまた別の情熱を持った人をひきつける働きをしています。またそれを飛び出して、コラボレーションや新しいアイデアが生まれるのです。「PechaKucha」はどんな建築家にとっても、素晴らしいインスピレーションの宝庫です。

MD　それに、これはエンターテインメントでもあるんです。最近私たちは思ったのですが、これ以上に面白いトイレのインスタレーションは出てこなかったでしょう。ドアに、その人がトイレに入っている時間を映し出す、というアイデアです。そうすれば、もし列があったときに、どのトイレが先に空くかが、すぐにわかるでしょう。「PechaKucha Night（ぺちゃくちゃないと）」は、私たちがミュージシャンやアーティスト、建築家たちのためにつくったクラブ（イベントスペース クリエイティブキッチン）「スーパーデラックス」で行われました。そうすると、クラブは人脈づくりの場所に早変わりです。面白い人たちが皆ここに集ってくるので、会いに行く時間の短縮にもなりました。

AK　しかし、どれだけ人脈が広くても、結局は一対一の関係だと思います。彼らと交流することによって、その場限りの熱狂ではなく、明日へとつながる真実をつかむことができるし、プラスになることがあると思います。

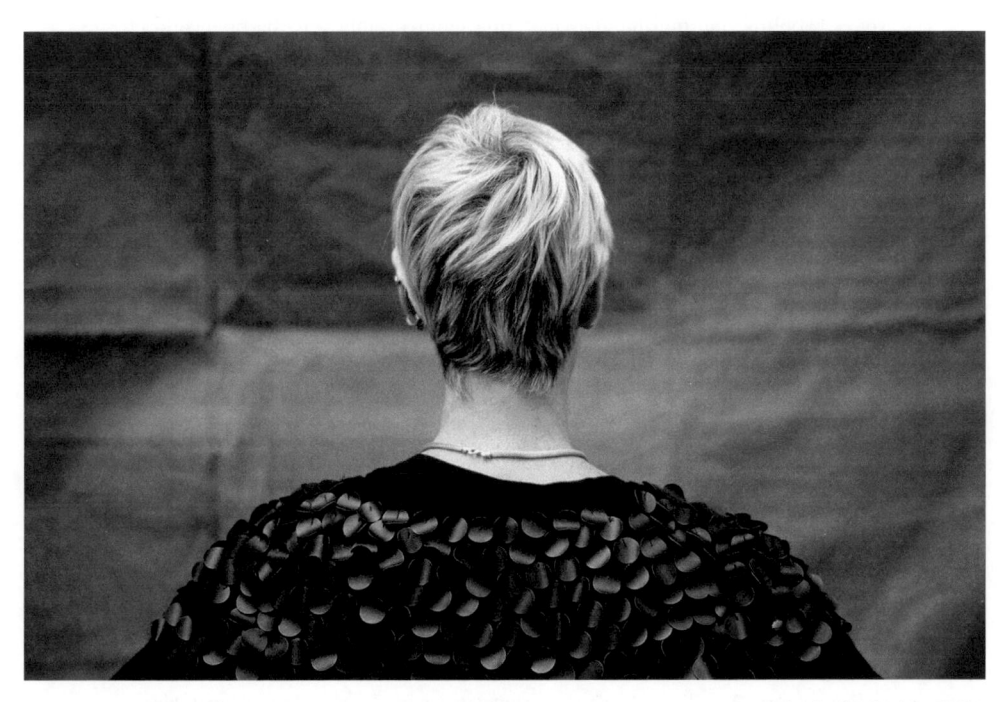

アストリッド・クライン | Astrid Klein

Astrid Klein and Mark Dytham

Like all brilliant ideas, Pecha Kucha is so simple that one wonders why nobody ever thought of it before: give a designer, an artist, or architect an extremely limited period of time to make a presentation, so he or she won't twitter on, ad infinitum, and bore the audience to tears. Pecha Kucha – a Japanese expression referring to voices babbling, murmuring and chattering unintelligibly – is the brainchild of Tokyo-based architects Astrid Klein and Mark Dytham.

At Pecha Kucha Night (PKN), speakers must make do with just 20 images for their entire presentation, and have only 20 seconds to explain each one. Go over the allotted time and the microphone is turned off, the next speaker takes the stage. This works wonderfully because no one wants to experience that sort of abject humiliation. "A laptop these days can save anything. There's no limit anymore to the amount of data, pictures and information you can accumulate," says Dytham, who hails from the UK. "We now stockpile things like hamsters and in the process we've completely forgotten how to edit, how to delete the unnecessary!" So successful have Pecha Kucha Nights become that the online magazine Architecture compared them to Apple products and Moleskine notebooks, items that have generated a similar self-sustaining momentum within the international design world. (Since then, PKN has spread to 210 cities worldwide.)

Twenty is a magic number for Astrid and Mark; exactly 20 years ago the pair relocated to Japan. Moreover, Tokyo reinvents itself every 20 years or so, and fashion trends too are characterized by two-decade cycles. As graduates of London's Royal College of Art, Astrid and Mark were acquainted with Japan only from magazines. To them it seemed like a land of boundless opportunity, but one where showing respect held precedence over elbow room. "When the architect Itsuko Hasegawa was awarded the Japanese Art Academy Grand Prize, all of her famous colleagues rushed to congratulate her," Mark tells. "In England it would be unthinkable for Richard Rogers to praise Norman Foster in a speech - even though both are world-famous architects." Mark and Astrid worked together for architect Toyo Ito for two years. When they eventually struck out on their own, Ito was instrumental in getting them their first architectural commission: a hair salon in the elegant Ginza shopping district.

Roland Hagenberg Before establishing Klein Dytham architecture (KDa) in 1990 you both worked for Toyo Ito. Are there any experiences from those two years that live on in your work today?

Mark Dytham I came from the Richard Rogers / Norman Foster school of thought, where you explore your gut feelings first – even when you don't know all the project details yet. And you take it from there, choose a direction and stick to it. At Toyo Ito's office it was quite common to turn projects upside down half-way through. They often took several turns along the way. The Western approach is to question the concept in a linear way. At Ito's, the constant input from all sides created this huge confusing cloud of thoughts that had to be process, but out of that would evolve a single distilled idea. Neither process is wrong, they are just different. We learned from Ito to keep on exploring, even when topics at hand might not relate directly to the actual project.

Astrid Klein Explore, question and input all into your mind's "data bank", and then, with the deadline-gun to your head, you can retrieve it and it will all fall into place.

MD British education teaches you that design evolves from structure and details. You figure out how the parts work together and this defines the architecture. At Ito's we were concerned about details too, but they were treated as functional parts, not steering elements and certainly not as starting points.

RH There are not many countries today which immediately evoke a brand image when tied to the word "modern architecture." Without the need to explain details, the term "Modern Japanese architecture" immediately conjures up a picture that people understand. Where does that come from?

MD Some of it has to do with this moment in time and the economic conditions, which allow only for certain houses with certain materials to be built, which drive similar construction methods. Look and feel is further defined by regulations.

RH You have these criteria in the US too, but "Modern American architecture" sounds pretty vague.

AK Japanese architecture of the 1960s and '70s is completely different from that of 2010. Trends influenced by different economic periods, clearly, inform architecture. But there is also something ingrained in Japanese culture that preserves its uniqueness – even when modern styles are globally re-mixed and mashed-up all the time. A simple, empty tearoom, for instance, can suddenly be full of surprises and tensions because of one oddly shaped little object placed inside it. Or, think of urushi lacquer bowls – of course, it's just a simple basic geometric bowl and the shape is not particularly noteworthy. But you soon become aware that the lacquer has been applied 30 times. You look closer and you are pulled into an invisible realm.

RH Speaking of invisibility, wasn't that your key concept when working on Tomamu Towers in Hokkaido?

AK Tomamu Towers are two 40 story buildings we have refreshed. We didn't build them. They were constructed during the bubble economy in the late 1980s. Twenty years later they looked dilapidated and the owner decided to put on an external insulation. He asked us for a color scheme and we came up with a camouflage pattern that correlates to the buildings' surrounding landscape. This kind of work will come up more and more in Japan. All the outdated giant buildings from the past cannot simply be torn down. So how do you update them and make them relevant again? This is a big challenge for the future.

RH Do you separate tasks at KDa? Are there female and male areas of responsibility?

MD Astrid takes care of colors; I don't touch them – well, OK… sometimes!

AK Shapes, forms, textures – we certainly approach them with different sensibilities. There is a "female vision," if you want to say so, but as a team we bring it all together and take more risks too because someone will always say "hang on a minute!" if ideas get out of hand. Ideas bounce between us constantly and the truth is exposed without exposing too much of ourselves in an unpleasant way. That's how it works.

RH Why do Japanese clients want to hire foreign architects who live in Japan?

AK With KDa they get a more encompassed view of things, a European background mixed with Japanese understanding. We see the "Japanese-ness" from a different angle and emphasize it in peculiar ways. It works the other way around too, when we go back to Europe. We have been in Japan over twenty years and when we re-experience London now, we do so with a wider perspective and from a remote point of view. Certain clients also appreciate that we are a woman/man team, like this cosmetic company which has recently started targeting male customers. I think our chemistry comes with a twist, and that's appealing for many people.

RH You are the inventors of "PechaKucha", a design event now presented regularly all over the world. Did this idea grow out of your profession?

MD I would say that we got tired of listening to presentations that dragged on and didn't get to the point.

AK PechaKucha is about communicating excitement and passion – and passionate people attract other passionate people. Out of that, collaborations and new ideas are born. PechaKucha is a fantastic treasure trove of inspiration for any architect.

MD And it is entertaining too. Just recently, we thought there was no way to come up with another funny toilet installation, when someone suggested projecting a clock on the door to show how long you've spent in the toilet. That way if there's a line, you can see immediately which toilet is most likely to be available first. PechaKucha night take place at Super Deluxe, an event space and creative kitchen, that we have established for musicians, artists and designers. It has turned out to be a great networking place. And it saves us travel time, because all these interesting people come to see us – at our place.

AK Still, no matter how big your network is, at the end of the day it all comes down to one-on-one relationships. In these, you can grasp the truth and feel that you can make a difference – and not with some hyped-up concept that will be gone tomorrow.

アストリッド・クラインとマーク・ダイサム 建設現場にて |
Astrid Klein and Mark Dytham at a construction site in Shinjuku, Tokyo (2010)

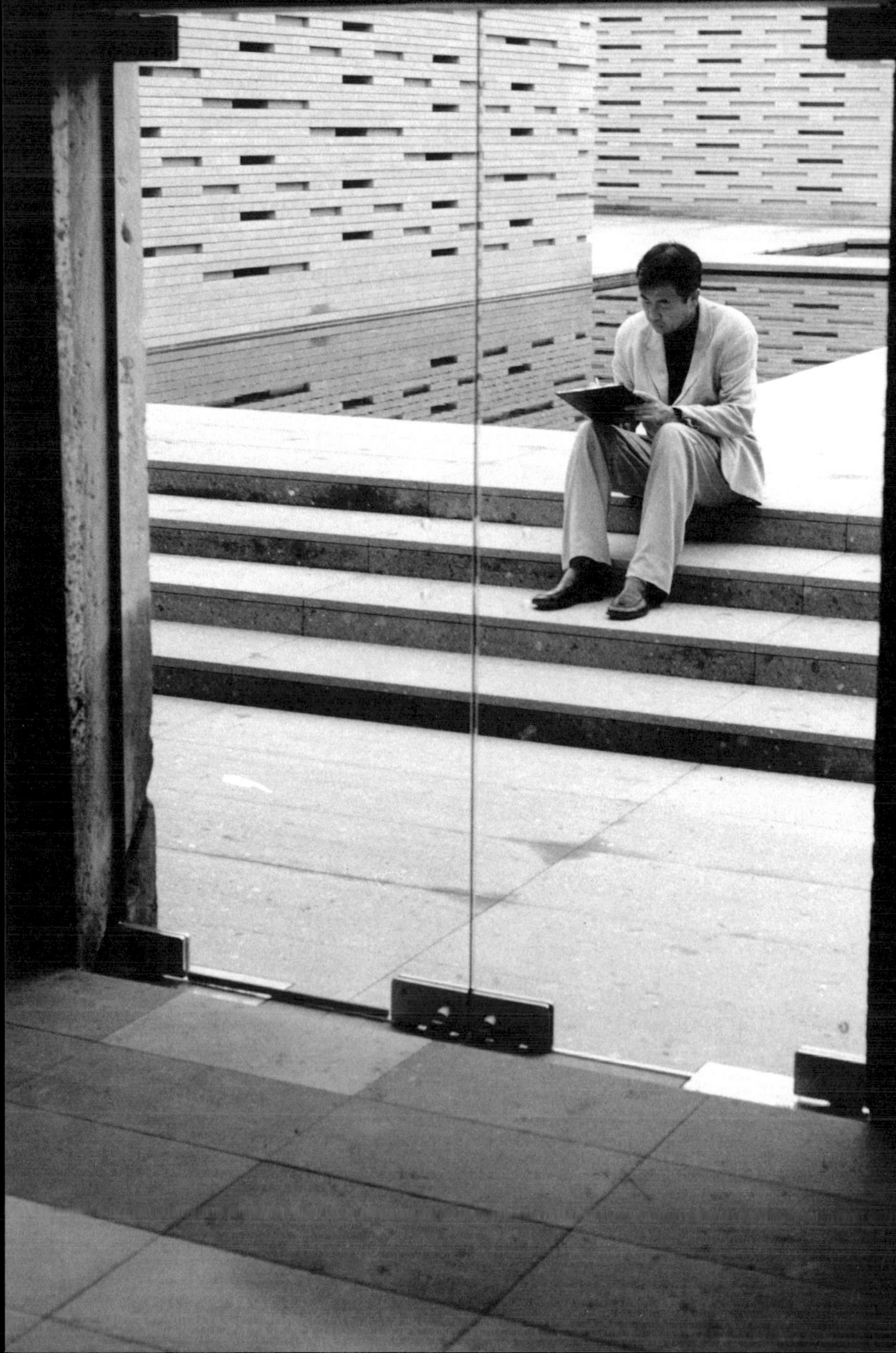

隈 研吾 | Kengo Kuma

私にとって、建築に関する最初のミーティングは、子供の頃の父との話し合いでした。
"My first architectural meetings were as a boy with my father."

1954年神奈川県生まれ。1979年東京大学大学院修了。1985年からのコロンビア大学客員研究員を経て、1990年隈研吾建築都市設計事務所設立。2009年から東京大学教授。日本建築学会作品賞、アメリカ建築家協会（AIA）デュポン・ベネディクタス賞、芸術選奨文部科学大臣賞など数々の賞を受賞。主な作品に、水／ガラス（静岡）、亀老山展望台（愛媛）、那須芦野・石の美術館（栃木）、馬頭広重美術館（栃木）、ロータス・ハウス（神奈川・鎌倉）、Great (Bamboo) Wall（中国・北京）、サントリー美術館（東京）などがある。

Born 1954 in Kanagawa Prefecure, Received Master Degree from University of Tokyo (1979). Visiting scholar at Columbia University from 1985. Established Kengo Kuma & Associates in 1990. Professor at University of Tokyo since 2009. Numerous awards such as Architectural Institute of Japan Award(AIJ), American Institute of Architects(AIA): DuPont Benedictus Award and Minister of Education's Art Encouragement Prize. Main works include Water/Glass in Shizuoka, Kirosan Observatory in Ehime, Stone Plaza(Nasu Ashino Stone Museum) and Bato Hiroshige Museum of Art in Tochigi, Lotus House in Kamakura, Great (Bamboo) Wall in Beijing and Suntory Museum of Art in Tokyo.

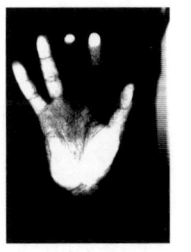

隈研吾 石の美術館にて | Kengo Kuma at Stone Plaza in Tochigi, Japan (2000)

隈 研吾

1980年代のことだ。金がありあまるほどあり、何を建ててもかまわないという時代が日本にもあった。計画それ自体がセンセーショナルになると確約できれば、許可がおりた。スタイルに関しては、あらゆることが可能だった。これが新しい世代に必要な資金やプロジェクト、そして建築家をしばらない（時には誤った方向へ導いたが）励ましを与えることになったのは確かだ。たとえば、妹島和世は、パチンコ業界から彼女に仕事の依頼があったことをいまだに感謝している。雑誌はこぞって表紙や特集で、若い建築家たちの作品を「ポストモダニズム」などともてはやした。それは、形だけが過剰に取り上げられて、その建築が何を意味するのかというところにまではいっていなかったが。しかし、すでに破壊されている日本の都市景観が、ずっと苦しんできたというわけでもない。もしアイデアが多く出過ぎているならば、それは切り捨てられるだけだ。引き裂かれた缶のような外観をした、鈴木エドワードのデザインの、麻布「ジュールA」。その中に植えられた木のように、経営者は文字通り掃除がしやすいという理由だけで木を切るのだ。

しかし、1990年代中頃になって日本の景気が行きづまると、建築家ももう一度考え直し、再評価をしなければならなくなった。隈研吾のように、その過程で本当の自己を見つけていった建築家も多い。1995年の「水／ガラス」は、彼自身の節目にもなった。太平洋に面した熱海の坂の途中に建てられた「水／ガラス」は、隈の現代建築の特徴となるすべての要素を持っていた。自然への開放性、ユニークな素材、建物の内部の心地よい雰囲気（風呂にたとえれば、熱すぎず、冷た過ぎず）。彼の建築の内部は、自然と人工の光が空間を満たしていて、それが癒しを与えるのだ（ファッションの大企業LVMHは、特にそれを気に入り、日本の本社を隈にまかせた）。

それに続くプロジェクトも、クライアントの要求にぴったりだった。北京近郊の「竹の家」、鎌倉の「Lotus House」、2007年に東京ミッドタウンにできたサントリー美術館……。家のことになると、日本はOECD各国の中で最低ランクだが、もし隈がすべての都市の責任者になれば、それはきっと向上するだろう。

現在東京で建設が進んでいる、浅草文化観光センターがいい例だ。「私たちはどうやったら、あの箱のような高層ビルという考えをから脱却することができるのか？」を自身に問いかけ、日本の伝統的な屋根を冗談半分に積み重ねてみたのだ。

個人の家である「Lotus House」を訪ねた。そこでは、浸透作用——生物学的なプロセスで、水が細胞膜にしみこむこと——について考えた。隈の建築でいえば自然は水であり、彼の建築にあるガラス窓と、複雑で様々な形をした穴がある壁が細胞膜だ。

[**パート1**]——2000-2007

ローランド・ハーゲンバーグ[以下RH]　建築家になろうと思ったのはいつですか？

隈 研吾[以下隈]　まだ子供の頃、1964年の東京オリンピックの時です。丹下健三設計の代々木の国立屋内総合競技場に行き、その形や新空間に感動しました。丹下さんが、設計コンセプトを説明するのをテレビで観て、自分も建築家になりたいと思ったのです。1970年の大阪万博の時もターニングポイントでした。黒川紀章さんがテレビでメタボリズムについて語り、建築は自然と共生しなくてはならないと説いていました。

RH　60年以上前、自然の精神と奇跡を表現できるのは曲線であると書いたドイツ人建築家、ブルーノ・タウトへの関心は深いと思いますが、熱海に設計したゲストハ

隈研吾 妹と ｜ Kengo Kuma and sister (ca. 1961)

ウス水/ガラスには曲線をあまり使用していませんね?

隈 ブルーノ・タウトの仕事は尊敬していますが、関心が深いのは、単なる偶然とは思えないぐらい接点が多いためでもあります。タウトは1933年から1936年まで日本に住んでいましたが、当時建設会社を経営する井上社長に支援されていました。後に、井上さんからホテルの設計を依頼されました。私はタウトを支援した社長の孫と親しくなったのです。
それから、私の父がタウトの作品を収集していた事実にも気づきました。
さらに、熱海では、タウトが設計した住宅があるとは知っていましたが、それがどこかはわからぬまま水/ガラスを建設していると、隣の建物から女性が出てきて、うちは有名な建築家が設計した、と何気なく話すのです。その建築家が、なんとブルーノ・タウトだったのです。

RH ユングなら「シンクロニシティ」と呼ぶでしょうね。よく、自然と調和する建築の重要性を語っていますが……。

隈 私にとって理想の建築とは、建物に気を取られず、まるで自然の中にいるような感じになるものです。
日本には建築家という存在はおらず、ランドスケープ・デザイナーという存在もいなかったわけです。同じひとりの人間が建物と庭を考え、両方を一体のものとして考えてきたのです。例えば、茶室を設計する場合、建物だけでなく、内装や茶器なども、同じ人がデザインしたのです。そういう発想で設計をして初めて、自然と人工物とがひとつの調和したものになるのだと思います。

RH 建築家の仕事は大変でしょうが、どのような苦労がありますか?

隈 個人の住宅の設計で、クライアントが神経質だと大変ですね。
日本では概して、夫より、妻の方が家の設計に影響力があるので、よく奥様と打ち合わせをしますが、理想のデザインと現実的な予算が噛み合わないことがほとんどです。
設計の際には、建物を使う人の身になって考え、そこでのストーリーも創ろうと考えています。素材は重要で、触れた時の感触や、そこから受ける印象を想像してみます。いわば、冬には何を着て、夏には何を着るかを考えるようなもので、木綿なのか、麻なのか、ウールなのかを選ぶような感じです。

RH　東京を見て、現在の都市開発をどう思いますか？

隈　日本の都市景観を変えるのは非常に難しいと思います。というのは、多くの建物は、建設会社の社内スタッフが設計しているためです。実は、それを禁止している国も多いのですが……。

加えて、日本では、いわゆる住宅メーカーが個人住宅を建てることが多いのですが、それがプレハブ式なので選択肢が少ないのです。とにかく短時間で安く造ろうと、外観の配慮より、工法に合う素材が優先されてしまいます。

戦後、西洋建築に刺激を受けた日本人は、伝統を忘れ去り、洗練された技術や素材をも失ってきました。最近になって、ようやく日本の良き感性が取り戻されつつあるのを感じています。

RH　東京の好きな場所と嫌いな場所を教えてください。

隈　川の上に架かる高速道路は嫌いです。オリンピックの前に、時間がなかったため、川を覆う決断を政治家が下したのですが、おかげで景観が完璧に損なわれてしまいました。高速道路は川の下につくるべきです。そうすれば東京の顔はガラッと変わりますよ。

RH　何か、好みの素材はありますか？　そもそも、素材というのは設計に影響するものですか？

隈　周りの環境だけでなく、素材によってイマジネーションが膨らむことはあります。例えば、熱海の水/ガラスは近くの海からインスピレーションを得ましたが、栃木の石の美術館では石や紙という素材からアイデアが膨らみました。

素材を選ぶ時に大切なのは、経験のある専門家に話を聞くことだと思います。石の美術館では、素材を知り尽くした専門家から、石を焼くと色が変わると聞いたので、その特性を内装に役立てました。低温で焼くと黄色がかり、高温では赤味がかるのです。

RH　熱海の水/ガラスはもちろん、一部が地下にもぐっている愛媛県今治市の亀老山展望台に見られるように、環境に溶け込む建築が多い中、石の美術館は異色ではないでしょうか？

隈　そんなことはありませんよ。石の美術館も、「反オブジェクト」を創るという私の信念に基づいています。水/ガラスも亀老山展望台も、環境そのもの、つまり庭をデザインするのが狙いでした。石の美術館も同じですが、もともと石蔵があったの

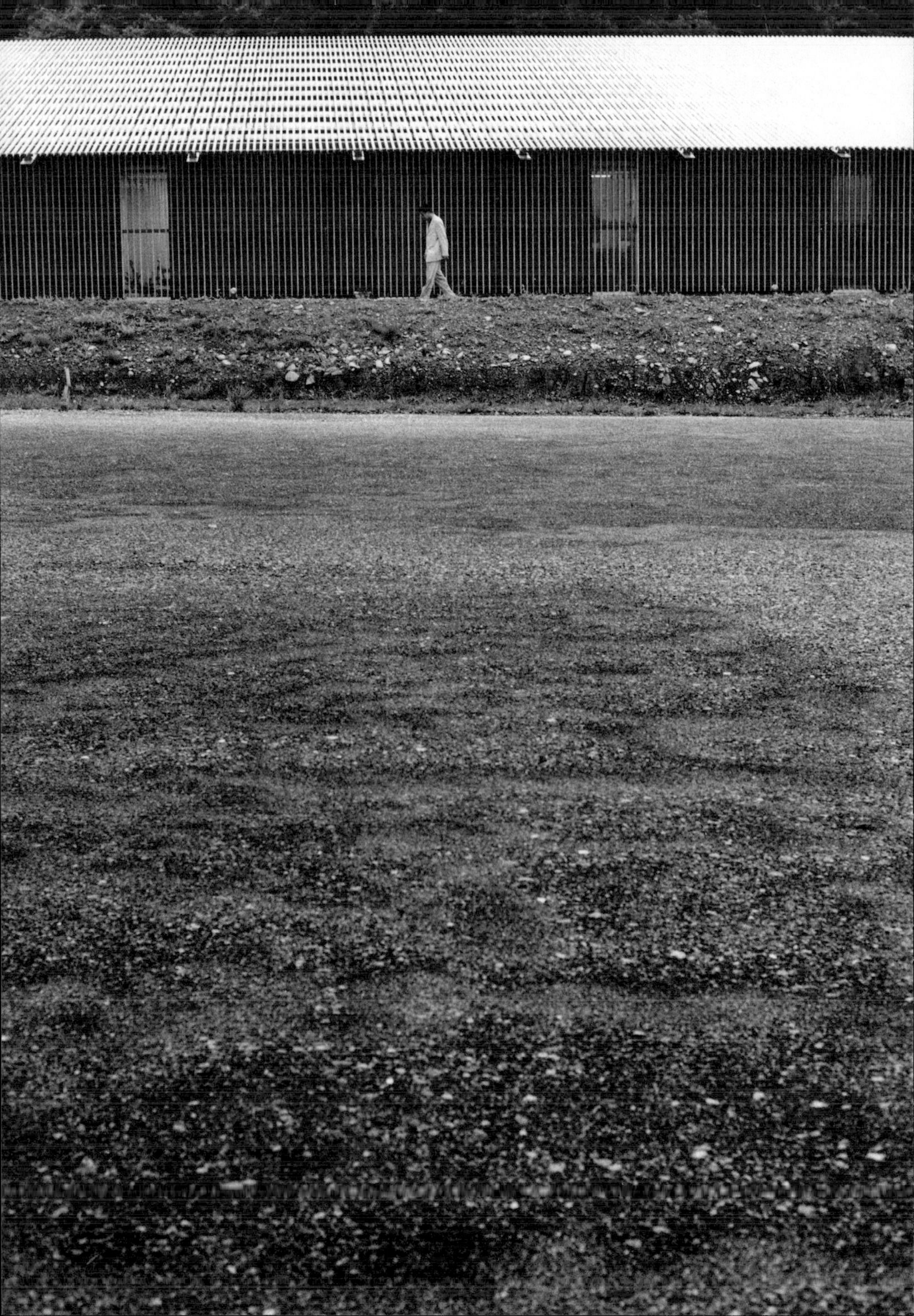

で、それを残して、周りに新しい環境を継ぎ足したのです。

RH　建築における安全性とは、どのようなものだと思いますか？

隈　私が考える安全な空間とは、竪穴式住居のようなものです。半分が地面に埋まっていて、土に触れることができ、その上には丸太がかかっていて、丸太に触れることもでき、全体が、土と丸太、そして周りの森に守られているという、安心感を与えるものです。

安全性とは安心感だと思います。したがって、心の平穏を保つ自然な素材を使うことは、安全性と深く関わっています。

縄文時代に建てられた日本古来の竪穴式住居には、大地に埋まっているという安心感がありました。また、紀元前250年頃の弥生時代に建てられた弥生式住居には、地上に浮いて、地上の動物たちから守られているという安心感がありました。コルビュジエに代表される、20世紀のモダニズム建築は、弥生式住居のように、地上に浮いた安全性を目指したのですが、私は縄文時代の住居のように、大地に抱かれ、周囲の森に守られる安心感を安全性と考えたいのです。

RH　これは、子供の頃好きだった横浜の公園を思わせるものですね。森に囲まれた公園だったと、以前、話していましたよね？

隈　長野宇平治が作った記念館の建物からそう遠くないところに実家がありました。彼は、建築史上の黄金期は、ヘレニズム期にあると考え、彼の作る建築はヘレニズム様式でした。子供の頃、記念館は、まだ戦争で廃墟となったままで——まあそれだから遊び場になったのですが——そこへたどりつくまでには、深い竹やぶを抜けていかなければなりませんでした。それがこの建物の視覚効果を高めていたのだと、森を出てから気づきました。この、実家近くの竹やぶが無意識のうちに記憶に残っていたのかどうかわかりませんが、2002年には、北京郊外に「Great (Bamboo) Wall」というヴィラを作りました。

RH　建築家としてのルーツは、子供の頃にあるんですか？

隈　父は三菱金属に勤めていました。デザインにとても興味があって、鉱山の現場にいるときは自分で照明器具まで作ってしまったようです。大倉山の私たちの家を少し広げることになったとき、私たちは皆で話し合って、どんな材料を使ったらいいか、どの作業を分担したらいいか決めました。いつも決めるのに時間が

かかったのは、どういう材料を使うか、ということでした。振り返ってみると、それが私にとって建築に関する最初のミーティングですね。まだ10歳そこそこの年でしたが。

RH そのときの材料というのは、種類の違う木材ですか？

隈 そうですね。木でした。最近になってようやくそのよさがわかってきた木材です。質素な私たちの家を拡張したり、再設計することによって、空間理解の生の感覚というものを身につけることができたと思います。こういう感覚は、直観的なもので、分析してわかるものではありません。建築を勉強し始めたときも、感情を呼び起こし、空間をある方法で感じさせる、その感覚をどういうものであるか、具体的に説明できませんでした。ターニングポイントとなったのは、1994年に、高知の梼原町地域交流施設をつくったときです。そこでは山の奥まで連れていかれて、町の人たちに、ここの木材をぜひ使ってほしいと言われました。私は、人間の暮らしを何千年にもわたって形作ってきた木材という素材をほとんど使った経験がなかったので、心配したんです。それまで木材を使った経験と言えば、子供の頃大倉山の実家を広げるときに使った木だけでしたから。私は、木材など使わない、モダンで現代的な建築家になりたいと思っていたんです。おそらく、無意識のうちに、自分が育った木の家というものの価値をゆっくり考えたこともありませんでした。でも、山奥にいてそういう状況になった時に、私は木という素材にもう一度向き合わざるを得なくなったのです。山をきっかけにして、私の建築に対する考え方は変わりました。木のおかげで、素材の力を再発見することができたのです。

RH スケールの大きさはとても魅力的ですが、同時に間違った方向へいくこともあります。とても大きな空間や、プロジェクトに携わってから、建築への姿勢は変わりましたか？

隈 個人的なレベルでいうと、私は規模が小さければ小さいほど、楽しみです。たとえば茶室のような。なぜかというと、それに関わる人とのやりとりが、より白熱し、真剣になるからです。彼らの思いや感性は、伝染していくんです。その雰囲気は電流が流れたように、もっとプライベートなものになるんです。

RH ある意味で、車は小さな建築ですよね。建築家として、車をどう関連付けていけばいいと思いますか？

隈 最近発見したことなんです。車のデザインはとても面白い。なぜなら、それが

外見の静的な形と、走っている時の動的な形のあやういバランスの上に成り立っているからです。これは常にこの2つの間を行ったり来たりする両極端なデザインですよね。でも、建物を建てる建築にそういうことは、あまりよくないですよね。外面をよくするのなら、内装もよくしなければならないから。1928年に建てられた、パリ郊外にあるル・コルビュジエの、サヴォア邸なんかは、本当にシンプルで、外側からは白い幾何学的な箱に見えます。でも、中に入り、階段を降りてガレージからエントランスホールを見ると、静かで、屋上庭園までのぼっていく構造が見えます。これは圧倒される眺めです。建築の中で動きを感じさせる体験で、まさに、とてもいい車に乗っているかのような感覚ですね。

[**パート2**]——2010

RH オーストリア・ライディングの村に、半透明のコンクリートでできた立方体のオブジェを作りあげましたよね。彫り出し、完成するまでに3ヶ月かかったと聞いています。これは、郊外の広大さに対して、コンパクトな都市部のメタファーですか？

隈 私が建築を始めたばかりのときに考えていたのが、壁が建築の背後にある力

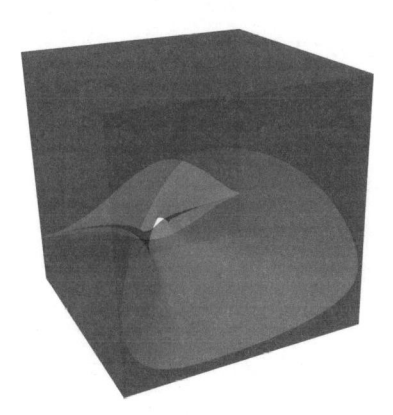

ライディングプロジェクトのための習作｜
Kengo Kuma study for Raiding Project (2010)

をコントロールしているということです。しかし今は、力を支配するのは壁ではなく、何もない場所の集合だと考えています。「Cube #6」で、私は空間の力を3次元のモデルで可視化しようとしました。これは、私の日本社会の理解ともかかわっています。一見すると平面のようなものも、内側はとても複雑で、でこぼこした穴があき、切れ込んだくぼみがたくさんあります。内側に隠れた複雑さが、人口が密集した社会をコントロールしているのです。外側からは、ヒエラルキーは見えません。立方体の表面の平らな部分は、そのことを表わしています。私にとって「Cube #6」は、世界中のどこにでもある隠れた力を表わすメタファーになりました。都市計画では、もっぱら「ゾーン(区域)」に関心を寄せますが、私は、町を穴の集合だと考えます。穴は、人々をどこか別の場所へ連れていってくれます。一本の道もまた穴なのです。都市計画も含めて、私が建築をデザインするとき、私はこの穴を可視化するのです。

RH このやり方は、ライディングのような村では変化しますか？

隈 都会であれ郊外であれ、基本的に、私は自分のアプローチを変えることはありません。人がたくさんいる街でも、風があります。光や木もあります。ポイントは、自然からある一部分を取り出し、それを私たちが生活している環境に組み込むということ。だから、ライディングの田舎での仕事は、私のこれまでの仕事と何の違いもありません。私はいつも、ひとつのプロジェクトを、その地域と私の間の信頼関係に根ざした共働の努力だと考えています。

RH グローバリゼーションによって、これからますます地域の文化的な個性というものがなくなっていくのでしょうか？ それとも、何かターニングポイントになるようなことが起こるのでしょうか？ 例えば、日本の畳の部屋はどうなるでしょうか？ 完全になくなってしまうのでしょうか？

隈 私は将来、畳の部屋や障子、縁側がもっと増えると思います。その理由は単純で、それが気持ちいいからです。障子はとてもいい陰影を作りますし、縁側は、家の外と中をうまくつないでいます。これは硬い壁には決してできないことです。だから私は、こういう日本の伝統的なものは、決してなくならず、むしろ増えると信じています。加えて、日本人は今よりもっと広い場所に住みたいとは思わないのではないかと感じます。ここで前提になっている感情は、狭いスペースを自分の好みのとおりにデザインするということこそが贅沢だと思われている、ということです。だから、日本

隈研吾 サントリーミュージアムにて | Kengo Kuma at Suntory Museum, Tokyo (2007)

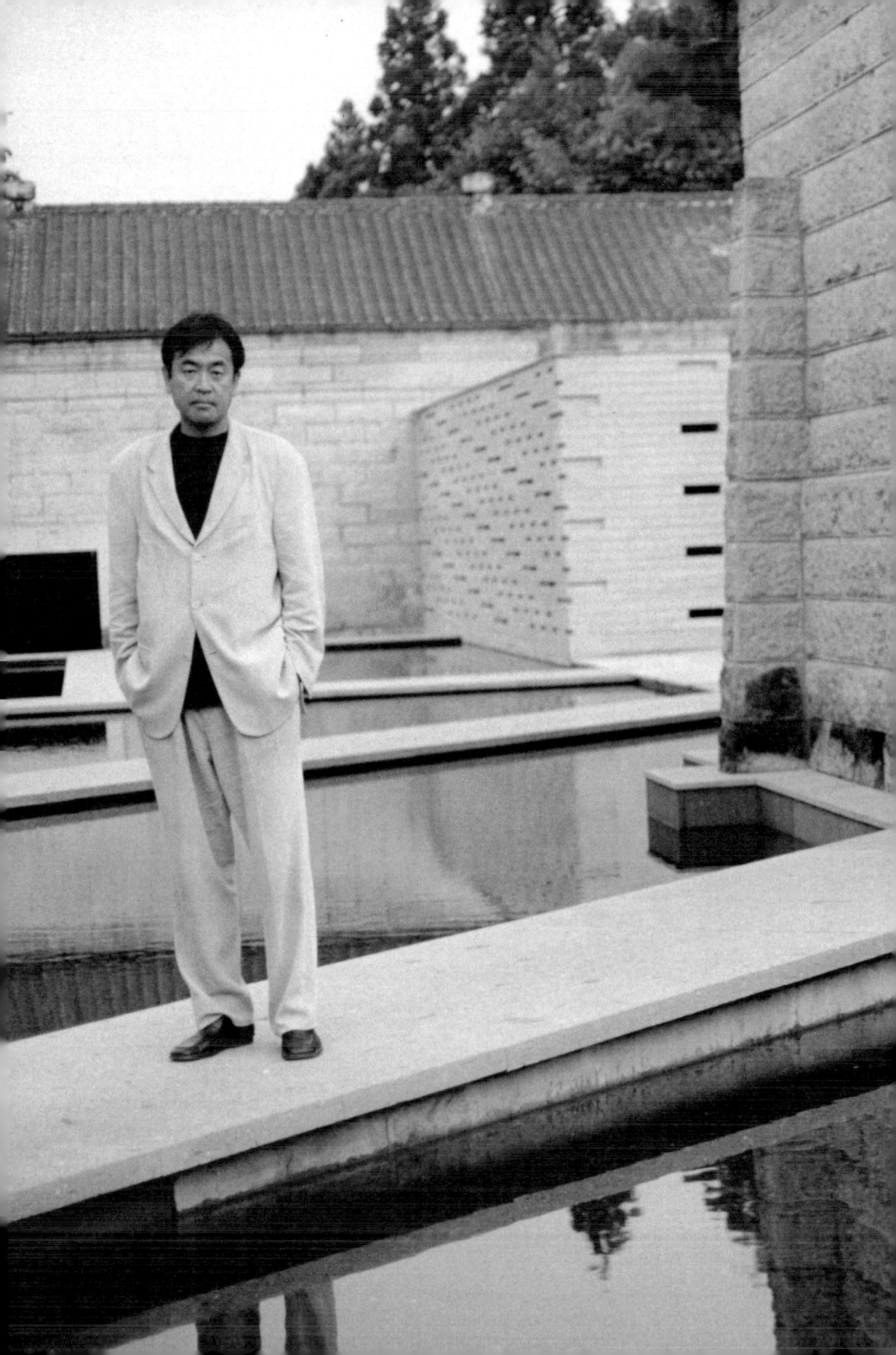

隈研吾 石の美術館にて | Kengo Kuma at Stone Plaza in Tochigi, Japan (2000)

の人口が減っても、それがそのまま、日本人がもっと広いスペースに住みたいと思うようになる、ということにはつながらないと思います。たとえ、広いスペースが手に入るようになったとしても。他の国や文化で、住む場所を小さくせざるを得ない人たちがいた場合、私たち日本人はそこへ行って、私たちの解決方法やノウハウを教えることができます。

RH　教えるということは、いつも建築と密接な関係にありますよね。今、学生たちと会って、一番関心があることは何ですか？

隈　この50年間、日本の建築教育というのは、コンクリートでできたビルを建てることばかり教えてきました。学生たちはこの枠組みからはみ出さないようにと言われ、教授たちも自分の手で建ててみるということの意味を教えようとはしなかった。それが最も大きな間違いだったと思います。私が一番伝えたいのは、自分の手で、自分自身で、家を建てることが可能なのだということ。例をあげるならば、ある学生たちはポリタンクを積み上げていって小さな小屋を作った。彼らにとっては、それが驚くべき体験だったんです。私にとっては、日本の建築教育の環境を変える、その第一歩といったところでしょうか。

RH　プロジェクトの中で、将来建築が発展していくいい例になるだろうと思うものは何ですか？

隈　最近、浅草文化観光センターのデザインをしたのですが、これまでの箱の形をして屋根が平らの高層ビルとは違うものを作りたかったんです。私はいつも思っているんですが、平屋で勾配のついた屋根がある家の方が、多層階で、天井がまっすぐな建物よりも心地よい。私は新しい方法で各フロアを作ることができるか試してみたいと思っています。新しい方法というのは、伝統的な、勾配のついた屋根を積み重ねていくという考えです。そうすれば、高層ビルより快適に生活することができるはずです。

RH　これもまた、将来、畳の部屋と障子が増えるのではないかということと同じく、未来へ一歩踏み出すのと同時に、過去も振り返る、ゆるやかな反改革運動のようなものですね。

隈　改革はいつも、中心人物が気づいているといないにかかわらず、歴史的な事実が基礎になっています。「太陽の下、新しいことは何ひとつない」。改革でさえも、

歴史的に何度も繰り返されているのです。私たちはいつも歴史を繰り返しているのだから、建築家もそのことを思い起こすべきです。

隈研吾と著者 隈の事務所にて | Kengo Kuma and Roland Hargenberg at Kuma studio, Gaienmae, Tokyo (2010)

Kengo Kuma

There was a time in the late 1980s when money was plentiful and questions were scarce in Japan's world of architecture; approvals were granted as long as proposals promised the sensational. Anything was possible in terms of style and this provided a new generation of talent with the necessary funds and projects, and with (sometimes misguided) encouragement. Kazuyo Sejima, for example, is still thankful today for the series of unglamorous pachinko parlors that allowed her to stay afloat. Magazines assigned the young architects' creations the convenient label of "postmodernism" and were often more concerned with style-hype than with the buildings' architectural implications. Not that the already damaged Japanese urban landscape would have suffered. If ideas stood out too much they were cut down, literally, like the trees planted inside the ripped tin-can façade of Edward Suzuki's Joule-A building in Azabu – the management sawed off the plants to make cleaning easier.

But in the mid-1990s, Japan's economy came to a standstill and its architects had to rethink and reevaluate. Some – like Kengo Kuma – found their true selves in the process. His 1995 Water/Glass house was a career milestone. Built on a slope on the Pacific seaside in Atami, Water/Glass features all the trademark characteristics of a contemporary Kuma design: openness to nature, unique materials, and a feel-good atmosphere comparable to taking a relaxing bath at the perfect temperature. In his environments, natural and artificial light flirts with space on a frequency that soothes the mind. (Fashion empires find this particularly appealing – LVHM hired Kuma to design its Japanese headquarters.) Other projects followed suit: the Great (Bamboo) Wall house near Beijing, Lotus House in Kamakura, and the Suntory Museum, which opened in 2007 in Tokyo's Midtown district.

When it comes to housing, Japan ranks on the bottom of the 30-member list of OECD countries. But if Kuma were in charge of entire cities today, the quality of living in Japan would certainly increase. The Asakusa Tourist Center – currently under construction in Tokyo – is a point in case. "How can I reinvent our boxy high-rise buildings?" asked Kuma, before deciding to stack angled roof-tops of traditional Japanese houses playfully over each other. A visit to Lotus House, a private residence, made me think of osmosis – the biological process whereby water permeates cell membranes. Kuma's water is nature. The cell membranes are the walls of his buildings, with glass windows and various intricate openings.

[**Conversation part one**]——2000-2007

Roland Hagenberg When did you decide to become an architect?

Kengo Kuma At an early age, at the Tokyo Olympics in 1964. Mr. Kenzo Tange designed the gymnasium, which I visited in Yoyogi. I was impressed by the shape and the new space. He explained his concept on TV. From then on I decided to become an architect. The 1970 Expo in Osaka was a turning point too, where Mr. Kisho Kurokawa talked about Metabolism on TV. He insisted that architecture should correlate to nature.

RH Sixty years ago German architect Bruno Taut wrote that "only round shapes are capable of expressing the spirit and miracle of nature". Your glass-house in Atami for instance ignores round shapes for the most part, Bruno Taut has been haunting you nevertheless. How come?

KK I have always admired Taut and I think, the way he entered my life is more than a coincidence. Taut lived in Japan from 1933-36. His sponsor at that time was Mr. Inoue, the chairman of a construction company, who once asked me to design a hotel in Thailand. His grandson then became a good friend of mine. After that I found out that my father had collected original Taut designs. I knew, that Taut had built a house in Atami, but I had no idea where. One day in the middle of constructing the Water/Glass House a woman came by who introduced herself as a neighbor. When she was about to leave she mentioned casually that a famous architect built her house and that architect turned out to be Bruno Taut.

RH Jung would call that "synchronicity". You always refer to the importance of establishing a link between nature and architecture.

KK The ideal building for me is where people are not aware of it, but only of nature. My dream actually is to create a new field of design. Architecture and landscape are different fields but I want to combine them. Traditionally the Japanese architect and landscape artist have been one and the same person anyway. When they designed a teahouse, they not only produced the hardware but also the software, the interior, the cups, the plates etc. I'd like to be that kind of designer and combine everything.

RH Architects often face tough times. Can you give some examples from your life?

KK In case of a private house, if the owner is too nervous, I have a tough time. Usually the Japanese wife has much more influence on the house design than the husband, so mostly I have meetings with the wives. I know the budget - and I know the dreams, which often never fit the budget.

When I draw up an architectural plan I create a story about the person who will live there. I think about his or her state of mind within this architectural environment. I also think of the materials, how they feel when they are touched, how they affect our moods and thoughts. It's like when people decide, what to wear in winter or summer. Should it be cotton or linen or wool? It works the same way in architecture.

RH Looking at a city like Tokyo, what does it say about today's urban planning?

KK It is very difficult to change the urban landscape in Japan – many buildings are designed by developers and construction companies, which have their own design teams.

That system is actually prohibited in many countries. On top of that, Japanese private homes and houses are built by so-called house-makers. It's a prefabrication system, - where you don't have many choices. The material is decided by the logic of fabrication and not by aesthetic considerations: "build it quickly and cheaply" is the main objective. After the war, people were shocked when confronted with the Western style of building. But then they gradually gave up their traditional ways and lost sophisticated techniques and materials. I feel, people's sensibility is changing now for the better again.

RH What sights do you love and hate in Tokyo?

KK I don't like the freeways over the rivers. Before the Tokyo Olympics, time was limited, so politicians opted to cover the rivers. That destroyed the old landscape completely. We should have built all the highways under the rivers. That would have changed the face of Tokyo drastically.

RH Over the years, have you discovered a material that became your favorite? Do materials influence shape?

KK In the past my imagination was triggered by materials and not by a particular environment alone. The ocean nearby inspired the Water/Glass House in Atami but the inspiration for the Stone Museum in Tochigi came from stone and paper. When you choose materials you should also talk to the craftsmen who have worked with them for a long time. I spoke with experts, who knew the characteristics of paper and stone. I found out that when stone is burned, it changes color. So I used this technique for the interior of the Stone Museum. Low temperatures trigger shades of yellow, high temperatures on the other hand can turn stones red.

RH You always try to make your buildings disappear in their own environment, the Water/Glass House for instance or the observatory in Kirosan, which is partly underground. In that respect your Stone Museum sticks out.

KK Not really. It too belongs to my philosophy of creating anti-objects. With the Water/Glass House in Atami and the Kirosan Observatory my intention was to design first of all an environment, a garden. The same goes for the Stone Museum, but there were already three old stone warehouses. So I just kept them and created a new environment around them.

RH What symbolizes for you security in architecture?

KK My ideal safe and secure house is like a pit dwelling, half buried in the ground. I can touch the soil and the wood logs and everything is protected by the surrounding forest. It's a secure space, because it provides peace of mind. Security can be achieved by means of natural materials. They help create this mind-set of peacefulness. Using

隈研吾 事務所にて | Kengo Kuma on the roof of his studio in Tokyo (2010)

natural materials that maintain peace-of-mind is intertwined with the safety of the building.

During the Jomon period (Japanese Stone Age) housing consisted of pit dwellings. It provided a feeling of safety and therefore peace of mind. It changed afterwards during the Yayoi period (around 250 BC), where buildings stood above ground and where the feeling of security started to "float". In the Yayoi-period houses you were above ground and you felt safe, because you were protected from any attacking animals on prowling below. With Le Corbusier the 20th Century architecture returned to this "floating" Yayoi-period-style security. At the moment I think, this sense of safety and peace of mind would be best provided by a Jomon pit dwelling, surrounded by earth and guarded by the forest.

RH This reminds me of your favorite childhood playground near Yokohama. You once mentioned it was guarded by a forest.

KK Not far from our family house was the Kinenkan Memorial Building, by architect Uheiji Nagano. He thought that the golden age of architectural history was Hellenism and so designed his buildings accordingly. In my childhood, the Kinenkan was still a war ruin and therefore a great playground, but to get there we had to fight our way through thick bamboo, which heightened the visual effects of the Greek ruins once we stepped out of the forest. I don't know if, subconsciously, the bamboo forest near my parents' house had been on my mind when I built a villa on the outskirts of Beijing in 2002 and called it 'Great (Bamboo) Wall'.

RH Looking back, can you see the roots of your architectural career forming in your childhood?

KK My father worked for Mitsubishi Metal as a salary man. He had great interest in design. He made his own set of lights when he worked in the mine and whenever he visited company sites he made drawings. When the time came to expand our house in Okurayama a little more we all sat down and talked over how we would do it, what materials we should use and who would take on what tasks. The longest discussions were always about materials. Looking back, I must say, those were my first architectural meetings, and I was not even a teenager.

RH At that time the materials were different kinds of wood?

KK Yes, wood, which I learned to appreciate only later in life. Expanding and redesigning our modest house equipped me with a raw sense of understanding space.

This sense was intuitive and not analytical. Even when I started to study architecture, I had difficulties pinpointing what it exactly was that could evoke emotions or make you experience space in certain ways. A turning point came when I built the Yusuhara Visitor Center in Kochi, in 1994. There I was in the deepest countryside, where all the town leaders wanted me to use wood and nothing but wood. I was afraid – I had no practical experience with a material that has defined the living conditions of humankind for thousands of years. My only close experience with wood was when we expanded our Okurayama home. I have never given deep thought to the values of the wooden house I grew up in. But, living in the mountains, I had no choice but to confront and reconsider wood and change my attitude towards architecture. As soon as I entered this new world with all its possibilities, my outlook on architecture changed. With the help of wood I rediscovered the power of materials.

RH Grandeur can be tempting, but also misleading. Does your attitude change when you deal with extremely large spaces and projects?

KK On a personal level, I have more fun with small projects – let's say a teahouse – because the interaction with all the people involved is much more intense. Their feelings and sensitivities are contagious; the atmosphere becomes electrified and very private.

RH In a way, cars are small architecture. How do you relate to them as an architect?

KK It's a recent discovery for me. Car design is exiting, because it thrives for a balance between the static shape of the outside and the moving dynamics that you experience inside when driving. It's a bipolar design, constantly shifting back and forth. But the same goes for the architecture of buildings. From the outside, Le Corbusier's Villa Savoye in the suburbs of Paris (built in 1928) is only a simple, white geometric box. But then you enter downstairs and from the garage, through the entrance hall, a quiet, ascending structure carries you through the building up to the roof garden – an overwhelming experience of movement within architecture, just like in a great car.

[Conversation part two]——2010

RH   For the village of Raiding in Austria you created a sculptural cube made of translucent concrete, which took three months to carve. Was it intended as a metaphor for metropolitan compactness confronting the spacious countryside?

KK   When I first started out I thought that walls were the controlling force behind architecture, but now I know it's actually a collection of empty spaces. With Cube #6 I tried to visualize the force of space in a three-dimensional model. It relates to my understanding of Japanese society, which looks flat from the outside but is very complicated inside – filled with uneven holes and curved pockets. This hidden complexity controls the densely packed society from inside. From the outside the hierarchy is invisible; the flatness of the cube's surface communicates that. For me, Cube #6 has become a metaphor for hidden controlling forces anywhere in the world. Urban planning has been mostly concerned with "zones", whereas I think of cities as a collection of holes. Holes take humans to other places. The street is a hole too. Architectural work, including city planning, would be impossible for me without visualizing holes.

RH   Would your work change in a village like Raiding?

KK   Basically, I don't change my approach whether the project is urban or rural. In crowded cities you have wind, light and trees too. The secret is to pick up certain elements from nature and incorporate them into your living environment – so the countryside setting of Raiding would not make a difference to my work. I always think of a project as a joint effort between the locality and myself, based on trust.

RH   Will globalization further water down local cultural characteristics, or have we reached a turning point? For example, will Japan's tatami rooms disappear?

KK   I think that in the future we will see more tatami rooms, shoji screens and engawa, simply because they make the body feel good. Paper screens create such nice shades of light, and engawa connect so wonderfully to the outside, which is something a solid wall can never achieve. That's why I believe these traditional elements will not disappear, but rather increase in popularity in Japan. Also, I don't think the Japanese want to live in larger spaces. The basic feeling here is that designing a small space according to your own detailed preferences is a desirable luxury. So, a decreasing Japanese population will not automatically make people want

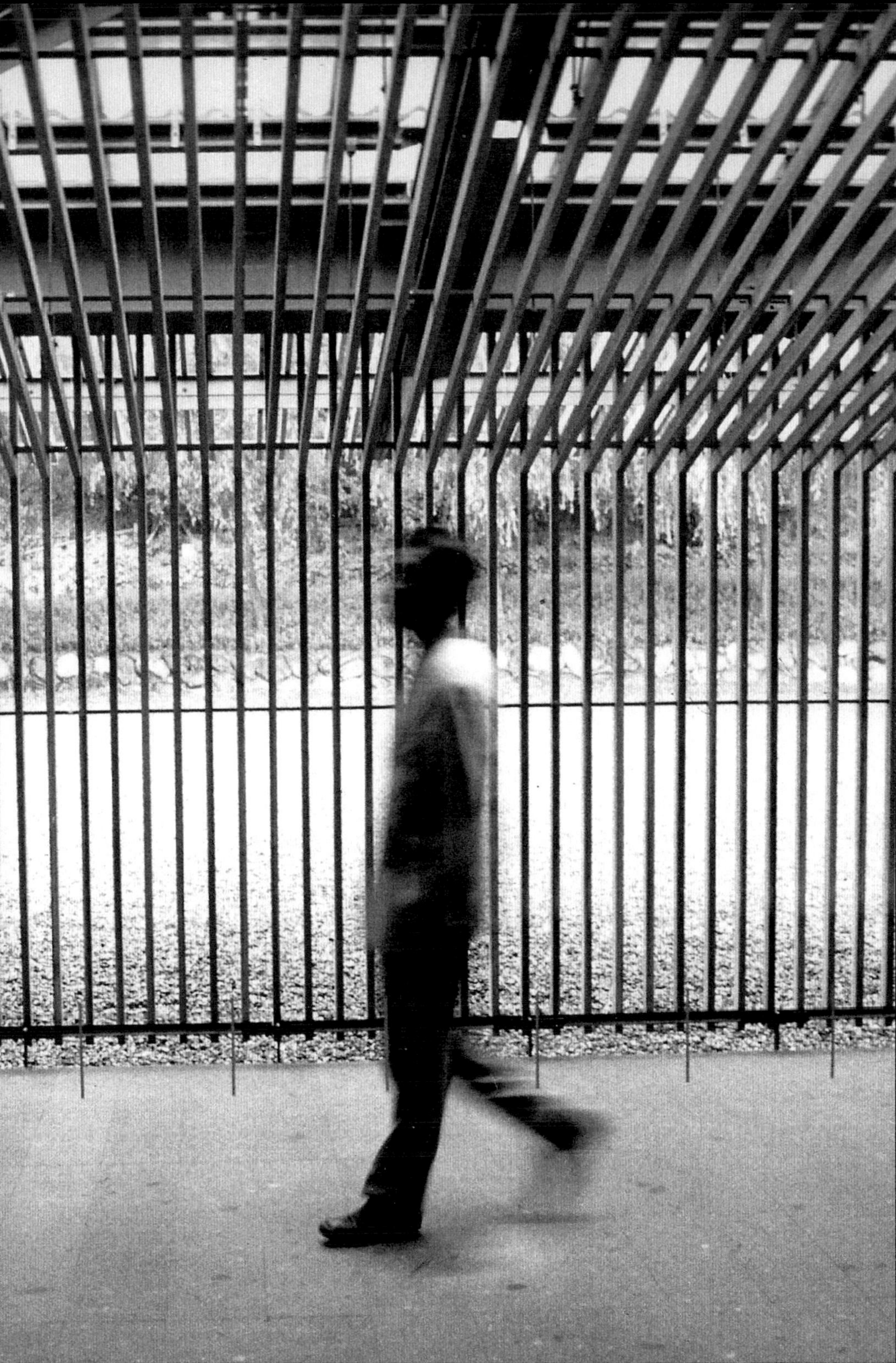

to live in larger spaces when they become available. When living space shrinks in other cultures and countries, we Japanese can be there to offer our solutions and know-how.

RH For you, teaching has always gone hand-in-hand with design work. What is your main concern when meeting with today's students?

KK For the last 50 years, the Japanese method of teaching architecture was to concentrate on buildings made of concrete. Students were not encouraged to think outside this frame and teachers did not explain what it means to build something by hand. That was a huge mistake. I want to emphasize that it is possible to create housing by hand, and by yourself. My students, for instance, just built a small hut with plastic water tanks. For them it was an eye-opening experience and for me a step closer to changing the learning environment of architectural schools in Japan.

RH Among your projects, which would you consider a good prototype for future architectural developments?

KK I recently designed the Asakusa Tourist Center to provide an alternative to the boxy, flat-roof high-rise buildings in Japan. I always felt that a one-floor building with a sloped roof was more comfortable than a multi-floor building with straight ceilings. I wanted to prove that, if we arrange floors in new ways and create alternative layers, like stacking traditionally sloped roof buildings over each other, then we can live more comfortably in high-rise buildings.

RH This – like more tatami rooms and shoji screens in the future – seems to be a step forward by looking back, kind of a of soft counter-revolution.

KK Revolutions are always based on historical events, even if the revolting person is not aware of it. There is the saying, "there's nothing new under the sun," which affirms the historic repetition of revolutions. So, since we are repeating history anyway, architects should know about it.

ライディングのための「Cube #6」|
Kengo Kuma, Cube #6 for Raiding made of Luccon translucent concrete.
Produced by Juergen Frei, Austria, 2010

黒川紀章 中銀カプセルタワーにて | Kisho Kurokawa taking a break during interview at Nakagin Capsule Tower, 2000

黒川紀章 | Kisho Kurokawa

キリスト教国は、自らの勢力範囲の中に、イスラムの文化を入れないでしょうね。

"Christian countries would never introduce the culture of Islam into their sphere of influence."

1934年愛知県生まれ。2007年没。1962年黒川紀章建築都市設計事務所を設立。1964年東京大学大学院修了。1987年に初版の著書『共生の思想』は世界中で翻訳。フランス建築アカデミーゴールドメダル、日本建築学会賞、日本芸術院賞など数々の賞を受賞。主な作品は、中銀カプセルタワービル(東京)、大阪府立国際会議場(大阪)、カザフスタンの首都計画、国立新美術館(東京)など。

Born 1934 in Aichi Prefecture. Died 2007 in Tokyo. Established his practice 1962. Received Ph.D. from University of Tokyo (1964). Published his Philosophy of Symbiosis in 1987. Numerous awards include Gold Medal from the Academy of Architecture, France, Architectual Institute of Japan Award (AIJ) and Japan Art Academy Award. Main works include Nakagin Capsule Tower in Tokyo and Osaka International Convention Center (Grand Cube Osaka), urban plan for Kazakhstan's capital and The National Art Center, Tokyo.

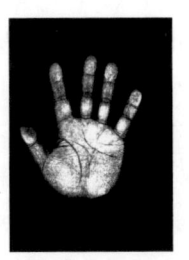

黒川紀章

東京の蒸し暑い夏でも、黒川紀章は黒いスーツを手放さない。秋になって、クーラーをきかせた、彼の涼しい事務所のデスクで、それは変わらない。ここでは、建築家と政府の要人との親密な関係を表わすように、壁に写真がところせましと並んでいる。それでもまだ黒川のすごさに納得しない人は、そこにある数々の賞状に納得させられることになるだろう。フランス建築アカデミーのゴールドメダル、日本とカザフスタンの首相顧問、中には1979年のブルガリア政府の勲章もある。

黒川は話上手で、講演会を断ったことがない。そして男性はそのユーモアで、女性には褒め言葉で、あっというまにひきつけてしまう。そんな彼にももうひとつの面がある。彼はかつて5000万円の賠償を求めて、建築評論家を訴えたことがある。彼がデザインした愛知の豊田大橋について、その評論家の文章が気に食わなかったのだ（その後、裁判所は800万円の賠償を認めた）。

私はあれこれ考えたが、結局尋ねてみた。その多くが壮大な、彼の建築の中で、どれが一番自分の心に近いのかと。クアラルンプール国際空港だろうか、いや大阪コンベンションセンターだろうか。東京・新橋の中銀カプセルタワーのひとつのスペースに座り、彼は心底うんざりしているようだった。72年に完成し、メタボリズム運動のシンボルだった13階建ての巨大建築は、時をへて老朽化していた。階段には

東京都知事選挙のポスター | Campaign poster: Kisho Kurokawa (bottom right) running for governor of Tokyo in 2007 shortly before his death.

ところどころかびが生え、エレベーターシャフトの雨水と鳩の糞で屋根は汚れていた。「中銀は世界遺産にするべきだ！」と彼は言った。「カプセルをチタンでできた豪華な部屋に作りかえたほうがいい。すぐにも改修が必要だ」

それが私と黒川との最後の会話になった。それからまもなくして、彼は東京都知事選に落選し、政府は中銀タワーを安全ではないと勧告した。かつての革命的な建築は、アスベストに汚染され、地震に耐えられないと判断され、取り壊されることになった。そしてそれを追うように、黒川も2007年10月12日、この世を去った。

東京、2000

ローランド・ハーゲンバーグ[以下 RH] 著書『新・共生の思想──世界の新秩序』を興味深く読みました。共時性と記憶領域についても言及していますが、超常現象を体験したことがあるのですか？

黒川紀章[以下 黒川] いいえ、そういったことには興味はありません。私が常に疑問に思っているのは、証明可能な事柄のみが事実とされる西洋哲学のありかたです。どうやって証明するかといえば、科学や数学、物理を使うわけですが、既存の科学的手法では証明できない事象も事実として考慮すべきだというのが私の持論です。

過去40年間にわたり、私が予言したことが次々に現実のものとなってきました。その理由はわかりませんが、もともと予言というのは感性に基づいた活動なのです。人間には理性と感性の両方が備わっています。にもかかわらず、近代社会においては、感性は非科学的だとされています。では、偉大なアーティストや音楽家の作品は、どうなるのでしょう？

RH アーティストでありながら理路整然とした建築家でもあるように見えますが、理性と感性のバランスは、どのように取っているのですか？

黒川 それこそ共生的なプロセスによってです。まず、私は頭の中で建物を建ててみます。これは昔からの癖で、少年時代には機械やロケット、飛行機を想像しては、頭の中でボルトのひとつひとつまで組み立てていました。建築家となった今は、実際の設計図に先がけて、すべてを想像しています。その作業は24時間休みなく続き、色や素材、デザインを毎日、段階を追って変えていくのです。同時に8つの建物

を頭の中で造ることもあります。そんな想像を終え、どのような建物にするかを自分で決めた後、初めて他人を交えたミーティングをするのです。

RH　すべてが頭の中で決定されるということは、他の人はそのプランに従うだけなのですか？

黒川　そうです。ですから、後は早いですよ。

RH　子供の頃から頭の中で何かを造っていたとのことですが、実際には何歳ぐらいからですか？

黒川　覚えていませんが、もしかしたら紙と鉛筆がなかったので、そんな癖がついたのかも知れません。

RH　兄弟はいますか？

黒川　はい。でも、なぜですか？

RH　ひとりっ子の方が、自分自身と向き合う時間が多いと思いますが……。

黒川　そういうこともあるのでしょう。

RH　西洋人が日本の建築家に求めているのは何だと思いますか？

黒川　日本文化に根差したものでしょうね。

異文化に惹かれるのは世界共通のメンタリティーだと思いますが、日本人がユニークなのは、憧れの外国文化を積極的に自分たちの文化に取り入れてしまうところです。仮にアメリカの建築家が日本の現代建築に惹かれたとしても、日本文化をアメリカに取り入れようとはしないと思います。それに比べると、日本はどうでしょう？　おそらく、日本の文化の80％程度は中国から入ってきたものです。それも、強制されたわけでなく、自主的に受け入れたのです。明治維新後にいたっては、靴から教育制度まで、文化の90％程度を欧米から輸入しています。にもかかわらず、日本人は外国の文化を自国の文化の中に消化吸収してしまったのです。なおかつ、日本であり続けています。これを私は共生と呼んでいます。

イスラムの国々も、ヨーロッパの国々も、こんなことはしません。古代のギリシャやローマ、エジプトで文明が滅びたのは、周縁の文化を取り入れなかったからだと思います。自己中心的な文化は滅びてしまうのです。

RH　総理府（現内閣府）のアドバイザーもつとめていますね？　日本の将来を予測することも仕事のひとつと聞いています。

黒川 日本は今、短期的な問題と長期的な問題に、同時に直面しています。行政改革も、地球上で日本の役割を見つけることも、等しく困難な課題です。この事態を解決するのは共生のみ、というのが私の考えです。日本の文化そのものを放棄することなく、異文化に同化し、異文化から学び、異文化を利用する。これだけが日本が世界に誇る要素なのです。科学技術は普遍的ですが、文化は固有のものです。そして、日本文化は完璧な共生文化なのです。50年後の未来社会で、この共生という文化の概念が世界の標準となっていても不思議はありません。

RH 自分の日常生活も予測のつくものなのですか？

黒川 私の生活は極めてシンプルですよ。オフィスから車で10分ほどの赤坂に住んでいます。人間、50歳を過ぎると運動はかえって毒で、睡眠をとることや頭を働かせることが長生きの秘訣だと思っています。事務所で夜の9時頃まで、場合によっては10時、11時頃まで仕事をした後、遅い夕食をとります。夕食後は、書類に目を通したり、ノートをつけたり、図面を描いたりで、午前2時頃に就寝。そしてまた、朝7時頃から新しい一日のスタート。この繰り返しです。

中銀カプセルタワー（黒い屋根が2つ見える、奥の建物）
Nakagin Capsule Tower (with two dark roof boxes) in 2001 near Shimbashi redevelopment construction site in Tokyo.

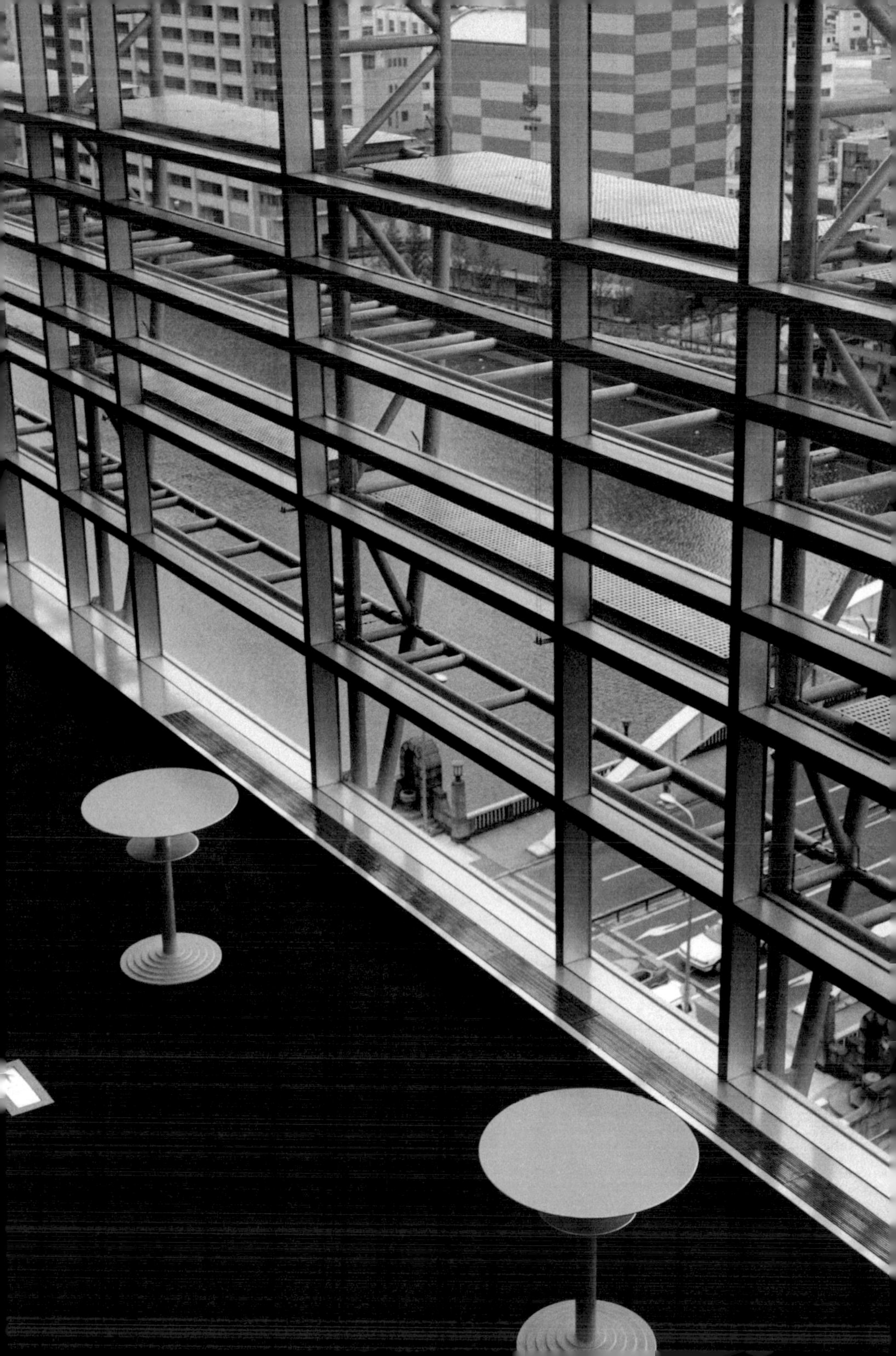

Kisho Kurokawa

Tokyo's hot and humid summers did not deter Kisho Kurokawa from wearing heavy black suits, and so the air-conditioning pumped icy winds over his ambassadorial office desk well into autumn. Here, photographs lined the walls as proof of the architect's closeness to heads of state. And if visitors to Kurokawa's office remained unconvinced of his importance, framed awards and certificates were there to convince them: a gold medal from the Academy of Architecture in France; an appointment to the advisory position for two Prime Ministers (Japan and Kazakhstan); the list was endless and also included a 1979 decoration from the Bulgarian Government.

Kurokawa was a born conversationalist and never refused speaking engagements, where he charmed men with humor and women with compliments. But there was also a darker side to him; he once sued a critic of architecture for half a million dollars because he didn't like the review of his Toyota Bridge in Aichi Prefecture. (The Japanese court awarded Kurokawa eighty thousand dollars.)

I wondered which, out of all his buildings – many of which are grandiose, like the International Airport of Kuala Lumpur or the Convention Center in Osaka – was the one closest to his heart. Kurokawa seemed weary when asked. He was sitting inside one of the cubicles of Nakagin Capsule Tower in Tokyo's Shimbashi district. The 13-storey high edifice from 1972, a symbol of the Metabolist movement, had deteriorated. There was mold in the stairways, rainwater in the elevator shafts and crusts of pigeon dirt on the roof. "Nakagin should become a World Heritage site!" he declared. "Maybe we should turn the capsules into deluxe cabins made of titanium. Renovation is needed now!"

It was our last conversation. Shortly afterwards, he ran unsuccessfully for Governor of Tokyo while the Ministry of Construction declared Nakagin Tower unsafe. Poisoned with asbestos and too weak to resist earthquakes, the once revolutionary modules were to be demolished. With them, Kisho Kurokawa passed away October 12, 2007.

Tokyo, 2000

Roland Hagenberg I read with great interest your book "The Philosophy of Symbioses". Among other things, you mentioned synchronicity and memory fields.

Have you experienced paranormal phenomena yourself?

Kisho Kurokawa No that's not what I am interested in. What I always question is the way of Western thinking that says if something is a fact, it must be proven first. But how? The only way is with the help of science, mathematics and physics. I say we also should take into consideration elements that have not been proven yet by traditional scientific methods. During the last forty years I made many predictions, and almost all of them were later proven right. I don't know why. Prediction is human activity based on feeling. We have both - reason and feeling, but in modern society feeling is not scientific. So how do you categorize the work of great artists or musicians?

RH You are an artist yourself, but also a rationally thinking architect. How do you balance reason and feeling?

KK This is a true symbiotic process. I usually build everything in my head. This is an old habit of mine. Even in childhood, when I imagined a machine or rocket or airplane, I actually constructed them bolt by bolt in my mind. And that's what I still do. I construct everything without drawings. It's pure imagination and a continuous, 24-hour process. Color, materials, and designs I change step by step every day. Sometimes I make eight different constructions. After that I decide and start meeting people.

RH Everything is fixed in your head. Other people just follow your plan?

KK They only follow. And from that time on everything goes very fast.

RH When did this technique evolve in your childhood?

KK I don't know the year - maybe it started because of the lack of pencils and paper.

RH Did you have sisters and brothers?

KK Yes, why?

RH Sometimes, if you are an only child, you start communicating more intensely with yourself.

KK That could have been a reason too.

RH What do Western people expect from a Japanese architect?

KK They expect something from their cultural background. Countries are always attracted to other cultures. The difference between Japan and the West, however, is that when we Japanese admire a foreign culture, we aggressively try to integrate it into our own. When American architects admire Japanese contemporary architecture, then this does not necessarily mean they want to import Japanese culture to America. But look at us! Probably 80% of Japanese culture originated in China. We were not

仮にアメリカの建築家が日本の現代建築に惹かれたとしても、日本文化をアメリカに取り入れようとはしないと思います。

When American architects admire Japanese contemporary architecture,
this does not necessarily mean they want to import Japanese culture to America."

forced to do so. We were willing to do so. After the Meiji restoration, maybe 90% of the culture became European, from shoes to education. We digested it but we still remained Japanese. This is unique and I call it Symbioses. Islamic countries don't do that. European countries don't do that. The reason for the end of Greek and Rome and Egypt was that those empires did not integrate the cultures at their periphery. Selfish cultures collapse. I have been watching Europe and America for forty years, but they never change their attitude – they never absorb other cultures. Christian countries would never introduce the culture of Islam into their sphere of influence. When I built the international airport for Kuala Lumpur it was never my intention to copy Islamic architecture, but Muslims nevertheless said they felt so close to it and they felt comfortable with it. This is an example of true symbiosis. If you just think of designing something beautiful, that's not enough. That's why I don't like Tadao Ando's architecture; a classic form of beauty, but meaningless if it cannot offer more than that to other countries.

RH   A long time ago, how was it working with Kenzo Tange?

KK   I never collaborated with Tange. His office was composed of two teams. One was paid and the other consisted of graduate students like me – unpaid. I spent a total of seven years there for my masters and doctorate course, independent from Tange's atelier. We never accepted money, neither me, nor Arata Isozaki. Of course, sometimes we helped on competitions, but I cannot define this as work.

RH   As an architect you are also an advisor to the Prime Minister's cabinet (sorifu). Among other things, your job is to predict the future of Japan. Will there be surprises?

KK   Japan now faces simultaneously short and long term problems. Reform of the bureaucracy is a difficult task but so is finding a role for Japan on this planet. I see the only solution in Symbioses. It is the only unique thing Japan can offer to the world: how to integrate, learn from and make use of other cultures without giving up its own. Science and technology have universality. Culture is different. Japan is so special, because it is a perfect symbiotic culture, which could serve as a planetary concept in another fifty years or so.

RH   Is your daily life very predictable?

KK   It is very simple. I live in Akasaka just ten minutes by car from my office. I believe that after 50 exercising doesn't do any good. Just sleeping and thinking is the best way to live long. I stay at the office until nine, ten or eleven in the evening.

Then my driver takes me to one of my three favorite restaurants. After dinner, I check documents, write notes, make sketches. Around two in the morning I sleep and start all over again around seven.

黒川紀章 大阪国際会議場にて
Kisho Kurokawa answers questions at Osaka International Convention Center, 2001

槇文彦 事務所にて | Fumihiko Maki in front of his office in Tokyo's Daikanyama district.

槇 文彦 | Fumihiko Maki

創造的であるために、いくつかを同時に進行させ、複数の建物の間を行き来しながら考えるのが私流です。

"To stay creative, I constantly have to shift my thoughts between buildings."

1928年東京都生まれ。1954年ハーバード大学大学院修了。1965年槇総合計画事務所を設立。ワシントン大学、ハーバード大学で教鞭をとり、1979年から1989年まで東京大学の教授をつとめる。シカゴ建築賞、プリツカー賞、日本建築学会賞など数々の賞を受賞。主な作品に、幕張メッセ(千葉)、風の丘葬斎場(大分)、ワシントン大学ミルドレッド・レーン・ケンパー美術館(米国・セントルイス)、テレビ朝日本社ビル(東京)、ヒルサイドウエスト(東京)などがある。

Born 1928 in Tokyo. Graduated from Harvard University in 1954. Established his practice 1965. Professor at University of Tokyo from 1979 to 1989. Numerous awards such as Pritzker Architectural Prize, Chicago Architecture Award and Architectural Institute of Japan Award (AIJ). Main works include Makuhari Messe in Chiba, Kaze-no-Oka Crematorium in Oita and Mildred Lane Kemper Art Museum in St.Louis, TV Asahi and Hillside West in Tokyo.

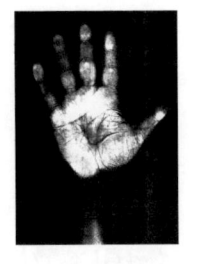

槇 文彦

彼は、流行の最先端、東京・代官山にあるオフィスの入り口に立っていた。その日はうす曇りで、彼はグレーのスーツにグレーのネクタイをしていた。ハーバードを出て、英語は完璧、プリツカー賞を受賞した槇文彦は、何年も前に、日本流のやり方というものを捨てていた。少なくとも海外の人と接するときには。まず、彼にはアシスタントがいない。どこにでもいる、よく気がきいて、お茶を出し、槇くらいの地位の日本の建築家には必ずいるあのアシスタントだ。そう、白髪の建築家は、彼の書くサイン——目に見えない定規で引いたように——まっすぐな人物なのだ。

私たちは、明るく手入れの行き届いた芝生を横切り、コンクリートの壁と、時を経てグレーになったウッドデッキを通り過ぎて、明るいスタジオに入った。そこでは、何人もの建築家たちが、白いシャツを着て、一心不乱に自分たちの模型に取り組んでいた。その雰囲気は、都心にある雑然とした事務所というより、アップステート・ニューヨークにある、ミニマリストの週末用別荘のような感じだった。

槇自身は何十年にも渡ってつながりを保ち続けている仕事が多い。建てられてから25年が経過して、改修が必要になったときに、槇にアドバイスを求めてやってくるのは、何も東京のオーストリア大使館だけでない。ある大使の家族は、槇の家族と一緒に休日を過ごしたこともある。そして、この代官山の半分を所有する朝倉家のために、槇は30年以上もの間、この土地を開発し続けてきたのだ。

ひとりの建築家のこのような一貫した姿勢は(おそらく、アメリカでの教育のおかげだろう)、もし答えたくないことを聞かれたときには、答えないという姿勢にも現れている。彼は、質問に対して質問で返すこともある。「ほんとうにそんなこと言いましたか？どこに書いてあるか見せてください！」将来日本にはどんな問題が起こるか尋ねると、彼ははぐらかして「私は日本についてはコメントしない」と言う。「私は日本の将来についてあれこれ言ったりしませんよ」。しかし、この筋金入りの厳しさも、やはり一時的なもの。彼はこう言うと、すぐに消えていってしまうのだ。「私は夜遅くまで仕事はしない。さもないと、夕食が冷めて、妻が怒るからね！」

[**パート1**]──2001

ローランド・ハーゲンバーグ[以下 RH] 建築様式に地域差がなくなり、グローバル・スタイルの時代に突入したと思いますか?

槇 文彦[以下 槇] そうは思いません。今でも地域の独自性や、そこに住む人々の感性に応じることは可能だと思います。

ただ、私は様式的な特徴よりも、空間的な特徴に関心があります。というのは、ある地域の文化が、より強く反映するのは空間の方だからです。例えば、日本の美意識は、その空間における奥行き、連続性、流動性に現れています。建物の内に入ったとたん、目の前に景色が開けるような空間は、日本の美感を反映していると思います。

そうしたことを考慮して、九州の風の丘葬斎場を設計しました。建物のどこにいても、次の空間が待ち受けていて、別の空間につながるように思える連続性が特徴で、使用している素材や技術は近代のものですが、日本の伝統的な美感を反映した空間です。

RH 幾つかの建物がぽつりぽつりと配置されていて、風の丘葬斎場は京都の石庭を連想しますね?

槇 日本人は近所に葬斎場ができるのを嫌がるものなのですが、風の丘葬斎場の敷地は広大で、建物の前が公園になっています。公園の敷地というのは市長の英断で、誰も葬斎場が近くにあるとは思いません。しかも、視界に入るのは、地面になかば埋もれた、抽象的でミニマルな立体です。こういう外観であれば、葬斎場も容認されるということです。

RH こんな所で火葬して欲しい、と見学に来た人がよく言うそうですが、自分でもそう思いますか?

槇 おそらく。でも、私は、まだ遺書も書いていませんよ。

RH 使用する素材の種類は多い方だと思いますが、好みの素材はありますか?

槇 例えば、ホテルであっても、美術館であっても常にコンクリートを使うというやり方は、私の感性には合っていません。小さな建物で、ある程度までの規模であれば、素材が1種類だけでもよいとは思いますが。

RH ある程度以上の大きさになると、素材が1種類ではダメということですか?

槇 コンクリートだけというわけにはいきませんね。

RH 仮に、今まで使用したことがない新素材を発見したら、どうでしょう？

槇 私が興味を持っているのは、素材そのものではなく、素材が、建物を見る人や使う人に、どういうメッセージを伝えるかということなのです。個人的な好みの問題だけでなく、もっと複雑な意味合いで素材を用いているのです。

ただ、素材の種類があまり多くない建築の方が、理解されやすいのは確かですし、予算に制約がある場合は、使える素材の種類が減るのも確かです。

RH 完成した建物に最初に足を踏み入れたとき、当初に予想していたものと違うと感じたことはありますか？

槇 あります。

RH 都会でも田舎でも仕事をしていますが、その方法は違うものなのでしょうか？

槇 それは何とも言えません。都市でも地方でも、生活の場から仕事の場まで、あらゆる種類の空間を創造するのが仕事なのですから。

都会の仕事の一例として、私の事務所も入っているヒルサイドウエストを見てもらえばよいと思います。私が幼い頃、東京にはたくさんの路地があったので、ここでも路地を造りました。それは、私の記憶の副産物ともいえるでしょう。

RH 日々の仕事時間は長い方ですか？

槇 建築のことは常に考えています。それも、ひとつだけでなく、いくつかを同時に進行させ、複数の建物の間を行き来しながら考えるのが私流です。

また、ある程度までは頭の中で設計もします。頭の中で、良いアイデア、さらに良いアイデアと発展させ、自然淘汰させていくのです。

一方、毎日、少なくとも6時間は睡眠をとっています。そのほか、友人と会ったり、テレビを観たり、本を読んだりもします。つまり、生活を楽しんでいるわけで、その意味では、普通の人間だと思います。

RH 外国での仕事より、日本での仕事の方が簡単ですか？

槇 外国の仕事の方がペーパーワークが多いと思います。というのは、しょっちゅう何をしてるのかを、施主に説明しなければならないので。ところが、日本の場合は、工事中も、ほとんど自分の仕事に集中できますね。

RH 外国のクライアントが求めるのは、「槇の建築」でしょうか？ それとも、「日本の建築」でしょうか？

槇　それは、もちろん「槇の建築」ですよ。

――――

[パート2]――2011

RH　今から40年以上も前にスタートした東京・代官山ヒルサイドテラス。このプロジェクトは、現在も続いています。その間、日本では様々なことがありましたが、ご自身の建築にその影響はありますか？

槇　外からの影響というものは、それほどないと思います。

RH　そのようなものからは距離を置いていたということですか？

槇　距離をおいていたということではないです。もちろんこの10年間は、さらなる経済の悪化に直面して、日本でのコミッションが減りました。それでも、私は海外に多くのプロジェクトを抱えているので、ほかの建築家にくらべて影響は少ないのではないかと思います。それと同時に、国内でも面白いプロジェクトに関わることができました。

RH　島根県立古代出雲歴史博物館や、三原市芸術文化センターなどですね。現在は30人から40人の人が東京のオフィスで働いていますが、世界中から集まってきているのですか？

風の丘斎場のコンセプトを説明する槇｜"Japanese usually don't like having a crematorium in their neighborhood"

槇　ある程度はそうですが、ほとんどは日本人のスタッフです。海外でプロジェクトを進めるときは、いつも現地のパートナーがいます。私たちの同僚は、働く国によって変わります。なので、その時、その場所によっては、多くの人たちと働くことになります。

RH　人々が言う「槇文彦のスタイル」とは、グレーと白の軽さ、微妙さだとおっしゃいました。これは外からの影響はないのですね……。

槇　私は、多くのものに影響を受けるということがないので、誰にも影響を受けていないと言えるかもしれません。

RH　プロの建築家というものは、とても大変な仕事だと思います。どうやって、ご自身のバランスをとっていらっしゃるのですか？

槇　わかりません。

RH　70年代、東京のオーストリア大使館のデザインをすることになったときのことを覚えていらっしゃいますか？

槇　誰かが私を推薦してくれたんです。当時のオーストリア大使は日本人が建てるのがいいと思ったのだそうです。今だったら、おそらくオーストリアの建築家が手がけることになるでしょうね。現代の大使館は、その国のショーケースになり得ると思っているので。

RH　長いキャリアを振り返ってみて、一番印象に残っていることは何ですか？

槇　建物を建てるときはいつも、クライアントとユーザーの満足のいくものができたときが、一番うれしいですね。建築家は自分のためにデザインするわけではありません。それを使う人のために、建築を作ります。もし建築家が、自分の虚栄心を満たすために建物を建てるのだとしても、クライアントの希望を忘れないでいる限り、それはそれでいいと思います。時には教養がなく、センスがない開発業者と仕事をすることもあります。そういうときにはできるだけ、その建物に住む、あるいは、働く人のことを頭に入れておかなくてはならないと思います。

RH　建築に関する最初の経験などという、いわば子供時代の決定的な経験はありますか？

槇　そのような、劇的な経験というものはありません。すみません……私の人生でこれまでそのような節目になるようなことなどないんです。建築は、私と私のまわ

りにあるものを結びつける、継続的なプロセスだと思います。ときにはうれしかったり、あるときはそれほどうれしくなかったり。でも、いつも私は次のプロジェクトを楽しみにしているんです。

RH お仕事がうまくいったときには、その幸福感はどのくらい続くのですか？

槇 代官山ヒルサイドテラスの場合、始まってからすでに40年間続いていますが、私は今も満足ですし、うれしいです。もちろん、そのほかにも多くの建物を作っていて、自分の関心の方向を変えていかなければなりません。でも、私は新しい建物を建てて、古いものはすべて忘れるということはできません。すべて自分の子供のようなものですから。

RH これまでこのような驚くべきお仕事をしてこられて、運はどれくらい関係あると思いますか？

槇 私は統計をとったりはしません。質問の意味がよくわからないのですが。それは量的に、ということですか？

RH これまでの人生の中で、これだけのことを成し遂げることができるなんて、本当に運がいい、と思ったことはありませんか？
同じような才能を持った建築家はほかにもいるかも知れないのに、どうして皆同じように幸運ではないのでしょうか？

槇 もしあなたの言葉で、建築家の運というものを計るとするならば、そうですね、私は幸運だったと思いますよ。私は今まで仕事がないときはなかったし、いつも仕事が向こうからやってきました。現在の状況が、若い世代にとって大変になってきているということは間違いありません。人口も、今の1億2000万人から、40年間で9000万人に減るといわれています。こういう状況からすると、建築家志望の若者たちは大変だと思います。

RH 彼らにアドバイスはありますか？

槇 私は誰かにアドバイスをする資格はないです。

RH でも、槇さんに触発されて、建築を専門に選んだ学生たちがたくさんいます。彼らは、槇さんからのアドバイスを期待していると思います。

槇 でも、これをやりなさい、そうすれば大丈夫でしょうということが本当にないんです。私は将来のことはわかりません……。

RH　槇さんは、本当に謙虚ですね……。

槇　うーん、すぐにアドバイスをくれる人なら、ほかに大勢いるでしょう。そういう人にインタビューしたほうがいいですよ。

RH　槇さんが建築家になる過程で、尊敬する人やアドバイスがほしいと思った人はいませんでしたか？

槇　もちろんいましたよ。ほかの建築家とも同じように。

RH　最も影響を受けたのは？

槇　このひとりだけに最も影響を受けたとは言いませんが、たくさんいます。ル・コルビュジエ、ミース・ファン・デル・ローエ、アルヴァ・アールト……。私をいつも駆り立てたのは、社会のために、人のために、クライアントのために、何か役に立ちたいということでした。いつの時代も、どこでも人間は同じだと思います。よいことが好きで、悪いことが嫌い。とても単純なことです。

RH　オフィスの建物や博物館に加え、スピリチュアルな建築もありますよね。例えば、東京キリストの教会や、カナダのイスマイリ・イママット記念館など……。

槇　東京では、シナゴーグが中にある日本ユダヤ教団のコミュニティセンターができました。

RH　宗教的な建築のデザインをするときには、これまでとはまた違ったアプローチが要求されますか？

槇　シナゴーグのデザインをしたとき、天井の高さをほしいと思ったので、様々な制約がある中で、どうしたら深みのある空間を作り出せるか考えました。

RH　計算されたアプローチですね……。

槇　すべてがそうではないですけれどね。

RH　スピリチュアルな面はどうしたのですか？

槇　それについては、光がとても重要です。でも、それを扱うためには何十もの方法があるんです。

槇文彦 事務所にて | Fumihiko Maki at his office, 2001

Fumihiko Maki

He stands at the entrance of his office in Tokyo's fashionable Daikanyama district – on a gray day, in a gray suit, with a gray necktie. Harvard-educated, English-perfect, Pritzker-prize-honored Fumihiko Maki did away with Japanese formalities a long time ago – at least as far as concerns his dealings with foreigners. To begin with, the ubiquitous attentive, green-tea-serving assistant usually present for a Japanese architect of Maki's stature is missing. Yes, the white-haired professor is as straightforward as his signature – an even line guided by an invisible ruler.

We pass a bright, manicured lawn, concrete walls and a wooden deck (withered and turned to gray) and enter the bright studio where dozens of architects in white shirts are glued to their models. The atmosphere here is more like that of a minimalist weekend-house in upstate New York than that of a cluttered office in the heart of Tokyo. Maki has maintained some working relationships with clients for decades. Not only does the Austrian Embassy in Tokyo still go to Maki for advice when repairs come up after 25 years, the family of one ambassador used to vacation in the same place as the Makis. And for the Asakura family, who own half of Daikanyama, Maki developed this part of the city over a period of three decades.

An architect of such consistency (perhaps a result of his American education) can afford to refuse to answer questions if he doesn't like them. He can also question the question: "I really said that? Show me where it's written!" When asked what the future challenges for Japan are, he sidetracks. "I don't comment on Japan," he states. "I don't speculate about its future!" This professorial strictness, though, is only temporary and dissipates quickly after one of his humorous remarks. "I cannot work late at night, otherwise my dinner gets cold and my wife, angry!"

[**Conversation part one**]——2001

Roland Hagenberg Have we reached a point in contemporary architecture where differences within a global style are not possible anymore?

Fumihiko Maki I don't think so. We are still capable of producing something unique to a particular region and to respond to the sensitivity of people in that area. I am more interested in the characteristics of space than the characteristics of form because within space individual cultures are expressed. For instance, a very Japanese aspect would be the depth, sequence and fluidity of spaces. Once inside, you can experience the unfolding of the scenery. I don't mind using this to certain extend. The crematorium 'kaze-no-oka' which I built in Oita features such a sequential development, where there is always the hint of the next space waiting for you, the hint of another space coming to appear. This sequential connectivity is very Japanese even though I use modern materials and modern technology to achieve it.

RH Kaze-no-oka is a very fragmented building, arranged like a stone garden in Kyoto.

FM In Japan people usually don't like having a crematorium in their neighborhood. The mayor of Nakatsu was wise to acquire a piece of property next to the site, which serves as a public park. From there people would not suspect they have a crematorium next door. Instead, all they see are abstract, minimalist forms half submerged in the ground.

RH People often come and say, "oh, that's a place where I want to be cremated one day." Do you feel the same?

FM Maybe yes, but I have not written my will yet.

RH You use all kinds of materials. Do you have preferences?

FM If you look at things like hotels and museums, everything is always made of concrete. That does not go with my sensibility.

RH From a certain size on you cannot use one material alone?

FM Only concrete - I cannot do that.

RH Let's say, you discover a new material that you have never used before...

FM ... I am more interested in what kind of message each material can give to the beholder or people using the building. I am using materials in a more complex way including my personal preferences. I must admit though, it is much easier for people to understand if there are not too many materials involved. Restraints on the budget can also be a decisive factor.

RH When you walk for the first time through the completed structure, do you sometimes think, this or that turned out completely different to how you originally anticipated it?

FM Yes!

RH Urban and countryside, you build in both environments. Does each require a different set of rules?

FM I can't strictly say that. I develop all kinds of active spaces, urban and rural for living and working. Hillside West, where I have my office, is a city place, so you can make your own judgment on what I have done. In rural areas I might make more pavilion-like buildings. When I was young, Tokyo had small alleys, and so we created another one around Hillside West. This is maybe a spin-off from my memories of the past.

RH Do you work long hours?

FM I constantly think about architecture, not only one but several projects at a time. I have to shift my thoughts constantly between buildings. To some extent I can design in my head. Some ideas are good, others better, and a natural selection process starts. I sleep at least 6 hours every day and I enjoy my life, talk to friends, watch TV, read a lot – which makes me a pretty normal person.

RH Is working in Japan easier for you than abroad?

FM It's much easier in Japan working with Japanese contractors and subcontractors. It is exciting to work in different countries and cultures – but it is not easy.

RH When foreign clients approach you, and ask you to build something, do they expect a Maki design or something Japanese?

FM They expect a Maki design of course!

[Conversation part two]——2011

Roland Hagenberg More than 40 years ago, you started the Daikanyama Hillside development project in Tokyo. It continues today. Was your architecture affected by the ups and downs of that time in Japan's history?

Fumihiko Maki I don't think it was much affected by outside influences.

RH You distanced yourself?

FM Not distanced… of course, we've faced further economic downturns during the last decade and commissions in Japan have decreased, but I have extensive projects abroad and have been less affected than other architects. At the same time, I've never stopped participating in interesting projects in Japan.

RH Like Shimane Museum of Ancient Izumo, or Mihara Performing Arts Center. Currently 30 to 40 people work in your Tokyo office – do they come from all over the world?

FM To some extent, but they're mostly Japanese. When we do projects abroad, we always have local partners. Our associates change depending on the country we work in.

RH You've said that your style – people might call it the "Maki-style", with its structured lightness and subtle grays and whites – is never influenced by outside forces.

FM I haven't been influenced by many sources, so you could say that I haven't been influenced by anybody.

RH The profession of architecture is very demanding. How do you balance yourself?

FM I have no idea.

RH Do you still remember the moment when you were selected to design the Austrian Embassy in Tokyo in the 1970s?

FM Somebody recommended me for it. At that time, the Austrian Ambassador thought the embassy should be built by a Japanese architect. Nowadays, the job would probably go to an Austrian architect. Modern embassies want to be showcases for their countries.

RH Looking back over your long career, what were the highlights?

FM Whenever I built something that satisfied my client and users, it was a high moment for me. If architects build to satisfy their vanity, that's OK too, as long as they keep their clients' wishes in mind. Sometimes you have developers that are not well educated, sophisticated, or cultivated. In that case, if possible, you have to think about the people who will live and work in your building.

RH Was there a defining moment in your childhood that was your first "architectural experience," so to speak?

FM I don't have such dramatic experiences, sorry; no milestones in my life. For me, architecture is a continuous process of associating myself with my surroundings. Sometimes I am happy, sometimes not so happy, but I always have an upcoming project to look forward to.

RH How long does your happiness last after the successful completion of a building?

FM In the case of Hillside Terrace, which has been going on for four decades now, I still feel satisfied and happy. Of course, many other buildings have been created in the meantime and I had to shift my interest towards them. But I can't say that I create a new building and forget all the others. They are all my children.

RH   In your career, how much luck has been involved in creating such an amazing body of work?

FM   You mean quantitatively?

RH   Haven't there been moments in your life when you've thought yourself quite lucky to have achieved everything you've achieved? There might be other architects out there with the same talent but less luck.

FM   If you measure the luck of architects in those terms then, yes, I was lucky. I've never had a time without work, something has always come up. The current situation in Japan has made it difficult for the younger generation, there's no question about that. We have a population of roughly 120 million that will shrink to 90 million in the next 40 years. If you look at things from this angle, aspiring architects are going to have a difficult time.

RH   Do you have any advice for them?

FM   I am not someone to give advice to people.

RH   But you have become someone who inspires students to choose architecture as their profession. They might expect advice from you.

FM   But I really can't say, "Do this and you will be OK." I have no vision.

RH   You are very modest.

FM   Well, I'm sure there are lots of other architects with advice at hand. You better interview them.

RH   Didn't you have someone in your formative years that you looked up to, and expected advice from?

FM   Sure, of course. Just like any other architect.

RH   Was there a single most important influence?

FM   I wouldn't say one most important architect. There are so many, like Le Corbusier, Mies van der Rohe, or Alvar Alto. What kept me motivated was that I always wanted to contribute something good to society; for people, for my clients. Human beings are the same across ages and places – they appreciate good things and dislike bad things. Very simple.

RH   Besides office buildings and museums, you've also created spiritual places, like the Tokyo Church of Christ and The Delegation of The Ismaili Imamat in Canada.

FM And I just completed the Jewish Community Center in Tokyo, with a synagogue inside.

RH Is a different approach required when designing a house of worship?

FM When I designed the synagogue, I wanted to give the ceiling a certain height. Under various restrictions I thought of a way to create depth in this space.

RH And how about the spiritual aspects?

FM Light is very important for that, but there are dozens of ways to deal with it.

代官山にある槇のオフィスの入口 |
Entrance to Maki office in Daikanyama, Tokyo

内藤廣 東京にて | Hiroshi Naito, Tokyo (2011)

内藤 廣 | Hiroshi Naito

建築の創造は、社会への参加である。
"Producing architecture is participating in society."

1950年神奈川県生まれ。1976年早稲田大学大学院修了。フェルナンド・イゲーラス建築設計事務所、菊竹清訓建築設計事務所の勤務を経て、1981年 内藤廣建築設計事務所設立。元東京大学教授。芸術選奨文部大臣新人賞、日本建築学会賞、毎日芸術賞などを受賞。主な作品は、海の博物館(三重)、安曇野ちひろ美術館(長野)、牧野富太郎記念館(高知)、倫理研究所 富士高原研修所(静岡)など。

Born 1950 in Kanagawa Prefecture. Received master degree of Architecture from Waseda University 1976. Worked at Fernand Higueras & Associates and Kiyonori Kikutake & Associates. Established his practice 1981. Former Professor at University of Tokyo. Many awards such as Best Newcomer Artists (Recommended by the Minister of Education), Architectual Institute of Japan Award (AIJ) and Mainichi Art Award. Major works include Sea-Folk Museum in Mie, Chihiro Art Museum, Azumino in Nagano, Makino Museum of Plants and People in Kochi and Fuji RINRI Seminar House in Shizuoka.

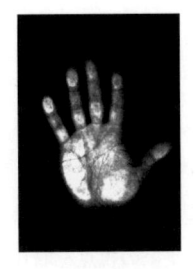

内藤 廣

「第二次大戦後、人々はもう一度生きたいと思ったんです。ただ生きたい！と。広島の中心にある丹下健三の作品は、その当時、希望の表現として理解されていました。でも今では、建築の哲学やムーブメントについて語るのはナンセンスだと思われているんです」。内藤廣は、他人とは違った考えを何気なく話す。まるで、悪い天気がそうすぐには変わらないと言うように。彼の第一印象は、とても穏やかな人。その姿は『悲しき熱帯』を書き、何年もの間熱帯雨林で暮らした後に、運命論者として文明世界に戻ってきた、あの人類学者のような感じを与える。内藤は、同僚であり、アフリカにシェルターをつくった坂茂の仕事を高く評価している。「あのような行動は、生か死かといった責任を引き受けることを意味すると思います。それはすべての建築の中心になければいけないものなんです」。東京・渋谷。都内で最もにぎわうこの地区を再開発するための検討委員会。ここではまとめ役として、役所を説得したり、隈研吾や妹島和世たちのような建築家の視点を取り入れようとしている。

内藤は、表面的で、スタイルのためのスタイルのような現代のデザインの世界には見向きもしない。雑誌の見開きページに夢中になっているようなものは嫌いなのだ。「新聞や雑誌は、人々を誤った方向に導く可能性があります」、そう警告する。内藤の一番有名な言葉はおそらく、「建築家は、未来のかけらを使って建築を組み立てる」というものだろう。彼は自分自身を、考古学を映し出した鏡の世界で働いていると考えている。つまり、過去の断片を集めて、現実を再構築するのだ。そして、その断片があるところでは、それをつなぐものが必要だ。それが内藤の建築を貫くテーマとなり、内藤のスタイルになっている（内藤に関して「スタイル」という言葉が適当であればだが）。東京大学の元教授でもあり、菊竹清訓の下で働いたこともある彼は、ビルへの信奉者たちによって見過ごされている「断片をつなぎ合わせる」という建築の冥府を心から楽しんでいる。内藤の建築は、ただ美を——それは技術に結びついている——賛美するために作られているかのように見える。鳥羽市にある「海の博物館」がいい例だ。何千本もの木の梁がめぐらされた複雑な屋根は静寂を生み出し、古代の大聖堂

内藤廣の建設現場 | Naito Coustruction site (2000)

の中にいるかのような感覚を引き起こす。

内藤にはもうひとつこだわりがある。ダンスだ。彼は、世界的な振付師ピナ・バウシュを崇拝している。「非人間化が建築にとって最大の脅威です」と彼は言う。「パソコンの前に一日中座っている人は、夕方には人間性を取り戻さなくては。だから私は、巧妙な身体の表現が好きなんです。そうでなければ、私たちはただの、バラバラなパーツの寄せ集めになってしまいますから」。

[パート1]── 2000-2007

ローランド・ハーゲンバーグ[以下 RH]　建築が時とともに朽ちていくのは運命で、時間の流れに抵抗しても、人間が老いていく自然の摂理のようなもの、というようなことを書かれていますね？　それは、自分が設計した建物が完成後、どうなっても気にならないという意味ですか？

内藤 廣[以下 内藤]　とんでもない。建物が完成した後の方が大切で、長い時間を生きてその寿命を迎える時が、私の手を離れる時です。建物がもともとの計画とは異なる使われ方をしたり、使う人にとってより快適になるように手を加えられてもあまり気になりませんが、それは建物への愛着がなくなったという意味ではありません。建築家と建物の関係は、親子の関係に似ています。子供が成人したり一定の年齢に達したりすると、親でもコントロールしきれませんが、だからといって子供への愛情がなくなるわけではありません。同じように、建物が成長する過程を見守るのも、建築家としての私の仕事だと思っています。よりよく育ってほしいとは願っていますけどね。

RH　そう考えない建築家も多いですよね？　自分の許可なく建物に手を加えられたとたん、「親子関係」をスッパリ切ってしまう建築家もいると思いますが……。

内藤　建築家は、いつまでも自分の作品に愛着を持ち続けるべきだと思います。そうすることで、使う人からのフィードバックを得ることができるし、社会における役割や責任も感じ取ることができますから。他人が手を加えたものは自分の作品ではない、と主張する建築家もいるかもしれませんが、それは、近代、とりわけ20世紀にはびこった「芸術のための芸術」という思想に根差した傲

慢な考え方だと思います。私は、建築の創造は社会への参加であると思うし、芸術と人間の協調を説いたカール・フリードリッヒ・シンケルや、ワルター・グロピウスなどの建築家にシンパシーを感じます。芸術と人間との関係には、20世紀の資本主義が、2つの足かせをはめたのだと思います。ひとつは、詳細な契約制度です。クライアントが契約書を用意して、建築家はその取り決めに従う義務を負う。もともと芸術はそんなシステムで生み出されるはずがない。契約は形式的なもので、信頼関係がベースにあるべきです。それがいつの間にか逆転してしまった。もうひとつは、マスコミの影響力です。近頃の建築家、とくに若い世代は、建物が完成すると、上手く写真を撮ってメディアに露出して、とにかく名前を売ろうと考えがちです。ものめずらしい情報を提供して売

内藤廣とスタッフのメンバー | Naito and his team (2001)

り上げ部数をのばしたいメディアと、そのメディアが生み出すスター建築家という構図の中で、ある種の共犯関係が成り立っているのです。近頃では、クライアントもこの関係に加わっています。そんな中では、建築は本当の意味での価値を発揮できていないのです。

RH　メディアが別の事実を作り上げてしまい、雑誌などに掲載される写真が、必ずしも現実の建築を忠実に伝えていない、ということですね？

内藤　それは根の深い問題です。ある出版社によると、年間4,000枚もの建築写真が持ち込まれるとのことです。もちろん、その出版社が4,000ヶ所を訪れ、すべてを実際に観るのは無理なので、建物の善し悪しを写真に頼ることになるわけです。結果として、写真映りが良いもの、メディアでわかりやすいものが流通していくのです。

RH　あなたの作品集の多くはモノクロですし、事務所にはアンセル・アダムスのモノクロ大判写真が飾ってありますが、なぜ白黒写真にこだわるのですか？

内藤　今の世の中に流通しているメディアでは、ほとんどの情報はカラーで伝えられています。けれども、カラーというものは、形やデザインは上手く伝えるのですが、その場所の空気やエネルギー、力を伝えるにはあまり向いていない。わたしは白黒写真が好きだし、わたしがこだわっているのも、その場所のエネルギーや空気の質感ですから、白黒写真にこだわるのです。

RH　今日のコンピューター・テクノロジーは建築家の仕事に、どのような影響を与えていますか？

内藤　この点に関しては楽観的に考えています。先程、芸術や建築と社会との関係についてお話ししましたが、インターネットによって、その関係性が改善するのではと考えています。建設の現場では、それぞれが非常に小さな専門分野に分かれているので、建物を作るという壮大な事業の中で、自分の仕事の位置を把握できる人がほとんどいないのが現状です。例えば、日本の原子力発電所で、小さな配管のひび割れが原因で事故が起こりましたが、その部品を作った職人が、事故のニュースをテレビで見て、原子力発電所に使われると知っていれば、もっと別のやり方で作った、と言ったそうです。つまり、ものづくりが細分化され過ぎていて、管理する機能ばかりが優先されているのです。イン

ターネットはこうした社会構造を変えていくはずです。つまり、細部と全体がインタラクティブにつながっていくのです。

RH テクノロジーがグローバル・スタンダード化を推し進め、建築の地域差を消し去る危険性はありませんか？

内藤 モダニスト的なインターナショナル・スタイルの建築が世界中に広まって、西欧でもアジアでも、猫も杓子も、同じスタイルを欲しがったのが今日の状況です。確かにインターネットは世界標準を推し進めるものですが、同時に世界中の誰もが特定の地域の文化的特色や伝統にアクセスできるものとなるのです。やがては、それぞれの文化的な特徴を相互に尊重し合う時代がくるのではないかと思っています。

RH ヨーロッパではエネルギー節約のために窓ガラスを二重にしていますが、自分の事務所に二重ガラスを使用していない点は気になりませんか？

内藤 このビルはそうとうボロボロですからね。でも、気に入っているんですよ。しっかりした箱を作り、内部空間をコントロールしようとするのは、いわゆる西洋的な近代建築の考えです。そこで空調や暖房器具、二重窓ガラスを用いれば、確かにエネルギーの節約にはなります。でも、そんな単純な話をエコロジカルと呼ぶことには違和感があります。真にエコロジカルな建築というのは、外部空間に向けて開かれているべきものです。これはわれわれ日本の文化の中で培ってきたものです。21世紀にわれわれが挑戦する新しいスタイルは、この考え方に基づくべきだと思っています。西洋の人は、日本の居住空間を非常に狭いといいますが、日本人というのは、もともと大きさに対してあまり関心がなかったのではないかと思います。日本人は、伝統的に内部空間と外部空間の関係がとても大事で、場合によっては、庭などの外部空間の方が大事だと考えてきたのだと思います。この考えを、建築でも都市でも活かすべきです。

RH もし自分のシェルターを作るとしたら、どのようなものになりますか？

内藤 コンクリートのような堅い素材で造られ、堅固でしっかりしたシェルターというコンセプトは好きではありません。防御の姿勢が強すぎるからです。結局、それは人目を引き、真っ先に破壊すべきターゲットになってしまうでしょう。シェルターは、ホームレスが使うような仮設のもので十分だと思います。

究極のシェルターとして関心があるのは、気候や自然に耐えられる身体そのものです。私が子供の頃、祖父が、早朝に氷点下の屋外に裸で出て、タオルで身体をこする乾布摩擦をして身体を鍛えていたことを思い出します。

RH　今、多くの日本人建築家は9.11に対して心を閉ざしています。建築雑誌を読んでも、誰も政治的な発言をしていません。あるシンポジウムで、9.11のようなテロ攻撃の対象となりうる透明性や開放性について、パネリストの建築家たちに尋ねたところ、沈黙が広がるのみでした。

内藤　透明性とは、現代建築における最も顕著な特徴でしょう。どういうわけか、それ自体が資本主義社会への恭順の姿勢をも意味しています。しかし、9.11以降、事情が変わってきたのではないでしょうか。より透明性を追求するべきなのか、そうでないのか。透明なシェルターなのか、堅牢な砦なのか、という問いかけは、建築家が社会にどう向き合うか、その姿勢の表明にもなってきているからです。

内藤廣 事務所にて｜Naito office Kudanshita, Tokyo (2011)

[パート2]──2011

RH 内藤さんは、渋谷の中心地区の再開発委員会の委員ですが、めまぐるしく変化する東京では、この20年間で建物が壊され、再び建てられということを繰り返してきました。そういう中で、結局、渋谷駅を中心に超高層建築が6棟も建つプロジェクトにかかわっています。そこで内藤さんが感じている一番の役割とは何ですか？

内藤 最近アジアの都市をいくつか見てきましたが、どこもグローバルな競争原理が最優先される、極端な商業主義に支配されていました。渋谷ではそれとは違ったアプローチをしたいと考えています。渋谷地域は多様性に溢れたビオトープのような場所で、それがあの街の個性になっています。店舗の隣に個人の小さな家、その隣に高層のオフィスビル、その隣に墓地、その隣には公園、というように、ともかくいろいろなものが共存しているのが魅力になっています。新しい開発計画は、こうした渋谷の特色を生かし、まったく新しい概念による都市空間を生み出そうとしています。日常的な生活感、伝統的な価値、質の高いデザイン、それでいてハイパーな機能性を持った、渋谷ならではの新しい都市空間を出現させたいと考えています。

RH それを決めるのは、内藤さんですか？

内藤 わたしもその一員ですが、もちろん、ひとりではできません。たくさんの人の合意が必要です。渋谷に住んでいる人たち、商業的な関心をもつ事業者、行政……そういう人たちの利害関係を無視して街はできません。また、事業的な側面や技術的な側面の合理性だけではなく、渋谷を訪れる人の気持ちや、そこで暮らす人の気持ちについても頭にいれておいてもらうよう、行政や事業者の人たちにお願いしています。そして、渋谷が若い世代に支持され、なおかつ生き生きとした多様性に溢れる街になるよう、10人あまりの日本の若手の建築家を招いて、デザインに加わってほしいと思っています。すでに素晴らしい実績をあげていますから、若手といえるかどうかわかりませんが、まずは隈研吾さんや妹島和世さんに参加してもらうことになっています。

RH 日本人は、20年間続いている経済の低迷にとらわれてしまっています。

そのような状態を考えると、次の20年間に向けて、何か楽観的なことを計画するというのは、とても挑戦的ではないですか？ それとも、これは現実を無視した希望ですか？

内藤 いやいや、私はリアリストですよ。私は20年前よりも今の方が面白いと思っています。この国は、これまでとは違った文化的なステージを迎えつつあるのです。日本は戦後、ひたすら経済復興を目指してきました。ともかく生きるために働かなくてはならなかったのです。ところが、この20年の停滞を経て、人々が生と死について考え始めています。問い直し始めているのです。会社のために働く以外に、どうすれば自分の存在に意味を与えることができるだろうか、と。「自分たちの文化に何が起きているのか？」「死について自分はどう向き合うのか？」「医学的な進歩はめざましいが、自分は本当に機械につながれてまで生きたいと思うだろうか？」かつては、それぞれの家には仏壇があり、寺や神社が近くにあって、一日の中で、短いけれど死者のために祈っていたものです。しかし、第二次大戦後は生きることに必死で、死を遠ざけてきたのです。当然のことながら、建築も都市も同様です。私たちは、生と死を100年前にわれわれの文化のなかで獲得していたような、バランスのとれたものにしたいと思い始めているのです。もちろん、昔に戻れと言っているのではありません。新しい時代の新しいバランスポイントを模索し始めているということを言いたいのです。それはまったく未知のものです。それは、十九世紀末、マーラー、クリムト、シーレ、フロイト、ホフマン、オルブリッヒ、ロースなどを生み出した、ウィーンで奇跡的に起こった文化の爛熟のようなものになる可能性だってあると思っています。

RH 日本がそのような新しい段階に入っているということに、いつ気がついたのですか？

内藤 以前から頭ではわかっていたのですが、はっきりと感じたのは2005年頃でしょうか。人口減少によって、将来社会的な変化が起こることを予想していた人は、当時はわずかでした。2005年から、この国の人口は減少に転じました。この傾向は、今後100年ぐらいは続きます。人口も経済もすべてのものが縮小していくのです。すでに中国に経済大国世界第2位の座を明け渡しました。

しかし、先ほども言ったように、文化的には、失ったものを通して、私たちが何者であるかを見つめなおすチャンスなのです。

RH 内藤さんが尊敬する、ダンサーで振付家のピナ・バウシュが2009年に亡くなりました。しかし、ダンスへの興味は依然失っていらっしゃらないですね。東京国立近代美術館で行われた展覧会で、何本もの赤い光の中で踊るダンサーたちのパフォーマンスがありました。建築とダンスを組み合わせた理由は何ですか？

内藤 建築をデカルト的なシステムの中だけで考えると、空間は精彩を欠いた冷たいものになってしまいます。しかし、肉体が介在することによって空間は新たなバランスを生み出し、さらに人間の特質をさらに深みのあるものにします。そのことを、やや極端な空間構成で表現したいと思いました。

RH 建築の中に、男性的な面と女性的な面の違いを見出すということはありますか？

内藤 そういう言葉を使うべきかどうかはわかりませんが、確かに2つの側面というものはあると思います。構造、そして壁や床や天井などのハードウェア、それらは構築的に作らざるを得ませんから、男性的な側面といえます。その一方で、私たちの建築の質を決めている目に見えない空間というのも存在します。やわらかく包み込むようで目には見えない。確かに存在するのだけれど、完全には理解することのできないもの。その意味で空間は女性的な存在だと言うことができます。建築家は、その両方の側面から建築について考えなければなりません。ですから、建築家はみんなバイセクシャル的な思考を持っていると言えるかも知れませんね。

内藤廣 東京にて ｜ Hiroshi Naito, Tokyo (2000)

Hiroshi Naito

"After World War II, people wanted to live again – just live! Kenzo Tange's work in the middle of Hiroshima, as an expression of hope, made sense at that time. But nowadays, to talk about architectural philosophies and movements is nonsense." Hiroshi Naito delivers his heretical opinion dryly, as if talking about bad weather with no change in sight. He projects the tranquil, Tristes Tropiques demeanor of an anthropologist who spends years in the rainforest and returns to civilization as a fatalist. Naito reveres the work of colleague Shigeru Ban, who builds shelters in Africa: "Such an act means taking on life-or-death responsibilities, the core – the heart of any architecture!"

As head of a committee for the redevelopment of Shibuya, one of Tokyo's busiest districts, Naito also tries to convince city officials to take into consideration the artistic views of architects like Kengo Kuma and Kazuyo Sejima. What Naito rejects is the superficial style-for-style's-sake approach of the contemporary design world, which is addicted to lifestyle magazine double-spreads. "Print media can be misleading," he warns. Naito's best-known statement is probably: "Architects assemble their work by using fragments from the future". He sees himself working in the mirror world of archeology, which re-assembles reality with fragments from the past. And where you have fragments, you need connectors – they form the spine of any Naito structure, the defining elements of his style (if 'style' can be used in relation to Naito). The former Tokyo University professor, who once worked for Kiyonori Kikutake, revels in this architectural netherworld of joining parts usually overlooked by admirers of buildings. At times Naito's structures appear as if created only to celebrate beauty – that of the connection techniques. The Sea-Folk Museum in Mie Prefecture is a good example; its intricate roof of thousands of wooden beams creates a sense of calm comparable to that inside an ancient cathedral. Naito has another obsession, too: dance. He adores the work of Pina Bausch, the famous choreographer, who passed away in 2009. "Dehumanization is the biggest threat to architecture," he says. "Sitting all day in front of a computer, you had better reconnect to humanity in the evening. That's why I love artful expressions of the body. Otherwise, we are just that – an assemblage of disconnected parts."

[**Interview part 1**]——2000-2007

Roland Hagenberg   In one of your essays you write, "It is the destiny of architecture to be eroded by time. Architecture should be like people, who age naturally even as they try to resist time." Does this mean you don't worry what might happen to your buildings once they are finished?

Hiroshi Naito   Not at all. When I complete a construction I let the building go. I really don't mind if people use it in a different way from what I had envisioned originally, or if it is changed so that people feel more comfortable in it. At the same time I am still attached to it. It's like a child-parent relationship. Usually parents try not to control their children, once they grew up or reached a certain age, which doesn't mean they stopped loving them. The relationship between an architect and his buildings is very similar. To observe this process of growing up is part of my work. I do hope that it ages in a healthy way.

RH   Not all architects would agree with you, some of them severe this parent-child relationship immediately, if their building is altered without their permission.

HN   I believe, an architect should always stay attached to his buildings. That way he can get feedback from the general public. It makes him aware of his social role and responsibilities. To think, that a building, which was changed by someone else, is no longer part of an architect's life, is an arrogant attitude, rooted in the 20th century, where the idea of art for art's sake was dominant. I feel closer to legendary architects such as Karl Friedrich Schinkel or Walter Gropius who said "producing architecture is participating in society". They established a link between art and the people. 20th century capitalism, however, put two restraints on this relationship. One is the so-called "detailed contract system", where a client prepares a contract and the architect has to follow it exactly, section by section, in order to satisfy the client's wishes. In this kind of system the architect became less society oriented. Art is never born of such systems. Contracts should only be a formality and the real foundation should be a relationship of trust, things are going in a different direction these days. The second restraint emerged with the influence of the media. Nowadays the ambition of many architects is to complete their buildings, shoot great photos and have them published in the hope to get famous. The media and the star architects created by the media are in cahoots. And lately, clients are also playing a role in this scheme. In such a situation the real value of architecture cannot be expressed.

RH   It creates a second reality. Buildings in magazines don't always look like those in real life.

HN   This is a fundamental problem. I once talked to an editor who said that every year he receives photographs of 4000 buildings. Of course he cannot visit all these sites personally. He relies on colorful pictures instead. As a result, buildings that look good in photographs, and are easier for the media to understand, become popular.

RH   Your own catalogues are in black and white. Your office is adorned with a big black and white Ansel Adams photograph. Why this monochrome obsession?

HN   Black and white photography is very good for capturing the feeling of air and space and it can trigger the imagination better than color. I like black-and-white pictures and I am very sensitive about expressing the energies and the atmosphere that surrounds a place. That's why I still go for black-and-white pictures.

RH   How does today's computer technology influence your work as an architect?

HN   I am pretty optimistic about that. I mentioned before the link between art, architecture and society. I believe that Internet technology can re-introduce this relationship again. In terms of constructing buildings, all the specialists in Japan are isolated in very small sections, in which nobody knows anymore what he or she is producing within the larger context. You probably remember the nuclear accident at a Japanese processing plant where a tiny light bulb cracked. When one craftsman saw the news of the accident on TV he said "Oh, if I could have known, that this bulb would be used for a nuclear plant, I would have produced it in a different way." The construction process is divided into so many segments. The priority now is how to manage the segments. I think the internet can change this structure. It allows the smaller parts to connect with the whole system in an interactive way.

RH   The windows in your office don't have double-glazing as is usually the case in Europe to conserve energy. Doesn't that bother you?

HN   I don't agree with you on this issue. You are referring here to a very Western idea of modern architecture, which basically is to construct a box and control the interior space. Within this control-oriented architecture people use air conditioners, heaters or double-glazed windows. It might be energy-wise but it's not ecological. Truly ecological architecture should be open to outside space and in that context I could see a new style develop for the 21st century. It is true that many Westerners

内藤廣 事務所にて ｜ Hiroshi Naito office, Tokyo (2011)

think our housing standards are quite low. Western people might say it's a pity to live in such small spaces. But Japanese are not so much concerned about scale. For them, how the building interacts with the outside space has always been more important. Eventually I think there will come a day when we all share and respect each other's cultural uniqueness.

RH If you would have to build a shelter for yourself – how would it look like?

HN I don't like the concept of a solid, fixed shelter made of hard materials like concrete. It's much too defensive. It attracts attention and makes an easy target for those who want to destroy it. A temporary shelter like the homeless use it would be enough. I like the idea of my body being the ultimate shelter which can withstand weather and nature. I still remember my grandfather who got up very early every morning, stepped outside in minus-degree weather and poured ice-cold water over his body to toughen himself.

RH Nowadays, many young Japanese architects close their minds. You look at architectural magazines and nobody addresses political issues. At symposiums I sometimes ask about the transparency and openness of society and face a wall of silence.

HN Transparency is the most important requirement of modern architecture. Somehow transparency became a flag to pledge allegiance to capitalism. However, after 9/11 the situation changed. Shall we respond with more transparency or with less, which would mean to build either transparent shelters or strong fortresses. It all depends on how architects commit themselves to our society.

[**Interview part 2**]——2011

Roland Hagenberg You are currently a member of a committee that represents the interests of the citizens of Shibuya. Within twenty years, this bustling Tokyo district will be razed and rebuilt. As a result, six new skyscrapers will be erected around Shibuya station. What is your role in this process?

Hiroshi Naito I've studied many modern cities in Asia and they're all defined by competitive commerce. I would like to take a different approach. The district of Shibuya is a biotope: small family houses next to shops, next to high rise office buildings, next to cemeteries, next to parks, and so on. Shibuya is a diverse town and the small private houses make it unique. They might sit next to a store, a high-rise building, or a cemetery, or park. The fusion of various types of buildings adds to the charm of a city. The new development project should preserve the unique charm of Shibuya. For that we need a new concept for the city landscape: a symbiosis that takes into account traditional values, the fabric of daily life and quality design, while adding the functionality of a modern city. I hope it can be achieved.

RH   And you can decide all that?

HN   Of course not. As chairman of the committee, I can make suggestions that are in the interests of the residents of Shibuya and those who will most likely be caught between commercial interest and government rules and regulations. I suggest to developers and the government that they keep in mind not only the functionality of the design, but also the feeling of the people who visit or live in Shibuya. And in order to make Shibuya a lively, diverse city that the younger generation also likes, I want to invite about ten young Japanese architects to contribute to the design. They are already established architects, so I don't know if they can actually be called

内藤廣 建設現場にて | Hiroshi Naito at construction site (2011)

"young". First on board will be Kuma and Sejima.

RH The Japanese are caught in an economic downturn that has already lasted two decades. With that in mind, is it a challenge to plan something optimistic for the next twenty years – or is that just blind hope?

HN No, no. I am a very realistic person. But I think the Japan of the present is more interesting than the Japan of 20 years ago. This country is entering a completely new cultural stage. Postwar Japan strove for economic success alone. There was no choice other than to work in order to live. For the first time in Japan's post-war history, people are thinking about life and death. They wake up and ask themselves how they can give meaning to their existence, other than through working for a company. "What has happened to my culture?" they ask. "What is my position on death? Yes, we have revolutionary medical solutions but do I really want to live on forever tied to a machine?" We must again find the right balance between life and the end of life as it was 100 years ago. Each house had its butsudan (place for offerings), a temple or shrine was nearby, and you had a short prayer during the day to remember the dead. But after WWII people were too focused on living from day to day and didn't give any thought to death. Cities and their architecture went in that direction too. Today we again feel that we want a balance of life and death, as we had it 100 years ago in Japan. Of course, I am not saying that we should turn back time. I am saying that we are beginning to search for a new balance in a new era – it's a big unknown. Eventually, this search could lead to a magical change in culture similar to what happened in Vienna at the turn of the 19th century when Gustav Mahler, Sigmund Freud, Gustav Klimt, Otto Wagner and many others emerged.

RH When did you become aware that Japan was entering this new phase?

HN I would say around 2005. At that time only a few people speculated about the coming changes due to the population decrease. Since 2005 pretty much everything has shifted into reverse. There's no more obsessive post-war growth, but instead, downsizing on all fronts: income, output, confidence. Last year, China took our old position as the second largest economy in the world. But, as I said, this is our chance to find out who we are through what we've lost.

RH You've always admired performance artist Pina Bausch, who died in 2009. Since her death you have not lost your interest in dance. In a recent exhibition at the National Museum of Modern Art in Tokyo you had dancers performing between

内藤廣 東京にて | Hiroshi Naito, Tokyo (2011)

bundled beams of red light. What did that have to do with architecture?

HN If you only think of architecture within a Cartesian system – in abstract terms, and number-dependant – it creates a lifeless and cold atmosphere. But a body traversing abstract coordinates creates a balance and adds a human dimension. I wanted to express that.

RH Can you identify male and female dimensions in architecture?

HN I don't know if I should use those terms, but there are certainly two aspects. One is the hardware with walls, structure, floor and so on – the male side, so to speak. On the other hand we have invisible space, which defines the quality of our architecture. It is invisible, but softly surrounds us. It is certainly there, but we cannot fully understand it. So, in that sense, space can be referred to as female. Architects have to think in both directions. So, architecturally speaking, they are all bi-sexual.

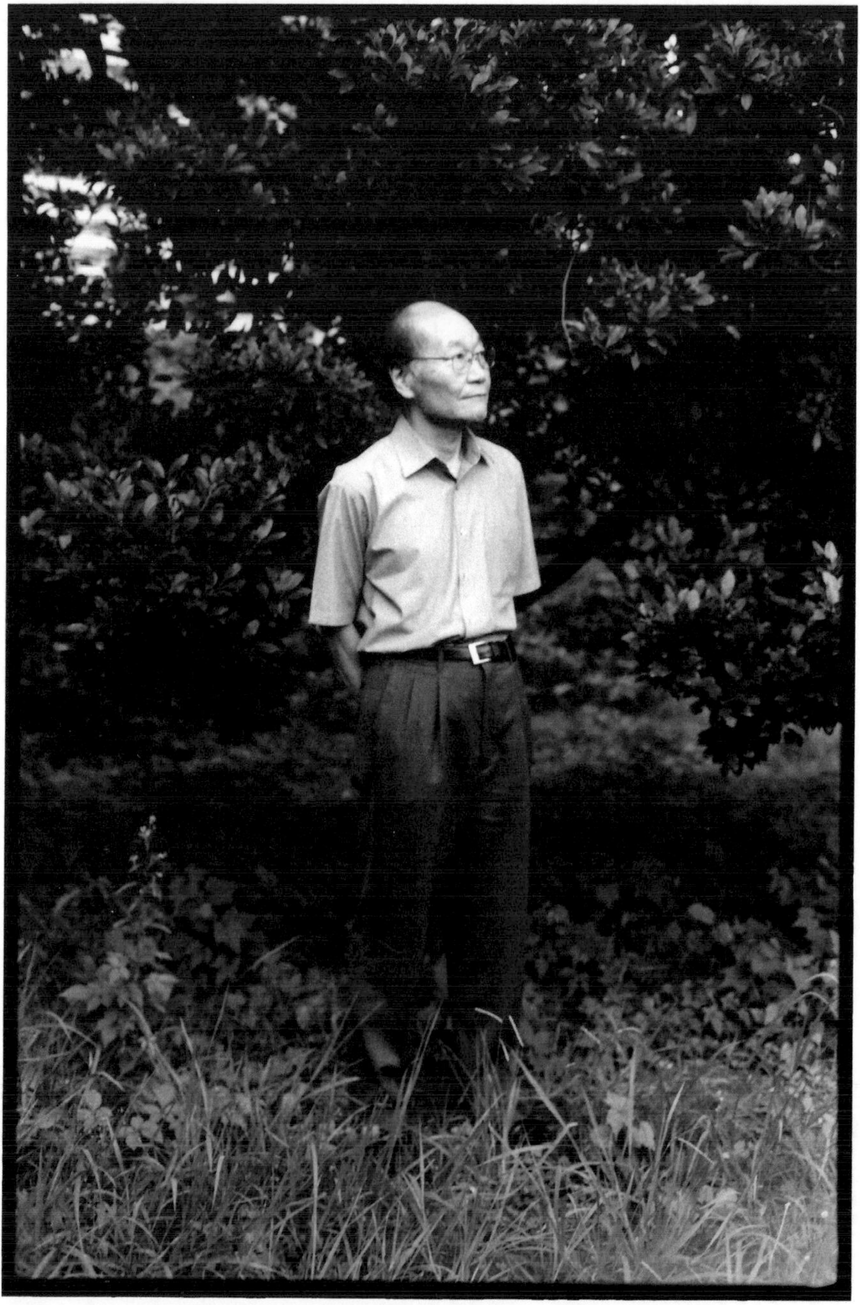

坂本一成 | Kazunari Sakamoto

建築家として、私は気持ちを数字に置き換えて伝えなければならないのです。
"As an architect I must translate feelings into numbers."

1943年、東京生まれ。1966年に東京工業大学建築学科を卒業して、1991年から2009年まで同大学の教授を務める。彼の住居のコンセプトは、批評家、多木浩二の「日常の中にある気づかない自由な空間」と、社会的な文脈に基づいている。彼の建築は、しばしば篠原一男の建築と比較される。村野藤吾賞、日本建築学会賞などを受賞。おもなプロジェクトに、「工作連盟ジードルンク・ヴィーゼンフェルト」(ドイツ・ミュンヘン)、Hut T(山梨)、プロジェクトUC(東京)などがある。

Born 1943 in Tokyo. Graduated from the architectural department of Tokyo Institute of Technology in 1966 and has been there as professor from 1991 to 2009. Sakamoto's residential building concepts are based on philosopher Koji Taki's recognition of "the unnoticed free space of everyday life" and its social context. Sakamoto's work is often associated with the "Kazuo Shinohara school of thought" He received numerous prizes like the Togo Murano Prize and the Architectural Institute of Japan Award (AIJ). Projects include Werkbundsiedlung Wiesenfeld in Munich, Hut T in Yamanashi and

坂本一成 東京工業大学にて | Kazunari Sakamoto in front of Tokyo Institute of Technology (2007)

坂本一成

夏も終わりに近づいたある日の夕方、坂本一成は東京工業大学の中にある公園を歩いていた。この時期になれば、蚊もほとんどいないはずなのだが、この時に限って大挙して押し寄せ、坂本の眼鏡の縁のまわりをぶんぶんと飛び回っていた。彼はそれを全く気にもせず、ポートレートを撮るために、じっとカメラを見つめ、散歩を続けてくれた。400戸のアパートに沿って歩きながら、彼の頭の中には、国際的なコンペで優勝したミュンヘンの工作連盟ジードルンクのことがあったのかもしれない。しかし、このプロジェクトは、保育施設をめぐる地元政治家と住民団体の間でもめ、着工が遅れていた。今回も、いつものように坂本は芸術的な直感に従って設計し、20人ほどのスタッフ（准教授、専門のアシスタント、大学院生）が彼の仮定した論理を数学的に実証していた。

坂本は1983年から最近まで、ここ東工大で教えていた（2009年に退官、同大学の名誉教授に）。彼のデザインは、空港や駅、高層ビルといった巨大プロジェクトではなく、小規模な住宅のつつましく実用的なスタイルで知られている。

坂本一成 「Hut T」| Kazunari Sakamoto, Hut T, Yamanashi, Japan (2001)

東京、2007

ローランド・ハーゲンバーグ[以下 RH]　ご自分の建築事務所を「実験室」と呼ぶのはどうしてですか？

坂本一成[以下 坂本]　私たちの建築設計する拠点が大学の研究室であるからです。ですから私たちは建築の設計だけでなく、建築のデザインに関する研究をしています。建築の設計は直感的に行うことが多いのですが、その直感が正しいかどうかの、証拠も見つけたいのです。

RH　あなたの直感が正しいという証拠ですか？

坂本　直感が正しいかどうかは、論理化できるか否かだと思います。ドイツ・ミュンヘンの「工作連盟ジードルンク」のようなコンペのプレゼンテーションで審査委員に私の直感を信じてくださいなんて言えません。結局、私は思いを論理化し、あるいは数字に置き換えて伝えなければならないのです。

RH　建築に対して——少なくとも、プロジェクトのスタート段階では——とても詩的なアプローチの仕方だと思います。「工作連盟ジードルンク」のプロジェクトのときは、いつ感情が数字におきかわったんでしょうか？

坂本　私たちは模型から計画の検討を始めることが多いのです。何がうまくいって、何がうまくいかないかを、個別のパーツごとに対応し、検討して、それらを鳥瞰的視点で観察します。おっしゃったように、詩を作るときに、言葉をあれこれ考えているようなものです。マニュアルにしたがって書いても、いい詩はできません。私の言葉は、道を歩いているとき、公園、陰影、ベランダ、素材や、いろいろな高さのアパートなどから出てきます。もし、それを1ページにおさめなくてはいけない詩として、建築に置き換えると、その1ページは予算の制約ということになるでしょう。何日も、何週間もかけて、ひとつの方向が定まってくるんです。私がバランスすなわち調和を感じたときが、その建築も釣り合いがとれているということです。「工作連盟ジードルンク」では、高さの違う3種類の住棟が敷地である場所に建っています。色々検討した結果、最後にはこの3つの異なる階数の建物の集合に落ち着くのです。このことは私自身が心地よいと思う構成にした結果です。その構成は、4、8、11階建てでした。なぜこの場所に4、8、11のフロアの住

棟が必要なのか、論理的な説明が必要です。そのプレゼンテーションが求められます。

RH こういう報告書は、何ページくらいになるのですか?

坂本 時には、何百ページにもなることもあるでしょうが、様々だと思います。フロアの階数などは単純な例ですが、さらに個々の問題もあります。たとえば、「工作連盟ジードルンク」の模型を見たときに、特に開放的な印象を持たれるでしょうが、同時に、そこに住むことを考えたとき、保護し守らなければならないことも多くあります。ここには塀もなく、守るという要素はないように見えるでしょうが、そのための対応が様々な部分にあります。

RH もし、坂本さんの直感が間違っているとチームの人たちが感じた場合は、どうするのですか?

坂本 そのときによると思いますが、直感と論理が争うのだったら、私は直感の方を信じます。

RH それでは、あなたの直感では、未来の東京の建築はどうなると思いますか? この都市の混沌とした空間——高速道路のランプが、居間のすぐ隣を通っているような——は、再生できるのでしょうか?

坂本 私は希望があると思います。解決方法もあります。そして、その新しいアイデアは日本だけでなくグローバルに有効だと思います。

RH ヨーロッパでは、やはり日本より仕事がやりやすいですか?

坂本 ヨーロッパでは、ディスカッションがより真剣で、深いところをついていると感じます。ひとりの人のアイデアに対して、特に敬意が払われ、吟味されていると思います。ヨーロッパの建築には長い歴史がありますからね。

RH もし日本人の建築家がヨーロッパのコンペで勝ったとしたら、それはヨーロッパの人々が日本人に日本的な美意識を求めているからなのでしょうか?

坂本 日本的、あるいは東洋的な曖昧さがヨーロッパの新しい建築、都市に有効だと思われたのでしょう。

RH 一日をはじめるとき、あらかじめ決められたことをてきぱきやるほうですか、それとも、直感的にやりたいようにやりますか?

坂本 朝は決められたとおりにやるほうですね。8時に起きて、朝食をとり、シャワー

をあびます。11時に家を出て大学に向かい、研究室には夜遅くまでいます。家に着くのはだいたい夜の11時頃ですね。

RH 8時から11時ですか……8と11という数字は、「工作連盟ジードルンク」と同じですね。

坂本 そうですね。スタッフにその時間で動いてもらわなければならないからではないでしょうかね。

坂本一成 東京にて│Kazunari Sakamoto, Tokyo (2007)

Kazunari Sakomoto

It is the end of summer and the sun is setting as Professor Kazunari Sakamoto walks through the park at the Tokyo Institute of Technology. At this time of year mosquitoes are rare, but today they are out in force, dancing randomly around the rims of Sakamoto's glasses. He ignores them, stares patiently into the camera for a portrait and continues his pensive walk. The Werkbundsiedlung in Munich is on his mind, along with an apartment complex of 400 units – the project that won him the international competition. But breaking new ground was delayed by local politicians and citizens' groups at odds over a childcare facility. With this project, as with all of his projects, Sakamoto worked by artistic instinct, and his staff mathematically verified his assumptions. Sakamoto has been teaching at the Tokyo Institute since 1983 and became professor emeritus after his retirement in 2009. He is not known for mega-projects like airports, train stations and skyscrapers, but for small houses, in which he cultivates a modest, practical style.

坂本一成 東京工業大学にて | Kazunari Sakamoto at Tokyo Institute of Technology, 2006

Tokyo, 2007

Roland Hagenberg Why do you call your architectural office a 'laboratory'?

Kazunari Sakamoto Because the center of our architectural design is located in the university laboratory, which means we not only design, but also study architectural design. My work is often based on instincts, so here I can find out if it is correct or not.

RH Proof that your instinct is correct?

KS I think you can say that if the instinct is correct you can explain it logically. For example, I can't enter a design in a competition, such as the one for the Werkbund Siedlung, and ask the judges to accept my instincts. It is necessary for me to logically put down my thoughts and explain them using numbers.

RH A very poetic approach to architecture – at least in the start-up phase of a project. In the case of your Werkbundsiedlung, when did emotions turn into numbers?

KS I often begin with models. We use a bird's eye view to examine individual parts and find out what works and what doesn't. As you say, it is like moving around words in a poem. You cannot write good poems if you go by a manual. My words are made of streets, parks, shadows, balconies, materials and apartment blocks with various heights. If the poem has to fit on one page, then, architecturally, this page translates into budget restraints. Over days or weeks a direction takes shape. If I sense balance and harmony it might confirm the correctness of architectural proportions. At the Werkbundsiedlung, there are three apartment blocks. After some consideration, I came to the decision to build three buildings of different heights. This was the outcome of my gut feeling. The answer in that case was to design buildings of 4, 8 and 11 floors. And to explain why 4, 8 and 11 floors are necessary in that area, a logical explanation is required.

RH How extensive is such a report......how many pages?

KS Sometimes hundreds of pages. The amount of floors is just a simple example – there are more intrinsic aspects, too, of course. Like, when I look at the model of the Werkbundsiedlung it has a very open feeling to it, but at the same time, when I imagine living inside it evokes an atmosphere of protection. Where does that come from? There are no walls; I have not considered defensive elements. To prove all that

坂本一成 事務所にて | Sakamoto Office Tokyo (2007)

I have to go beyond the beauty of geometry.

RH What happens if your team finds out that your instinct was wrong?

KS That depends. My instinct cannot be muted easily by formulas. If it really comes down to a conflict between instinct and logic, I would say I make sure that my instinct prevails.

RH And what does your instinct say about the architectural future of Tokyo? Can this urban chaos – with highway ramps passing by next to living rooms – ever reinvent itself?

KS I think there is hope and there are solutions. However, to implement those solutions in Japan they must first be tried abroad. If the Japanese see that a new idea is successful in other countries they suddenly want to make use of it at home, but only then. If someone tries to implement a new idea first in Japan, he or she will most likely fail.

RH Is working as an architect in Europe easier than in Japan?

KS In Europe, discussions are more serious and profound. More respect is shown towards your ideas and you are more scrutinized, I guess, because of Europe's long architectural history.

RH If a Japanese architect wins a competition in Europe, is it also because Europeans expect from a Japanese architect Japanese aesthetics?

KS It's probably that Japanese or Asian "fuzziness" must have been considered useful to Europe's new architecture and cities.

RH Do you start your day systematically or by intuition?

KS I would say very systematically. I get up at eight, have my breakfast and then a shower. I leave my home at eleven and stay at the university, where I have my office-laboratory, until late at night. I am back at home again around eleven.

RH I noticed the numbers eight and eleven – just like in your Werkbundsiedlung!

KS You are right. I guess I have to let my staff work on that.

西沢立衛と妹島和世 東京にて | Ryue Nishizawa and Kazuyo Sejima, Tokyo (2007)

妹島和世 | Kazuyo Sejima
西沢立衛 | Ryue Nishizawa / SANAA

私たちの意見が全く同じだったら、沈黙するでしょう。
"If our opinions would be the same, we would be mute."

妹島和世

1956年茨城県生まれ。1981年日本女子大学大学院修了。伊東豊雄建築設計事務所勤務を経て、1987年妹島和世建築設計事務所設立。1995年西沢立衛とSANAA設立。主な作品に、再春館製薬女子寮(熊本)、西沢立衛と共同で、飯田市小笠原資料館(長野)、金沢21世紀美術館(石川)、ニュー・ミュージアム・オブ・コンテンポラリー・アートなどがある。

Kazuyo Sejima

Born 1956 in Ibaraki Prefecture. Received master degree from Japan Women's University in 1981. Worked at Toyo Ito & Associates. Established her practice 1987. Established SANAA with Ryue Nishizawa in 1995. Major works include Saishunkan Seiyaku Women's Dormitory in Kumamoto, O-Museum (Ogasawara Museum)in Nagano and 21st Century Museum of Contemporary Art, Kanazawa in Ishikawa and the New Museum of Contemporary Art in New York.

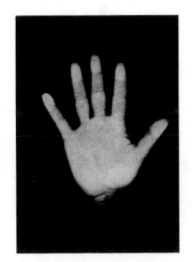

西沢立衛

1966年神奈川県生まれ。1990年横浜国立大学大学院修了。妹島和世建築設計事務所勤務を経て、1995年妹島和世とSANAAを設立。1997年西沢立衛建築設計事務所設立。主な作品に、ウィークエンドハウス(群馬)、森山邸(東京)、妹島和世と共同で、国際情報科学芸術アカデミーマルチメディア工房(岐阜)など。妹島と共に、プリツカー賞、日本建築学会賞(1998、2006年)などを受賞。

Ryue Nishizawa

Born 1966 in Kanagawa Prefecture. Received Master Degree from Yokohama National University 1990. Worked at Kazuyo Sejima & Associates. Established SANAA with Kazuyo Sejima in 1995. Established his practice 1997. Major works include IAMAS Multimedia Studio in Gifu, Weekend House in Gunma and Moriyama House in Tokyo. Numerous awards together with Kazuyo Sejima such as Pritzker Architectural Prize, Architectural Institute of Japan Award (1998, 2006).

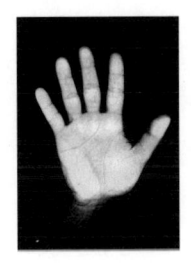

妹島和世、西沢立衛

ニューヨークのダウンタウン、工場を改装したロフト風のアトリエは、アーティストなら世界中の誰もが憧れる。しかし、彼らの多くにとって、そんな夢のような環境には手が届くはずもない。東京であればなおさらのこと。生活空間も足りないのに、ロフトをもつなんてもってのほかだ。しかし、妹島和世と西沢立衛は、東京・辰巳にちょうどいい場所を見つけた（品川の倉庫、セメント工場の隣り、ファッションデザイナー山本耀司のところから歩いてすぐのアトリエからは引越した）。

彼らの実習生がアトリエの場所を教えてくれたのだが、そこにたどりつくのは簡単ではなかった。やっとアトリエにたどり着いた時、スプレー缶のシューッという音とともに、シンナーと糊のにおいが鼻をついた。世界各地からきている実習生たちが、まるで幼虫を持ったアリのように、白い発泡スチロールのボードの回りに群がっていた。ここで、ニューヨークのニュー・ミュージアム・オブ・コンテンポラリー・アート（豆腐の塔のような形をしている）や、金沢21世紀美術館、ローザンヌのロレックス・ラーニングセンターなどのプロジェクトが形づくられるのだ。

木の棚がある長い廊下をぬけると、ようやくSANAA（イエメンの首都ではない。Sejima and Nishizawa Associated Architects の略）の聖域だ。西沢用のスペースはさらに木の棚で区切られていて、折りたたみ式のベッドが置いてある（寝ることは死ぬようなものだと西沢は言った）。天井は数メートルもの高さがある。そこでは、何人もの意欲的な建築家たちが、ものでいっぱいになったデスクにかじりついていた。彼らは皆、黒い色を着ていて、目の下にはくまができていた。徹夜をしたり、床に寝るのも、締切を目前にした彼らにとっては当たり前のことだ。そして、いつかプリツカー賞をとった妹島と西沢のように自分のデザインした建築が「Architecutural Digest」に載る日を夢見ている。

[パート1] —— 2000

ローランド・ハーゲンバーグ[以下RH]　自分たちの建築を日本的だと思いますか？

妹島和世[以下 妹島]　特に日本的とは思っていませんが、外国の人は、そう思うのかも知れません。日本で創っているのは事実ですから。

西沢立衛[以下 西沢]　僕たちは日本的な建築だとは思っていなくても、外からそう言われるのです。

RH　でも、なぜ外国人はそう言うのですか？

西沢　よく分かりません。言葉が違うからではないでしょうか？

妹島和世 東京にて | Kazuyo Sejima, Tokyo (2010)

RH　設計のプロセスを通して、デザインやスタイルが決まってくるものですか？

妹島　まず、クライアントからの条件に則って、スタッフ全員がたくさんの模型を作ります。それを比較検討して、可能な限りのオプションを考えます。この段階ではスタッフひとりひとりが個別に仕事をしていますので、それぞれが異なった視点を持ち込むことになります。それぞれが模型を持ちよって話し合いをするということを何度も繰り返します。こういった一連のプロセスの中で建物の性格を決定するアイデアが生まれてきます。

西沢　例えば、僕がアイデアを思いついたとしても、模型にしてみないことには判断がつきません。今日はA案が一番だとしても、明日にはD案が一番ということになるかも知れませんし、判断するには時間が必要ですから。

RH　建築家の仕事の中で、どの部分が一番好きですか？

西沢　好きなところが2つあります。ひとつは、自分でスタディをしていて、良いアイデアを思いついたときです。2つめは、建物が立ち上がったときです。躯体が立ち上がった時はいつも、それを見に行きたくなります。自分が考えていたことが、どういった形で実現されているか、どういう形で立ち上がったのかを見るのが、すごく好きです。

RH　写真撮影もしますか？

妹島　ええ。後から写真を見るのが楽しみです。カメラの種類は関係なくて、インスタント・カメラでもいいくらいです。写真を整理したり、ラベルを貼って分類する時間がないのが問題で、靴箱に入れっぱなしの写真がどんどん増えています。

西沢　妹島さんは仕切るのが上手というか、全体をコントロールするタイプなのですが、写真ばかりはコントロールできてないという感じです。

RH　建築写真は真実を伝えるものでしょうか？ それとも、真実を曲げてしまっているのでしょうか？

西沢　ケース・バイ・ケースだと思います。一般論でいえば、写真と現実は完全に別のものですが、写真が伝える世界が現実の世界にインスピレーションを与えることはありますし、現実の世界が優れた写真を誘発する場合もあります。つまり、お互いは常に影響しあっているのです。

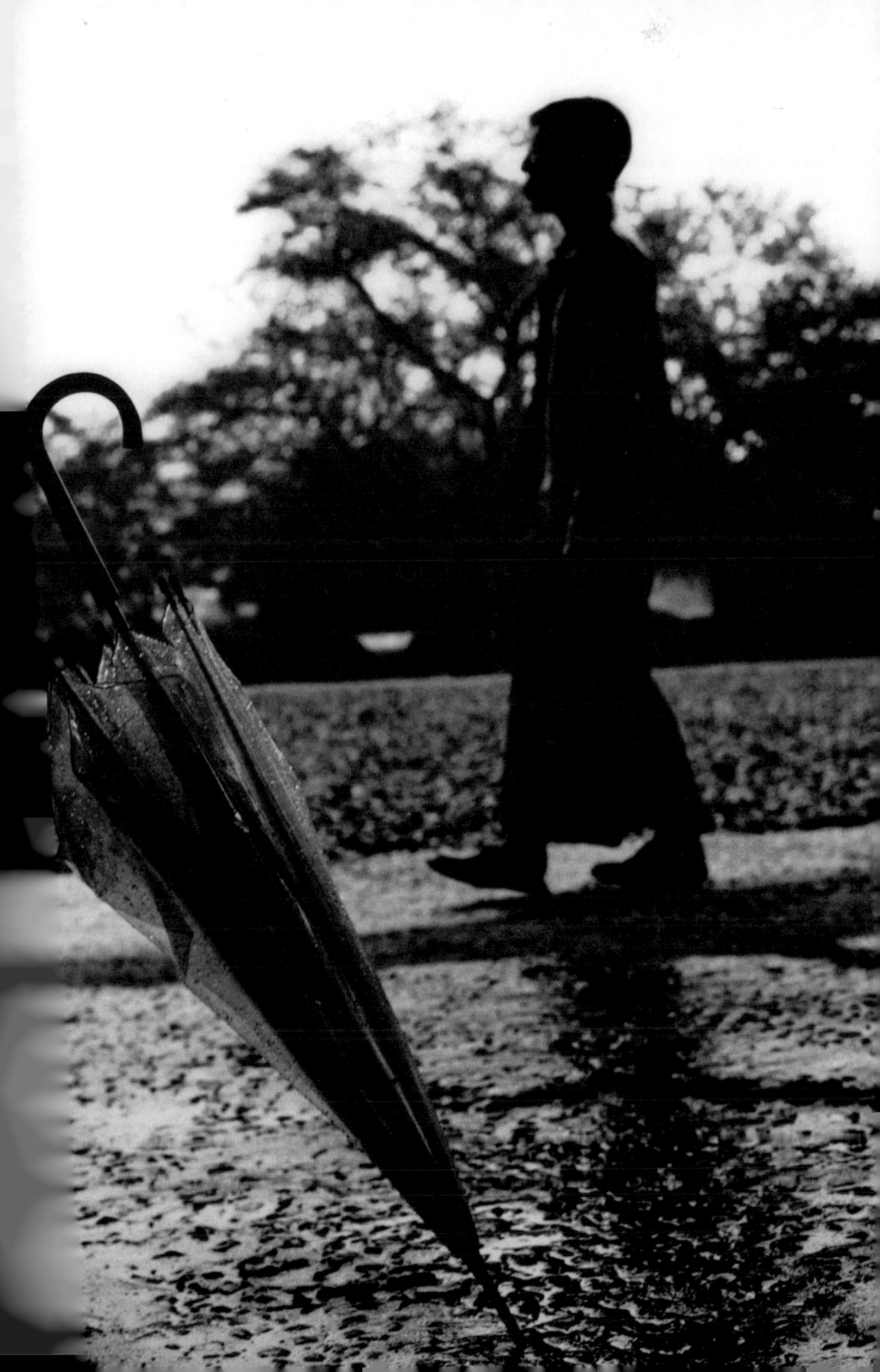

例えば、写真家が僕たちの建築を撮影する場合、僕たちが思ってもみなかった角度から撮ることがあります。それが、僕たちの後の仕事に影響を与え、写真家のおかげで新たな視点を獲得することもあります。そこでは、写真家がよき評論家となったわけです。逆に、建築が写真家を刺激して、写真家の見方を変えるということもあります。つまり、お互いに異なるからこそコミュニケーションが発生するということで、双方向に影響するのです。

———————

[パート2]——2010

RH 2010年、妹島さんは、西沢立衛さんとともに、プリツカー賞を受賞しました。将来の建築の方法として、今世界は、日本流のやり方に期待しているのでしょうか。

妹島 日本的な、もしくはアジア的なといったほうが良いかもしれませんが、建築の内部空間と外部空間のやわらかな関係のあり方について興味をもたれていると思います。それから、小ささということ、体と建築のスケールの関係についても私たちには独自のやり方があるように思います。

RH 畳や障子などの伝統的な生活必需品はいつまで残るでしょうか？

妹島 10年前まではクライアントから、使うかどうかわからないにもかかわらず、ほとんど100パーセント畳の部屋を作るように言われたと思います。今はそういう要求を受けることはほとんどありません。現実的には畳は少なくなってきていると思います。でも、畳や障子が作り上げていた様々な関係性は、今でもいろいろな形で私たちの生活の周りにあります。

RH 日本の伝統的な要素が姿を消しつつある一方で、ヨーロッパの人々の日本建築の美学への興味がこれほどまでに強い時代はなかったのではないでしょうか？　これについてはどう思われますか？

妹島 今までにそれほどなかったかどうかはよくわかりません。今は、日本の建築が持つまわりとの関係の中にある軽さ、多様さというものに興味がもたれているのではないかと思います。

RH あなたの基本方針となるテーマの、もうひとつの新しいプロジェクトに、

瀬戸内海でのプロジェクトがありますね。犬島という小さな島には、約30の家族が昔からの木造の家に住んでいる。島民の平均年齢は70歳をこえていて、若い人は皆島を出ていってしまったそうですね。でも、島内に分散する美術館として10軒の家を改築、改装したいと考えている、と。これは失われつつある生活様式を懐かしむということですか？

妹島　この計画は、小さな集落の中のいくつかの民家をギャラリーに改装し、集落全体が美術館になるというものです。そこにある木造建築は、別に建築的に価値があるというものではなく、ごく一般的なもので、何年か前まで普通に使われていたものです。ですが、注意深く見てみると、材料や部材の大きさな

妹島和世 飯田市小笠原資料館にて ｜ Kazuyo Sejima at Ogasawara Museum, Japan (2000)

妹島和世 飯田市小笠原資料館にて | Kazuyo Sejima at Ogasawara Museum, Japan (2000)

ど様々なものが犬島の風景を作り上げることに大きく関わっているのに気づき、できるだけそこにあるものを使おうと考えました。その上で新しいものが必要なところには、アクリルやアルミなどの現代的な要素を取り入れて、既存の集落の風景とアート、そしてそこにある島の生活が交じり合った、新しい風景を作れないかなと考えました。

RH　学生や若いスタッフの中に、将来への発展のヒントとなるような、新しい姿勢を見つけることはありますか？

妹島　基本的には若い人の方が新しいことを考えられる可能性を持っていると思います。

SANAAライディング・プロジェクト展覧会のための模型 建築博物館、ウィーン |
SANAA model for Raiding Project Exhibition, Architecture Museum Vienna, 2010

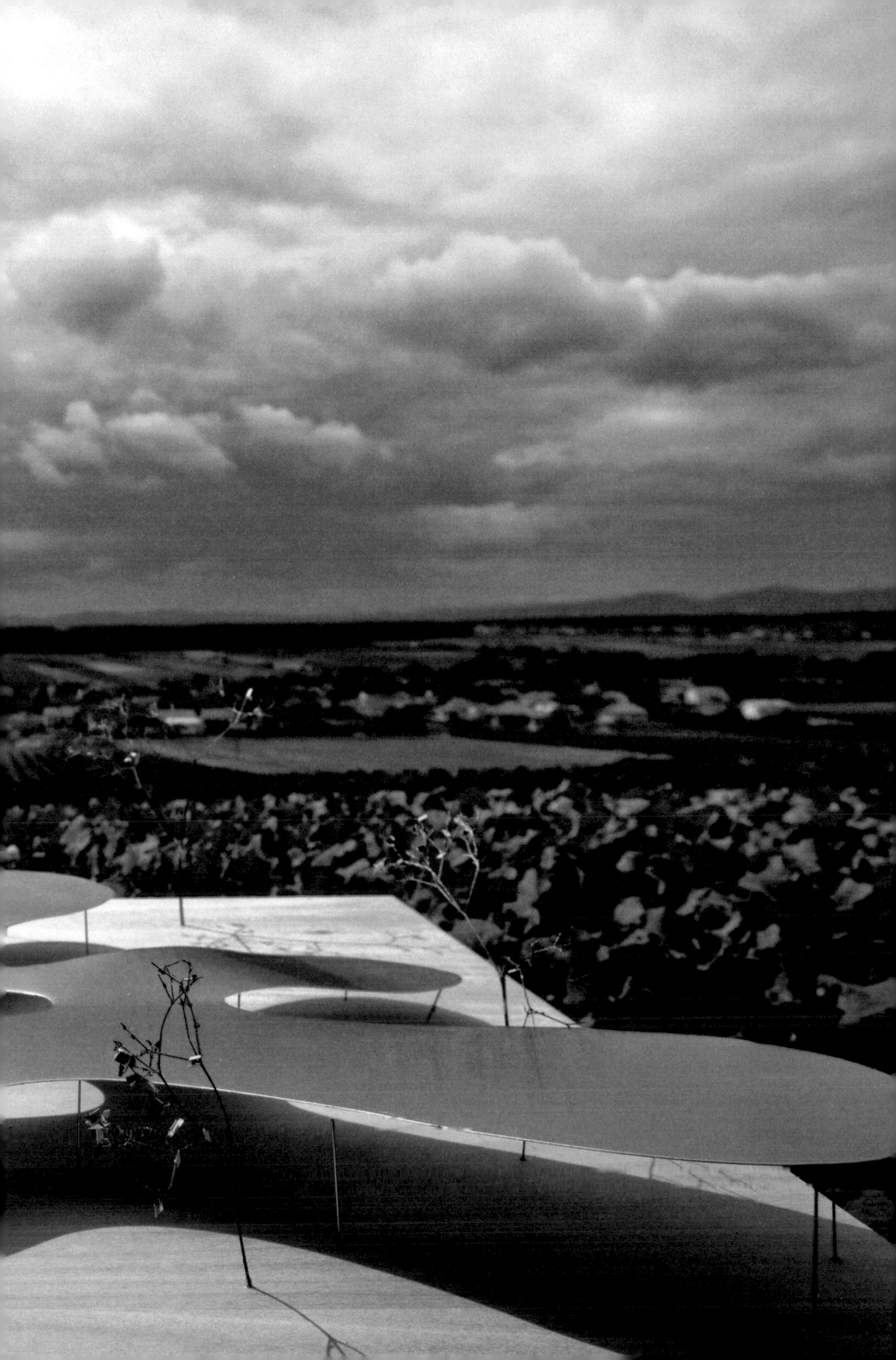

妹島和世 モデルとともに | Kazuyo Sejima with model, Tokyo (2005)

Kazuyo Sejima and Ryue Nishizawa

Fashioned on converted factory spaces in downtown New York, lofts have become the style of choice when it comes to studios for artists all over the world. For many of them, however, such a dream environment is financially out of reach, and if you are in Tokyo, with its lack of living space, a loft looks even more remote. But Kazuyo Sejima and her partner Ryue Nishizawa, 10-years her junior, have found just that – in Tokyo's Tatsumi district (they have just moved from a warehouse in Shinagawa that was next to a cement factory and walking distance from the studio of fashion designer Yohji Yamamoto). The place is not that easy to find, and so one of their interning architects will brief you beforehand. When you finally walk into their studio, the sound of hissing spray-cans will greet you, followed by a punch to your nose with a mix of spray-paint, thinner and glue. The interns come from all over the world, swirl around with white foam boards – like ants on their way to the sun with their larvae. It is here where projects like the recently opened New Museum in New York (which looks like a pile of tofu cubes) start taking shape. Or the Kanazawa Museum of Contemporary Art and the Rolex Learning Center in Lausanne.

Through a long corridor of neck-high wooden shelves, one finally enters the sanctuary of SANAA (which is not the capital of Yemen, but stands for Sejima and Nishizawa Associated Architects). Nishizawa's corner is enclosed by additional wooden shelves and features a camp bed (sleeping is like dying, he confesses in the interview). The ceiling is several meters high. Dozens of aspiring architects hover over their crammed desks, dark is their dress code and so are the rings under their eyes. Staying over night and sleeping on the floor is acceptable in this world born out of espressos, sleep deprived deadlines and the romantic vision to have one's building depicted in Architectural Digest one day.

[Conversation part one]——2000

Roland Hagenberg Are your buildings typically Japanese?

Kazuyo Sejima I don't think so, but foreigners might say that. There is always a certain mixture with some Japanese elements.

Ryue Nishizawa We don't say our buildings are Japanese. Outsiders say that.

RH Why would foreigners assume that?

RN I don't know. Maybe because of the cultural differences.

RH Maybe the question of style could be explained through your work process?

KS In the beginning our staff produces many models based on the requirements of the client. This is the starting point for everybody in the office. After that we compare. We think about as many options as possible. Everyone works by himself. Everyone produces something with different aspects. Then we discuss again and again. Somewhere along this process ideas evolve that later shape the character of a building.

RN I might have a great idea, - but in reality I cannot understand if it's good or not, or useful, until the model is made. Today option A could be the best, - but tomorrow it's maybe option D. To evaluate what is best I need some time in-between.

RH Which part of your work as an architect do you like best?

RN Two points. One is the moment where I think I came up with a great idea. The other is the experience watching the final construction of a building's frame. I mean, to be there - not to see the finished house, but the raw structure. That is for me a very exciting moment. When that time in construction happens, we always go there together and watch.

RH Do you take pictures then?

KS I do and I just love looking at these photographs later. It doesn't matter what camera I use, sometimes even an instant camera works. The problem is, we don't have time to sort and label the photos afterwards, so we just keep them in shoeboxes.

RN Basically Sejima loves to organize everything, to be in control, but that doesn't work with the photographs!

RH Is architectural photography always telling the truth or is it sometimes misleading?

RN It depends. Generally the photographic and the real world are completely different. Sometimes the world of photos can inspire new possibilities in the real world, and sometimes the real world makes good photographs. They are constantly communicating with each other. Often photographers take photos in a way which surprises us, like when they find new angles of a building, which we never thought of ourselves. This can influence our work later on. Photographers help us find new ways. They can also be good critics. On the other hand, buildings also can influence a photographer so that he begins seeing differently. It works both ways.

Only different views are able to communicate. If they are completely the same, they would be mute.

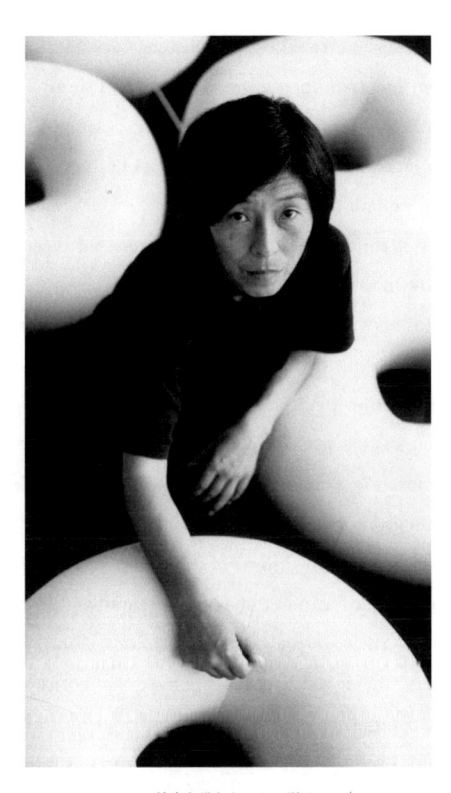

妹島和世とドーナツ型チェア |
Kazuyo Sejima with doughnut chairs (2000)

[Conversation part two]——2010

RH In 2010, you were awarded the Pritzker Architecture Prize along with Ryue Nishizawa. Does the world now expect building solutions for the future to come from Japan?

KS The Japanese way, or a certain 'Asian' way, has been the focus of international interest lately. I think that's because of the tender relationship that exists here between the inside and the outside of a building, and because of all the small-scale structures. The relationship between small-scale architecture and our bodies leads to unique design.

RH Up to the point where traditional essentials like tatami and shoji will disappear?

KS Everybody still likes tatami. Ten years ago, clients always asked explicitly for a tatami room, even when they didn't know if they would use it. Nowadays, I seldom get such requests. The reality is, tatami is in decline. However, the various relationships and lifestyles created by the existence of tatami and shoji paper screens in the past will continue to influence the way we live, I think.

RH On one hand, traditional elements are disappearing. On the other hand, the West's interest in Japanese architectural aesthetics has never been stronger than it is today. How do you explain that?

KS I don't know if the Europeans were less interested before, but now I feel that many people are drawn to the lightness of Japanese architecture, and the nature of the various relationships between the architecture and its surrounding environments.

RH This is also a guiding theme for your new project in the Japanese inland sea. There are only 30 families living in traditional wood houses on the small island of Inujima. The average age is over 70. The young all have left. And still, you want to reconstruct and renovate ten houses here to create a museum scattered over the island. Is this a sentimental gesture towards a disappearing lifestyle?

KS In this project, we've turned some of the houses in a small village into a gallery, and the whole village into a museum. Architecturally, the wooden houses are not especially valuable – they are pretty normal houses – and, until a few years ago, people lived in them. But if you take a closer look, you notice that the specific size of the parts and the materials that are used are contributing to the whole landscape of Inujima. That's why I wanted to use original structures as much as possible. And, in instances where new materials were needed, I added (for instance) aluminum and acryl. In that way, I created a new image that is a blend of the original village and the culture of the island.

RH Have you discovered new attitudes among architecture students or among your younger staff members that might give you hints as to future developments in Japanese architecture?

KS Basically, I think younger people always have the ability to think of 'the new.'

妹島和世と著者 | Kazuyo Sejima and Roland Hagenberg, Tokyo (2010)

直島、2010

ローランド・ハーゲンバーグ[以下 RH] 　以前、生活にはスーツケースがひとつあれば十分だとおっしゃっていましたが、今もそうですか？

西沢立衛[以下 西沢] 　20代の頃は確かに、部屋の中には旅行カバンしかありませんでした。ただ、今も持ち物はそんなに多くありません。ひとつには僕は借家に住んでいて、しばしば引っ越すので、引っ越すたびにモノを捨てて、あまりモノが部屋の中に増えていかないのです。しかし、自分で家を作ったら、もう引っ越さないでしょうから、モノは徐々に増えていくだろうなと思います。いつか自分の家を作ってみたいと思っています。昔はそういうことは考えていませんでしたが、いくつかの住宅を訪れるうちに、徐々に自分の家を作ってみたいと思うようになってきました。自分の持ち物がどんどん増えていって、部屋がモノで埋まっていくということを自分でやるのは、楽しそうな気がします。

RH 　私たちは一生のうち、半分の時間を寝室で過ごす計算になります。このことを考えると、寝室は建築の教科書では見落とされがちです。これは、個人的すぎる問題でしょうか？

西沢 　寝室は重要だと思います。ルイス・バラガンの寝室が、まるで死の部屋のように暗くて、驚いたのですが、それまで僕はそんなに暗い部屋を作ってこなかったので、非常に新鮮でした。それに影響されて、僕も自分の住宅を作るとしたら、寝室はすごく暗い部屋にするかもしれません。暗い部屋で寝ると、まるで死んでしまうように深く眠ることになる気がします。今の世の中は便利な時代で、どこでもネットに繋がる時代なので、そういう隔絶された世界が住宅の中にあってもいいかもしれませんね。

RH 　これまでで一番大きなコラボレーションといえば、妹島和世さんとの活動だと思います。妹島さんとおふたりでの活動は、どのように進めたのでしょうか？作業を分担していたのでしょうか？いつ話し合いをしていたのですか？

西沢 　妹島さんは、僕が最も影響を受けた建築家です。また、いつも的確な批評をしてくれる人でもあります。僕が西沢事務所のあるプロジェクトにとりかかっていて、行きづまってしまったとき、妹島さんにアドバイスをしてもらう

ことが少なくないです。一方、隣の部屋で妹島さんが妹島事務所のプロジェクトの議論をしているのが聞こえると、そちらへ行って、いろいろ口出しすることもあります。

SANAAの仕事としては、とくに作業分担というのは決めていません。決めていることは、なるべく対等にやるということくらいでしょうか。

RH プリツカー賞を受賞したとき──槇文彦さんと安藤忠雄さん以来──日本の学生たちにとってのはげましになると思いましたか？

西沢 それはまったく思いませんでした。僕はあまりいい先生ではないのだと思います。でも最近は、建築科の学生たちは、あまり建築に大きな夢をもっていない感じがします。要領のいい利口な子供たちは皆、建築家より、IT関連の道に行くんじゃないでしょうか。

RH 20年前とは大違いですね。

西沢 そうですね。20年前というと1990年ですが、それは日本ではバブルと呼ばれた時期で、僕はその頃大学教育を受けました。その頃は日本全体が狂っていて、毎日がお祭り騒ぎでした。今の時代の学生は全体的に展望を持つことができず、悲観的ですが、でもあの頃にくらべれば、今はまだいい時代なのではないかと思います。景気は悪いですが、でもそれは逆に、冷静に物事を考えることができる時代です。就職難だと学生は嘆くけれど、それも、自分で自分の道を作っていけるということでもあるから、意志がなくても生きていけたバブル期よりも、生きていく環境としてはよい時代だと思います。

西沢立衛と著者 | Ryue Nishizawa and Roland Hagenberg, Tokyo (2010)

西沢立衛と著者 豊島美術館にて
Ryue Nishizawa and Roland Hagenberg at Nishizawa's Teshima Art Museum, Japan (2010)

Kazuyo Sejima and Ryue Nishizawa

Naoshima, 2010

Roland Hagenberg   You once prided yourself on the idea that all you needed in life was a suitcase. Has that changed?

Ryue Nishizawa   When I was in my twenties, a suitcase was the only thing in my room. Even now, I don't own a lot of stuff. I live in a rented place and I move a lot, and every time I move I throw away a lot of things so that I can keep my possessions to a minimum. If I were to build a house of my own I wouldn't move and my possessions would gradually pile up. I really would love to build a house for myself in the future. I never thought of doing it until I was inspired by visiting a few important buildings. To see things filling up my rooms now seems like a fun idea.

RH   Even though we spend half our lives in the bedroom, it's generally neglected in architecture books. Is the topic too private for the public?

RN   Bedrooms are very important. Luis Barragán's bedroom was very dark, like a chamber of death. This surprised me. I've never built a dark space like it in my career and seeing where he slept was inspiring. I might build something like it in my house. I assume you'd fall asleep deeply in this space – kind of close to the experience of death. Nowadays we are connected with the world wherever we are, so maybe a room with such a level of privacy might be a very important element in the house.

RH   The longest collaboration in your life has been with Kazuyo Sejima. How does that relationship work? Do you separate certain tasks? When do you consult each other?

RN   For me, Sejima is the most influential architect in my life and she has always been the greatest person to go to when I need suggestions. When I am at a dead-end with one of my projects, I just walk over to her – we share the same studio space – to find out how she thinks and feels about it. Her comments are always honest. Conversely, when I overhear a discussion next door I might join the meeting to tell her my preferences. In regards to SANAA projects, we don't really divide our roles – the only rule is that we put in the same amount of work.

RH   You received the Pritzker Prize – after Fumihiko Maki and Tadao Ando. Do you think the prize is an encouragement to Japanese students?

RN   I did not think so at all. Maybe I am not a very good teacher, but I feel that students these days don't have 'big dreams' about architecture – smart children seem to be drawn to IT-related fields rather than architecture.

RH Quite different from 20 years ago...

RN That's right. About 20 years ago, during the bubble economy in Japan, the whole country was crazed. Every day was a party. Nowadays, students cannot have a broad view of their future; they are pessimistic. At the same time, I still think today's situation is better than yesterday's bubble economy. It's true – business is bad – but we are also able to think in a calm way, without being distracted, which was not possible back then. Students say they struggle to find work, but that also means they are paving their own distinguished path. In that way, we are living in a better environment compared to the days when nobody was thinking at all.

西沢立衛 豊島にて | Ryue Nishizawa, Teshima island, Japan (2010)

丹下健三 ミラノのBMWイタリア本社前にて │ Kenzo Tange at the construction site of BMW Headquarter Italy in Milan 1998. Photo: Thomas Kohnle

丹下健三・丹下憲孝
Kenzo and Noritaka Tange

写真を見せ、それと同じようなものを建ててほしいという依頼は、たいてい失敗します。

"If someone comes up to you with pictures and says, 'build me something like this,' then you will most likely fail if you try."

丹下健三

1913年大阪府生まれ。2005年没。1938年東京大学卒業。前川國男の建築事務所勤務後、1942年東京大学大学院に入学。1961年丹下健三・都市・建築設計研究所設立。文化勲章をはじめ受賞多数。主な作品に、国立屋内総合競技場(代々木体育館・東京)、東京都庁舎、東京カテドラル聖マリア大聖堂、BMWイタリア本社ビル(イタリア・ミラノ)などがある。

Kenzo Tange

Born 1913 in Osaka. Died in 2005 in Tokyo. Graduated from University of Tokyo in 1938. Established his practice in 1961. Numerous awards such as Order of Culture, Japan. Major works include Yoyogi National Gymnasium for Tokyo Olympics, Tokyo Metropolitan Government Office, St. Mary's Cathedral, Tokyo and BMW Italy Headquarters Building in Milan.

丹下憲孝

1958年東京都生まれ。1985年ハーバード大学大学院修了、丹下健三・都市・建築設計研究所入社。1997年同社代表取締役社長。2003年丹下都市建築設計代表取締役。主な作品に、フジテレビ本社ビル(東京)、モード学園コクーンタワー(東京)などがある。

Noritaka Tange

Born in 1958 in Tokyo. Received master degree of Architecture at Harvard University in 1985. He has been with Kenzo Tange & Associates since 1985. President of Tange Associates since 2003. Major works include Fuji Television Building in Tokyo and Mode Gakuen Cocoon Tower in Tokyo.

丹下健三、丹下憲孝

2008年冬の寒い朝、私たちは、東京にある50階建てのモード学園コクーンタワーにのぼった（当時、まだ工事中だった）。丹下健三の事務所によってデザインされた校舎は、私の性分にはあわなかった。ここ数十年、新宿の高層ビル街はほとんど変わらずにきた。箱の形の、統一されたオフィスタワーが、まるで墓石のように、疲れたサラリーマンの前にそびえ立っている。それは、1990年代の「失われた10年」、日本の経済低迷を思い出させた。しかし今、そんな四角い冷蔵庫のようなビルを尻目に、一見すると、切り刻んだ紙に包まれた、曲線状の太い万年筆のような建物が空に向かって伸びている。東京の中で最も慌ただしいこの一角に立てば、突如として現れたこの建物に不意に気を取られてしまう。

「私は、夕方家に仕事を持って帰らない建築家はいないと思います」丹下憲孝はそう言った。私たちはコクーンタワーのてっぺんにいて、どこまでも続く東京の地平線を見降ろしていた。それは、彼の父親のモノリスのひとつによって、あちこちで、際立っていた（憲孝は2003年、丹下事務所の社長になった）。しかし、もし普通の建築家が夕方に仕事を家に持ち帰るとすると、「あの」丹下の息子はさらに重荷——それは、彼の父の影だ——を持って帰らなくてはならないのではないか、と私は思った。戦後日本の景観に、丹下の父親ほど影響を与えた建築家はいない。彼は1964年のオリンピック体育館で、新しいスタンダードを打ち立てた。革新的なデザイナーであった上に、やり手の政界人でもあり、イタリアのコミュニストのみならず、かつて東京をその官僚的方法で支配した鈴木俊一のような日本の保守派をも、自らのプロジェクトに取りこんでいった（広島の平和記念資料館の仕事をどうして取ることができたのか聞かれたときに、健三は「なぜなら、私はかつて広島の学生だったから」と言ったという）。

2005年に健三が亡くなった後、丹下の事務所には、古い期待と思考パターンの影が一時的に存在したが、それは憲孝によってすべて消えた。「人々はいつも私のところにきて言うんです『そうですね、丹下さんだったらこうしたでしょう。あなたのお父さんなら、ああしたでしょう！』って」。憲孝は覚えている。「大変だったのは、私たちの会社をどうやって新しい世界に再び順応させていくのか、考えることでした。アジアの国々に、もっと注目していかなくてはならない——たとえば中国など。この3

年間だけで、私たちは23件の大型プロジェクトを終えました。複合マンション、ショッピングモール、そしてコクーンタワーのような超高層ビルです」。

コクーンタワーのほかにも、息子が父の影を越えようとしている兆候がある。私たちが11年前にイタリアで初めて出会ったとき、彼は健三と同じような暗い色のスーツを着ていた。しかし、今やスーツの色は明るいベージュ、そして黄色いタイとスカーフ、それにシルバーのリング——日本の実業界では珍しい——をしている。しかし最も印象的だったのは、日本の官僚を批判する彼の率直な言葉だった（「長い申請のプロセスが、日本の産業をだめにするんだ」）。これは、丹下の父親があえて口にしなかったことだった。それは健三自身が——ある意味で——官僚主義の申し子だったから。「お父さんは、コクーンを認めると思いますか？」との私の質問に憲孝は、顔をあげて、素敵な笑みを浮かべた。彼の父がそうだったように。「そうですね。天国で、誇りに思っていると思います」。

モード学園コクーンタワー｜
Clouds over Tokyo: Tange's Mode Gakuen
Cocoon Tower in Shinjuku,
Tokyo (under construction, 2008)

イタリア・ミラノ、1998

ローランド・ハーゲンバーグ［以下 RH］　50年以上にわたり、古代エジプトの王もうらやむほどのコンクリートや花こう岩を、それこそ何万トンも積み上げてきましたね？ かなり多忙だと思いますが、睡眠に費やす時間はあるのですか？

丹下健三［以下 丹下］　人は年をとるほど早起きになるといいますが、私は夜型人間なので、早起きは苦手です。そもそも、私には、きっちりとした日課はないのです。日課ほど、私の生活にそぐわないものはありません。状況の変化に自分を適合させていく方が好きです。

RH　履歴を見ると、勝利のマニュアルができるほど、建築コンペを勝ち抜いていますが、その成功の秘訣は何ですか？

丹下　私の成功は、決して自分の力だけによるものではありません。これまでの人生で、私は終始チームワークの大切さを説いてきました。同僚たちと互いに支え合うことで、広く、緊密なチームワークを築いてきたのです。

その哲学は、今日でも私たちの企業戦略として生き続けています。むろん最終決定を下すのは私の責任ですが、開発段階では仲間たちが、それぞれ独自のアイデアを出し合います。仕事の過程で、不要なものをふるいにかけて取り除き、最高のアイデアだけを融合させ、具体化するのです。私たちの仕事に対する姿勢は、不要なものを取り除く不断の努力といえるでしょう。

RH　創造をインスピレーションだけに頼ることもありますか？

丹下　もちろんインスピレーションを感じる瞬間はありますが、それは、突然スケッチブックに殴り書きして、「これがベストだ！」というようなものではありません。建築とは、それよりはるかに複雑で、多くの要素から構成されていますので。

RH　その、ひとつの要素がクライアントの存在ですね？

丹下　その通りです。建築家は、クライアントにとって、何がよいことなのかを、常に自問自答しなければなりません。同時に、それは環境やビジュアル・コミュニケーションにとってもよいことなのか、予算的に実現の可能性があるのかも突き詰めなければなりません。東京都庁の設計図がミラノに適合するはずはありませんし、高速道路脇に位置するBMWイタリア本社の社屋をそのまま他に移しても、全くの場

違いになるはずです。建築は、特定の場所にあってこそ、持ち味を発揮するのです。

RH BMWイタリア本社ビルには、2つのコンセプトが同居していますね？ クライアントが要望した、可動性があり、動的な要素ともいえる「モビリティー」に対し、固定性があり、静的な要素ともいえる「インモビリティー」を提示して、デザインに融合させているように見えますが、クライアントとは、どのような関係を築き、プロジェクトを進展させたのですか？

丹下 お互いに、複雑な問題の扱いには豊富な経験がありましたが、このミラノでのプロジェクトは、何といっても敷地がハイウェーに隣接していることが難問でした。まず、その解決策を考え、それからクライアントのコーポレイト・アイデンティティーを高めるには、どういう建物が最適か考えました。建築によって、どうスピードを表現するかも大きな課題でした。

RH しかも、あらゆる方向から見られる建物なのですね？

丹下 そうです。建物の正面に立つ人だけでなく、ミラノとボローニャを結ぶハイウェーを走る車の中からも見られるわけですから、建物が視点に入った時、誰もがスピードを感じるデザインにしなければなりません。それに関しては、側面の壁を湾曲させ、鋭く尖ったポイントを創造することで、上手く解決できたと考えています。静と動の外観に加え、ミラノ空港からそれほど遠くないので、建物が俯瞰されることも考慮に入れました。上空から見ると、ショールームのアーチ型のガラス壁が車の後輪となり、建物全体はコンセプトカーのような形のデザインにしています。

RH ヨーロッパでの仕事は日本での仕事と違いますか？

丹下 それぞれの国の伝統や文化を念頭に置いて仕事はしますが、根本的には何の違いもありません。仕事のアプローチはいつも同じで、クライアントの考えを理解するのが最初のステップです。そのためには、常に施主と話し合うことが、何より大切だと思います。

例えば、BMWイタリア本社ビルのデザインにしても、私と日本のスタッフだけでなく、イタリアの施主側と何度も意見交換をする中で生まれています。本人は認識していないかも知れませんが、先方の企画責任者の役割は大きく、プロジェクトの本質と目的を私たちが理解するのに、多大な貢献をしてくれました。

RH つまり、建築の仕事はクライアントに妥協しなければ成り立たない、というこ

とですか？

丹下 誤解してもらっては困ります。私は決して妥協しません。先程お話ししたことと矛盾して聞こえるかも知れませんが、クライアントの要望に深い理解があるからこそ、妥協のない設計を貫徹することができるのです。

RH クライアントを理解して、綿密なプランを作るという必然性と、遊び心に満ちた創造性とは、両立するものですか？

丹下 私は偶然を固く信じています。ただ、一般的に考えられている偶然とは少し違いますが……。

若い建築家たちには、設計が始まったら、集中力を保ち絶え間なく考え続けるように強く言っています。製図板の前や仕事場にいる時だけでなく、目が覚めている時は四六時中考え続けることで、初めて回答が得られるのです。

その回答というのは、全く思いもしない瞬間に、偶然、得られることも多々あります。地下鉄に乗っている時かも知れませんし、朝食の最中かも知れません。誰にもわからないのです。突然、ひらめいたように思うかも知れませんが、実際は、そうでなく、無意識のうちに働き続けていた感覚の信号が、正しい答えを察知して、偶然のように、インスピレーションとして提示されるのです。

それを実践してきたのが、私の成功の秘訣かも知れません。

RH 学生時代は、ドイツ語を学び、トーマス・マンを読み、文筆家か芸術家への道を考えていたと聞きますが、その希望を変えたのは何ですか？

丹下 片田舎の子供だった私が、建築を志そうとは、夢にも思いませんでした。当時は、むしろ大空に輝く星の方が身近なもので、毎晩、手製の望遠鏡で星座を観察していました。

大きな心境の変化が起きたのは、高校生の頃、海外の雑誌の特集でコルビュジエの建築と設計図を見た時です。タイトルはソビエトの宮殿といい、今でも明確に覚えています。

RH コルビュジエの何に魅せられたのですか？

丹下 不必要な飾りや伝統的な装飾をすべて取り払いながら、完璧な美の調和を創ることに成功した建築家がいたという事実です。

その後、東京大学の学生時代に友人の立原道造（昭和の詩人・建築家）から刺激を受

け、建築家になることを最終的に決意しました。彼は詩人ならではの観察力で、「僕は北からやって来た一介の貧乏人だ。北の人間は、とにかく物事を観念的に捉えがちなので、物書きや哲学者に向いている。しかし、丹下くんは南の温暖な地方からやってきたから、視覚的に物事を捉え、考える。地中海に沿った、あのギリシアやローマの素晴らしい建築物を見ればわかるじゃないか」と、言ったのです。

RH　息子さんが建築の道に進むにあたり助言もしたと思いますが、その中で最も大切なことは何ですか？

丹下　私の世代は工業の時代にルーツがあり、日本では高度経済成長期における東京タワーの鉄骨構造に象徴される時代でした。しかし、私は、もうひとつの側面である情報化社会との関連を考えていました。とにかく、情報化社会を構成する必要条件が何かを突き詰めたかったのですが、やがて、それはアイデアや情報を交流させる空間の創造へとつながりました。

例えば、学校においては、教室が重要なのはもちろんですが、本当のコミュニケーションが行われるのは廊下や校庭なのです。それは、もっと大きな規模や高い次元で考えてみても同じでした。東京都庁には何千人もの職員が働いていますが、理論的には、職員は教室に座っているようなものですから、ちょうど学校における廊下や校庭と同じように、近隣の人々と自由に触れ合える広場や公園を、そこに盛り込んだのです。これこそ、未来に向けてすべての都市が選択すべき道だと思います。

ですから、息子に助言したのは、コミュニケーションをとり、アイデアを交換し合う自由な環境を創造するということです。

丹下健三の葬儀 東京カテドラル聖マリア大聖堂にて |
Kenzo Tange's funeral at Saint Mary's Cathedral, Tokyo (2005)

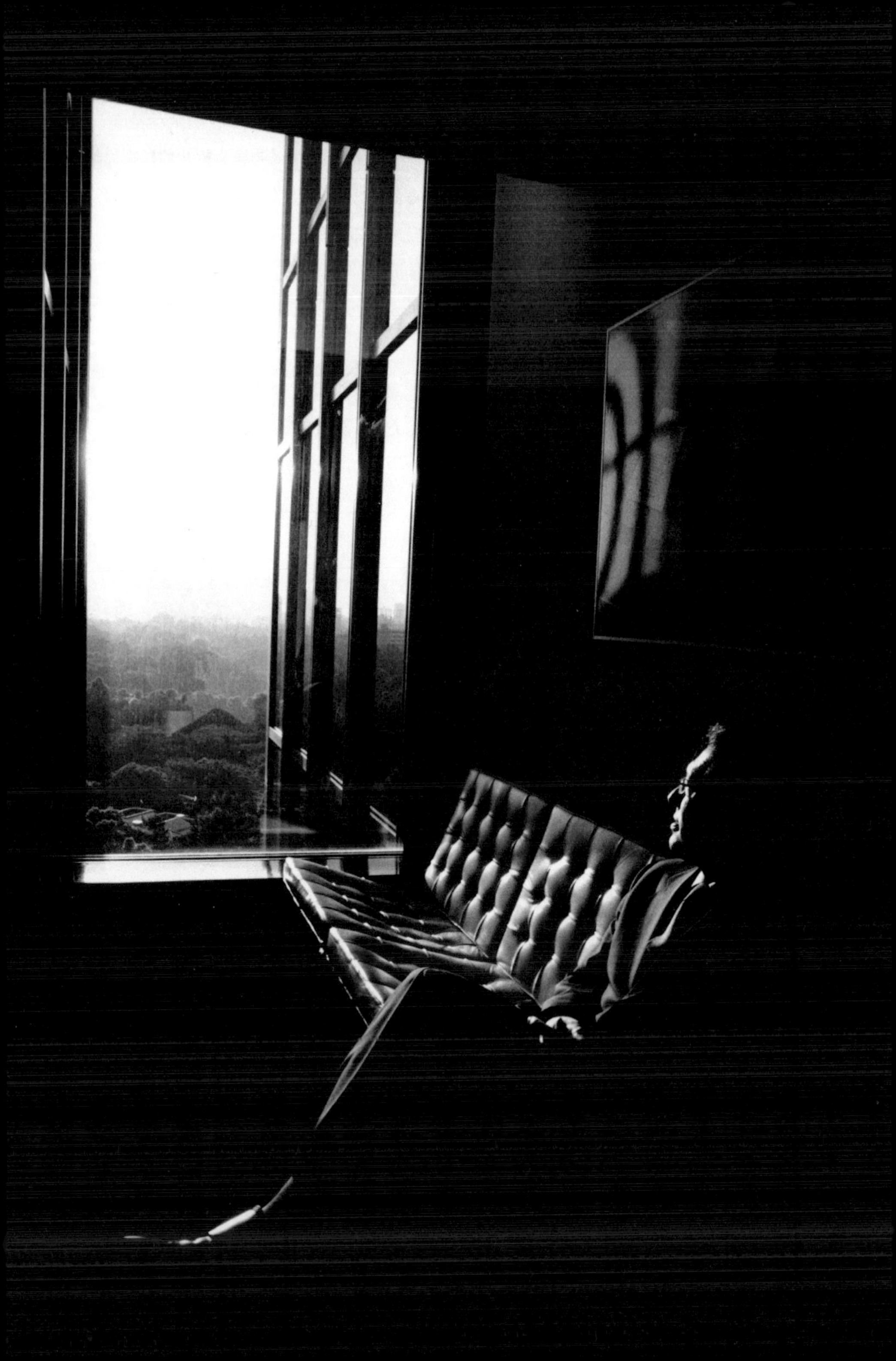

東京、2007

ローランド・ハーゲンバーグ[以下 RH]　よく聞かれることだと思いますが、丹下都市建築設計の社長として、父と自身の関係をどう位置づけていますか？

丹下憲孝[以下 丹下]　確かに、よく尋ねられますね。建築家になろうと決めた日から、その質問は覚悟していましたが……。
私はハーバード大学に行きましたが、そこには有名な建築家の息子も何人かいて、シーザー・ペリの息子、ラファエロ・ペリとはクラスメイトでした。そういう二世建築家は、楽ができてラッキーだと思われがちですが、親の会社に就職ができるという点では幸運ですけれども、有名な父親とは別に自分自身のアイデンティティーを持つという、極めて困難な課題とともに生きることになるのです。その意味では、二世建築家は、皆、大変だと思います。

RH　建築家になることを期待されて育ったのですか？

丹下　いいえ、自分で決めました。進路を決めなくてはいけない年の夏のことです。父の出張について、30年来、父がプロジェクトを手がけていたボローニャに行きました。暑い日、ふたりっきりで昼食をとっている時に、建築をやりたいと打ち明けました。父は、しばらく無言になりましたけれど、一生のうち一度やる仕事だとすれば、建築はすごく面白い仕事だ、と言いました。その無言の数秒間の中には、息子が同じ道を歩みたいということへの父としての喜びと、逆に建築家の大変さを身にしみてわかっている、父としての親心のふたつが、入り交じっていたと思います。そんな中で、人生は一度しかないのだから、やりたいことをやってみろ、と父は快く私が建築に進むことを認めてくれました。父と真面目な会話をしたのは、この時が初めてだったと思います。

RH　1985年に丹下健三・都市・建築設計研究所に入社していますね？　そして、1997年にフジテレビ本社ビルを完成させていますが、あの建物がポスト丹下健三時代の幕開けだと思いますか？

丹下　丹下健三・都市・建築設計研究所としての建築哲学は父が築いたもので、今でも、あまり変化はしていないと思います。ただし、時代が変わりましたので、私たちも視野を広げ、新しい考えを取り入れています。例えば、現在では高層住宅を数多く

手がけていますが、それは丹下健三が得意としない分野といわれてきたものです。フジテレビ本社ビルが、会社の転換点だったかどうかは、はっきりとはわかりませんが、私が入社した当時は、「丹下先生ならこうする」という言葉を、よく耳にしました。スタッフが、父の好むやり方に傾いていたのです。しかし、現在では、どうするのが適切か、とチーム全員が自問するように変わりました。

丹下都市建築設計は、チームワークを重んじる会社です。建築はひとりでは作れません。そこを勘違いすると、失敗します。スタッフには、私のことを親友だと思って説得するように、と言ってます。厳しいことを言うのは嫌いだからではなくて、理解しようとつとめてるからだ、と。

RH　フジテレビ本社ビルの設計では、どのような点に苦労しましたか？

丹下　私にとって初めての大規模なプロジェクトで、条件も厳しかったです。まず、フジテレビの企業のイメージをどう考えていくか、その中で、21世紀の放送局はどうあるべきかを念頭に入れたうえで、開かれた放送局というコンセプトを考えました。建物は、スタジオ・スペースのほか、様々な機能を持っていますが、どこででもスタジオとして機能するような、オープンな感じのものを造りました。

RH　フジテレビ側が「こんな感じでお願いします」と、カタログを見ながら言うような進め方だったのですか？

丹下　基本的には、「どんどん進めて欲しい」という感じでした。写真を見せ、それと同じようなものを建てて欲しいという依頼は、たいてい失敗しますよ。

RH　欧米のクライアントは、日本の建築会社に何を求めていると思いますか？

丹下　何とも言えません。

日本は、国土のサイズの割には、優れた建築を多く生んできました。丹下都市建築設計は、長年、アジアで建物を創る機会に恵まれてきましたが、1980年代の中頃になると、アメリカの建築会社もアジアに進出してきて、競い始めたという感があります。1990年代においても、その傾向は続いていますが、アメリカの会社だからといって、建物を創れる時代ではなくなりました。確かに、アメリカは経済大国ですが、すべての問題を解決できるわけではない、とアジアの人は気づいたのです。その結果、アジアの内部に目を向けたのではないでしょうか。例えば、土地の有効活用法をとってみても、狭い国土に慣れた私どもの方が得意なわけですし。

RH　ごく普通な一日の過ごし方を教えてください。

丹下　朝は7時に起きて、娘が出かけるまでの時間を一緒に過ごすようにしています。妻がイタリア系アメリカ人なので、娘は3ヶ国語を話しますよ。事務所の始業は9時半で、毎週月曜の朝は全体ミーティングがあります。事務所では歩き回って、複数のプロジェクトの進行具合を確認します。私のデスクはアトリエの真ん中にあり、個室は持っていません。日中はほとんどミーティングなどに追われ、デザインなどは夜になることが多いです。帰宅は夜10時を過ぎることがほとんどです。健康管理という意味で、週3回はスポーツ・ジムに行くようにしています。

フジテレビ本社ビル　スケッチ
Fuji Television Building, drawing (1997)

フジテレビ本社ビル |
Fuji Television Building, Tokyo

Kenzo Tange and Noritaka Tange

On a freezing winter morning in early 2008 we climbed up the fifty floors of Mode Gakuen Cacoon Tower (still under construction) in Tokyo. Designed by the firm of late architect Kenzo Tange, the school building goes against the grain. Shinjuku's high-rise district has not changed much in decades: the boxy, standardized office towers that once loomed like tombstones over the lives of exhausted 'salary-men' stand as reminders of Japan's economic downturn in the lost decade of the 1990s. But now, instead of another square refrigerator, a curved, fat fountain pen sprouts into the sky seemingly covered with webs of shredded paper. Wherever you stand in Tokyo's busiest ward, your attention is inadvertently drawn to this breakout structure.

"I think there is no architect who doesn't take home work in the evening," said Noritaka Tange, as we stood at the top of Cocoon and gazed over Tokyo's never-ending horizon –accentuated, here and there, by one of his father's monoliths. (Noritaka became president of Tange Associates in 2003.) But if an average architect takes home a workload in the evening, I reflected, the son of 'The Tange' has to carry additional weight – that of his father's shadow. No architect had more influence on Japan's postwar cityscapes than Tange père, who set new standards with his Olympic gymnasium in 1964. Besides being a revolutionary designer, he was also a shrewd political animal who could win over Italian Communists as well as Japanese conservatives like Shunichi Suzuki, the once omnipotent bureaucrat-ruler of Tokyo, with his projects. (Asked why he should get the job of building the Hiroshima Peace Memorial, Kenzo is reported to have answered, "Because I once was a student in Hiroshima!")

After Tange's death in 2005, shadows of old expectations and thought patterns lived on briefly in the Tange organization but were cut short by the heir apparent. "People always came up to me and said, 'Oh, Mr Tange would have done this. Your father would have done that!'" remembers Noritaka. "The struggle was how to best readjust our firm to a new world, turning more attention to Asia – to China, for instance. In the last three years alone we have finished 23 large-scale projects, apartment complexes, shopping districts and skyscrapers like Cocoon Tower!"

Besides Cocoon, there are other signs that the younger Tange has outgrown his father's shadow. When we first met fourteen years ago in Italy, he wore the same dark suits as Kenzo. Now, the colors are light; the suit is beige, with matching yellow tie and kerchief and he wears several silver rings – a very unusual choice in Japan's corporate world. Most striking, however, is his outspoken criticism of the Japanese bureaucracy ("The long application process hurts the industry!"). This is something the elder Tange would never have dared to voice, being himself – in a way – a product of the bureaucracy. "Do you think your father would have approved of Cocoon?" I enquired. Noritaka looked up and flashed a charming smile – all the diplomat his father had been. "I hope, in Heaven, he is proud of it!"

著者 モード学園コクーンタワー前にて |
Roland Hagenberg in front of Mode Gakuen Cocoon Tower (2008)

Milan, Italy (1998)

Roland Hagenberg Mr. Tange, over the last 50 years you have piled up so many millions tons of concrete and granite that the Egyptian pharaohs themselves would be envious. How much sleep do you actually get?

Kenzo Tange People always say that the older you get, the earlier you get up in the mornings. But I say, the longer I sleep, the longer I will live. I am a night person, and so it's difficult to get out of bed in the mornings anyway. I don't have a strict daily routine, because everything is changing all the time. Routine would be entirely inappropriate in my life: I prefer adapting to circumstances as they arise.

RH Your biography reads like a catalogue of victories which you have carried away from architectural competitions. Is there a secret recipe behind your success?

KT You must not put my success down to me alone. Throughout my life I've been preaching teamwork and I've built up a wide, close-knit network of colleagues based on mutual support. That remains our corporate strategy to this day. Of course I am the one responsible for the final decisions, but during the development phase my associates go their independent ways. Later on the most brilliant ideas will merge into a compact substance and anything extraneous will fall away. I would describe our approach to work as "mutual effort with uncountable eliminations".

RH Do you ever rely on pure inspiration?

KT Of course, there are inspirational moments, but not in a sense, that I will suddenly scribble a drawing into my sketch book and say: "That's it and nothing else!" Architecture is far too complex for that, it relies on more than a few components.

RH One of them being the client....

KT Indeed. We have to ask ourselves: what is good for our client? But also: What is good for the environment and for visual communication. Is what we are planning actually affordable? And so on. Our design for Tokyo Metropolitan Government Office simply wouldn't fit into Milan, and all the other Tange buildings would be equally inappropriate if transplanted to another location. BMW's Italian headquarters is in Milan, situated right here next to the highway. It serves a specific purpose at this specific site.

RH Two interesting elements overlap in the design of this structure: one is mobility, as represented by your client, and the other is static, immovable architecture, as represented by you. When one of the world's best car manufacturers gets together with one of the best architects, what kind of ideas are at the basis of such a partnership?

KT Well, both partners are very experienced in handling complex tasks. And this project was quite a challenge: after all, the Milan construction site next to the highway isn't quite as designer-friendly as one might wish. That alone presented us with a number of challenges. Then we had to consider how the BMW corporate identity could best be conveyed through a building, and especially how one could express speed through architectural means...

RH ....and from various perspectives....

KT ...that as well. The BMW headquarters will not only be seen by people facing the building, but also by motorists traveling along the Milan-Bologna highway. Both are supposed to experience the same sense of mobility when they look at the design. I believe we have solved that quite successfully with an elliptically bent side wall and the sharp-edged "nose" which we have attached. In addition to the static and mobile perspective, we have also taken account of the bird's-eye view, bearing in mind that Milan Airport isn't far away. If you look at our constructional plans, you will see that the building can be perceived as a BMW concept car from above, with the arched glass wall of the showroom representing the rear wheel – a little surprise for airline passengers.

RH How would you say working in Europe differs from working in Japan?

KT Fundamentally there is no difference, but I do take each country's traditions and culture into account. Our procedural approach is always the same: the first step is to try to understand our client's corporate philosophy. Constant consultations with company representatives are a must. For instance, my colleagues and I weren't the only ones who came up with design ideas for the Milan project. In the course of our numerous conversations, BMW's project manager was probably not even aware of the extent to which he actually contributed to our understanding of the nature and purpose of the new Italian headquarters and how much this has helped the overall design process.

RH Does that mean, architecture would not be possible without compromises?

KT Here you seem to misunderstand me. I never make compromises. That may sound like a contradiction to what I said just now, but not making compromises is possible because my work is based on a deep understanding of my clients' whishes.

RH Next to this understanding and a microscopically detailed plan, is there still room for playful, creative coincidence?

KT I firmly believe in coincidence, but it happens in a different way than you might expect. From the very beginning I urge my architects to concentrate and think non-stop — not just at the drawing board, not just in the office. I mean all the time, as long as they are awake. Only then will we find answers to all our questions. Those answers might come at the most unexpected moments — in the subway, during breakfast, when shopping at the supermarket, who knows. When that happens, you might think of it as a sudden flash of inspiration, but in reality it was the product of permanent alertness on an unconscious level which helped you to recognize and seize the right solution. That's my recipe for success. Nobody can claim that I have had a bigger share of luck in my life than anyone else, because we are all allotted the same amount of luck. But if you said that I was better at recognizing luck than others, you would be hitting the right spot.

RH As a student you learned German, read Thomas Mann, and were thinking of a career as a writer or artist. What made you change your mind?

KT I was a boy from the country and it would have been sheer madness to cherish any hopes of becoming an architect. Architecture was quite simply beyond my wildest dreams. Even the stars in the sky were much closer to me, much more tangible. I used to observe them every night through a self-built telescope. The big change of mind set in during high school, when I happened to come across a foreign magazine featuring illustrations of a Le Corbusier model. It was called Palace of Soviets. I remember it quite clearly.

RH What was it that fascinated you about it?

KT The fact that here you had an architect who dared to sweep aside all unnecessary ornamentation and traditional embellishments, and yet managed to imbue this naked structure with a perfect aesthetic harmony. It was later on at Tokyo University that I was finally prompted into becoming an architect by my friend, the poet Michizo Tachihara, who came up with an interesting poetic observation: "I'm only a beggar from the North," he said, "and people from the North tend to think in conceptual ways: they are good writers and philosophers. But you, Tange-san, you come from the mild climate of the South, you think visually. Just look at the fantastic Greek and

Roman architecture on the shores of the Mediterranean!"

RH Looking at the lives of great architects, it is striking just how many of them lost their father at an early age. This could be an invitation to draw psychological conclusions…

KT My parents both died within days of each other at the end of the Second World War, my mother when an incendiary bomb exploded in the garden. They were both very open-minded people who would never tell me which path to choose, who supported all my endeavors, morally as well as financially. So I don't really feel that my architecture was a way of compensating or trying to prove anything.

RH Your son Noritaka is also an architect and already has a leading position in the Tange company. What is the most important piece of advice you have given him for his career?

KT The roots of my generation go back to the industrial age.

In Japan that era is perhaps best symbolized by the steel construction of the Tokyo Tower. In my case, I set out early on to forge links with the information society. I wanted to create the architectural prerequisites for it, space for the exchange of ideas and information. Let me put it this way: of course at school the classroom is important, but the real communication takes place in the hallways and schoolyards. The same happens on a grander scale as well. Thousands of people work at Tokyo Metropolitan Government Office, and theoretically they're also sitting in "classrooms". So I have also built "school-yards" and "hallways" for them, in the form of plazas and parks that reach out into the neighborhood. That's how all cities should grow in the future. My advice to my son was: communicate, create an environment in which nothing can interfere with people exchanging thoughts and ideas.

丹下健三と著者 |
Kenzo Tange and Roland Hagenberg, Milan (1998)

Tokyo, 2007

Roland Hagenberg You probably get this asked all the time: as president of Kenzo Tange Associates, how do you manage the legacy of your father's reputation on a personal level?

Noritaka Tange Many people ask me that. When I chose architecture as my profession, I knew that this issue would come up one day. I went to Harvard and there were other sons of famous architects, like Rafael Pelli, Cesar Pelli's son, he was my classmate. Many people think these guys are lucky, have an easy way out. In some way they do, when there's already a company waiting for them. But to try to have your own identity away from a famous father is a difficult endeavor. In this regard, all of us have different problems and we must live with it.

RH Was it expected that you would become an architect?

NT Nobody pushed me. One summer, when I had to decide which way to go, I went with my father on a business trip to Bologna. We had been building there for thirty years. It was very hot. We went to a restaurant and I told him that I wanted to apply to architecture school. I think, he was a little confused, when he heard that. He was happy that his son was following in his footsteps and unhappy, because he knew what I would have to face. At the end he said, "well, you only live once - you might as well do what you like to do. There are already too many people in this world who are committed to something they don't want to do!" I think that this was the first time as father and son we had a really serious talk.

RH You joined the company in 1985, so you were already involved in the Fuji TV building, which was completed in 1996. Does this building mark the beginning of the post-Kenzo Tange era?

NT Our architectural philosophy as a company was instigated by my father, and that has not changed much. Times, however, have changed. We widened our view and started implementing new ideas. For instance, we are building a lot of high-rise residential towers now, which were not considered to be Kenzo Tange's cup of tea. I can't say clearly if Fuji TV was the turning point. When I joined the company, people often said, "Oh, professor Tange would like it this way....". People had the tendency to please my father by doing things they knew he would like to see. That has changed. Everybody in our team now just asks what is the right thing to do.

KTA is now a team oriented company. You cannot create architecture just by yourself. If you do that, mistakes will happen. I always say to my staff "try to convince me - I am your best friend who wants to understand you and don't think I don't like you when I say something harsh!"

RH   What were the challenges you faced with the Fuji TV building?

NT   It was my first large-scale project. The requirements were tough. Lots of special spaces were needed and juxtaposed. The concept was that no matter where you are, you should always be able to turn the place into a TV studio. With the design, we wanted to express that Fuji TV is part of the mass media of the 21st century.

RH   Did Fuji TV come up to you with one of your catalogues and say, "we would like to have something in this direction, can you do it?"

NT   Basically, they said, just go ahead. But honestly, if someone comes up to you, shows you a picture and says, please make something like that for us - then you most likely will fail.

RH   What do Europeans or Americans expect, when they hire a Japanese architectural firm?

NT   It's difficult to make a generalization. For its size, Japan has produced quite a lot of good contemporary architects. In Asia, our company was fortunate to be able to build for many years. In the middle of the 1980s many American architects began doing business in Asia, and many of the American firms were competing with us. I think in the 1990s this trend was still there, but not everybody could come in just because he had an American flag on his back. Asians have realized that the United States is an economic powerhouse, but that does not mean it can solve all the issues. I think Asia is looking inwards again. We just know for instance how to best utilize land, which is so scarce in Asian countries.

RH   How does a typical day go for you?

NT   I wake up at 7 o'clock. I try to spend the morning with my daughter before she leaves for school. She is actually growing up tri-lingual, - my wife is Italian-American. The office starts at 9.30. Every Monday morning we have a general meeting. I usually walk around and see how other projects are doing. I don't have my own office separated from the others. I just sit in the middle of the studio. During the day I'm mostly occupied with meetings. I am more an evening person and get home around 10pm. And three times a week, I try to make it to the gym.

丹下憲孝 | Noritaka Tange, Tokyo (2009)

手塚貴晴 | Takaharu Tezuka, Vienna (2011)

手塚貴晴 | Takaharu Tezuka

私たちにとって屋根は大切です。
屋根には人の姿勢を変える力があります。

"The roof is an important part of our work.
It can change attitudes of people."

1964年東京生まれ。武蔵工業大学卒業。ペンシルバニア大学大学院修了。1990年から94年まで、ロンドンのリチャード・ロジャーズ・パートナーシップ・ロンドンに勤務。1994年、妻の由比と手塚建築研究所を設立。2009年からは東京都市大学教授をつとめる。

Born 1964 in Tokyo. Graduated at Musashi Institute of Technology. Masters of architecture from University of Pennsylvania. Worked at Richard Rogers from 1990 to 1994 in London. Established Tezuka Architects with his wife Yui in 1994. Since 2009 professor at Tokyo City University.

手塚貴晴

手塚貴晴と妻の由比に日本での独立のチャンスが持ち上がったとき、彼らは師のリチャード・ロジャーズのもとで働いてから4年が経っていた。貴晴はロジャーズに尋ねた。「リチャード、興味あるオファーを受けたんだ。でも、あなたが望まないのであれば、もちろん私たちはそれを断る。どう思う？」。ロジャーズは答えた。「問題ないよ！　何年か経って、君たちはきっとまたここに戻ってくる。これまでほかの人たちがそうだったように、君たちも失敗するだろうからね。いいデザイナーがいいビジネスマンであるとは限らないんだよ」。それは1994年のことだった。今日、手塚たちはその革新的で、モダンなデザインで、日本で最も成功した建築家のひとりに数えられる。しかし、彼らのデザインは、同時代の現代建築家と簡単に比べられるものではない。たとえば、妹島・西沢のコンビは、個人的な生活臭のない、知的なアバンギャルドととらえられたが、手塚のデザインは、もっと地に足がついた実用的な面を強調したもの、世界に向けて家族の生活部分をさらけ出すようなものなのだ。

夜の10時、東京・等々力にある小さなロフト・スタジオ。10人ほどの若い建築家とインターン——そのうちの何人かはヨーロッパから来ている——が模型やパソコンにはりついて働いていた。玄関を入ってすぐのところに、フィットネスマシーンがあり、事務所の中は、糊とカレーの匂いが充満していた（誰かが奥で料理をしていた）。貴晴が「すみません、すみません、子どもを寝かせないといけないんで」と言いながら入ってきた。彼は日焼けしていて、実際の年齢より10歳は若く見える。「うちの家族は皆90歳まで生きているんですよ。父の叔父なんか、100歳を越えても、ボランティア活動でコミュニティーセンターまで自転車で通っていましたからね」。貴晴は、毎日青い色のものを着る。Tシャツ、靴下、iPhoneまでが青いケースに入っている。妻の由比は赤、娘の無捺は黄色、息子の士惟は緑色だ。「本当は、私たちはこのひどい東京には戻りたくなかったんです。ロンドンでは、決して豊かではなかったですが、満ち足りた生活でした。週末には、自転車でリッチモンドパークに行き、ピクニックもしました。この生活の質を、東京でも手離したくはなかったんです。だから、ここに自分たちだけの世界をつくって、ほかの人が私たちのことをどう思うかなんてことは考えないことにしたんです」

彼らに転機が訪れたのは、「屋根の家」という、プライバシーを重要視する日本では大胆ともいえる建築をデザインした時だ。「屋根の家」では、日常の生活は、巨大で、少し傾斜のある屋根の上で行われることになり、そこには手すりもなく、外を歩く人からは全て見える構造になっていた。「クライアントとは、ずいぶん長い時間を一緒に過ごしました」と貴晴は言う。「一緒に旅行に行ったり、食事をしたり、彼らのライフスタイルを知るためにたくさん話をしました。それらが、私たちの建築のスタートなんです」。手塚たちは、クライアントの家族が、小さな窓から傾斜のきつい瓦屋根に登って、そこでご飯を食べるのが好きということに注目した。それが、「屋根の家」のコンセプトにつながっていったのだ。

ローランド・ハーゲンバーグ[以下RH]：ロンドンのリチャード・ロジャーズ氏の下で働いたという経験は、その後の手塚さんの建築にどんな影響を与えましたか。
手塚貴晴[以下TT]：多くの人がリチャードを、「ハイテク」建築家と呼びますが、私はそうは思わないんです。彼は真のモダニストです。彼のプロジェクトでは、人々の生活を理解することが、すべてに優先します。これが彼の建築に意味を与えているのです。いつだったか、1960年代の終わりに彼が両親のために建てたウィンブルドンの家に連れていってもらったことがあります。ハーブガーデンとお母さんの陶芸のアトリエ、そして住居部分がすべてひとつのフロアにあって、両親の年齢と興味、気持ちに合わせて作られていました。細かいところを知らなくても、家に足を踏み入れたときに、すぐわかりました。私と妻は1994年にリチャードの下を離れて、東京で仕事を始めましたが、それが彼から受け継いだ建築の本質だと思います。
RH　それで、まず依頼主の生活を知るということから始めて、最初の段階ではラフスケッチや模型もないのですね。
TT　建築は人がいなければ成り立ちません。ここが彫刻とは違うところです。依頼主の持っている歴史や日々の仕事、好みなどを知ってはじめて、ラフスケッチを描くことができます。ひとつのプロジェクトについて、平均して50くらい、時には100もの模型を作ることがあります。コンピュータは、模型の代わりにはなりません。

RH　「屋根の家」は海外でも有名です。

TT　そうですね。そのほかにも「越後松之山『森の学校』キョロロ」や、「箱根の森　ネットの森」「ふじようちえん」などが紹介されるようになりました。

RH　「屋根の家」が面白いのは、ほかのどの建築よりも、手塚さんの建築の本質を視覚化しているからだと思います。同時に多くのアレゴリーがある。「デートについての普遍的な黄金律」というものも入っているんですよね！

TT　シエナやローマ、メルボルンなど、世界の有名な広場を見ると、それらが少し傾いていることに気づきます。平らな場所の端に座るより、坂になっている場所の端に座るほうがいいんです。このことは「屋根の家」を作る上でとても参考になり、コンセプトのひとつでもあります。わたしはいつもカップルに、最初のデートをカフェで顔を突き合わせて会うことをすすめないんです。それは災いのもとになります！　話題も限られているところで、小さなテーブルを挟んで、お互いを見なければいけない状況……。もし話題がなくなってしまったら、絶対に気まずい雰囲気になってしまいます。だから、初対面のときには、少し傾斜のある川の土手をおすすめします。日本のカップルたちがどうして多摩川でそうしているか、考えたことはありますか？　彼らは同じ方向を向いているので、息をつく暇があるんです。

RH　最近「ふじようちえん」がOECDの学校施設好事例に選ばれました。これも、少し傾いた屋根が特徴です。

TT　私たちの建築では、屋根がとても重要なんです。なぜなら、屋根のデザインによって、日常生活の中での柔軟性が決まるからです。それは、人々の姿勢を変えます。「ふじようちえん」では、子供たちが突然歩き出したり、走ったりする回数が、普通の場所の５、６倍も多くなるそうです。それも誰かに言われたからそうするのではありません。彼らが皆自分でそうするのです。「屋根の家」の場合も、自然が向こうからやってくるという、現代の私たちの考えを逆転させているんです。今、家主は、日本で遠い昔から行われてきたように暮らしています。つまり、自然に合わせるという姿勢です。夏には、彼らは暑さを避けるために、早めの時間に朝食を摂ります。冬には、日が昇ってから朝食にします。ひとつ心配だったのが、ある時妻が言ったことです。「冷たい台風が来ている中で、熱いシャワーを浴びるほど気持ちいいものはないのよ」。私は「気をつけてよ」と言ったのですが、彼女は「心配しなくてもいい。私は

手塚貴晴 ウィーン工科大学にて
Takaharu Tezuka at Technical University of Vienna (2011)

いつもTシャツを着ているから」。彼女は私が心配していたような風や雷については考えていなかったんです。

RH 「屋根の家」での生活には、防護柵もないですよね……。

TT あるとき依頼主が、家族が2階の上の瓦ぶきの屋根の上で朝ごはんを食べている写真を見せてくれたんです。子供たちは、そこが彼らの遊び場や庭、そして青空の下にある自分たちの部屋であるかのように遊んでいました。そこで、私たちはこのアイデアにこだわることにしたんです。私たちは、防護柵をつくることも提案しました。しかし、依頼主は「どうして屋根に柵がいるんですか？ 屋根に柵がある家がありますか？」と言ったんです。私たちは建築計画を提出するときに、同じことを話し、最後には許可がおりました。

RH いつも青い色のものを着ていますよね。靴下、Tシャツ、iPhoneまでブルー。いつからですか？

TT リチャード・ロジャーズ氏はいつも青い色を着ていて、スタッフも少しずつ青いものを着るようになっていったんです。ある時、リチャードはそれをうるさく感じて、結局はピンクを着るようになってしまったんですけれどね。1992年に、由比と結婚してからは、青と赤をそれぞれのトレードマークにしようって決めたんです。

RH 子供たちも、それぞれの色が決まっているんですよね。

TT 実は、家族皆のものは全部黄色なんです。たとえば車は黄色いシトロエン2CV。黄色は、娘の無捺の色でもあるんです。でも、弟の士惟が生まれ、黄色を着せたときに、彼女はそれに反対して、彼女の黄色いおもちゃを全部弟の士惟にあげてしまったんです。だから、私たちは、士惟は緑色と決めました。もちろん、いつも本気ではないんですよ。これは時間をかけてできあがった一種のゲームみたいなものですから。私がもし青い色に飽きたとしても、それはそれでいいんです。

RH それは、イブ・クライン・ブルーですよね？

TT イブ・クライン・ブルーが大好きなんです。表面を見ただけで、その深みの幅が広がる色は、息をのむようです。残念なながら、その効果を損なわずに、100パーセントTシャツへその色を移すのは、ちょっと無理です。以前クラインブルーのボトルを買ったことがあります。金以上に高いアフガニスタン産の宝石の粉が入っているらしいと聞いたことがあります。

RH　いつも、教えることは生活と仕事の一部だと言っていますよね。ウィーン工科大学ではその様子を見せてもらいましたが、とても楽しそうでした。学生たちも、ワクワクして、熱心な様子でした。

TT　おっしゃるとおり、教えることは人生の大切な一部です。そして、学生たちがコンペに勝つと、とてもうれしいんです。400人以上もの応募がある中から、2年続けて最優秀卒業研究に選ばれました。そしていつも——たとえば2004年や2008年、2010年の学生など——彼らは、どこでこんな奇抜なアイデアを思いつくんだろうと不思議に思います。学生のひとりは、氷で家を建てるにはどうしたらいいか研究しています。別のひとりは、少しずつ分解するプラスチックを使って、最後はなくなってしまう家を作ってみたいと言っています。建築家にとって、たとえそれに住むことができなくても、アイデアを実験してみることはとても大切だと思います。私もいつも学生たちに挑戦し、質問をします。けっこう厳しいんですよ。休む暇も与えませんからね。例えばフランツ・リストが生まれたライディングという小さな街にできるプロジェクト。担当所員の斎藤裕美さんは、完璧を求めるあまり一週間毎日模型を磨き続け、ついには爪が削れ指紋がなくなってしまいました。その一方で、私は、レム・コールハースとは違って、いつでも学生たちのために時間をあけています。コールハースが教えていた頃、自分がアメリカで学生だった時のことをよく覚えています。ワークショップの後、自分たちは伝説的な建築家と仲良くなったのだ、ということで彼のところに行き、ヨーロッパでもう一度会えないかと聞きました。それを聞いた彼は「無理だよ」と言いました。「なぜかって？　私は有名人だからね」。

事務所の風景 | Tezuka office, Tokyo (2010)

Takaharu Tezuka

Takaharu Tezuka and his wife Yui had been working in the practice of London architect Sir Richard Rogers for four years when the opportunity arose to open a practice of their own, back home in Japan. Takaharu approached his boss, "I've received an interesting offer, but if you'd prefer, Richard, I will of course decline. What do you think?" The Englishman replied, "No problem. After a couple of years, you'll come back anyway, as all my architects do, because you'll be broke. You're a good designer, but that doesn't mean you're a good businessman!"

That was 1994. Today, the Tezukas run one of the most successful architectural practices in Japan, specializing in innovative, modern design. The public image of the couple's working relationship, however, is very different to that of their contemporaries. Whereas, for instance, the Sejima-Nishizawa partnership is perceived to be "avant-garde-intellectual" and void of any kind of private life, the Tezukas appear to be down-to-earth pragmatists who don't shy away from exposing their family life to the entire world. It is ten o'clock in the evening. In a small loft-studio in Tokyo's Todoroki district, a dozen young architects and interns – some from Europe – labor away on models or stare into their computers. A fitness machine leans next to the entrance. The air is filled with glue and curry (someone is cooking out the back) as Takaharu rushes in: "Sorry, sorry. We had to put the kids to bed!" He is well tanned and appears ten years younger than his years. "In my family, everybody makes it to at least 90," he says. "I still remember an uncle of my father who rode his bike to the community center to do volunteer work when he was over 100." Takaharu wears blue everyday: blue t-shirt, blue socks, blue rubber iPhone case. Yui prefers red, and yellow and green are reserved for their daughter Buna and son Shii. "We actually didn't want to return to Tokyo. In London we were poor, but it was a rich life. On weekends we took our bicycles and went to Richmond Park for picnic. We didn't want this quality of life taken away from us ever again, not even in Japan. And so, we created our own world here and we just ignore what other people think of us."

The Tezuka team's breakthrough came with Roof House, a daring structure if you consider how much Japanese people value their privacy. In this building, daily family life is visible to all passers-by as it happens, on a giant, slightly angled, flat roof without railings. "We spend a lot of time with our clients," says Takaharu. "We travel with them, we eat together and share stories so we can get acquainted with their lifestyles – this forms the starting point of our architecture." At one such gathering, the Tezukas learned that their client-family loved to climb through a tiny window on top of their steep tiled-roof to eat – and this led the architects to the concept for their acclaimed project.

Roland Hagenberg How did working at Richard Rogers' practice in London shape your outlook on architecture?

Takaharu Tezuka Many people say Richard is a high-tech architect. But I don't think so. He is a true modernist. Understanding people's lives precedes all his projects and this gives his architecture meaning. He once took me to the house he built for his parents in the late 1960s in Wimbledon. The herb garden, his mother's pottery studio, the open plan single-floor living area – all was attuned to their age, interests and feelings. I could sense it immediately when entering the house, without knowing the details. I think that's the essence my wife and I took away when we left Richard in 1994 to open our own practice in Tokyo.

RH So no sketches, no models as your starting points, but just getting to know the lives of your clients first...

TT Architecture cannot live without people. That makes it different from sculpture. After we make ourselves familiar with our clients' history, daily routines, and likes and dislikes, we commence with sketches. On average, we produce at least 50, sometimes 100 models for each project. Computers alone will never replace models.

RH Your "Roof House" has become well known internationally...

TT I guess so. But other projects too, like the Matsunoyama Natural Science Museum, the Woods of Net at the Hakone Open Air Museum, or the Fuji Kindergarten.

RH What makes "Roof House" so intriguing is that it visualizes – more than other Tezuka projects – this essence of architecture you talk about. It is also full of allegories. You even integrated a "universal golden rule about dating"!

TT If you look at famous plazas all over the world – be they in Sienna, Rome or Melbourne – you will notice they are inclined. It just feels better to sit on the edge of a slope then on the edge of a flat one. This conclusion was part of our Roof House research and formed one of the building's many concept layers. I always recommend that couples on their first date do not meet face-to-face in a café. This spells disaster: you have a very limited amount of available topics anyway, and when you are forced to look at each other over a small coffee table the whole time and you run out of topics, the situation becomes awkward. So, I recommend couples first meet on the side of an inclining riverbank. Have you ever wondered why so many couples in Japan do this, like at the Tama river? When they look in the same direction, their romance has time to breathe.

RH The Fuji Kindergarten was recently selected by an OECD committee as a most recommendable kindergarten building. It also features a slightly tilted roof.

TT The roof is an important element in our work. The way we design them allows for maximum flexibility in daily life. It can even change people's attitudes. Kids at Fuji Kindergarten suddenly walk or run around five, six times more than they would in a conventional place, without being ordered to do so. In the case of the Roof House it also reverses our modern attitude that nature should come to us, which is wrong. Now, the owners of the house do as it was customary in Japan a long time ago – they adjust to nature. In summer they eat breakfast earlier on the roof to avoid the heat, in winter they eat later when the sun's up. It has come to a point where I get worried. One day my wife told me, "Nothing feels better than a hot shower in a cold typhoon." And I said, "Please be careful." And she answered, "Don't worry, I always wear a T-shirt." She was not thinking about the winds and lightning that I had in mind.

RH Life on top of Roof House happens even without a guardrail...

TT The future owners showed us pictures of their family having breakfast on the steep tiled roof above the second floor of their old house. The kids behaved as if it was their playground, their garden, their own room under the sky. So we tried to stick to this arrangement in our design. When we suggested a handrail, the client said, "Why a handrail? Do you see any houses around with handrails on the roof?" We submitted the planning application and succeeded with the same reasoning.

RH You always wear blue: socks, T-shirts, even your iPhone is blue. When did that start?

TT Richard Rogers always wore blue and gradually all his associates also switched. At one point Richard got annoyed and began to dress in pink. In 1992 I married Yui and we decided to make red and blue our trademark colors.

RH And your kids have their own colors too...

TT Actually, everything Yui and I share is yellow, like our car, a Citroen 2CV. And Yellow is also our daughter Buna's color, but then her brother was born and when we dressed him in yellow she rebelled and gave all her yellow toys to Shii. So we chose the color green for him. Of course, I don't take all that too seriously. It's a game that's developed over time. And if I get tired of blue one day, so be it.

RH It's the Yves Klein blue, isn't it?

TT I love Yves Klein blue. The depth that opens up just by watching the surface of an object this color is breathtaking. Unfortunately, transferring it to a T-shirt is impossible without losing some of the effect. I once bought a bottle of Klein blue. I heard, this kind of blue used to be made out of gem stones in Afghanistan and was valuable like gold.

RH You always emphasize that teaching is part of your life and work. And, as I have witnessed at the Technical University of Vienna, you also enjoy it. The students were thrilled and enthusiastic when working with you.

TT Yes, it is an important part of my life. And I am always proud when a student of mine wins a competition. For the second year in a row, one of my students was awarded the best diploma project out of more than 400 submission in Japan. And every time one of them wins – which happened 2004, 2008 and 2010 – I wonder where they get all their strange ideas. One student is now researching how to construct a house of ice. The other wants to use plastic that slowly degrades until the house finally disappears. It is important for architects to experiment with ideas like that; even though it is impossible to live in such edifices. I also challenge and question my students whenever I can. I am hard on them. I don't give them a break. For the Raiding Project, for instance, one of my staff members worked on a model for a small cube-house in the village where Franz Liszt was born. Yumi-san polished the model for a week, everyday, to perfection. At the end she had scrubbed off her nails and the skin of her fingers. On the other hand, I am also very accessible, not like Rem Koolhaas. I remember my time as a student in the US very well. Koolhaas was teaching. After a workshop, I thought we'd all become very close with the legendary architect, so I went up to him and asked if I could see him again in Europe. "No way," he said. "And you know why? Because I am too famous!"

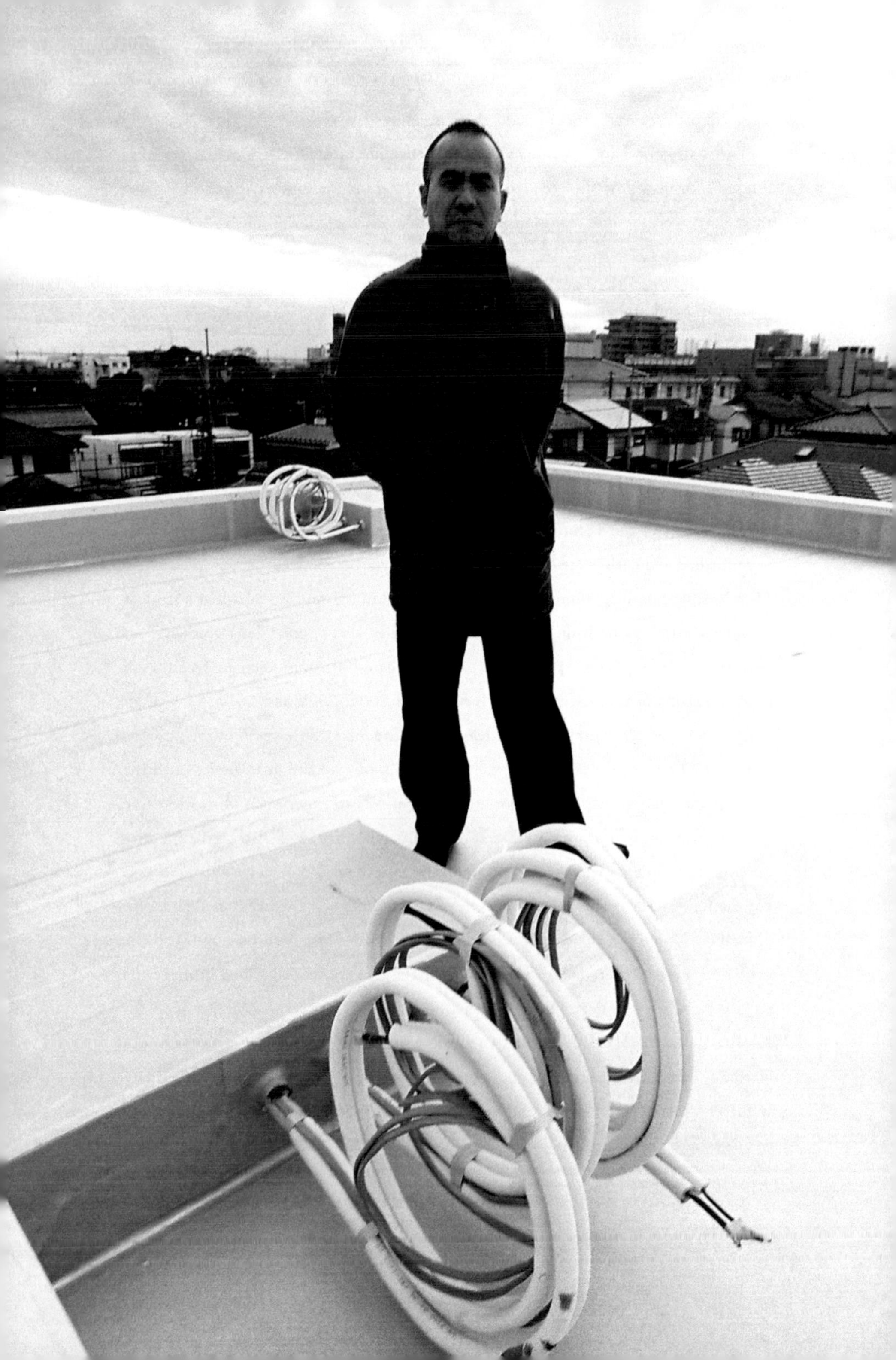

山下保博 | Yasuhiro Yamashita

新しいアイデアがすべて都市から出てくるという考え方をもうやめたほうがいいと思います。

"We have to stop looking at urban centers as the cradles of all new ideas."

1960年、鹿児島県生まれ。1986年芝浦工業大学大学院工学研究科建設工学修士課程修了。1991年に建築事務所を設立、95年にアトリエ・天工人(テクト)と改称。東京建築士会住宅建築賞・奨励賞、第26回INAXデザインコンテスト・銀賞、第11回空間デザイン・コンペティション作品部門・金賞など。おもな建築作品に、「Lucky Drops」「クリスタル・ブリック」「チカニウマルコウブツ」「aLuminum-House」「ref-ring」がある。

Born 1960 in Kagoshima Prefecture. Graduated in architecture from Shibaura Institute of Technology. Received master degree in 1986. Established his office in 1991 and renamed Atelier Tekuto in 1995. Numerous awards including Tokyo Society of Architects & Building Engineers: Housing Construction Encouragement Prize in Japan, Silver Prize from 26th INAX Design Contest and Gold Prize from 11th Space Design Competition (Nippon Electric Glass). Selected buildings in Tokyo include Lucky Drops, Crystal Brick and Reflection of Mineral as well as aLuminum - House and ref-ring.

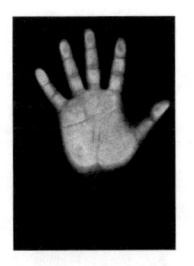

山下保博 建設現場にて | Yasuhiro Yamashita at construction site in Tokyo (2008)

山下保博

何百個もの白い小さな模型が木の棚に並んでいた。山下保博の事務所、アトリエ・天工人。もし見たいと言えば、そのこわれやすい模型をひとつひとつ手の上にのせて、いろいろな角度から見せてもらえるだろう。「Lucky Drops」「Mineral House」「セル・ブリック」……そのどれもが、親しみを感じさせ、コメントや提案を次々と生み出す。そして、本来の目的からは脱線してしまうくらい想像力を働かせる建築だ。最後には、その模型が好きになって持って帰りたくなってしまうか、本物を建ててもらいたいと思わせる力を持っている。こうして、山下のクライアントは、山下の手引きで、自分がデザインしているような気持ちになるのだ。山下は言う。「最後はすべて信頼の問題です。そして、コストを下げるという問題も、ただ単に安い建材を使い、安い業者を選べばいいということではない。多くの場合、多機能のデザインがすべての解決方法になるんです」

日本の多くの若手建築家のように、山下もアジアの国々で新しい仕事を見つけようとしている。日本の現代建築の環境はとても限られてしまっているからだ。しかし、インターネット上での、彼の存在は、積極的で、驚くべきものがある。今やその半分以上はインターネット経由の仕事なのだ（数年前までは、その数字は一けた台だった）。

1960年生まれの山下は、自然や環境がすでに本質的な問題ではなくなってしまった世代にあたる。なぜなら今どんなデザインでも、それについて考えることが当然になっているからだ。

[**パート1**]──2008

ローランド・ハーゲンバーグ[以下 **RH**]　「Mineral House」のユニークなデザインと機能性は、国際的にも高い評価を得ました。新しいプロジェクトを始めるときはいつも、ダイヤモンドが落ちてくるのですか？

山下保博[以下 **山下**]　いいえ、今回だけです。毎回見ることが出来たら、お金持ちになって設計を続けていないかもしれませんね（笑）。冗談はともかくとして、ダイヤモンドの形をした石をイメージして、それがどうやって地面に突き刺さるかを考えました。その考えが「フォルクスワーゲンをどこに置いたらいいか」という問題に対する解決法にもなったからです。この住宅の敷地の面積は駐車スペースも含めて、45平方メートルと、とても小さいです。そのため、ダイヤモンドのような削ぎ落とされたカットは、クライアントの車のための屋根になりました。地震によって車がつぶれないように、そして、全体のバランスが崩れないようにコンクリート構造を慎重に考えました。

RH　クライアントの要望は、ほかに何がありましたか？

山下　キッチンをシンプルにしてほしいと言われました。クライアントのご夫婦は広告業界につとめていて、帰りは遅く、料理はあまりしないからです。それならば、美術館のインスタレーションのような形にしたらどうかと思いました。カウンターと換気扇は、アメリカのアーティスト、ドナルド・ジャッドの彫刻のように、白い壁の前に浮かべました。また、クライアントが冷蔵庫を買う時は、その背中が美しいものを買ってくださいとお願いしました。空間が限られているので、冷蔵庫を階段のすぐ横に置き、彫刻作品に見えるようにしたかったのです。それには、空間を広く見せるために私のデザインのキーワードである、「視線の反射」「反重力」を利用しました。

RH　上手くいきましたか？

山下　はい、キーワードが効果的に使われたと思います。コンセプトやデザインを伝えるたびに思うのですが、クライアントやスタッフに思いを伝えるのは難しい。でも、キーワードが建築のエッセンスを抜き出すフィルターの役割を果たすのだと思います。「視線の反射」「反重力」に加えて、「レイヤー」「構造

山下保博 建設現場にて | Yasuhiro Yamashita at construction site in Tokyo, 2008

と工法」「環境」「多様性と多機能性」などというキーワードを使います。

RH もうひとつの国際的な賞を獲得した「セル・ブリック」ではどういうキーワードを使ったのですか？

山下 そこでは、「レイヤー」「多様性と多機能性」「環境」を使いました。これらのシステムを応用することでコストも下げることができました。270個の鉄の箱は外壁になって、夏の間は日光を反射する役割をし、内側は収納棚の機能を持っています。それに加え、冬は保温の役割をします。

「構造と工法」というキーワードからは、「aLuminum-House」を発展させることができました。敷地が山の上にあって、トラックやクレーン車が入りにくい場所でした。そこに、とても軽くて持ち運びのしやすい素材を持ち込んで組み立てることにしたのです。建築材料としてのアルミは、その当時、国に認められたばかりでした。コストの問題から、中国でアルミ材をつくり、日本に運んだのです。プロジェクト全体の費用はトラックがそこへ乗りつけるために道路を強化する費用より安くすみました。

RH 話は変わりますが、山下さんは、日本の社会が学校を中心にコミュニテ

ィーが形成される社会になってきていると以前に話していました。それは建築とどのような関わりがありますか？

山下 長い間、日本は家族関係を基本にした社会でした。オープンで、他の家族とのつながりもダイレクトでした。だから、仲介者は必要ありませんでした。そこに、家族のあり方に異変が起きました。緊張関係に満ちた都市型の生活が、家族と他者の関係をバラバラにしてしまったのです。以前は地域のコミュニティーがしっかりしていましたが、現在は子供の行く学校を通して家族同志の関係性が作られています。私はこれを、学校中心社会と呼んでいます。このことが、個の孤立と視野の狭さを生んでしまうのです。これは、私の建築家としての仕事に直接影響を与えているわけではありませんが、自分の建築家としての社会的責任と、世界の中の日本人という立場について考えさせられます。私は孤独の中に引きずり込まれたくはありません。外へ向かって一歩踏み出したいと思っています。エチオピアでのプロジェクトはその一環です。そこでは日本の伝統と技術、エチオピアの技術の両方を使っています。建築における社会的責任をどう表現するかに重きを置いています。

一方、日本では100年以上経った伝統的な古民家について考えています。樹齢100年以上の木で作った柱や梁を使っている古民家は、日本にまだ100万棟ぐらい残っています。しかし、すごい勢いで壊されています。なぜかと言うと、水回りの不便さや構造強度に対する不安、断熱性能の弱さなどが影響していて、若い人たちが住まなくなってしまうからです。それに加えて、50坪の木造の住宅が壊されると、30トンもの二酸化炭素を排出することになるのです。私の考える古民家保存の方法は、その家を住みやすくし、そこに住む家族と他の家族間のネットワークをつくることです。そのような建築を通した社会的ネットワークが、視野の狭くなってしまった都市のダイナミズムを変えることができると思います。

RH 建築家になることは、ずっとあなたの夢だったのですか？

山下 いいえ、まったくです。中学生までは画家になりたかった。でも高校生の時に、友人の絵を見てショックを受けました。とても上手だったので、私は一生かかっても追いつけないと思い、建築の道に転向しました。私は建築家で

1964年当時の山下保博 |
Yasuhiro Yamashita, 1964

あることには後悔はしていませんが、思っていた以上にハードな職業であることと、経済的に恵まれないことは歯がゆいですが(笑)。

RH 自分が設計した家に住みたいと思いますか？

山下 あまり、思わないですね。多分、一年間に20棟近い住宅をクライアントのために創っていますし、それらは私自身が住みたい家でもありますから。でも将来的には、今までにありえなかった素材を使って作るかもしれません。例えば、土構造のような（笑）。

[パート2]——2010

RH 以前お会いした時に、エチオピアでプロジェクトを始めたとうかがいました。今、そのプロジェクトを終えて、それが将来へのよい例になるとおっしゃっています。それはどうしてですか？

山下 まず、日本のことを話しましょう。島国である日本が、有史以来押し寄せてくる情報を編集する方法はとてもユニークであり、優秀だと思います。そんな、情報を編集するための専門の知識は、海外に輸出できるのではないかと思います。経済的輸出ではない、モノを再編集する「知の輸出」です。

今回、私が設計したミレニウム・パビリオンは、その具体例です。エチオピアの伝統的な住宅と日本の伝統的な住宅を融合し、既存の塀を利用しながら囲い

こんだものです。エチオピアの住宅の編集の仕方に、私がやりたかったことが表現されています。つまり、その地域の材料と工法が、その地域の時間（伝統や気候性）を帯びている。そのポテンシャルを少ない言語で引き出していくという方法です。具体的に言うと、捨てられている石造りの民家の材料を移動し、積み上げる。その上に、日本から運び込んだガラスブロックを積み、淡い光を入れる。天井を現地の昔の工法で編み込む。その屋根を支えるために軽やかな梁と束のみにする。そうすることによって、貧しい住宅の象徴として見放されていた建築に再び光が当たりました。完成後、このギャラリー空間には申し込みが殺到していると現地からの連絡で知りました。

RH オーストリアのライディングという村で、都市と郊外の相互関係から成り立つ、新しい街づくりへ移行しようと提唱する実験的な立方体を作りましたよね。山下さんにとって、将来へ向けてのもうひとつの重要なテーマだと思いました。

山下 これまでの街づくりのコンセプトは、東京のような都市から発展して、地方へ広がっていくというパターンがほとんどでした。そこでは、既存の地域ネットワークと価値が見捨てられてきました。私は今までの、都市の経済を優先した考え方はもう破綻していると思っています。しかし、私のアイデアは経済をないがしろにしているわけでもないし、昔への回帰でもありません。新しい価値のあり方が問われていると思うのです。そのための提案として、ライディングのプロジェクトを考えているのです。今回の実験的な立方体は「万華鏡と走馬灯のような」と名づけました。立方体の表面は、64個の反射する三角形のブースにわかれています。そこに、石やネジ、葉、貝殻など、日常にあるものを使って球体になるようにしました。そして、中から明かりで照らし、立方体が万華鏡のような模様を作り出す仕掛けになっています。同じ球体であることから、素材の違いに差異はないということを表現しています。また、中心に照明があって、走馬灯のように外部の壁に影を映し出します。ミクロ（万華鏡）とマクロ（走馬灯）が同列になるのです。最近、私が講演等で述べている「価値のパラダイムシフト」は全てのモノが等価であるということからスタートするのです。私たちがローカルのレベルでも、グローバルなレベルでも同じ地球

を共有しているのと同じように、どちらの世界も同じ球体を共有しています。それは900人の住民が住むライディングの村であろうが、1200万人いる東京だろうが「豊かさ」という面では、同じように見える「新たな価値観」がどこかにあるのです。物の見方を変えることによって、新しいライフスタイルが生まれてくると思うのです。

RH たとえば、どのようなことですか？

山下 私は、人々がそう簡単に、大都市をあきらめ、都市を去っていくとは思いません。でも、私は想像できるのです。人々が今までの生活を振り返る。なぜ自分たちが食べるものを都市で作らないのか？ そして近い将来、都市の中で個人のレベルで食料を生産することのできるシステムを考えつくだろうと思

山下康博 ／トリエにて | Yasuhiro Yamashita at his studio in Tokyo, August 2010

います。これは、私たちのリビングルームにまで入り込み、都市の「田園化」につながっていきます。もうひとつの可能性は、私たちのライフスタイルが、「移住を続ける生活」という形に変わるかもしれないということです。交通の発達により、都市と郊外の間を簡単に移動する。不必要なものはほとんど持たずに、しかし、より質の高いものを持つという形です。

RH 日本人である山下さんを、明確に日本人たらしめているものとは何ですか？

山下 おそらく、物によるものではなく、素足で畳の上を歩くといった習慣や態度と、そこに付随する五感が私を日本人たらしめているのだと思います。私は文化の中にこういう何か理解しがたい五感のようなものはなくならないと思っています。おそらく私たち日本人は、これからもずっと家の中に入るときは靴を脱ぐでしょうし、触覚による官能性や、触れることによる高度な感覚も持ち続けるでしょう。こわいのは、そういう感覚を私たちがなくしてしまうことです。

RH 今もいくつかの大学で教えていらっしゃいます。最近、学生の建築に対する態度は変わったと思いますか？

山下 彼らは、個人の空間と彼らの身近にあるものに、より関心を持つようになってきているのではないかと思います。一方で、都市の構造など、スケールの大きなものには興味がないと感じます。彼らにはよく言うのですが、グローバルな視点でプロジェクトを見ないとだめなのです。もちろん、経済が低迷している中、いつも外へ向かっていく姿勢でいるというのは大変なことです。自分が建築家として働けるかどうかもわからないのですから。しかし、景気の後退をポジティブに考えるしか方法はありません。時代的には、産業革命・明治維新の時のように大きな変革の時期ですから、チャンスも多くあると思います。先ほども話したように、これからは世界や価値のあり方を違った目で見る必要があります。万華鏡を通して、あるいは走馬灯の力を借りながら。

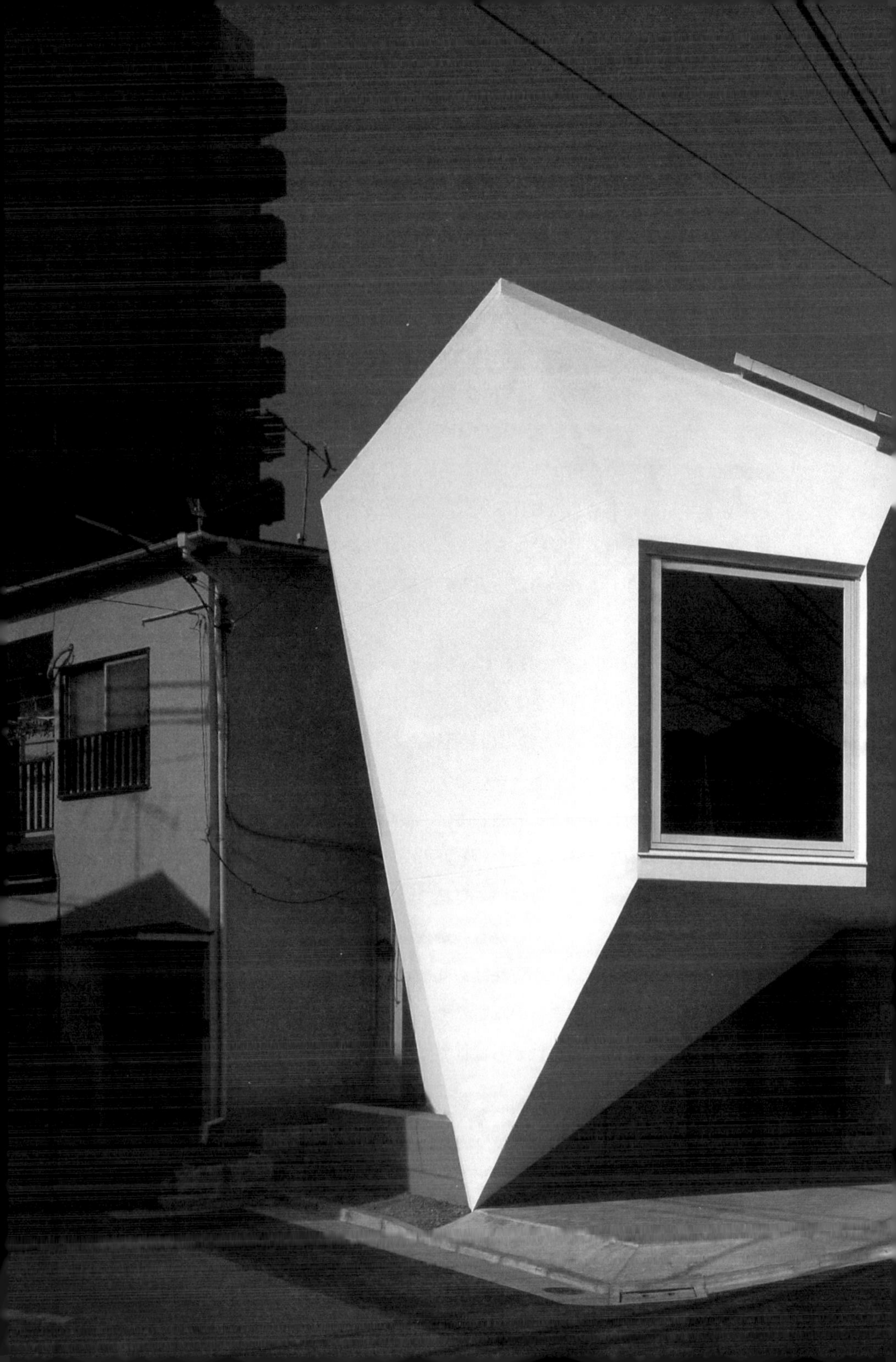

Mineral House, Tokyo

Yasuhiro Yamashita

Hundreds of small white models line the wooden shelves at Atelier Tekuto – Yasuhiro Yamashita's crammed office in Tokyo. If you want to, the architect will let you balance the fragile sculptures in the palm of your hand to better observe their intricacies from various angles. Lucky Drops, Mineral House, Cell Brick – they all radiate intimacy. You're encouraged to comment, to make suggestions, to let your own imagination spin off on tangents. In the end, you feel so attached to the little structures that you want to own them, if not have the real things built. Yamashita's clients feel as if they are the ones who design the house and that he is only a guiding bystander. "In the end, it all comes down to trust," he explains. "And to how to bring down costs, which doesn't simply mean finding cheap suppliers and builders. Most of the time a multi-functional design is the solution for everything." Like many Japanese architects of the younger generation, Yamashita is on the lookout for opportunities in other Asian countries because the climate of the construction industry has become restrictive in Japan. A positive and surprising development, however, has come from the internet; more than half of Yamashita's business originates from his web presence, compared to single-digit numbers just a couple of years ago. Born in 1960, Yamashita belongs to a generation for whom nature and the environment are not real issues anymore, since they are an integral part of any contemporary design decision.

[Conversation part one]——2008

Roland Hagenberg Unique design and functionality made Mineral House an instant success – internationally. Do you always watch diamonds falling when starting a new project?

Yasuhiro Yamashita In that case, only. If I were to do that every time, I would probably be too rich to work. I dropped a diamond shaped stone hundreds of times, watched how it struck the ground and studied its position after impact. One particular angel caught my attention, because it presented itself as the solution to the question, "Where to put the Volkswagen?" I had a 45-meters-squared piece of land on which to build the house, including space for parking. For that reason, one side of the diamond became the roof of the garage. I thought carefully about the concrete structure, to provide the whole building with a solid balance and to make the garage earthquake proof.

RH What did the client want?

YY He requested a simple kitchen. The couple works in the advertising industry, comes home late, doesn't cook but wants a kitchen, nevertheless. I thought, "OK, in that case why not make it appear like a museum installation?" A counter and a ventilation box float in front of white walls like sculptures by American artist Donald Judd. When my clients bought their refrigerator I asked them to get one that looks nice from behind! I placed it next to the stairway, where you can see it as a sculpture when ascending – it hovers a couple of centimeters over the floor. For this, I used "anti-gravity" and "reflection of the line of vision" as–keywords for this particular design.

RH Keywords keep you on track?

YY Yes, they turned out to be quite effective. Every time I try to explain a concept or design to a client or to my staff, it is very difficult for me. Keywords serve as filters that distill the architectural essence. Besides anti-gravity and reflection of line of vision, I use the terms, "layers", "environment", "materials", "structure", "construction method", "diversity" and "multi-functionality."

RH For your national-award-winning Cell Brick House, which keyword did you apply?

YY Layers, diversity, multi-functionality and environment. 270 steel boxes serve as outside walls that reflect the sun in summer – inside they can be used as shelves. Plus, they conserve heat in winter. For Aluminum House, I used "structure" and "ways of construction." The plot of land was at a mountain side and difficult to access with trucks and cranes. The solution was to use a very light material easy to transport and to assemble. Aluminum as a structural material was only recently approved by the ministry of construction. We took our chances, producing the aluminum parts in China and transporting them to Kawasaki. The project as a whole was still cheaper than building fortified access roads for the trucks.

RH On another subject, you mentioned that Japan is becoming a school-network-based society. How is that affecting you as an architect?

YY For so long our society has been a family-network based society, with families very open and directly connected to other families. There were no intermediaries necessary – everybody knew everybody. Then something interesting happened: the intense urban way of life disrupted family fabrics. Why and how certain families come together now is decided by their children at school; they are the ones that determine with whom their mothers associate and whom they can meet at and after school. This is what I call the school-network based society of Japan. It creates isolation and an insular way of thinking. Not that it affects my work as an architect directly, but it makes me question my own social responsibilities and my place as a Japanese person in this world. I don't want to be drawn into isolation; I want to step out. My project in Ethiopia is such an effort, where I use Japanese technology and traditional Ethiopian expertise. In Japan I was also thinking of all the hundred-year-old traditional houses – the Kominka. Theose old houses were made of 100-year-old trees and there are about a million of them still left in Japan. My guess is there are still about a million around, built with beams from 120-year-old trees – the best construction material you can think of. But few people want to live in a Kominka with no water, no utilities and an ice-cold winter, so they leave. In addition, if such a 150 square structure is torn down and a new apartment complex is erected instead, we emit up to 30 tons of carbon dioxide and that's really not necessary. My idea is to preserve the Kominka, make them comfortable to live in and establish a network of families who live there. Such a social network could reverse the insular dynamism of our cities.

RH Was it always your dream to become an architect?

YY Not at all. First I wanted to be a painter. But one day I saw the works of an artist friend and was shocked, because the paintings were so special that I thought I would never be able to achieve such quality in my life. On the spot I decided to choose another profession and I have never regretted that I became an architect, instead. But the work is harder than I thought it would be, and I didn't become rich, as I thought I would!.

RH Do you live in a place that you designed yourself?

YY No, not really. I build about 20 houses every year for my clients and each of those houses are houses I would love to live in. But in the future I might build one for myself using the most unusual materials – for example, mud.

[**Conversation part two**]——2010

RH Last time we talked, you had just started a project in Ethiopia. Now it is finished and you say it is "exemplary for the future." Why?

YY The island nation of Japan is unique in the way it edits all the information that washes to its shores. Our information-treatment expertise is exportable. In the case of my Millennium Pavilion, I took an Ethiopian house and a traditional Japanese building and connected them. I fenced them in and the fence has a very Japanese look, although we used Ethiopian weaving and tying techniques. In the future we will make much more use of cross-cultural elements, but for that we have to know how to edit, filter, and adjust. That's what I wanted to explain with the project in Ethiopia.

RH And for the village of Raiding in Austria, which is also located in the countryside, you created an experimental cube that refers to the shifting interdependence between city and countryside. You consider this another important issue for the future.

YY In the past, new concepts evolved mostly in cities like Tokyo and then spread to the countryside. They also spread old city problems. I think we have to stop looking at urban centers as the cradle of all new ideas and instead seek local innovations outside urban parameters. I called the experimental cube for Raiding Kaleidoscope and Revolving Lantern. Its surface is divided into 64 reflecting triangles. I filled them with everyday objects, like stones, screws, leaves, blossoms, and shells. Lit from inside, the cube creates patterns as a kaleidoscope does. This represents the micro world of society and the changes in how we look at things in the 21st century. At the same time, the cube projects enlarged images to the outside like a revolving lantern – representing the macro world. Both universes share the same sphere, as we share the same planet on local and global levels – be it in Raiding with 900 inhabitants, or in greater Tokyo with 30 million. Changing the way we look at things leads to a new lifestyle.

RH Can you give an example?

YY I don't think that people can be easily motivated to give up the mega-city and leave, but I can imagine that they look at the micro world in the countryside and ask why they don't grow their own food in the city. And then they come up with systems that make it possible to produce food in an urban setting and on an individual level. It could lead to a "ruralization" of the metropolis that reaches into our living rooms. Another possibility is that our lifestyles will incorporate a permanent state of relocation,

Yasuhiro Yamashita and his team with study for cube in Raiding at his studio in Tokyo, August 2010

which means we live, fluctuate and travel "light" between city and countryside; give up unnecessary products; have fewer things that are of higher quality.

RH Which traditional Japanese elements would you keep?

YY I would not so much keep a physical object, but rather keep an attitude, like enjoying walking barefoot on a tatami mattress. I hope this part of our culture will not disappear, that we will continue to take our shoes off when entering a house; that we will keep our tactile sensuality, our advanced sense of touching. The danger that we will lose it is there.

RH You teach at several universities. Have students changed their attitude towards architecture in recent years?

YY I feel they are more and more concerned with personal space, with their immediate surroundings, and less concerned with larger scales – the structure of cities and city blocks. I urge them to perceive projects from a global point of view. I understand that it is not easy to keep an outwardly focused attitude during an economic downturn when you don't even know if you will get work as an architect. But there is no other way than to perceive the recession as a good thing. As I said, from now on we have to look at the world differently, be it through a kaleidoscope or with the help of a revolving lantern.

1960年以降の建築家の系譜とムーブメント

作成：五十嵐太郎　村越怜

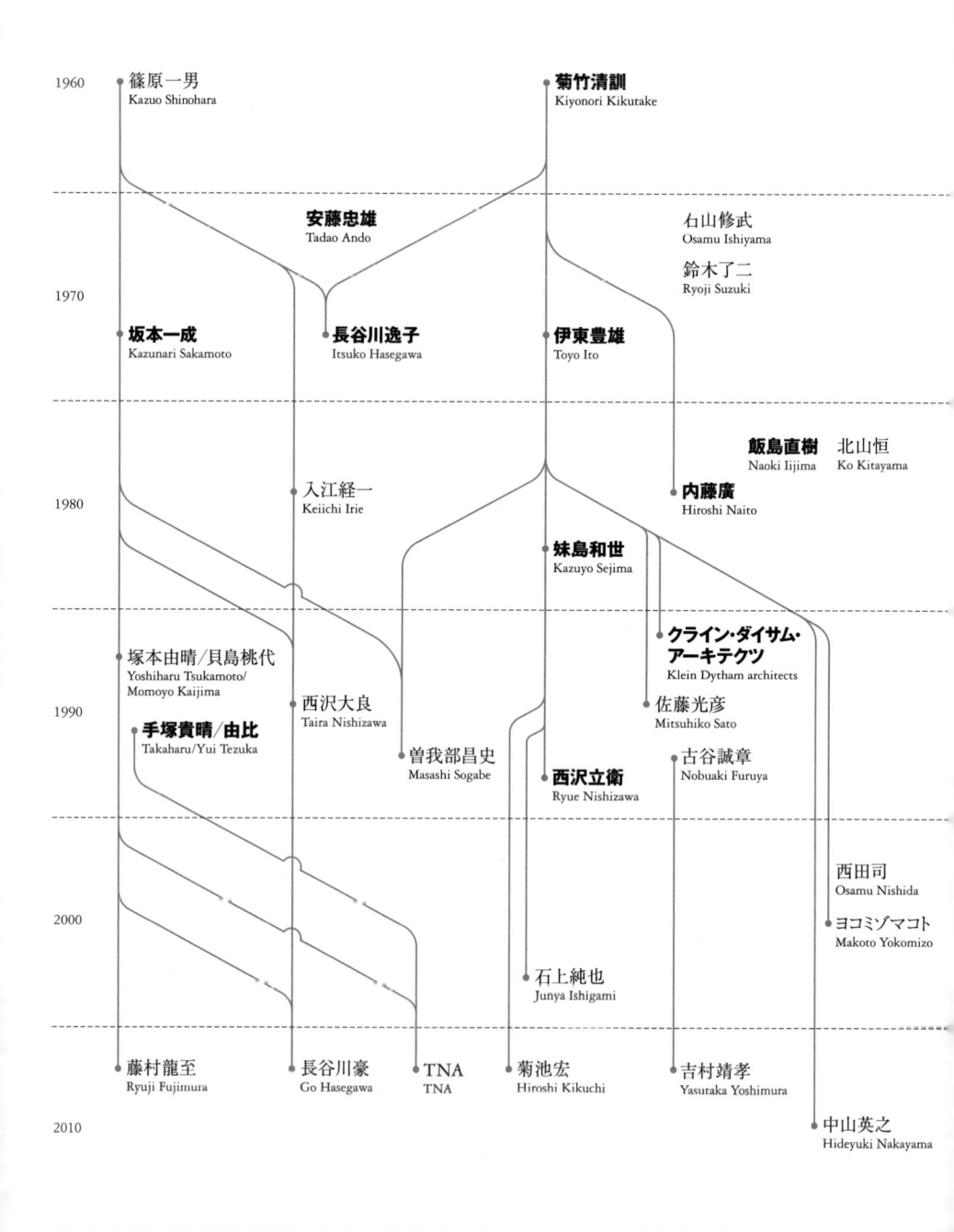

1960
- 篠原一男 Kazuo Shinohara
- 菊竹清訓 Kiyonori Kikutake

1970
- 安藤忠雄 Tadao Ando
- 石山修武 Osamu Ishiyama
- 鈴木了二 Ryoji Suzuki
- 坂本一成 Kazunari Sakamoto
- 長谷川逸子 Itsuko Hasegawa
- 伊東豊雄 Toyo Ito

1980
- 入江経一 Keiichi Irie
- 飯島直樹 Naoki Iijima
- 北山恒 Ko Kitayama
- 内藤廣 Hiroshi Naito
- 妹島和世 Kazuyo Sejima

1990
- 塚本由晴／貝島桃代 Yoshiharu Tsukamoto／Momoyo Kaijima
- 西沢大良 Taira Nishizawa
- クライン・ダイサム・アーキテクツ Klein Dytham architects
- 佐藤光彦 Mitsuhiko Sato
- 手塚貴晴／由比 Takaharu／Yui Tezuka
- 曽我部昌史 Masashi Sogabe
- 西沢立衛 Ryue Nishizawa
- 古谷誠章 Nobuaki Furuya

2000
- 西田司 Osamu Nishida
- ヨコミゾマコト Makoto Yokomizo
- 石上純也 Junya Ishigami

2010
- 藤村龍至 Ryuji Fujimura
- 長谷川豪 Go Hasegawa
- TNA
- 菊池宏 Hiroshi Kikuchi
- 吉村靖孝 Yasutaka Yoshimura
- 中山英之 Hideyuki Nakayama

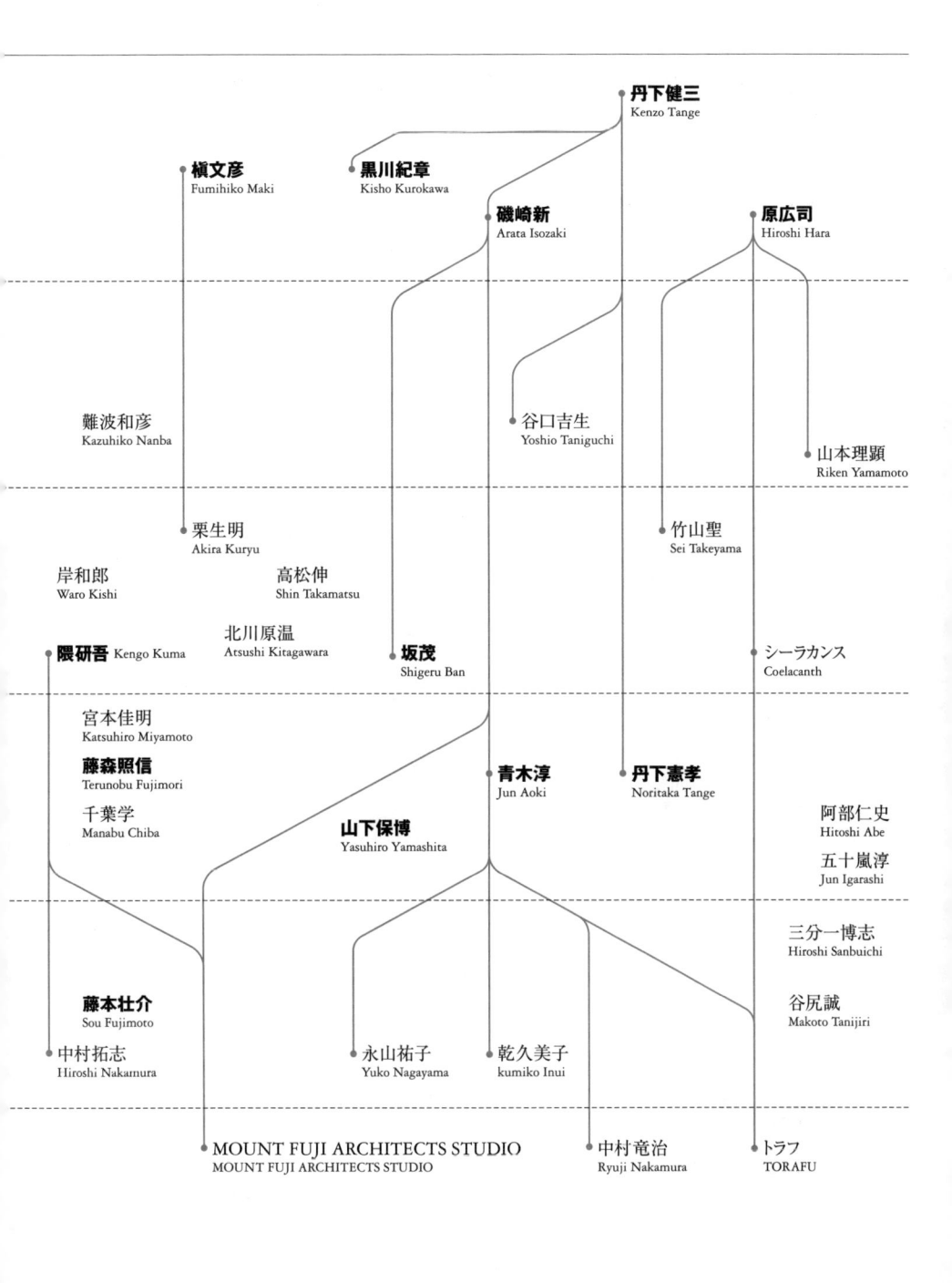

丹下健三	Kenzo Tange
槇文彦	Fumihiko Maki
黒川紀章	Kisho Kurokawa
磯崎新	Arata Isozaki
原広司	Hiroshi Hara
難波和彦	Kazuhiko Nanba
谷口吉生	Yoshio Taniguchi
山本理顕	Riken Yamamoto
栗生明	Akira Kuryu
竹山聖	Sei Takeyama
岸和郎	Waro Kishi
高松伸	Shin Takamatsu
北川原温	Atsushi Kitagawara
坂茂	Shigeru Ban
シーラカンス	Coelacanth
隈研吾	Kengo Kuma
宮本佳明	Katsuhiro Miyamoto
藤森照信	Terunobu Fujimori
青木淳	Jun Aoki
丹下憲孝	Noritaka Tange
阿部仁史	Hitoshi Abe
千葉学	Manabu Chiba
山下保博	Yasuhiro Yamashita
五十嵐淳	Jun Igarashi
三分一博志	Hiroshi Sanbuichi
藤本壮介	Sou Fujimoto
谷尻誠	Makoto Tanijiri
中村拓志	Hiroshi Nakamura
永山祐子	Yuko Nagayama
乾久美子	kumiko Inui
MOUNT FUJI ARCHITECTS STUDIO	MOUNT FUJI ARCHITECTS STUDIO
中村竜治	Ryuji Nakamura
トラフ	TORAFU

［ブックガイド］建築家と建築学がわかる100冊 | 五十嵐太郎　平野晴香　市川紘司

［凡例］書名｜著者名｜出版社名｜刊行年

登場建築家などによる書物

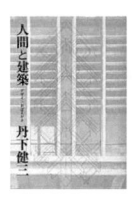

001
人間と建築　デザインおぼえがき
丹下健三
彰国社｜1971

002
新・建築入門——思想と歴史
隈研吾
筑摩書房（ちくま新書）｜1994

003
新 共生の思想
——世界の新秩序
黒川紀章
徳間書店｜1996

004
空間へ
——根源へと遡行する思考
磯崎新
鹿島出版会｜1997

005
住宅——日常の詩学
坂本一成
TOTO出版｜2001

006
記憶の形象
——都市と建築との間で（上・下）
槇文彦
筑摩書房（ちくま学芸文庫）｜1997

007
集落の教え100
原広司
彰国社｜1998

008
紙の建築 行動する
——震災の神戸から
ルワンダ難民キャンプまで
坂茂
筑摩書房｜1998

009
建築を語る
安藤忠雄
東京大学出版会｜1999

010
建築のはじまりに向かって
内藤廣
王国社｜1999

011
生活の装置
長谷川逸子
住まいの図書館出版局 | 1999

012
透層する建築
伊東豊雄
青土社 | 2000

013
建築家 安藤忠雄
安藤忠雄
新潮社 | 2008

014
妹島和世+西沢立衛/
SANAA works 1995-2003
妹島和世+西沢立衛
TOTO出版 | 2003

015
青木淳完全作品集 第1集
青木淳ほか
INAX出版 | 2004

016
負ける建築
隈研吾
岩波書店 | 2004

017
手塚貴晴+手塚由比
建築カタログ
TOTO出版 | 2006

018
アトリエ・ワン・フロム・ポスト・
バブル・シティ
アトリエ・ワン
INAX出版 | 2006

019
原初的な未来の建築
藤本壮介
INAX出版 | 2008

020
-FUL
クライン ダイサム アーキテクツ
TOTO出版 | 2009

建築家の自伝／伝記

021
評伝ミース・ファン・デル・ローエ
フランツ・シュルツ／沢村明=訳
鹿島出版会｜1987

022
未完の建築家
フランク・ロイド・ライト
エイダ・ハクスタブル
TOTO出版｜2007

023
ルネサンス彫刻家建築家列伝
ジョルジョ・ヴァザーリ／
森田義之=監訳
白水社｜1989

024
ピーター・ライス自伝
——あるエンジニアの夢みたこと
ピーター・ライス／
岡部憲明=訳
鹿島出版会｜1997

025
建築家たちの20代
東京大学工学部建築学科
安藤忠雄研究室
TOTO出版｜1999

026
丹下健三
丹下健三・藤森照信
新建築社｜2002

027
東京駅の建築家 辰野金吾伝
東秀紀
講談社｜2002

028
ブレイキング・グラウンド
ダニエル・リベスキンド
鈴木圭介=訳
筑摩書房｜2006

029
にほんの建築家 伊東豊雄・観察記
瀧口範子
TOTO出版｜2006

030
磯崎新の「都庁」
平松剛
文藝春秋｜2008

建築家による建築論

031
ウィトルーウィウス建築書
ウィトルーウィウス／森田慶一＝訳
東海大学出版会（東海選書）｜1979

032
建築論
レオン・バティスタ・アルベルティ／
相川浩＝訳
中央公論美術出版｜1982

033
パラーディオ「建築四書」注解
アンドレア・パラーディオ／
桐敷真次郎＝訳
中央公論美術出版｜1986

034
建築をめざして
ル・コルビュジエ／吉阪隆正＝訳
鹿島出版会（SD選書）｜1989

035
建築の多様性と対立性
ロバート・ヴェントゥーリ／
伊藤公文＝訳
鹿島出版会（SD選書）｜1982

036
ルイス・カーン建築論集
ルイス・カーン／前田忠直＝編訳
鹿島出版会（SDライブラリー）｜1992

037
建築意匠講義
香山寿夫
東京大学出版会｜1996

038
住宅論
篠原一男
鹿島出版会｜1970

039
錯乱のニューヨーク
レム・コールハース／
鈴木圭介＝訳
筑摩書房（ちくま学芸文庫）｜1999

040
斜めにのびる建築
クロード・パラン
戸田穣＝訳
青土社｜2008

建築ガイド・フィールドワーク

041
「建築MAP東京」
ギャラリー間=編
TOTO出版 | 2003から

042
路上観察学入門
赤瀬川原平　藤森照信
南伸坊
ちくま文庫 | 1993

043
「建築グルメマップ」シリーズ
建築知識=編
エクスナレッジ | 2001から

044
「ヨーロッパ建築案内」シリーズ
淵上正幸他
TOTO出版 | 1998

045
環境ノイズを読み、
風景をつくる。
宮本佳明
彰国社 | 2007

046
ペット・アーキテクチャー
ガイドブック
東京工業大学塚本研究室＆
アトリエワン
ワールドフォトプレス | 2001

047
東京リノベーション——建築を
転用する93のストーリー
フリックスタジオ／SSC=編
廣済堂出版 | 2001

048
北京論 10の都市文化案内
松原弘典
丸善 | 2008

049
東京建築ガイドマップ
倉方俊輔＋斉藤理
エクスナレッジ | 2007

050
超合法建築図鑑
吉村靖孝
彰国社 | 2006

都市論

051
都市のイメージ
ケヴィン・リンチ/丹下健三=訳
岩波書店 | 1968

052
アメリカ大都市の死と生
ジェイン・ジェイコブズ
鹿島出版会 | 2010

053
上海——都市と建築
1842-1949年
村松伸
パルコ出版 | 1991

054
街並みの美学/
続・街並みの美学
芦原義信
岩波書店(岩波現代文庫) | 2001

055
要塞都市L.A.
マイク・デイヴィス/
村山敏勝ほか=訳
青土社 | 2001

056
都市のかなしみ
鈴木博之
中央公論新社 | 2003

057
趣都の誕生
森川嘉一郎
幻冬舎 | 2003

058
アースダイバー
中沢新一
講談社 | 2005

059
徹底討論
私たちが住みたい都市 身体/
プライバシー/住宅/国家
山本理顕=編
平凡社 | 2006

060
東京から考える
東浩紀+北田暁大
NHK出版 | 2007

評論系

061
マニエリスムと近代建築
コーリン・ロウ/伊東豊雄＝訳
彰国社 | 1981

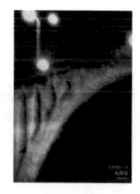

062
現代住宅研究
塚本由晴＋西沢大良
INAX出版 | 2004

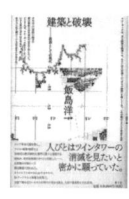

063
建築と破壊――思想としての現代
飯島洋一
青土社 | 2006

064
言葉と建築――建築批評の史的地平と諸概念
土居義岳
建築技術 | 1997

065
セヴェラルネス　事物連鎖と人間
中谷礼仁
鹿島出版会 | 2005

066
トラヴァース
南泰裕
鹿島出版会 | 2006

067
建築はいかに社会と回路をつなぐのか
五十嵐太郎
彩流社 | 2010

068
アルゴリズミック・アーキテクチュア
コスタス・テルジディス
伊東豊雄＝監訳
鹿島出版会 | 2010

069
1995年以後
藤村龍至他編
エクスナレッジ | 2009

070
建築家の読書術
倉方俊輔編
TOTO出版 | 2010

歴史系

071
日本建築史序説
太田博太郎
彰国社 | 1989

072
日本の民家
今和次郎
岩波書店(岩波文庫) | 1997

073
「図説世界建築史」シリーズ
エンリコ・グイドーニ/
桐敷真次郎=訳ほか
本の友社 | 1996から

074
現代建築史
ケネス・フランプトン
青土社 | 2003

075
近代建築史
鈴木博之ほか
市ヶ谷出版社 | 2008

076
「磯崎新の建築談議」シリーズ
磯崎新／篠山紀信=写真
六耀社 | 2001

077
思想としての日本近代建築
八束はじめ
岩波書店 | 2005

078
人類と建築の歴史
藤森照信
筑摩書房 | 2005

079
批評と理論
磯崎新+鈴木博之+
石山修武=監修
INAX出版 | 2005

080
伊勢神宮
井上章一
講談社 | 2009

構造・環境・構法系

081
環境としての建築
──建築デザインと環境技術
レイナー・バンハム/
堀江悟郎=訳
鹿島出版会 | 1981

082
自然な構造体──自然と
技術における形と構造、
そしてその発生プロセス
フライ・オットー/岩村和夫=訳
鹿島出版会(SD選書) | 1986

083
「建築学」の教科書
彰国社 | 2003

084
「住宅」という考え方
──20世紀的住宅の系譜
松村秀一
東京大学出版会 | 1999

085
宇宙船地球号操縦マニュアル
バックミンスター・フラー/
芦沢高志=訳
筑摩書房(ちくま学芸文庫) | 2000

086
小住宅の構造
池田昌弘
A.D.AEDITA TOKYO | 2003

087
フラックス・ストラクチャー
佐々木睦朗
TOTO出版 | 2005

088
インフォーマル
セシル・バルモンド
山形浩生=訳
TOTO出版 | 2005

089
建築の四層構造
サスティナブルデザインをめぐる
思考
難波和彦
INAX出版 | 2009

090
都市この小さな惑星の
リチャード・ロジャースほか/
野城智也ほか=訳
鹿島出版会 | 2002

関連分野

091
陰翳礼讃
谷崎潤一郎
中央公論新社
(中公クラシックス) | 2002

092
パサージュ論(全5巻)
ヴァルター・ベンヤミン/
今村仁司ほか=訳
岩波書店(岩波現代文庫) | 2003

093
世界の調律——サウンド・スケープとはなにか
マリー・シェーファー/
鳥越けい子ほか=訳
平凡社 | 1986

094
アートレス
——マイノリティとしての現代美術
川俣正
フィルムアート社 | 2001

095
家族を容れるハコ
家族を超えるハコ
上野千鶴子
平凡社(平凡社ライブラリー) | 2002

096
カワイイパラダイムデザイン研究
真壁智治
平凡社 | 2009

097
戦争と万博
椹木野衣
美術出版社 | 2005

098
写真な建築
増田彰久
白揚社 | 2003

099
映画的建築/建築的映画
五十嵐太郎
春秋社 | 2009

100
空間の詩学
ガストン・バシュラール/
岩村行雄=訳
筑摩書房(ちくま学芸文庫) | 2002

ローランド・ハーゲンバーグ　Roland Hagenberg

オーストリア生まれ、ウィーンで育つ。マルチメディアアーティストとして、"VOGUE"や"Architectural Digest"などに寄稿。1995年より日本に移り、建築とデザインの世界を追っている。そのほか、WOWOWのTVドラマ用楽曲の歌詞を執筆するなど、幅広い活動を続けている。2010年には、作曲家、フランツ・リストの生地でもあるオーストリアのライディングにて、10人の日本人建築家によるマイクロ・ハウス建造のプロジェクトを開始、現在進行中。

ホームページ http://www.hagenberg.com

Writer, photographer and filmmaker Roland Hagenberg grew up in Vienna, Austria. His stories and photographs are featured in magazines such as "Vogue" and "Architectural Digest". He currently lives in Japan where he has been documenting the world of architecture and design since 1995. WOWOW commissioned him to write songs for TV dramas. In 2010 Hagenberg invited ten Japanese architects to create micro-houses for Raiding, the birthplace of composer Franz Liszt in Austria.

五十嵐太郎（いがらし・たろう）

1967年パリ生まれ。東京大学工学部建築学科卒業。同大学院修了。現在、東北大学大学院工学研究科教授。第11回ベネチア・ビエンナーレ国際建築展では、日本館展示コミッショナーを務める。主な著書に『終わりの建築／始まりの建築』（INAX出版）『戦争と建築』（晶文社）『現代建築のパースペクティブ』（光文社）などがある。

村越怜（むらこし・れい）東北大学大学院工学研究科
平野晴香（ひらの・はるか）東北大学大学院工学研究科
市川紘司（いちかわ・こうじ）東北大学大学院工学研究科

なりたいのは建築家（けんちくか） 24 ARCHITECTS IN JAPAN

2011年6月25日 第1刷発行

著　者　ローランド・ハーゲンバーグ

発行者　富澤凡子
発行所　柏書房株式会社
　　　　東京都文京区本駒込1-13-14（〒113-0021）
　電　話　03-3947-8251（営業）
　　　　　03-3947-8254（編集）

装丁　木ノ下努（ALOHA DESIGN）
DTP　有限会社共同工芸社
印刷・製本　共同印刷株式会社

©Roland Hagenberg 2011, Printed in Japan ISBN978-4-7601-3964-4

なりたいのは
建築家